Serving the Underserved

SERVING THE UNDERSERVED

∎

CARING FOR PEOPLE WHO ARE BOTH OLD AND MENTALLY RETARDED

∎

A Handbook for Caregivers

∎

edited by Mary C. Howell, Deirdre G. Gavin, Gerard A. Cabrera, and Henry A. Beyer

Exceptional Parent Press
Boston

cover and text photos: Mary C. Howell
text design and production by Ellen Herman
cover design by Andrea Golden

ISBN 0-930958-08-x
Library of Congress Card Number: 89-084088
Library of Congress Cataloguing-in-Publication Data

Serving the Underserved: Caring for people who are both old and mentally retarded: a handbook for caregivers
    Edited by Mary C. Howell ... [et al.]
    Bibliography: p.
    1. Mentally handicapped aged--Services for--Massachusetts.
    2. Kennedy Aging Project.   I. Howell, Mary C.
    HV3009.5.A35S46   1989
    362.3'084'6--dc20   89-84088

Thanks to a grant from the Joseph P. Kennedy, Jr. Foundation, limited funds are available for subsidies to non-profit organizations. To qualify for a subsidy, please send a letter to The Publisher, Exceptional Parent Press, 1170 Commonwealth Ave., Boston MA 02134.

**To Rosemary Kennedy,
whose life inspired this work.**

Acknowledgements

■

Thanks to Kristen Hager, for spending most of her summer typing for us, and for her useful comments on the text, to Diane Arnt and Cynthia Dunn for help with typing, research, and editorial comments.

Kathy Smith did essential work for us by editing all the pieces with a nice eye for balance between individual expressive style and usage conformity. Stanley Klein, and, especially, Max Schleifer of Exceptional Parent Press gave us a free hand and a great deal of encouragement, as well as substantive and technical support. David Jones, also of the Exceptional Parent Press, went well beyond the call of duty to see this project through to the end. Ellen Herman designed and coordinated the production process with a *sympatico* heart.

We owe an intellectual and emotional debt to Gunnar and Rosemary Dybwad, Ruth Snider, Father Henry Marquardt, Dale Anderson, and Peg Pyne for helping us to see and understand.

The Handbook would have come about were it not for the funding and encouragement given to the Kennedy Aging Project by the Joseph P. Kennedy, Jr., Foundation, and the Department of Mental Retardation of the Commonwealth of Massachusetts.

Table of Contents

PART 5: REFLECTIONS AND RECOMMENDATIONS

PART 6: AFTERWORDS

■

A word about our words:
The use of non-sexist pronouns is never as smooth and easy as reliance on the conventional HE. We believe, however, that it is worth some effort on the part of both writers and readers to search for linguistic forms that do not perpetuate sexist habits, and that remind us how "naturally" sexist we have been. In this book we have elected to alternate the use of HE and SHE from one example or instance to the next, to remind us that the "generic HE" is not interpreted by many readers as making reference inclusively to all of us.

We hold to other linguistic choices out of respect. For instance, we make an effort, whenever it is stylistically possible, to talk about "People with…" or "People who are" when we are discussing disabilities. We use the direct and simple words OLD and MENTALLY RETARDED, believing that euphemisms ("developmentally disabled," "older") soon also become denigrated. Our effort must go to honoring and giving value to the status of being old and being mentally retarded, not to avoidance and looking away.

Whenever clients and their stories are discussed, names are changed to protect privacy. In some instances, where an account seems so revealing as to lead to identification of the client, other details have been altered. Their stories, however, are still true to the course of their lives and experiences.

Some of these chapters have appeared in modified form in other publications: "Decision-Making by and for Individuals of Questionable Competence" (#23) appeared in *The Exceptional Parent*; "Eating for Good Health: A Diet Program for Older Adults in Special Olympics, 1987" (#31) is a booklet distributed by Exceptional Parent Press in Boston (617) 730-5800; "Depression in the Mentally Retarded Elderly: Implications for Treatment Care and Research" (#37) appears in Harper M.S., Ed. *Mental Health and Mental Illness of the Mentally Retarded Elderly*, Washington, D.C.: U.S. Dept. of Health and Human Services, 1988; "Estate Planning: Providing for Your Child's Future" (#49) appeared in *The Exceptional Parent*, 1986, 16:8:12-19; "Ethical Dilemmas Encountered in the Care of Those Who Are Mentally Retarded and Also Old" (#52) appears in Rose, T. and Ansello, E.F., Eds. *Special Issue on Aging and Developmental Disabilities, Educational Gerontology: An International Bimonthly Journal*, 1988; 14; "Ethical Dilemmas in Caregiving: A Guide for Staff Serving Adults Who Are Mentally Retarded" (#56) appears in a handbook published and distributed by Exceptional Parent Press, 1988; "A Support Group on the Issues of Death and Dying With Mentally Retarded Adults" (#67) appears in the *Journal of Gerontological Social Work,* The Haworth Press, Inc., Vol. 13, 3 and 4, 1988.

During the period the Kennedy Aging Project operated, the Department of Mental Health (DMH) became the Department of Mental Retardation (DMR). The new DMR retained the organizational structure established while it was a Division within the DMH. It was, however, in the process of reorganization and, to some extent, redirection in its service priorities. We have solved the confusion of referring to one or the other by referring to the Division and the newly created Department in the text as DMR in every case.

We want to thank the following people for helping us to make arrangements for photographs: Alan Beauchesne, Ann Marie Homsey, Fran Wiltsie, Harrison Glavan, Trish Bligh, Karen Sedat, David Ziegler, Deborah O'Neill, and others too many to name.

We would like to thank all the members of our Kennedy Aging Project team who did not contribute to this book: Robert Burdick, Judy Diamond, Maureen McCann, Mary Mello, Patricia O'Brien, Jean St. Pierre, Philip Reilly, Laura Rotenberg, Elizabeth Smears, Joyce Stamp, Mark Goodwin, David Stone, Karen Sedat, and Louis Aucoin. Finally, we would like to thank all our friends at Shriver and Fernald who have been so supportive in these past three years.

Finally, we should note that this book is the work of thirty-one independent authors. The views expressed are our own, and not necessarily those of the Joseph P. Kennedy, Jr. Foundation, the Massachusetts Department of Mental Retardation, the Eunice Kennedy Shriver Center, or any other affiliated or supporting organization. In fact, not even all of the book's contributors subscribe totally to all of the opinions put forth by all other authors. We are, nevertheless, united in our general philosophy of caring. Through this handbook, we hope that others will learn and share that philosophy, and that individuals who are both old and mentally retarded will be the beneficiaries.

PART 1
FOREWORDS

PART I

FORWORDS

FOREWORD

Eunice Kennedy Shriver, Executive Vice-President, The Joseph P. Kennedy, Jr. Foundation

■

The great Irish poet, WIlliam Butler Yeats, looked around him as he grew old and wrote in "Sailing to Byzantium," "That is no country for old men." The world, he felt, was for the young. The old no longer had a place or purpose. An aged person was "a paltry thing. A tattered coat upon a stick."

For the aged mentally retarded, the world has been doubly cruel. Ostracized because of their handicap, shunted aside because of their years, people with mental retardation who are old have had almost literally no place to call their own—few services, few opportunities, few supports.

As this very important handbook illustrates, that situation is rapidly changing. Thanks to extraordinary people like Mary Howell and her staff, elderly people with mental retardation not only have a place and a purpose—but talented people in a variety of disciplines who are devoted to enhancing and enriching the quality of their lives.

For anyone concerned with the fate of our intellectually disabled senior citizens, this book offers detailed analysis, reflection, and recommendations concerning all the areas of experience affecting the lives of our special friends and neighbors. It offers options, fosters choice, dispels the myths and fears that even professionals may have when confronted with a crisis in the life of a person who is both mentally retarded and old. The importance of providing companionship to counter the loneliness of old age is stressed. Specific information about services—where to go and how to get them—is detailed. For anyone concerned with integrating elderly mentally retarded people into the community, this book is an indispensable guide.

Professionals, family members, and community leaders will want to have this book as a ready reference. It is both important and timely, for like the aging population as a whole, the population of elderly people with mental retardation is increasing. Modern medicine, corrective surgery, education for health and fitness, all combine to increase the years and enlarge the horizons of our mentally retarded friends and neighbors.

In his most famous lines of poetry, Robert Browning wrote, "Grow old along with me—the best is yet to be." Of all these words, "along with me" are the most beautiful. Loneliness and exclusion are the curses of old age. By learning more about the needs of our special friends, by enriching our programs and opening our lives to them we are saying, "Come in." Only then will we fulfill Browning's promise that "the best is yet to be."

2

Foreword

Mary McCarthy, Commissioner, Department of Mental Retardation, Commonwealth of Massachusetts

■

The needs of our citizens who are old are changing the way we view human services and the way we view ourselves. National demographics suggest that the unique needs of people who are old will be among our most pressing social needs in the future. Citizens with mental retardation who are old have presented a challenge to our profession for the last two decades. This book is about how we have responded to that challenge. It is a creative collection of opportunities and ideas that help to ensure the best quality of life possible for people who are mentally retarded and old.

I am honored to have the opportunity to speak to readers of this extraordinary work. In Massachusetts, we have long enjoyed a leadership role in providing services to people who are mentally retarded. In

1848, the Commonwealth of Massachusetts established the first publicly funded service delivery service system in the nation. In 1974, we were the first state to put in place a guarantee of special education services to children with disabilities. Ten years later, we were the first state to establish a bureau of transitional planning for special education students who were turning 22. And in 1988, Massachusetts became the first state in the nation to create a mechanism whereby people with disabilities and others who lack adequate health care coverage could, for the first time in the United States of America, access affordable and comprehensive health insurance.

In providing services to people who old, we have organized options and choices around three guiding principles:

• Principle I—Individualization

Achieving relevant, individualized services for people who are mentally retarded and old will depend significantly upon changing widely held stereotypical views, especially among planners, coordinators, and service providers.

• Principle II—Options

Exemplary programs need to be developed that focus on aggressively enabling people who are mentally retarded and old to enter valued roles in their communities, especially employment roles. These programs would be designed to meet an individual's needs based on their interests and capabilities rather than on role expectations based on their age.

• Principle III—Choice

In making recommendations around the principle of normalization and program design, we are not trying to impose any constraints on people who are old and mentally retarded or to dictate how they should lead their lives. Rather, our goal is to provide increased opportunities to people who are both mentally retarded and old and to enable them to make choices about their lives.

Along the way the Commonwealth has enjoyed the cooperation, assistance and support of two University Affiliated Programs and some of the most talented and dedicated professionals in the field of human services. One of these people is Mary Howell. Dr. Howell, through her affiliation with the Eunice Kennedy Shriver Center, has helped guide our service development to persons with mental retardation who are old. She has developed program strategies and service models that have helped to emphasize the competencies and potential of our older population. Her clinical experience in working with people who are old has given focus to our initiatives for integration and for enabling healthy and active lives for people who are mentally retarded. She is recognized nationally as an expert who is guided by principles that value each and every individual as complete and whole.

Each page of this work reflects her commitment to these principles and to the possibilities for people who are old to be full participants in the economic, social, recreational, spiritual, and civic life of the community. She continues to play an important role in how our profession thinks about the opportunities that are presented to us today and the potential for tomorrow.

I hope that you are challenged in reading this collection of ideas and insights. I hope that you come to expect more from yourself and those you work with, in expecting more from those we serve. And ultimately I hope that the menu of services and opportunities for participation that we create for people who are both old and mentally retarded are the same kinds of services you would create for yourself.

Dr. Howell has given of herself in making these ideas realities. She has stretched the artificial boundaries we often create for people. She has taken risks in designing therapies that are new and innovative. And she has put herself on the line in direct services each and every day of her professional life. Enjoy this book, use it, take a risk and discover the possibilities we each carry into our later years as full participants in life.

Foreword

Peter O'Meara, Superintendent,
The Walter E. Fernald State School

■

As we reflect on the contribution of the Kennedy Aging Project to the Walter E. Fernald State School over the last three years, it is clear that Mary Howell and her staff created an environment in which we had an opportunity to learn and to increase our sensitivity on issues of aging in our society, especially with regard to citizens with mental retardation.

We at Fernald were fortunate to be the home of the Kennedy Aging Project. A striking change has occurred in these short years. Our values and attitudes about the rights of our senior citizens are changing. We recognize the imperative of their rights to lead a dignified life and to be recipients of services supportive of their individual emotional and physical needs.

The Kennedy Aging Project has helped us to learn, in an innovative forum, that

- A person who is old has the right to remain, if possible, in a familiar environment with familiar staff and peers.

- It is important to develop values about our citizens who are old that recognize the individuality and uniqueness of each; this must be the cornerstone of a service delivery plan.

- Rigidity in program models and systems is always counterproductive.

- In spirituality, a bond exists between our senior residents and ourselves that must not be taken for granted, a lesson we learned through the efforts and sharing of Fr. Henry Marquardt.

- Our success in meeting the needs of our clients is rooted in the way the larger system and society perceive the needs of those who are old; we have a responsibility to share values with the broader community.

- We have to take time away from the rigors of our daily routine to reflect on what we are doing, and why; the conference series of the Kennedy Aging Project provided a forum for reflective thinking about the needs of our aging clients.

- We don't have all the answers, but with a collective and cooperative effort we can change attitudes and improve services through mutual sharing.

- We are proud to care about people, our jobs are extremely important to society, and sometimes we undervalue ourselves.

- Small projects that are relatively free of the trappings of bureaucracy can be effective incubators for innovation.

The Kennedy Aging Project had a significant impact on the Fernald community and on the entire service-providing system, and I am grateful that our staff, our clients, and their families had an opportunity to participate. The challenge for all of us is to carry the work forward.

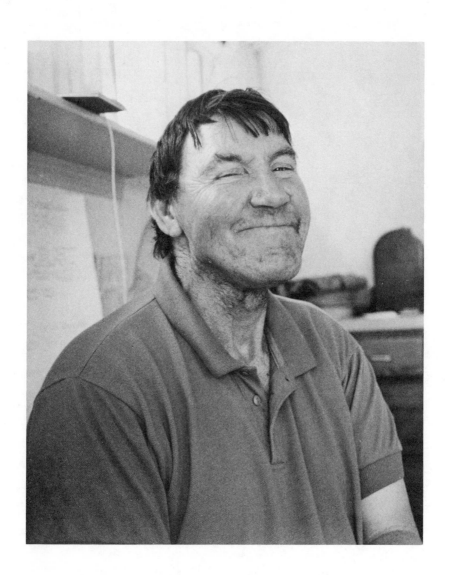

PART 2
INTRODUCTION

WORKING WITH PEOPLE WHO ARE OLD AND MENTALLY RETARDED

Mary C. Howell

■

Our work with people who are mentally retarded encourages us to challenge and question what we take for granted as given and fixed in human capacities, potentials, and yearnings. Watching the growth and development of a developmentally delayed child, we can observe—teased apart and proceeding at different rates—both the interdependence and the separateness of cognitive competence, affective maturity, social skills, communicative adaptability, neuromotor abilities, and other skills. In a similar manner, as we observe the developmental progress of the adult and aging person who is retarded, we become aware of separate threads of change in the raveling fabric that represents the approach to the end of life.

Erik Erikson, writing about the stages of the life cycle, proposes that in each stage there is a predominant conflict between two forces—one positive and one negative. We all resolve these conflicts in some fashion and to some degree, and from the resolutions we acquire certain strengths. In Erikson's last stages of Adulthood and Old Age, respectively, the conflicts are between generativity and stagnation, and integrity and despair. Out of the resolution of these conflicts will arise, if we are lucky, the strengths of *care* and *wisdom*. Erikson always reminds us that he speaks of a life course of cycles, each stage spiralling and overlapping with all the others over and over again. He also speaks of epigenesis, a concept that brings to mind both the progressive differentiation and diversification of the embryo, and the formation of mineral crystals—structures of increasing orderliness and complexity—in response to external pressures.

It is useful, in work with people who are mentally retarded and old, to think about progressive differentiation and unfolding; about the interaction of external forces and given potentials; about becoming "more like ourselves," more complex and more orderly, as we age; about life cycles spiraling around again, each superimposed on what has gone before; and about the meaning of the Eriksonian conflicts in the life of someone who is mentally retarded.

Ed is now sixty. He was born in 1928, after his mother had experienced four normal pregnancies. When he was born his mother was 38 and his father 41. Ed is said to have walked at the age of two-and-a-half and to have started to talk at the age of four. When he was seven he began school, but was soon returned to the home. They said he was "inattentive, listless, apathetic, and withdrawn."

At about that time his parents took him to a doctor—we do not know whether this was his first visit to a doctor—and he was diagnosed as a "hypotonic mongoloid, male." It was recommended that Ed be placed in an institution, but his mother found him easy to care for and wanted him to stay with the family. The following year, when he was eight, he was sent again to school, but the results were the same and after that he stayed home.

When Ed was 30 his mother became ill and was unable to care for him any more; she was then 68 years old. Ed was placed in a state residential school for the mentally retarded, and he lived there for almost 20 years. When he was 49, Ed moved to a community residence, where he now lives with four other men. He works at a sheltered workshop and earns pocket money. His parents are both dead now. One sister, who lives nearby, serves as a family contact person, but there are no family visitors for Ed.

We expect that Ed, with Down syndrome, will age ten to twenty years earlier than people who do not have Down syndrome. Like all people who are old, Ed has a variety of body changes that constitute some degree of "health problems." He has a growing cataract in his right eye; last November he had the cataract in his left eye removed and replaced with a lens implant. He has aortic and mitral cardiac valvular disease, and also a cardiac conduction defect; these are now asymptomatic, but must be watched and they may cause him some trouble as time goes on. Ed also has chronic constipation, a hiatal hernia, and rather fragile skin.

In the past few months there have been some subtle changes in Ed's behavior that make us wonder if the process called Alzheimer's disease is beginning. Ed used to look out the window and comment on the world going by, and he used to be able to hold an appropriately responsive conversation. Now, however, his spontaneous speech is quite restricted and what he says is increasingly limited to pat or rote phrases like "See ya later, alligator." He used to be something of a wanderer, traveling on occasion as far as five miles to the nearest shopping center, but recently he appears to be both more physically quiet and less curious. There are stories from the past of rather skillful social manipulation on Ed's part—feigning illness to get out of workshop early, for instance—and that sort of behavior has also very much diminished. There has also been some flattening of his emotional expression.

We know that a high proportion of those with Down syndrome, if they live long enough, are afflicted with a disorder that appears to be Senile Dementia of the Alzheimer's Type. Although we know something about the beginnings of Alzheimer's disease and its subsequent course in the non-retarded population, we need to understand better the earliest beginnings of this process in patients like Ed, so we can be of maximum help in arranging programs and living circumstances, and also in predicting, for family and caretaking staff alike, the probable course of the disorder.

We do not know with any certainty how many people there are who are mentally retarded and also old. This is a population that, years ago, we assumed would never exist. Calculating from the proportion of our population known to be retarded, and from estimates of longevity, we can guess that there are between 150,000 and 500,000 retarded citizens older than fifty-five; this group, as with the general population of old persons, is growing larger. The largest part of this number is mildly or moderately retarded, and is living in the community with relatives, friends, or alone.

Doris was born in 1912, the ninth and last child of her thirty-three-year-old mother. The pregnancy was uneventful, but the birth was difficult. Forceps were used, the occiput and the bridge of the baby's nose were crushed, and it was evident from the start that the infant was in trouble. They gave her her mother's name.

Doris has never walked or talked. She can feed herself slowly, she laughs and grumbles, and she has a strong sense of personal possessions and space, objecting to violations with angry pointing and loud vocalizations. Often she looks for a quiet space to escape from noise; there, she withdraws and covers her ears and eyes with her arms. She has warm social relationships and interacts by reaching out, hugging, and pinching. She stayed at home with her family until she was twelve, when she was admitted to a state residential school for people with mental retardation. Her older sisters said that she had a wonderful sense of humor and was a very special part of their family circle.

Doris' parents visited her almost weekly for five years, until her father died. Then her sister Dorothy accompanied her mother on monthly visits. Her family had always been concerned about her well-being, her clothing, her appetite, and her behavior. After their mother's death in 1950, her sisters Dorothy and Mary, who live together, have continued these visits, which now take place once a year. In 1982, at the age of 70, Doris moved to an Intermediate Care Facility, especially designed and built for people who are mentally retarded, in the same community where her sisters live.

Doris suffers from various rashes and sores, some of which are related to her incontinence. There is atrophy of her leg musculature and also contractures. She has been operated on repeatedly for cysts of her eyelids; she rubs her eyes and has frequent bouts of conjunctivitis. But in general, Doris has remarkably good health for her age.

It is likely that, one of these days, Doris will have a severe pneumonia or some other life-threatening acute medical problem. Important decisions will have to be made promptly at that time. For instance, should she be transferred to an Intensive Care Unit in one of the teaching hospitals with which we are affiliated? Doris is fortunate to have family members actively involved in her life—her two sisters are co-guardians—and these are questions that need to be brought to their attention before such a medical crisis arises.

For some residents in institutions, as well as some elderly persons living in their homes, a hospice approach to care, which emphasizes comfort, support, and the assurance of familiar surroundings, may be most desirable. As professionals charged with supervision of Doris' ongoing care, we are responsible for helping family members—including members of the direct-care staff, who constitute a *de facto* family of care—to consider all options and facets of the goals of comfort, dignity, and autonomy for the patient in the care we give.

Margaret was born in 1919, the second of two daughters. Her mother thought that something might be unusual about this baby when Margaret was six months old and unable to be propped into a sitting position. From birth her limbs were spastic and weak. She walked with help at the age of four-and-a-half years. She has never really talked in the usual sense, although she speaks a sort of musical gibberish and says several repetitious phrases like "I'm all right, dear."

Margaret was admitted to a state residential institution when she was 34, 39 years ago. Her father had died nine years before that and for a while her mother struggled to care for Margaret with the help of a daily attendant, but her mother was 66 and ill when Margaret was finally brought to the school.

Margaret's mother visited her regularly and also wrote her letters until her own death in 1961. Since then there have been no visitors and no letters until just a few months ago, when Margaret's sister began to take more account of Margaret's health problems.

When Margaret was admitted to the school she was confined to a wheelchair, and she remains so. She has regular physical therapy to help her retain what motor function she has. After a lifetime of chronic and recurrent urinary tract infections Margaret now has severely damaged kidneys—small and shrunken, by X-ray—and she appears to be headed for renal failure. She also has chronic bronchitis, osteoporosis, occasional bleeding from her gastrointestinal tract, and chronic skin irritation and infections.

Some decisions will need to be made about the desirability of medical procedures that might prolong Margaret's life, without cure, procedures that are almost certain to be uncomfortable and restrictive and perhaps even painful.

For patients like Margaret, as for instance with our patients with incurable cancer, we are concerned with the need for establishing an appropriate process of deciding—in concert with the wishes of the patients, if possible, and the families and also their guardians, if need be—on a reasonable balance between those medical procedures that might prolong life, and other medical procedures that are thoughtfully and vigorously planned to make the patient's final months, weeks, and days as comfortable and reassuring as possible.

> *Harold has always lived with his mother. When he was born in 1922, his father and two sisters also shared the family home, but now only Harold and his mother survive. Harold attends a day program in a nearby church every weekday; his mother shops and cooks, and a homemaker comes twice a week to help with the housework. Harold has never had services from the state Department of Mental Retardation. His nephew, who is Harold's co-guardian along with Harold's mother, is concerned that some arrangements be made for Harold's care when, in the foreseeable future, his mother becomes too frail to continue to provide care and a home for him.*
>
> *Harold is moderately retarded. He has never learned to read, but he can follow simple instructions and does helpful chores around the house. In the day program, also, he assumes janitorial responsibilities and is well-regarded as helpful and reliable. His health is good except for a limp (the residual of a poorly healed fracture suffered when he was young), some arthritis of both hips that is exacerbated by rainy weather, and diminishing hearing that is only partly remedied by hearing aids.*
>
> *His mother is adamantly certain that she does not want Harold to move out of her home. She seems to be unable to make plans for him, nor to allow her grandson (Harold's co-guardian) to begin to explore options for Harold's placement. When asked what she imagines will happen, she says that she hopes that "Harold will die right after I do."*

Erikson proposes a spiraling of life cycles, each conflict returning again and again so that each strength is reinforced and elaborated in different contexts across the lifespan. The strength that arises from the conflict of the first stage, the conflict between trust and mistrust, is the strength of *hope*, a strength we need to be able to fall back on throughout life and especially at the end of life. Hope is built out of and defined in part by the experience of the trustworthiness of others.

For people who are mentally retarded, who need to rely to some degree on the care of others through the whole life span, trustworthiness is a critical and recurrent issue. Those who choose to provide care for them do so in community, which is knit together with a bond of trustworthiness.

Care, which includes caring for and taking care of, is the strength that Erikson posits as the result of the resolution of the conflict of the adult stage—the conflict between generativity and stagnation. Working to provide care for clients who are old and mentally retarded provides daily illustrations of this Eriksonian dictum.

People who are mentally retarded are not only on the receiving end of care, but also they offer care to each other. They give and accept it between themselves both in pairs (in long-time relationships arising in the workplace or in shared residence), and in the family groupings that evolve over time. Not long ago, one of the residents of a state facility died in his own bed, in his own room, after a prolonged illness with metastatic cancer. His housemates knew that he was ill and was dying. They would come home from work and ask how he was doing, "shhhh" each other when he was sleeping, and bring him glasses of juice. They knew when he died, cried appropriately because they missed him, and attended his funeral. It was altogether a familial occurrence.

Erikson's last strength is *wisdom,* born of the conflict between integrity and despair. I also acknowledge the wisdom of my friends who are old and mentally retarded, even though that wisdom may not be entirely shared with me because of the nature of their communicative abilities. But I am confident that there *is* wisdom after six or seven or eight decades of seeing and hearing, touching and being touched, moving in space and relating to others.

5

THE EDUCATIONAL COMPONENT OF THE PROJECT

Mary C. Howell

■

The charge from the Kennedy Foundation for our Project was to teach health professionals about the problems and care of people who are both old and mentally retarded. We chose to define "health" broadly, to include well-being in every arena of life, to go beyond purely medical considerations.

We envisioned an Interdisciplinary Team composed of representatives from a variety of health-related professions. We sought to assemble, on a part-time basis, faculty who would serve as mentors to students studying in their various fields.

We intended to teach in many contexts. Graduate students in professional training were invited to join us for sixteen hours a week over an entire academic year, with a modest stipend. These students would function as full members of the Team, learning not only from the professional faculty member representing their own discipline, but also from faculty members representing all the other health-related disciplines.

Further, we anticipated opportunities to publish literature and to present at professional meetings. We planned to visit community residences, workplaces, day programs, and area offices of the state Department of Mental Retardation. Three one-day conferences were planned for each year, with presentations from our faculty (and students, as they became ready to present) for mixed audiences of professionals and paraprofessionals working with this group of clients.

Clients who are already in the care of publicly-supported service systems are growing old, and agencies charged with caring for people who are mentally retarded often claim that they know little about people who are old. Conversely, agencies providing care for old people maintain that they do not know about people who are mentally retarded.

Finally, people with mental retardation who have never come to the attention of formal caregiving agencies, who have remained with family and other private arrangements for care, are very likely in their old age to request services of one sort or another from formal agencies. Like all old people, those with mental retardation differ broadly within groups, depending on the nature of their physical and mental disabilities, their life experiences, and their opportunities for health-promoting activities such as physical exercise, participation in a community, and close personal relationships.

We recognized several themes that would shape our work. Health promotion—physical activity, a nutritious diet, optimal use of leisure time, engagement in work and other esteem-generating activities—became a central focus. The need for community integration, long an important concern for those working on behalf of people with mental retardation, is especially poignant when clients are old, for our society tends to segregate and exclude all people who are old. In old age, experiences of loss and the attendant mourning are constants; anticipation of one's own death is a universal developmental task. Yet our contemporary culture makes it difficult for us to look at death as an expected transition; in preliminary conversations with individual caregivers, a recurrent request centered on the need for training on issues related to death and dying. In addition, we recognized as a central theme the preoccupation of "doing the right thing" in situations where there were dilemmas of an ethical nature.

The content of our teaching was to a large extent determined by the disciplines in which our various faculty members were trained, and by the specific experiences each of us brought to the project. For instance, the physicians on the team had had direct day-to-day experience in diagnosis and care of patients with Alzheimer's disease, the attorneys were expert in disability law, and the nurse practitioner was knowledgeable about community resources for the care of clients who are old and mentally retarded.

In addition to the knowledge and skills that each of us bought to the Project, we referred constantly to our clients and caregivers for direction as to the educational needs in which they had special interest. This may be best seen in the organization of our conferences (see Figures 1-8), which were planned in direct response to needs expressed by the community of caregivers we wished to address. The organization of this handbook reflects our understanding of what we can teach that will most support the service efforts of many dedicated and hardworking caregivers.

Figure 1
Program
Maintenance of Function in People
Who Are Old and Mentally Retarded

9:00	Introduction: What Are People Who Are Old and Mentally Retarded Like?	
	Group Characteristics and Service Needs	Mary Howell, M.D., Ph.D.
9:30	Community Resources and Financing	Alice Wells, M.S.W.
10:00	Leisure and Recreation Programming	Elizabeth DeBrine, M. Ed.
10:45	Spiritual and Religious Concerns	Fr. Henry Marquardt
11:15	The Alzheimer's Down's Connection	Mary Howell, M.D., Ph.D.
11:45	Behavior Problems: Analysis and Management	Frank S.G. Wells, M.D.
1:30	Guardianship	Louis Aucoin, J.D.
2:15	Estate Planning for Families	Henry Beyer, J.D.
3:15	Legal and Ethical Problems of Privacy and Confidentiality	Eric Harris, Ed.D., J.D.

Figure 2
Program
Who Are Our Clients Who Are Old and Mentally Retarded?
What Are Their Needs?

9-9:30	Special Problems and Benefits Working with the Clients Who Are Both Old and Mentally Retarded...Mary C. Howell, M.D., Ph.D.
9:30-10:00	Primary Health Care Needs...Fran Wiltsie, R.N.-C., N.P.
10:00-10:30	Dimensions of Well-Being...Edith Finaly, M.Ed., M.Sc.
11:00-11:45	Cognitive Changes in the Aging Process...Arianna Fucini, Ph.D.
11:45-12:15	Options in Recreational Programming...Liz DeBrine, M.Ed.
1:15-1:45	Vocational and Recreational Settings...Mary Howell, M.D., Ph.D.
1:45-215	Guardianship...Louis Aucoin, J.D.
2:15-2:45	Estate Planning for Families and Clients...Henry Beyer, J.D.
3:00-3:15	Spiritual Concerns...Marjorie Rucker, S.L.P.N.

Figure 3
Program
When Are Current Services Not Enough?
Innovative Approaches for Clients
Who Are Both Old and Mentally Retarded

9:00	Introduction: When Are Current Services Not Enough?...Mary Howell, M.D., Ph.D.
9:30	Use of Generic Senior Day Programs...Gary Seltzer, Ph.D.
10:30	Elder Enrichment Programs...Marylee DeLaiarro, LPN
11:00	Maintaining Safety in Community Residences...Fran Wiltsie, RN-C., N.P.
11:30	Psychological Perspectives...Arianna Fucini, Ph.D.
1:00	Health Related Treatment Approaches... Staff from Wallace Building, Fernald School
2:00	Alternative Housing...Henry Beyer, J.D.
2:45	Retirement: Now or Never?...Elizabeth DeBrine, M.Ed.

Figure 4
Program
What Services Are Available for Persons
Who Are Both Mentally Retarded and Old?

9:00	Maintenance of Function...Mary Howell, MD, PhD
9:30	Community Residences and Workshops...Marsha Seltzer, PhD
10:00	Religious Communities and Recreation...Liz DeBrine, EdM
10:45	Support to Caregivers...Edith Finaly, EdM
11:15	Desensitization to Health-Related Tests and Procedures ...Alison Boyer, NP
12:45	Hospice for Institutionalized Older Adults...Mary Howell, MD, PhD
1:15	Funeral and Memorial Services...Tom Barbera
1:45	Affective Disorder and Proxy Decision-Making...David Stone, MA, Henry Beyer, JD
2:30	Break
2:45	Physical Activity Programming for Older Adults...Liz DeBrine, EdM

Figure 5
Program
Retirement: Developmental Issues

9:00	What Is Meaningful Work?	Mary C. Howell, MD, PhD
9:30	History of Retirement:	
	Problems and Issues	Liz DeBrine, MEd, CTRS
10:00	Double Jeopardy: Origin and Impact	Bruce Blaney, MA
11:00	Current Service Trends	Bruce Blaney, MA
1:00	The Future We Are In	Bruce Blaney, MA
2:00	Guidelines for Planning	Bruce Blaney, MA
3:00	Designing Creative Options	Bruce Blaney, MA
		Liz DeBrine, MEd
		Mary C. Howell, MD, PhD

Figure 6
Program
Hospice Care

9-9:30	Hospice care for adults who are mentally retarded and old	Mary C. Howell, Md, PhD
9:30-10	How cognitive limitations affect one's thoughts about death	Gary B. Seltzer, PhD
10:10:45	Nursing needs and issues	Barbara Parton, RN, BS
1? 11:30	Death and dying as a process	Mary C. Howell, MD, PhD
11:30-12	Funerals and memorial services	Rev. Henry Marquardt, MEd
1-1:45	Guidelines for training direct care staff	Tom Barbera
1:45-2:30	Symbolic listening	Virginia Fry, BGS
2:45-3:15	Loss and creative survival	Virginia Fry, BGS
3:15-4	Constellations in grief	Virginia Fry, BGS

Figure 7
Program
The Promotion of Spirituality
in a Secular Service Environment

9-9:45	Spirituality in a secular service world	Mary Howell, MD, PhD
9:45-10:30	How to modify religious services for people who are both old and mentally retarded	Fr. Henry Marquardt, MEd.
10:45-11:15	How to conduct a spiritual assessment in an Interdisciplinary Team	Sr. Bridget Bearss, MEd
11:15-12:00	"I Should Know A Lot, I Been Around So Long"	Videotape
1-1:45	Sexuality: Unifying body, mind, and spirit	Stephen Draft
1:45-2:30	Intimacy issues with clients and caregivers	Sr. Bridget Bearss, MEd
2:45-3:15	Carl's Story: The church as advocate	Liz DeBrine, MEd

Figure 8
Program
Care and Nurturing of People
Who Are Mentally Retarded and Old

9:30-10:00	Cognitive Approach to Understanding Death and Dying Among Clients with Mental Retardation	Gary Seltzer, Ph.D.
10:00-10:30	The Utility of Rehabilitation Philosophy in the Care of Clients with Mental Retardation	Keith Robinson, M.D.
10:45-11:15	Physical Fitness for Clients Who Are Old and Mentally Retarded	Elizabeth DeBrine, M.Ed., C.T.R.S.
11:15-12:00	Memorial Services	Father Henry Marquardt, M.Ed.
12:00-1:00	Lunch	
1:00-1:30	Programming for People Who are Developmentally Disabled, Old, and Frail	Tom Barbera
1:30-2:00	Interdisciplinary Teams	Mary Howell, M.D., Ph.D.
2:00-2:30	Protecting the Rights of the Person with Alzheimer's Disease	Deidre Gavin, M.A.T.
2:45-3:15	Housing Alternatives	Henry Beyer, J.D.

6

THE CONTEXT OF EXEMPLARY SERVICE

Mary C. Howell

■

It is a tradition of the Community Evaluation and Rehabilitation Center of the Eunice Kennedy Shriver Center, the parent organization in which the Kennedy Aging Project was housed, that student training and education takes place in a context of exemplary service. The Aging Project readily adopted this educational format.

Our field placement students were all enrolled in graduate training programs in their specific clinical disciplines; all had experience in providing direct service; and all had immediate supervision not only from the faculty member of their special discipline, but also from all faculty members representing the entire range of disciplines on the Team. Therefore we were able to enroll them as members of the Interdisciplinary Team in providing services.

One of the pleasures of advocating for and inventing services for previously underserved clients lies in the opportunity to think about ideal models. Clients who are both mentally retarded and old have truly been underserved. Their very existence was hardly acknowledged prior to the last decade; in addition, like every other subgroup of our population, their group longevity is increasing, so their numbers—and needs—are expanding.

There were several areas of intervention that we anticipated as foci of our efforts as a service project. While we could envision neither all the problems nor all their resolutions, we had some clear ideas of the kinds of services that we would search for and strive to promote.

Residential placement, for instance, is a universal need. Everyone has to have a place to live, and the housing needs of people who are both old and mentally retarded are more like the housing needs of everyone else than they are different. There is a need for security—a reasonable guarantee that one will not have to move suddenly or capriciously. An aesthetically pleasing and valued neighborhood, access to transportation, and private personal space where one's belongings are safe, are valid expectations.

Most people enjoy some contact every day with others who are their age-peers, and some contact every day with people who are older and younger than they are. Unfortunately, much housing has predetermined age limits, and thus results in *de facto* age segregation. Age segregation in residential facilities may also be set by limits established by other regulations. Even though most of the frailties of old age are not medical problems, funds to hire extra helping hands are often provided only for medically diagnosed "illnesses" that are amenable to remedy. For instance, arthritic joints that limit ambulation, and diminishing acuity of vision, hearing, and touch, call for extra help—not expensive professional help, but help from caregivers who are thoughtful, kind, and energetic. Such extra help may have to be fought for, as it runs counter to our established funding conventions.

Other amenities of housing that we all need include the provision of fresh, locally available food of the highest variety and quality. Frail old people cannot afford to waste their energy eating food of poor quality. Opportunities for self-determination and choice, opportunities to make significant contributions to group welfare, and opportunities to participate in meaningful group decision-making are reasonable priorities in a welcoming home. And the environment—inside and outside—should be free and protected as much as possible from chemical pollution, including that of tobacco smoke.

Another area of intervention was work, the answer to the question "What do you do during the day?" We all need to have daytime occupations that are interesting and varied, that provide opportunities for productivity, and that reward us with self-esteem as demonstrated by status, pay, advancement, and recognition. Work brings opportunities for socialization and the establishment of long-term friendships. One definition of "right livelihood" is that it gives us the possibility of doing something worthwhile, and doing it well. People who are mentally retarded and old need these values in their lives as much as we all do. Finding appropriate daytime activities for our clients proved to be an arena of service need that cried for intervention.

Play was an equally important area of service. We all require opportunities for vigorous physical exercise and for out-of-doors experience, in and out of the city. We need access to activities in the community that are "open to all"; often this access requires not only transportation, but also a friend who can help facilitate integration. We need the experience of making friends in the course of play, and the privilege of choosing our own times and places for leisure activities.

We foresaw other major areas of intervention in the course of trying to arrange the best possible service provision for our clients. One was the clarification and defense of the client's legal rights. We had often seen that people who were old and mentally retarded were not treated with the dignity and privilege that was their right by law. Another area was attention to the client's needs for spiritual and religious participation in community. Support for the development and maintenance of social relationships was known to be a fragile area of need for people whose care was provided through an institutionalized system. And, finally, we would be concerned with securing provision of enough—but not too much—medical service.

With these areas of intervention in mind, we undertook to teach our students by inviting them to be members of our Clinical Team, and made it known to the wider caregiver community that we were a new resource for assessment and recommendations.

7

THE INTERDISCIPLINARY TEAM: TWO PERSPECTIVES

Mary C. Howell and Henry A. Beyer

■ 1. Commencing and Developing the Content and Process of Working Together
by Mary C. Howell

The Kennedy Aging Project began with certain requirements and expectations with regard to faculty, students, and staff. We were to assemble a faculty who could teach students who were enrolled in professional training, on a field-placement model. We wished to bring together as broad a spectrum of health-related professions as possible. There were exigencies of time (the team needed to be assembled in a matter of a few weeks), of geography (we had time only to recruit faculty participants from the Boston area), and of funds (even with the generous funding of the Kennedy Foundation and the Department of Mental Retardation, we needed to find faculty who would be willing to work with us for only a few hours a week).

Further, in 1985 when the Aging Project began, there were no accessible models for an interdisciplinary team that functioned in the area of service to clients who were both mentally retarded and old. Few professionals considered this area of expertise to be a primary identification. For all of these reasons, assembling a smoothly functioning team was partly a matter of serendipity.

Individuals who were excited by the venture of a new project and who were willing to set out in uncharted waters came together to evolve a project by their joint efforts. Certain assumptions were represented by the Project Director; a sense of affiliation or attachment to these assumptions may have been a primary organizing principle of the team as it assembled itself. These assumptions related less to content (which we would discover as we began our work) than to process. They included:

- An intent to avoid a "medical model" of working, in which single diagnoses were sought, intrapsychic explanations were regarded as especially significant, and the authority of the physician was dominant in team deliberations.

- A curiosity about the extent to which interdisciplinary cooperation and learning could be pushed. It is notable that almost all members of the Project were trained, and exercised expertise, in at least one discipline other than the disciplines they represented in the Project; apparently, interdisciplinary people enjoy interdisciplinary work.

- A strong personal need to "serve the underserved."

We began without a preordered plan of how to work together. One of our early concerns was to devise instruments for collecting information about the clients that we would be seeing. This we did both as individuals representing specific disciplines (the member of the Team who was a nurse evolved a nursing assessment instrument, the lawyers developed a procedure for legal assessment, and so on) and also as a team.

The assessment procedures that evolved from the work of the Team as a group were based on a conception of a person and the various domains of his or her life, arranged as concentric circles of decreasing personal salience and intimacy to the most distant, the domain of the law, ethics, politics, and culture (See Figure 1). This visual representation was then used to array domains against disciplines, so we could ask, what information would a social worker—or clinical psychologist, or a pastoral counselor—want to know (for instance) about the client's personal relationships, integration in the community, or sensory capabilities? (See Figure 2).

Following this conceptual guide, we evolved a series of questions designed to elicit information that we believed we needed to know about our clients. The questions themselves were later divided into three categories: (1) information that was most efficiently provided in paper-and-pencil questionnaire form, such as the names of medications that the client was presently using, his Medicaid and Medicare numbers, and the names and addresses of the client's nearest family members; (2) information that could comfortably be provided in a telephone interview, such as the client's activities of daily living, leisure and recreation interests, and usual means of transportation; and (3) information that was best requested in a face-to-face interview, such as current behavior problems, caregiver stress and burden, and the client's satisfaction with his living arrangements, work, and leisure opportunities.

Figure 1
Domains of Function

As we developed these information-collecting procedures we also learned a great deal about how we worked together. We began to function as a Team. Throughout the three years of our relationship as members of the Project, we continually refined our ways of working together (see Figure 3). Our individual processes of evaluation became refined and were enriched by our growing experience and the observations of fellow Team members. We learned to teach and support each other, sharing the concepts and language of our particular disciplines.

Figure 2
Traditional Areas of Functioning

	Physical	Mental	Service	Housing	Legal	Work/Voc	Nutrition	Financial	Social Support
Person	1. Health Status Items 2. Medical Assistance 3. Drugs 4. Health Problems	1. Adaptive Behavior Assessment 2. Health Problems 3. MR Client Interview	Medical Assistance Equipment	MR Client Interview		MR Client Interview	Dietary Needs Survey		Spiritual MR Client Interview
Interactions With Environment	1. Health Status Items 2. Medical Assistance 3. Drugs 4. Health Problems	1. Adaptive Behavior Assessment 2. Health 3. Behavior Problem Checklist	Basic Needs Scale	Residential and Housing Questions	Service and Assistance Scales	Work/Voc Program Questions		Financial Status Questions	
Family/Caregivers Coping Support		1. Behavior Problems 2. Service and Assistance 3. Adaptive Behavior		Residential and Housing Questions					Social Resources Questions Family Burden Interview

Figure 2, cont.
Traditional Areas of Functioning

	Physical	Mental	Service	Housing	Legal	Work/Voc	Nutrition	Financial	Social Support
Community Resources Access Adequacy			Service and Assistance Scale	Residential and Housing Questions	Financial Status	Work/Voc Program			
Culture Law Policy Ethics			Service and Assistance Scale		Legal Issues Questions				Spiritual Needs

We evolved new ways of working together—pure process. And as we became more skillful, we shared with each other the nuances and subtleties of asking questions and understanding answers in the various information-gathering instruments. All of these different aspects of our work proceeded simultaneously and in tandem, alternately and repeatedly. At the end of three years, we worked with much greater ease, subtlety, and efficiency as a Team. With a longer passage of time, we might have developed these qualities to an even greater extent.

Figure 3
Interdisciplinary Team Process

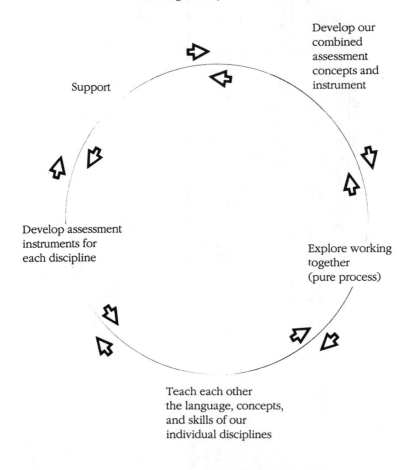

Develop our combined assessment concepts and instrument

Support

Develop assessment instruments for each discipline

Explore working together (pure process)

Teach each other the language, concepts, and skills of our individual disciplines

Finally, we agreed that the work we did was indeed collaborative work. Nothing was exclusively in the service of individual academic promotion, personal gain, or public approbation. We took seriously the problems and pleasures of working as a Team.

■ 2. "Who Is Our Client?" by Henry A. Beyer

Lawyers, in general, have probably even less experience than other professionals in serving as "co-equal members" of an Interdisciplinary Team. Although lawyers frequently work with physicians, psychologists, social workers, or other professionals in developing or pleading a client's case, these other professionals are typically viewed as expert resources to be used only if and when the attorney determines, to provide support or credibility for the client's position. On those occasions that lawyers do serve on an equal footing with professionals from other disciplines, it is usually as part of a board or committee addressing business, organizational, or public policy issues, not on a group seeing and serving individual clients. Working on the Kennedy Aging Project was therefore a novel experience for the lawyers.

One question that surfaced in various guises throughout the Project's three years, and that appeared to trouble the lawyers especially, was that of identifying which of the various participants in a case was the Team's "client." The American Bar Association (ABA's) Model Code of Professional Responsibility places heavy emphasis on the fiduciary nature of the relationship existing between an attorney and her client.[1] It stresses that clients must feel free to discuss whatever they wish with their lawyer,[2] and that lawyers must act scrupulously in making decisions that may involve the disclosure of information obtained in a professional relationship.[3]

These maxims, which of course are present in all professions, but which appear to weigh more heavily in the legal field, raised certain concerns for the Team's lawyers. These arose from the fact that the Team was to interview and provide advice not only to people who are old and mentally retarded, but also to their families, professional caregivers, and to representatives of state service-providing agencies. In order to eliminate confusion over who enjoyed a fiduciary relationship—whose disclosures must be treated confidentially—the lawyers wished to establish from the outset which of these players would hold the status of "client."

Lawyers who had previously worked with public interest advocacy organizations, such as a legal services office or a protection and advocacy (P&A) system, initially believed that the person with mental retardation should be designated as the Team's client in all cases, except where that individual had a legal guardian, in which case the guardian would enjoy that status. Other Team members pointed out, however, that: (1) in virtually all cases, it was another party who would be requesting the Team's services[4]; (2) the problem(s) underlying a presenting complaint would frequently turn out to reside in persons or agencies other than the person with mental retardation (or in interactions between these others and the person with mental retardation), and the Team's services should be directed toward assisting those other parties to address those problems; (3) in many cases, the person who was mentally retarded and old would be functionally incompetent to retain legal counsel and would have no legal guardian to represent him.

This last situation presented, perhaps, the greatest ethical and practical problem for the approach espoused by the attorneys.[5] The mechanism traditionally used for dealing with this situation is the creation of a legal guardianship.[6] Establishing even a limited guardianship for the purpose of our Interdisciplinary Team evaluation in such cases appeared, however, an excessively intrusive, cumbersome, and expensive solution to the problem. The experience of several Team members also indicated that finding enough suitable individuals or organizations to serve as guardians would be virtually impossible. Furthermore, if the person with mental retardation were to be considered the Team lawyer's "client," it is even possible that any measures the attorney might take toward imposing guardianship might be considered violative of his fiduciary duty to the client.[7]

It was noted, however, that the ABA Code also recognizes that "[t]he responsibilities of a lawyer may vary according to the intelligence, experience, mental condition or age of a client...or the nature of a particular proceeding."[8] Furthermore, "[i]f a client under disability has no legal representative, his lawyer may be compelled in court proceedings to make decisions on behalf of his client...If the disability of a client and the lack of legal representative compel the lawyer to make decisions for his client, the lawyer should consider all circumstances then prevailing and act with care to safeguard and advance the interests of his client."[9]

After considerable discussion, the Team decided not to establish an inflexible rule for denoting the Team's "client," but to make this decision on a case-by-case basis. It was also noted that, in many cases, the "client" might not even be a single individual, but might consist of the several people constituting the family or caregiving unit. Although this was, in fact, how the Aging Project operated throughout its three years, Team members generally used the term "client" to refer to the individual who was old and mentally retarded. That usage is retained throughout this book.

The Team's lawyers stilled their ethical and legal qualms by reasoning as follows: (1) the relationship between the Team and its clients (whomever they turned out to be) was not that of an attorney and client in the legal sense, and nothing in the Project's statements or literature would portray it as such; (2) all parties would be informed, verbally and in writing, of the Team's composition (including its student membership) and its function, and of the right of all persons interviewed by the Team to decline to answer any of the Team's questions; (3) as a program of the Massachusetts Department of Mental Retardation, the Team would be authorized by state regulations to read and interpret the records of the clients with mental retardation that it served, and to provide proxy consent to routine or preventative medical care[10]; and (4) any individuals whom the Team believed to be in need of legal representation or continuing counseling would be referred to attorneys independent of the Project for such services. Several such referrals, to both private and public interest lawyers, were made in each of the Project's three years, with the Legal Aid Clinical Program of Boston University School of Law serving as the most frequent referral.

8

THE CLIMATE OF OUR WORK

Mary C. Howell

■

Ethical values embodied in workplace environments facilitate productivity, genuine and growth-enhancing personal relations, and an
awareness that we all struggle in our work to define and follow a
spiritual path.

These connections can be made explicit by pairing specific ethical
tenets[1] with certain domains of workplace values that appear to correspond, as an ethics in-the-field. The first tenet is that relationship with
other beings, rather than the declaration, defense, and exercise of
individual rights, is the central priority of ethical enactment. In the work
of the Kennedy Aging Project, the participants (professional and nonprofessional, faculty and students) chose to work with recipients of their
service who were not only mentally retarded but also old, a group that
is doubly disparaged and neglected by most of the professional community. The charge to the Project by the funding agency was to teach
health professionals about these people as clients; the Interdisciplinary
Team chose to do that teaching in a context of direct, face-to-face
service. Most settings for health care focus on the curing (transformative) transaction. The Kennedy Aging Project, in contrast, accepted
profound levels of disability and handicap as givens, and worked to
better the quotidian context of lives that were recognized to be triumphs
of a human survival spirit.

A second ethical tenet is that the giving and receiving of care,
appropriate to specific persons and their situations, is the measure of
outcome of ethically determined behavior. By contrast, other systems
of ethical measure look to the autonomy or liberty of the individual. In
the Kennedy Aging Project, the central focus of our work was to take
care of our clients (and their caregivers) and each other. The office was
planned so that waiting clients and caregivers could be amused and
pleased. Waiting itself was kept to a minimum. Telephone contacts and

opportunities of introduction were consciously courteous and welcoming. Our lunchtimes were deliberately social times, occasions for expression of a familial interest and concern. No effort was made to bolster a sense of the autonomy of individuals working in the Project, except in our intent to respect the work efforts of each other—in the sense that each was an independent and self-regulating worker and none was exclusively the waitperson for any other.

A third ethical tenet emphasizes interdependence over individualism, and a mutuality of giving and receiving over entitlements to taking nurture from others. The manifestation of these emphases in a day-to-day work environment appears most consistently as a leveling of status. Every faculty person and administrator in the Kennedy Aging Project participated in direct, face-to-face contact with clients who were old and mentally retarded; each also was personally responsible for telephone calls to caregivers, contact agencies, and family members on behalf of clients, and for summary letters that described in detail the findings and recommendations of the Interdisciplinary Team. The Interdisciplinary Team itself played out the themes of interdependence and mutuality, as no single discipline was preeminent, and as each representative of a distinct discipline (law, medicine, leisure, social work, ministry, nursing, psychology, and rehabilitation medicine) was responsible for teaching all other team members a rudimentary familiarity with special disciplinary language, concepts, and processes.

A fourth ethical tenet is a focus on a concrete and particular other, in contrast to an ethics that speaks of the other as generalized, faceless, and impersonal. The Kennedy Aging Project steadfastly refused to reduce the clients that we worked with to a statistically blended "population." In fact, one treasure that each of us takes from our work in the Project is a compendium of interviews, home visits, and accounts of life histories of intensely memorable individuals. The power of this experience would be reduced if it were to be leveled into impersonal generalities, as is the common manner of research.

A fifth ethical tenet counters the process by which other systems of ethics propose formulaic, deductive decisions. Instead, decisions are sought that are rooted in context and are responsive to the particularities of the individual case. In the Kennedy Aging Project, this preference was played out in meticulous examination of the life circumstances of each client, with detailed consideration of every aspect, not only of dysfunction, disability, and handicap, but also of resource and capability. We were helped, of course, by the fact that each case presented dilemmas of care and required thoughtful brainstorming to search out all possible avenues of solution for finding needed services.

In the sixth tenet, the characteristic processes of this ethical system are circular rather than linear, atemporal rather than time-bound, and accepting rather than transformative. These characteristics of process were played out at the Kennedy Aging Project in the establishment of rituals, repeated acts of mutual help, and social exchanges based on story-telling. For instance, a potluck party was celebrated every three months, with ritualized formalities of invitation, decoration, and food specialties. Every Monday morning, two or three of us brought freshly baked breads as part of Team meeting. We served as an interdisciplinary clipping service for each other, bringing items of interest not only in direct relation to our shared work, but also in response to personal interests such as quilting, backpacking, and vegetarian cooking. And we told and retold stories of our families, especially our children, and our own hobbies and avocations, so that we all became observers of each other enmeshed in the small everyday details of our individual lives.

Finally, it is a tenet of our ethics that virtue is seen as the highest good (an emphasis that takes precedence over justice) and that at every juncture, exploitation and hurt are to be avoided. I believe that this perspective also was embodied in the work of the Kennedy Aging Project by our devoted attention to provision of the best possible service to our clients and the best possible education for our students, both those with whom we worked directly and those with whom we communicated by written materials. By this firm attention to service and education—the *content* of our appointed work—we deemphasized any focus on power relations either within our project or as we were embedded in a larger agency. We wasted little energy firming our position in the agency; we did not need to maneuver for power with each other within the Project.

These characteristics of our work resulted in an energetic devotion to the Project by almost all participants. I believe that the Kennedy Aging Project can be seen as a model of a workplace environment that embodies many ethical values, and that offers an environment that feels welcoming, appreciative, and appropriate.

9

THE STRUCTURE OF OUR WORK

Gerard Cabrera

■

In its three-year existence, the Kennedy Aging Project served a varied clientele and became a link in a network of service providers, scholars, and professionals that has crossed international boundaries.

The Kennedy Aging Project was always seen as a multi- purpose, multi-function endeavor. As a training project, it was intended to teach health professionals (including graduate students) about the needs and care of people who are old and mentally retarded. As a service project, the Interdisciplinary Team Evaluation Clinic was created to provide a holistic evaluation approach for our clients. Our goal was to take into account as many facets of the clients' lives as possible and to address their needs as comprehensively as we could. Maintaining function by the least restrictive and most appropriate means was one of our primary goals.

A process was set up to refer and assign clients to a faculty case manager and a student case worker. Referrals were made by telephone to the intake worker, who did a preliminary screening to ascertain the appropriateness of the referral: Could we do anything to help? Was the client's presenting problem one that could be related to aging and decline of function? Was the client diagnosed as being mentally retarded? The intake worker asked for preliminary information (birthdate, addresses, whether the client was a "class client" under the Consent Decrees approved by the federal court (see Chapter 19), what medications she was taking at the present, and finally, what did the caregivers expect and want as a result of the evaluation). After the preliminary intake interview, a questionnaire was mailed to the caregiver along with a release form to obtain records, and an appointment date was set. (See Appendix)

On the day of the initial visit, the client and caregivers met the faculty person and student to whom the case had been assigned and were interviewed by them to learn further details about the client's circumstances and needs. After about an hour of interviewing, the faculty person and student reported to the Team and the case was discussed. Plans were then made for additional evaluations (as needed), such as an interview and testing session with the psychologist, a leisure assessment, or a pastoral care assessment. The result of the Interdisciplinary Team evaluation, usually arrived at several weeks later, was a final report that summarized the Team's recommendations and included all individual reports and results. The Team met twice a week during the academic year (September-May).

Another of the Aging Project's services was the Case Conference. The Case Conference served as a smaller-scale, more focused version of the Interdisciplinary Team Evaluation Clinic. For caregivers who were concerned about a particular dilemma of care, or who wanted interdisciplinary consultation because of some particular change in their client, the Case Conference provided a forum in which several individual experts could consult as a group. Clients were not present at Case Conferences.

After a preliminary telephone interview and intake, an appointment date was set and the release-of-records form was sent. The lengthy questionnaire was not used. We requested a letter from the caregiver detailing the issues to be presented and particular questions to be asked, in addition to a brief history of the client. This resulted in a final report that could be delivered much sooner than an Interdisciplinary Team Evaluation Clinic report. This format also served as an emergency consultation team, as there were many occasions when a Case Conference could help resolve and give second opinions to rather immediate problems. Case Conferences were scheduled as needed, but the official day and time was on Wednesday mornings.

Another service provided by the Aging Project was the Ethics Conference. The Ethics Conference, whose origins are discussed in another chapter, was an open forum that could be attended by anyone in the community interested in ethical dilemmas that arise in the care of people who are old and also mentally retarded. Cases were presented in confidence, preserving the client's anonymity. Members of the Kennedy Aging Project Ethics Committee and all others in attendance discussed the ramifications of the case, such as legal, medical, and spiritual issues, communication with and between family members (including the "surrogate family" of direct-care staff) and creative utilization of a wide range of services to assist the client and caregivers. As a rule, the purpose of the discussions of the Conferences was educational; the transcripts of the discussions were used for that purpose. Final decisions about a case were virtually never made at an Ethics Conference. The only exception to this was that on rare occasions the committee members present and the participants of the Conference would come to consensus on an issue, and an advisory letter would be sent to the appropriate person specifically on that issue. It would be written by the chairperson and sent with the understanding that it represented the voice of those assembled at that particular Conference. It should be noted that in this way, the group effectively retained its credibility and non-partisan reputation.

Finally, the Kennedy Aging Project initiated a service of lectures and inservice teaching whereby Dr. Howell, Ms. DeBrine, Dr. Fucini, and various of the students traveled to workshops, residences, and program sites to give talks on a variety of topics, including aging and mental retardation, staff training sessions on death and dying, dealing with ethical dilemmas, devising creative new services, and the Alzheimer's-Down syndrome connection. Group counselling sessions for staff, and peer support after a client had died, were also given on request. In the first year, Dr. Howell made twenty-three visits to programs and residences to talk about these various aspects of aging and mental retardation. In the second year, Dr Howell again made twenty-three visits to residences and programs to discuss and lead inservices on issues of aging and mental retardation. In the third year and final year, Dr. Howell made fifteen visits. This smaller number is attributable to the work on this book.

In the first year of the Kennedy Aging Project, forty-three clients were seen by the Team for full assessments and for Case Conferences. Clients' average age was sixty-two years. In the second year, the Team saw forty-two clients in full Team and Case Conferences, with the average age being fifty-nine years. In the third year, we saw fifty-four clients for full Team and Case Conference evaluations. The average age was fifty-seven years. Roughly half our clients in each year were women and half were men.

The unevenness of our intake can be attributed to a number of things: firstly, record-keeping was sporadic in the first year, as we debated the usefulness of these kind of numbers; and secondly, there were many cancellations due to clients changing their minds, or bad driving conditions in the winter, or other emergencies.

As we can see from these approximations, there has been a general increase in interest in our services, and an increase in clients both seen by the Team and referred to the Team. These numbers are only meant to give an impression of the burgeoning demand for services for people who are both mentally retarded and old. We hope these services can continue.

10

THE STRUCTURE OF THIS BOOK

Mary C. Howell

■

For three years, the staff of the Kennedy Aging Project worked with people who are both mentally retarded and old. This direct, face-to-face understanding is what we want to convey in this volume. Sharing our accumulated experience is a way for us to pass on what we learned so it can be preserved, commented on, challenged, and added to by others whose work is similar.

This Handbook, like the work of the Project, begins with the contributions of individuals who represent separate disciplines. Each of these (Chapters 11 through 21) presents a way of working that evolved from direct clinical contact with clients who are both mentally retarded and old. The approaches vary. The lawyers, for instance, search for specific problems. The pastoral counselor elicits a spiritual history in order to create a portrait of the client's experience of the sacred. The leisure specialist, by contrast, assumes that some improvement in the client's opportunities to make use of leisure time and energy is inevitably to be discovered by probing the present utilization of resources.

These chapters on disciplinary assessment are written to be understood and used by everyone who works with this group of clients.

Family members and staff, lay workers, and professionals from all fields can learn the concepts and language of, say, law, or rehabilitation medicine, to a degree that will be useful in offering assistance to a client. These chapters are written for the generalist and we encourage all readers to become generalists with regard to this special population of clients.

The Handbook continues to follow the progress of the Project by presenting topics that are, necessarily, interdisciplinary. When we are concerned with housing, safety, or care for the client who is dying, our perspective is enriched by the varied contributions of the several disciplines. Although each chapter is written by only one or two Project members, the perspectives represent the interdisciplinary focus of the entire Project.

Our orientation combines an examination of the relationship between studying and serving both people with mental retardation and people who are old—realms that rarely overlap except with reference to this special population of clients. We consider the difficult dilemmas of confidentiality in the provision of maximally responsive service. The application of the perspective of functional assessment is presented in overview, and the dangers of ageist stereotyping are outlined.

A holistic view of health and well-being includes a broad spectrum of information on health promotion, disease and accident prevention, and care within the established medical system. Overviews of mental health disorders and dementia are included.

In the section entitled "Living in Community," there is a broad variety of information on matters ranging from housing to day programming, sexuality, legal issues, participation in the life of religious congregations, and behavior shaping. The section ends with an account of a friendship with a person who became much more than a "client."

Soon after we began the work of the Project, we were struck by the presentation of dilemmas of action that represented choices between two or more ethically-ordered preferences. These ethical issues framed all of our subsequent work.

Not everyone who dies has reached old age, but everyone who reaches old age looks forward to dying. The disciplines of medicine, psychology, social work, pastoral care, law, and staff development are combined in this section.

Certain conclusions and recommendations grew from our work, especially from our appreciation of the resources that are now available to our clients and the resources that are needed. Included in the section on "Reflections and Recommendations" are observations of the work we accomplished—from the difficulties encountered in collecting data for research purposes, to the special and distinct trajectory of a Project that was funded only for a duration of three years. The Handbook concludes with personal statements from many of the participants—faculty, staff, and students.

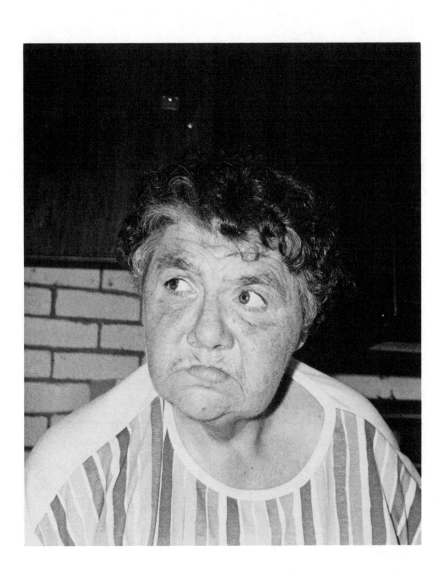

PART 3
ASSESSMENT BY
INDIVIDUAL DISCIPLINE

11

THE NURSE AND
THE NURSING ASSESSMENT

Frances Wiltsie

■

The nurse on the Interdisciplinary Team must rely heavily on both community health and primary care skills. One's idea of the "scope of nursing practice" must be very broad, as is evident from the following discussion. This perspective allows for numerous areas of collaboration with other Team members. Skill in acute care of the medically ill is sometimes useful here, but knowledge of more general health promotion is essential.

This chapter will describe a nursing assessment process taking place in the context of an Interdisciplinary Team evaluation. Some information can be included in written, pre-appointment questionnaires; some is easily obtained in Team discussion after the intake interview; and some may require direct investigation by the nurse.

The first area to be considered is the client's general level of wellness. Is the person healthy? This includes assessment of mental alertness, mood, level of comfort or distress, presence or absence of fatigue, and degree of physical endurance. These may or may not be independent of specific medical problems. Some people with long lists of medical problems appear and feel well; others have fatigue and malaise in the absence of disease. One must consider the perceptions of client, family, staff, and one's own direct impression (even if based on a brief observation). These may be contradictory, in which case the varying impressions should be noted.

Next, evaluate the person's gait and any physical limitations or adaptive equipment, such as a walker. Is there a history of repeated falls? A recent increase in falls? How and where do falls occur? What does this person want to do, physically, that he or she cannot do now? Direct observation of gait—walking down the hall with the client—can be invaluable when a gait problem is suspected. The physical therapist, physiatrist, and generalist physician may also play an active role in gait evaluation.

After this overview, assess what health care services have been and are now being utilized. It is important to identify the presence or absence of a primary health care provider. This is usually, but not always, a physician; it may be a nurse practitioner or physician's assistant. It is the person consulted for general, new, or minor health problems, and for the annual physical exam typically required by Department of Mental Retardation (DMR) programs. Also determine what, if any, medical specialists or habilitative therapies such as physical therapy and occupational therapy are involved, and how actively. Ideally these should be coordinated by the primary care provider. Is this the case? And finally, does the client have adequate health insurance?

Elicit any chronic medical problems as presented by the client, the caretakers, and the record. Many clients will bring a formal list. Consider relevant laboratory work, such as anticonvulsant drug levels. The objective here is to understand how others understand this client's health, not what the assessor (you, the nurse) thinks the problems are. If there is a question of dementia, has there been a standard medical evaluation for treatable causes?

Along with the recognized chronic medical problems, review the client's medications, if any. It will sometimes be useful to get a history of medication changes, especially if behavior or seizures are a concern. Is there a clear relationship between the medications and the identified medical problems? Again, look for relevant lab work. Is the client taking numerous medications? Consider the possibility of drug interaction and side effects. Make sure the medication list is complete, accurate, and up-to-date. The physician on the Team is an active participant in the review of chronic medical problems and medications.

At this point, the assessment moves into less medical areas. Evaluate the client's oral and personal hygiene. What assistance does the person receive in this area, and from whom? How do staff or family view the client's nutritional status? Is the diet varied and generally balanced? Is the client obese or underweight, gaining or losing weight? Who cooks? Are there any special meal problems? What are his sleep patterns? Is sleep, or wakefulness, a problem? Has there been change in any of these areas of hygiene, nutrition, or sleep?

Ask for and observe any general problems with vision or hearing. Have ophthalmological and audiological evaluations been done within the last one or two years? What were the findings? Are formal test results consistent with informal findings at home and work? Are glasses or hearing aids, if advised, actually in use and serving their designed function (glasses not badly scratched, hearing aid batteries not exhausted)? Has there been a dental exam in the past year? Are there any dental problems? Can the person chew adequately, given whatever diet texture she theoretically needs? Have there been choking episodes?

Determine what self-medication skills the client is reputed to possess and what plan for medication administration exists now. What is the actual practice? Review what, if any, skilled nursing services are presently provided in the home and workplace or day program. What are the nursing objectives?

Briefly consider general safety issues such as street crossing, behavior in the car, use of the stove, smoking, pica (eating non-edible things such as paper clips), and so on. Has the client had accidents? Specifically check whether the client has passed self-preservation tests (fire drills) if living in a setting where self-preservation is required. Ask what the client does for work, and consider occupational health risks, such as pesticide use.

For the areas just discussed, the nurse will be the primary (but not sole) organizer and interpreter of information usually obtained by questionnaire, intake interview—not necessarily done by the nurse— and limited direct nursing observation. There are other areas where more active collaboration with other Team members is needed. In these areas the nurse will have a particular perspective and skill but less unique expertise. Other Team members are likely to assume a greater role.

Areas where the nurse's role is more collaborative and less independent include social and family relationships, factors influencing self-esteem, communication and language skills, spiritual needs, issues of grief and loss, sexuality, and vocational concerns. The nurse should also participate in consideration of the client's legal status, especially with regard to psychotropic medication or other need for medical guardianship.

This wider role on the Team will be partly determined by the individual nurse's particular interests and skills in these and related areas. This list is certainly not complete. Similarly, the interests and skills of other Team members may help determine the role of the nurse as Team members grow increasingly to complement each other. The nurse may be particularly involved in sexuality training, birth control, and prevention of sexually transmitted diseases, including risk-reduction for AIDS.

Up to this point, the role of the nurse has been investigative; she collects information and organizes it. After all of this is brought together, the nurse steps back and asks himself a series of questions that form the actual nursing evaluation. These are questions that are initially considered by the nurse alone, although they may become topics of wider Team discussion.

First, what are the person's health problems? Does the existing list of chronic medical problems appear accurate and complete? Should something be added? Deleted? Or is there a need for further investigation, perhaps including a physical exam or formal consult by the Team physician?

Second, what does this nurse assess the person's skilled nursing needs to be? Are they being met? Is the medication administration plan appropriate?

Third, are the existing health care services, individually and as a package, adequate and appropriate? If not, are family and staff willing to consider change?

Fourth, what are the health-related education and training needs of the person with mental retardation? Of the staff? Of the family?

Fifth, is the person safe? What are the risks? Are these risks recognized and accepted? By whom?

Finally, what are the needs for consultations with other Team members, or for outside referrals?

This is the point at which consideration naturally goes back to the Team as a whole. Other persons on the Team may take an active interest in some, or all, of the preceding questions, as the nurse may take an active interest in evaluation by other Team members.

In conclusion, the role of the nurse in the Interdisciplinary Team is based on a broad definition of nursing, the ability to assess a wide range of health-related factors, and the skill and interest to collaborate with other Team members.

12

PSYCHIATRIC ASSESSMENT

Frank S.G. Wills

■

As an approach to thinking about elderly people with mental retardation who have behavioral problems, the disease entity, major depression, will be used as illustration. The first questions I wish that all of us would always ask are, *"Is the person suffering?" "Is there evidence of internal distress?" "Is there physical pain, emotional distress, or both?" "What makes you think so?"*

The next several questions are subquestions of the last question. *"What do you see that makes you think so?" "What do you hear that makes you think so?"* and *"What do you feel that makes you think so?"* That may puzzle you for a moment. However, if someone's muscles are very tense you can tell a lot more by feeling them than you can by just looking at the patient.

The next subquestion deserves special attention. *"What do your 'innards' tell you?"* Many of us are reluctant to pay close attention to those impressions that we cannot really put a finger on, that we cannot objectify, so to speak, but that our heart, our gut, or whatever part of our innards talks to us best, tells us is surely going on. Sometimes we have a sense of what is going on even though we may have a terrible time divining or articulating what it is.

It is crucial, when you get that sort of strong impression, to pay close attention to your intuition, take it seriously, try to listen to your innards, decipher what may be going on, and share your impressions with other people, such as your consulting experts. Some people will tell you that they do not want to hear vague impressions. It obviously does not pay to pursue them with people like that. But I hope you will not give up at that point. Ask the next person. Those intuitive impressions are important.

The next question is, *"What is the patient doing that upsets others?"* Here we get to the concept of "problem." *"Does the person's behavior* *appear to be in response to something or does it appear to be 'out of the blue'?"*Your impression regarding that can help the psychiatrist a great deal. *"If it is in response to something, is it too much of a response, too little a response, or too different a response from what you would ordinarily expect?" "If it is 'out of the blue,' what is it about the behavior that you are concerned about?" Again, "Is it too much, too little, or is it too different?"*

*"How long has it been going on?"*There is a big difference between something that has been going on for an hour or even a day and something that has been going on for a week, month, or a year. *"Has it happened before?" "If it happened before, when—at least approximately—did it happen?" "Has it or something similar happened to other family members?"* It is important to try to find this out to the extent that you can. *"When and where did it happen?" "What were the circumstances under which it happened?" "What was the context in which it happened?"*

The main thing I want to emphasize about management and treatment is that they depend on diagnosis. I am not using diagnosis as a medical term here but as a synonym for the product of good analysis. Good analysis really is an understanding of the state of affairs that exists. When a behavioral psychologist has done a detailed behavior analysis, his statement of the problem behavior is, in medical terms, a diagnosis. If you accept the word *diagnosis* in that very broad sense, you see that anyone can arrive at a diagnostic statement of a particular state of affairs and, therefore, can begin a rational course of management and treatment.

The hallmarks of major depression are depressed mood and loss of interest or pleasure. There is always some degree of distress or suffering but it is not always the classic "blues." Emotional discomfort is often expressed in physical complaints. It is common for depressed people who are mentally retarded and old to express their sad feelings in physical complaints. Some suffer from both emotional and physical problems.

Part of our task is to determine whether both are present and what is the cause of each complaint. If the person looks sad, says he feels "blue," has lost interest in things he has usually found pleasurable, and has begun to smell bad because he is not taking care of himself, it is easy. But he may just look "out of sorts," complain more than usual about aches and pains, the food, staff, family, or peers, and refuse activities stubbornly or angrily. Then it is not so easy. He may continue to do things, but without his usual enthusiasm. Sometimes there is "just something about him" or "he is not his usual self," but defining it more specifically is difficult.

More than one depressed person who was helped a great deal by treatment was brought to appropriate professional attention through just such an intuitive statement. The loss of interest can look like forgetfulness and the person can be thought to be suffering from early dementia, rather than treatable depression. Internal distress can be hard to see because the person's behavior has become obnoxious. Complaining, irritable behavior with episodes of assaultiveness is the only way some depressed people express their distress. If the behavior is different than the person's usual manner; if it is not necessarily related to understandable antecedents or is very disproportionate to the stimulus; if there has been a previous period of such behavior that went away; if family members have had depressive disorders, the behavior is likely to represent depression.

The relationship between any specific behavior and any specific disorder or treatment is not simple. A behavior can be a manifestation of many different psychiatric disorders, and a psychiatric disorder can be manifested by many different behaviors.

What I am concerned about is a methodical approach that, at a minimum, asks the basic questions previously mentioned and then tries to analyze each of the simplest elements. This should help in your own work with clients, and it will certainly help the psychiatrist you call on for assistance.

13

OCCUPATIONAL THERAPY ASSESSMENT

Linda S. Corman

■

The image of the person with mental retardation as eternally youthful and joyous is a false one. People who are mentally retarded grow old and face many of the difficulties, life changes and decisions that the "normal" adult faces in old age. My role as an Occupational Therapist is to evaluate my clients, encourage their uniqueness and self-esteem as individuals, and enhance their well-being.

When assessing the adult with mental retardation you need not always focus on the diagnosis of mental retardation. For instance, your clients will face the same health issues as clients who are old and not mentally retarded. They may experience decreased vision, loss of hearing, sensation, and mobility, osteoporosis, arthritis, stroke, heart disease, diabetes, and cancer. The diagnosis of mental retardation assists you in understanding your clients' abilities both to interact with you and others, and to understand the changes they are undergoing.

Knowing your clients' functional and cognitive skill levels will assist you in determining the type and level of assistance that will be needed. Take, for example, a client with mental retardation who is old and suffering from rheumatoid arthritis. A client with limited cognitive functioning may only know that her hands feel better after paraffin (wax) treatments. Another client may understand a simple description of arthritis with its "sore fingers"; a third client may be taught energy conservation and joint protection techniques.

Occupational therapists use a holistic approach when assessing clients. The client requires assessment of her physical, functional, psychosocial, and cognitive abilities. Sensory systems are examined to determine if there is a change or a decrease in vision or hearing. Is the client having trouble seeing her work or doing a familiar self-care task? Is she missing directions or not participating in tasks to her previous potential? In the area of nutrition and oral motor skills, is the client missing teeth, does she wear dentures, or is she without teeth altogether? Has she decreased her food intake? Is the client refusing to eat previously favorite foods or difficult-to-chew foods? Sensation needs to be evaluated to see if the client can distinguish hot from cold, to ensure safety in the kitchen and bathroom.

Mobility is evaluated to assess whether the client can ambulate independently and safely. He may need a walker, cane, or a manual or motorized wheelchair to enable him to ambulate or mobilize himself in his home environment and in the community-at-large.

Self-care tasks, such as bathing, grooming, eating, and toileting, are assessed to determine the client's level of independence and whether the performance of these tasks has changed either suddenly or over time. If there are changes, the cause should be determined; they may be due to changes in motoric ability, decreased range of motion due to arthritis or hip fracture, or cognitive changes such as decreased attention span or diminished ability to remember multi-step tasks.

Fine motor skills are assessed to determine eye-hand coordination, grasp patterns, and hand dominance. Is there a tremor? Are there contractures interfering with grasp? Is the client able to use both hands or is she one-handed due to disability? Can the client manipulate small items (buttons) as well as large items (faucets)?

Cognitive skills are assessed to determine the client's attention span, ability to follow directions, and memory of multi-step tasks. Can the client read or write? Can he learn through verbal instruction, demonstration, or modeling? Have there been recent changes in his learning style?

Psychosocial skills are assessed to determine how the client interacts with her environment and the people around her. Does she respond to her surroundings by looking or verbalizing? Can she make her needs known? Does she initiate interactions with peers or staff? Have there been recent changes in her interaction style?

When all information is gathered, the occupational therapist can assist the client and the staff and family working with the client to deal with the changes that are taking place. For instance, adaptive equipment can be used to facilitate independence when the client experiences decreased range of motion caused by longstanding contractures or illness. Utensils with enlarged handles provide less pressure on arthritic joints. Raised toilet seats will help clients who experience decreased mobility at the hip joint because of arthritis or hip fracture. The occupational therapist can discuss with staff and administration how highly waxed floors can be frightening and dangerous for a person with cataracts and decreased mobility. Contrasts of color such as red or yellow can help aging eyes find doorknobs and toothbrushes; the standard institutional colors of beige or white are difficult for clients to distinguish. A client who in the past needed only verbal instructions at his worksite in order to perform multi-step jobs may need printed instructions or cue cards because of decreased hearing and loss of memory. A client who was quiet and waited to be spoken to when he was younger may become more isolated as he grows older because of changes in vision and hearing. An occupational therapist working with clients who are mentally retarded and old can assist staff and administration by describing the changes occurring with the clients, providing necessary therapeutic interventions and adaptive equipment, and advocating for environmental modifications to assist the clients.

Many of my clients spent most of their early years in large, impersonal institutions where conformity was the rule rather than the exception. There was little room for individual personality and uniqueness. There were few day programs and workshop placements. Opportunities to make choices and decisions were infrequent. Time was marked by the arrival of the meal truck. A few decades ago, all institutions had insufficient staff and materials. The person with mental retardation who is old and who resided in an institution may have had little opportunity to make choices and decisions or to develop leisure skills or hobbies.

In the late 1970s and 1980s, most institutions obtained more staff and money to develop programs and materials. Large wards were converted into smaller, more private living spaces. Day programs and sheltered workshops were developed to provide activities and jobs that were appropriate for their clients' functional levels. However, depending on the age of the client, there had already been years with very little meaningful activity in their lives.

Occupational therapists can help staff develop programs for clients with mental retardation who are old. When looking at program development for this population, whether living in an institution or a community setting, it is important to discover as much about a client's background as possible. Record and archive reviews are essential. Just as important, however, are conversations with family, significant others, and staff people who have known the client for a number of years. Family and staff who know the client provide a human anecdotal approach to the client that is not usually found in the files.

Record reviews and staff interviews will tell you information about the client's religious, ethnic, and family background. Was the client admitted to an institution as a child, adolescent, or young adult? Was there any family contact after admission—intermittent, continuous, or none? How were the client's years spent in the institution, and with what peers? What is the client's functional, cognitive, and psychosocial skill level? Also, where applicable, the client should be interviewed. What does she like to do? What does she dislike? What would she like to learn to do? Would she like to go out to eat, go to a movie, or go to the park?

The answers to these questions will help staff develop programs to meet the needs of their older population and to initiate activities that are meaningful. Assessing clients' skill levels will assist staff in deciding the program's focus. For instance, the focus of a program could be either maintenance of function and skills, or maintenance and enhancement of skills, leisure choices, and socialization.

Other issues to consider in program development are space and time. Is the projected program site accessible to all its participants? Are tables adjustable to accommodate wheelchairs? Are bathrooms and kitchen facilities accessible? Will clients need to be transported to the program site?

A client who is old may not be able to tolerate a full day of activity. Many work part-time instead of full-time, or take part in activities in the morning and nap in the afternoon, pacing activities to meet needs. The client who is mentally retarded and old may be able to choose between a whole day program and a morning or afternoon program. The latter would allow for a nap or provide more time in the morning to get up, get dressed, and go to the program. Also, a flexible structure allows the more independent client to make choices about how his day is spent and what activities he would like to do. This may include watching the "soaps" or puttering around. Sessions within the program should vary in intensity or pace to allow for both quiet and robust times.

In developing activities and groups to meet a client's needs and interests, all the information that has been gathered about the client— history, functional level, tolerance to task, and communication style— comes into play. Staff can use the client's history to help develop programs that include music of their generation, and ethnic celebrations that incorporate food, music, and dance. Reality orientation groups can deal with topics that are meaningful to the client, such as holidays, birthdays, and seasonal changes. Depending on the client's functional and cognitive level, groups can be used to expose him to activities he has never seen or tried, such as bowling, croquet, knitting, or needle-point. Activities should promote the client's self-esteem and feeling of uniqueness. Clients should feel a sense of accomplishment or satisfaction from their work.

Occupational therapists can assist staff in adapting activities to clients who have various physical limitations and various functional and cognitive skill levels. They can also provide input to enhance the participation of everyone. As an example, painting is an activity that most clients enjoy. The client with no physical limitations and with a good grasp and good eye-hand coordination may be able to hold the paint brush, dip the brush in the paint, and make brush strokes on a piece of paper or canvas. However, the client with poor grasp, strength, and coordination can also paint. Instead of using a paintbrush and paper or canvas, a cardboard box and a small rock can be used. A piece of paper is placed in the cardboard box, along with a few drops of several colors of paint and the rock. The client needs only to shake the box to paint the picture; the shaking of the box and the rock will create the picture. Both clients are painting a picture, have a sense of accomplishment, and receive recognition as creative artists.

Gardening can be an enjoyable activity, but tending to a garden in the ground can be very tiring and difficult for those who are old. Window boxes can be used so that clients can stand and tend their flowers and plants. They can be placed on the inside or outside of a window. Indoor window gardening can be enjoyed by many clients.

Occupational therapists can assist staff to analyze an activity, breaking it down into its component parts. They can help staff decide which steps a client can learn to do himself and which ones require the assistance of adaptive equipment. How can weaving be adapted for the blind client who is old? How can a client who has had a stroke continue to do her needlepoint using only one hand? An occupational therapist can help answer these questions and make suggestions.

Throughout program development, staff should allow for as much client choice and decision making as applicable. There can be choices even within a structure. During reality orientation, should we talk about today's weather or tomorrow's trip to the park? Should we bake brownies or a cake? During art group, would you like to paint or use clay? The client who has lived in an institution for a long time has had very little experience or opportunity to make choices. Clients may have difficulty making choices and decisions for themselves. However, staff can encourage this by their patience and by providing a supportive environment.

Occupational therapists working with people who are mentally retarded and old should encourage their clients and provide them with a sense of self-worth and uniqueness. Program planning is one way in which occupational therapists can bring their creativity and knowledge of purposeful activity, adaptive equipment, therapeutic interventions, and environmental modifications to develop programs that have meaning to all who participate in them. These skills are also used to consult with staff, family, and administration on the changing needs of clients.

However, just as important as encouraging skills is the need to be an advocate. Occupational therapists should explain changes they see in their clients, but also should observe what remains the same. John's illness may prevent him from physically engaging in many activities; however, he still likes slapstick humor and watches the Three Stooges, likes classical music and hates rock and roll.

Occupational therapists must advocate for the fact that *old* does not mean sitting around watching television all day. The person with mental retardation who is old is capable of enjoying life to the fullest.

14

PHYSICAL THERAPY EVALUATION

Stephanie Bowen

Physical therapy services are utilized both in the generalized problems associated with normal aging, and in the specific problems associated with disease processes commonly occurring in old age.

A clinical specialty in geriatrics is not required in order to be able to address the needs of people with mental retardation who are old, but the norms and expected evaluation results are best analyzed, and

---

treatment plans most effectively applied, when the clinician has some experience in the area of geriatrics. Although greater attention is now focused on old age in people with mental retardation, this is an area that is not yet well researched. Norms, therefore, are still the product of various therapists' experiences, based on their own work, rather than on data.

■ Effects of Aging

As with the normal population, there are generalized effects of aging in people with mental retardation that occur without the presence of a specific disease process. Included in these effects are decreased strength and decreased flexibility. These factors can lead to other problems, including a decrease in or loss of the ability to ambulate, an increased need of assistance during activities of daily living (ADLs), and a decreased ability to perform sections of the developmental sequence such as crawling and rolling, which contribute to one's ability to complete more complicated activities such as walking. Also noted are a general decrease in balance and coordination that can lead to falls, a leading cause of dysfunction in people who are old.

Aging alone, however, would not have an effect on a specific neurological function such as muscle tone or the protective extension reaction (the extending of one's arms to catch oneself when falling), nor would it account for the development of primitive reflexes like those found in newborns (such as a hand grasping reflex). Development of these types of symptoms are usually correlated with specific disease processes, not simply normal aging.

The aging process seems to put people at a higher risk of specific disease processes such as osteoporosis and fractures, strokes, cardiac disease, and Alzheimer's disease. All of these processes include a greater decline in gross motor functioning than is generally seen in normal aging.

■ Evaluation Components and Expected Findings

A physical therapy evaluation for people with mental retardation is similar whether one is evaluating a child, an adult, or an older individual, but the evaluation results need to be interpreted according to the person's age level.

As with any comprehensive evaluation, a record review will be important. This review is the best place to start when working with people with mental retardation because it makes one aware of any behavior problems before the actual evaluation. It is important to gather information regarding existing medical problems, visual or auditory deficits, cardiac and pulmonary status, as well as language skills and any potential contraindications to activity that have been identified by any of the team members. The record is also a good place to obtain a neurological history; information should be found there about onset of symptoms of Alzheimer's, Parkinson's, or other disease processes, descriptions and frequencies of seizures, and effectiveness of medications. Previous physical therapy or occupational therapy evaluations can also be helpful in establishing a pattern of degeneration. The importance of documenting baseline information should also be remembered when writing up the evaluation.

Interviews with staff can be useful because staff may be able to tell you of methods that have proven effective in dealing with the client, and to give you some help in establishing rapport. A favorite staff person may help to put an anxious client at ease during the evaluation.

A good place to start the "hands-on" portion of the evaluation is to measure the client's range of motion; this will give you clues about results you will get later. If a client has a severe lack of motion at the shoulder, for instance, you can expect limited results when testing for protective extension. While an exact recording of the range of motion (ROM) is important when there are existing deficits, a client who can actively demonstrate full ROM can be graded simply as "within normal limits." In people who are older it is common, especially with a wear-and-tear type of arthritis, to find slight limitations in range; however, as long as the limitations do not interfere with function, the joint can be graded as "within functional limits."

Measurement of ROM can be important in establishing baseline information as well as in determining required treatment. Once the availability of range is established through passive range of motion (therapist moving the part), then it is important to establish usage of that range through active range of motion (client moving the part).

In the evaluation of usage, the therapist is examining not only range but also strength. When working with clients with mental retardation, the subjective evaluation of the therapist is usually the only tool available to measure strength. In physical therapy work in a hospital or in private practice there are machines to judge strength and to compare muscles that flex to muscles that extend; however, these machines are of little use for people who do not have the cognitive skills to understand either the procedure or the reason for the test.

The subjective tool used is a manual muscle test. It involves evaluating the amount of resistance a muscle or group of muscles can stand, and grading that muscle (or group of muscles) on a scale of 0-5. Zero is the assessment when no muscle contraction is felt; five is a normal measure. This scale has a limited usefulness, though, and if grades are given at all to people with severe mental retardation, they are usually extrapolated from functional movement. For instance, if the client is able to bend from the waist, pick up a ball, and stand without assistance, the back muscle can be graded at least 3 or 4.

Generalized arm strength can be extrapolated by arm-wrestling with the client. This method will not work if the client cannot understand the procedure or if weakness in a specific muscle group needs to be evaluated, but it can be a fun break for the client who may be apprehensive about the evaluation. Clients might also enjoy shaking an instrument; they can be coaxed into rubbing their faces after being tickled by a light stroke on the face. These methods can all be graded as motion against gravity and are useful in evaluating strength. Strength usually decreases with age, but I can remember several clients who were old but whose strength was enough to give me a challenge.

Muscle tone must be taken into account in the evaluation of strength, as it can significantly interfere with strength testing. Muscle tone is the response that a particular muscle or group of muscles demonstrates when being passively stretched. While there are several methods for testing muscle tone, rapid, passive flexion and extension of the part being evaluated is most often used. This is also a subjective measurement; I am not aware of any instruments available to measure muscle tone.

Old age does not seem to have any noticeable effect on muscle tone. Clients who are spastic (high muscle tone) generally stay that way as they age, and clients who are hypotonic (low muscle tone) also tend to stay that way. When a client's muscle tone changes from its usual state, she should be referred to a physician (perhaps to a neurologist) because it usually indicates that something besides normal aging is going on.

For the sake of establishing baseline information, muscle tone should be recorded in fair detail and should include the effect the muscle tone has on functional mobility. Does the muscle tone keep the client from walking, eating, dressing, or communicating?

Gait is a very important area to consider in people who are old. Physical therapists and caregivers can have a dramatic effect on the independence and quality of life of a client by working as a team to keep the client walking. The details of a full gait evaluation are complicated; many joints are taken into consideration in the evaluation, including ankles, knees, hips, spine, arm position, and head alignment. This is an area where baseline data can be critical in determining changes. When baseline data are absent, the client's care providers should be questioned about whether his gait looks different, or whether he is falling more frequently. Caregivers are usually the first to notice these changes.

Because of the decreased strength and decreased flexibility caused by aging, clients may lose the ability to climb stairs. They can lose the ability to walk on level surfaces when there are fewer opportunities to do so. As a client's gait slows down, it becomes easier for staff to take her to the dining room in her roommate's wheelchair, or in the wheelchair that is only intended for her housemate to use on long trips; her showers might be given in the shower chair, if time is short. She also loses opportunities to walk when day program staff decide that she is not "safe" (fast enough) to travel to day program without a wheelchair; when staff decide she cannot go on a walk because she cannot keep up; and when staff find it easier to bring an object to her rather than having her go to the object. Every time staff tacitly agree to let one of these opportunities go by, they also agree to help her stop walking.

Once a client is in a wheelchair, it is very hard to get him out. If a client works with a physical therapist as much as thirty minutes a session and up to five times a week, and sits or lies down for the rest of the day, the therapy is not enough to offset the loss of muscle strength and ROM during the rest of the day. Physical therapists may have clinical knowledge to design a program, but only the effort of the direct care staff will provide opportunities to make that program successful.

An evaluation of coordination is another area in which a physical therapist can gather information to help address functional deficits. The results of this evaluation can provide the therapist with information about a client's quality of movement and motor planning (the brain's ability to map out the order of movement necessary to complete a given sequence). As clients age they experience a generalized slowing of movement, but they should not experience a deterioration in motor planning (the ability to carry out a complex chain of motor activity), nor should they develop any shaking, writhing, or other movements associated with brain disease, if none previously existed.

A sensory evaluation can also be helpful in determining goals that are geared toward independent functioning. The client's ability to sense hot and cold, her ability to sense where her arms and legs are without looking at them, and her ability to feel pain, can all provide valuable information toward goal setting. There seems to be little that can be done to restore sensation in areas where it is not intact, but information about deficits can be valuable to caregivers when considering the client's daily activities.

Finally, an assessment of the client's ability to carry out his own activities of daily living (ADLs) such as washing his face, brushing his teeth and hair, dressing, and feeding himself, can be useful in either identifying areas of direct treatment, or identifying areas in which the caregivers can maximize the client's ability to care for himself and to prevent loss of skills because of aging.

When all the information that has been revealed during an evaluation has been correlated, and time constraints on the part of the staff and client have been considered, a plan of action can be implemented that focuses efforts toward maximizing independence and fostering an attitude of self-reliance on the part of the client.

The elderly client seems to be at risk for these specific disease processes:

Alzheimer's Disease

The evaluation results in Alzheimer's are often difficult to pinpoint because of the slowly declining level of awareness in the client on a day-to-day basis. Over a period of time, however, a client would be expected to slowly lose cognitive function (i.e., losing his way to the bathroom, forgetting the names of the staff, perseverating on a particular activity) before losing motor function. Motor changes are often shown first by a fear of uneven terrain and stairways, and will eventually lead to a need for assistance to ambulate on level surfaces and finally the cessation of all walking activities. I have never seen a client with Alzheimer's, who has recently lost the ability to walk, be able to learn wheelchair mobility. By the time he needs the wheelchair, his ability to learn new motor tasks is severely impaired. He will generally become incontinent before he stops walking.

In terms of treatment, there are three major goals. The first is to maintain range of motion; this is accomplished by moving all the limbs in all potential directions each day. The second goal is to prevent skin breakdown; this is accomplished by using adaptive seating equipment and providing changing positions for the client throughout the day. The third goal is to maintain or improve respiratory status; this is accomplished through positioning and chest physical therapy. Other activities assist with circulation. Maintenance of socialization will continue to be an important goal.

Stroke

Clients who are referred to physical therapy after having a stroke will usually have an inability or a decrease in ability to move the arm and leg on one side of the body. In the beginning, we work to maintain the client's range of motion and to facilitate what little movement there might be. After the body starts to repair itself, the client will develop an increase in muscle tone that may cause the arm to position itself in seemingly odd positions. In this stage, we work on relaxing the muscle tone and facilitating normal movement. In cases in which there might be complete recovery, the client will then start to develop some control over muscle tone. Complete recovery would be total control and normal muscle tone.

In persons who have mental retardation, recovery from a stroke seems to happen at a slower rate than in the general population. There are several instances of clients who spent a full year in that first stage of having no control and odd posturing. Were this to happen in the general population, the patient's chances of any kind of recovery would be very dim. But in this population, recovery to a good degree cannot be ruled out even after a year of little or no improvement. A good example of this is a 55-year-old client who has Down syndrome, who is fifteen months post-stroke, and who is just beginning to be able to overcome the muscle tone in her leg and to be able to take a few steps.

Parkinson's Disease

Parkinson's disease usually has a fairly slow onset; it begins with a slight shaking of the hands and can end with a complete inability to move. The most effective management seems to be through the use of medications. The role of physical therapy is to help maintain range of motion and to encourage independence in ADLs. Caregivers can also be shown ways to foster independence.

There are many areas in which physical therapy intervention can be applied to benefit the client who is old. Indirect services from caregivers supplement direct treatments to help ensure success. Assistive devices such as canes and walkers can be utilized to help maintain independent ambulation. Increased staff-to-client ratios ease the burden that clients who are old and frail can place on staff resources because of their need for assistance.

15

PSYCHOLOGICAL ASSESSMENT

Arianna Fucini

■

Very little has been written on how to assess the client who is mentally retarded and old from the perspective of psychology. The task is not simple and requires a thorough understanding of this particular population.

Usually, if any previous cognitive assessment is available it reflects the cognitive abilities of the client at an early age. In the majority of the cases that we saw at the Kennedy Aging Project, past cognitive and even performance data were sketchy or nonexistent. Therefore whenever staff reports a recent decrease in the client's functional abilities, it is difficult to determine, without any prior data or previously-available record, at just what level the client functioned before the lamented "decrease in ability."

Further, the lack of previous cognitive assessments makes testing burdensome. At times it is necessary to adjust the testing materials to the same modality in which the client "functions best" in his actual environment. For example, for one client who was evaluated, the entire test had to be presented in written form. This particular client could not retain verbally-presented material because of her own interfering verbal behavior. In other cases verbal stimuli had to be replaced by concrete and meaningful forms, while at other times paper-pencil subtests were replaced with more simple fine motor skills. In each of these substitutions the formal requirements of the task were not altered.

Last but not least is the fact that, while most of the previously available assessments were performed by very competent psychologists, most had not had extensive experience with people with mental retardation. In a few cases the psychological report under-evaluated a client's ability; in almost all cases the report did not include the scores of the various subtests or a detailed description of the tasks that were performed. This insufficient and often inadequate background material made a comparison of current evaluations very difficult. There ia also a current tendency to overlook the specific client's competencies and learning style.

When a psychologist is faced with the problem of evaluating an individual who is old and mentally retarded, just which is the best approach?

At the Kennedy Aging Project, the standardized initial telephone interview and the client and caregiver interviews were helpful in offering a general picture of the client, his environment, reasons for referral, and staff involvement. Following this general outline, it was then necessary to examine the client's record for reports of any previous psychological, neurological, or vocational assessments. Care was taken also to watch for any record of behavior patterns or problems and behavioral interventions. The caregiving staff was again interviewed by the psychologist, in person or by phone, in order to clarify questions or discrepancies between the initial interview and the record examination, and to evaluate the personality and the emotional state of the communicating staff member. The final step was the actual testing of the client.

The major goal of testing was to document and evaluate the cognitive and learning capabilities of the client. Special attention was given to each client's cognitive style, in order to evaluate the client's functional adjustment to the environment.

The testing session generally lasted two hours. It started with a Mini Mental Status examination, followed by other tasks, such as sorting and crossing off a printed letter from a series of printed letters, recollection of narrative material (three-sentence stories), ability to copy two simple designs, memory for digit sequences, single digit repetition (both forward and backward), and the Performance subtests of the WAIS-R.

During the Mini Mental Status examination, emphasis was placed on the number of trials necessary for the client to learn and repeat the names of three familiar objects (table, telephone and ball), the number of those names recalled after 2, 5, and 10 minutes delay, the backward recitation of automatized series (days of the week), and the addition and subtraction of single digits. As previously mentioned, some verbal tasks were replaced with more concrete and meaningful stimuli. Clients with language difficulty were asked to perform an auditory-visual delayed matching-to-sample task in order to document their recollection. Clients with auditory problems were asked to perform a visual-visual delayed matching-to-sample task.

At times the staff member accompanying the client was asked to remain during the testing session because the examiner could not understand what the client was trying to say when the client's verbal behavior was indistinct. On a few occasions, during testing, clients tried to leave the testing room or actually struck the examiner. In these situations, reinforcement (e.g., food, praise, or an interesting object to play with) was used to keep the client in the testing room and to avoid aggressive behavior. Reinforcement was delivered between tasks and was not contingent on task performance.

When the referral was also for an intellectual evaluation, then the entire WAIS-R or the Stanford Binet Intelligence Scale were administered. If the client's verbal skills were limited, the Peabody Picture Vocabulary Test was given and the Bender Visual Motor Gestalt Test was used to document visual-motor perception deficits and/or emotional difficulty.

These tests proved to be very useful in the documentation of a client's confusion, memory impairment, and learning ability, as well as the client's adjustment and interaction with the environment. The testing was also instrumental in identifying behavioral and cognitive deficits related to emotional distress such as depression, anxiety, and delayed grieving.

In many cases, a single testing session was not sufficient to diagnose a Senile Dementia of the Alzheimer's Type. Every time there was a strong suspicion of this condition (usually based on a poor performance in tasks using short-term memory), the suggestion was made to test the client again after a twelve-month period in order to compare performances and to document increased confusion and further memory impairment.

SERVING THE UNDERSERVED

Once testing was accomplished and the data examined, a written report was sent to the original referral source. In the report was a comprehensive description of the tasks performed by the client and the scores on the different subtests. The report was written in detail to minimize interfering variables in the next testing situation, and to make it possible for another evaluator to obtain, in the future, a more reliable picture of the client's functional abilities. The final part of the report included suggested interventions and other recommendations. These often turned out to be helpful in improving client-staff interactions and in changing the client's dysfunctional behavior.

For clients with initial symptoms of Senile Dementia of the Alzheimer's Type, interventions were mainly directed to the caregivers. Several staff training sessions were held in various group homes. One of the most frequent problems among workshop and residential staff was the lack of knowledge about the slow and progressive process of dementia. Frequently, residential staff who were inexperienced at working with dementia were actively considering nursing home placements rather than initiating a simplification of the client's present environment. At the training sessions, staff were informed about the course of dementia and the value of maintaining the client in a familiar environment as a means of slowing the progression of the disease. At times there was almost an active resistance by many of the staff who were simply unwilling to accept evidence of the dementia.

Sometimes staff came to the Aging Project asking for behavioral interventions for the observed behavioral changes and were distressed to learn of the possibility of the client's dementia. At other times, staff tried to force their clients to perform complicated tasks that were once familiar to them. It seemed as if these staff members believed that practicing a task could somehow help to slow down the process of deterioration. Staff responding in this fashion gave insufficient weight to the client's emotional response and frustration and attributed the associated behavior problems to other causes.

Sometimes workshop staff did not adjust the work demands to the client's cognitive decline but continued to require the same production quotas and to penalize the client for slow performance and the behavioral outbursts associated with such expectations. An important component of the training was the emotional response of the staff to the client's deterioration. Some staff were quite open about their feelings of frustration and about being overwhelmed with the need for close supervision of these clients. This was especially true when the client exhibited behaviors like hoarding of food and other objects, misplacing clothes and other possessions, incontinence, poor performance of adaptive behaviors, falling, or wandering away.

When staff came to the Kennedy Aging Project with a complete knowledge and acceptance of a client's decline, the training involved teaching appropriate interactions with the client and the other residents along with some information about the support groups that are available in our greater metropolitan area.

The assessment of clients who exhibited behavioral or cognitive deterioration as a result of depression or anxiety included a functional analysis of the client's emotional state and suggestions on how to alleviate the symptoms. It was often found that the depression or anxiety stemmed from a perception of loss. There may have been loss of a family member, loss of a friend or roommate, loss of a job, loss of a working relationship, a change in residence, retirement, or the replacement of a paying job with a day program.

For the person with mental retardation, aging could simply mean an increase in deficiencies that were exhibited from birth. With aging we cannot escape the reality of a general decline in most, if not all, functional modalities. Vision and hearing become less acute, the ability to move is reduced, fine motor skills decrease. At the same time, it may appear that the demands from the environment do not decrease or lend themselves to the inescapable result of simply...getting older. For example, some clients, with increased hearing and vision impairments, were forced to lip read or to listen to directions expressed with a very loud tone of voice. In these cases, the performance difficulties were eliminated and the depression lifted when the same requests were made using, as a prompt, photographs of the client actually performing the desired task.

The main general suggestion to the referral sources is to seek immediately a psychological and cognitive evaluation at the first sign of behavior deterioration. In some cases, the Kennedy Aging Project was used as the last resort to try to address long-standing staff frustrations and exasperations. At other times, clients came to the intake meetings already labeled by staff as being demented, without the support of a formal cognitive evaluation; often, in these cases the client was found by testing to be depressed, anxious, or very angry, but cognitively intact.

Another important suggestion to the referral source is to document with data the client's actual decline, along with a functional analysis of the client's behavior; that is, to record what happens before and after the behavior in question is demonstrated. Sometimes the client's inability to perform serves two functions: first, to get attention from staff, and second, to provide staff with the satisfaction of being needed. This is a subtle symbiotic relationship that is not easily detected and is often overlooked.

The experience of the Kennedy Aging Project makes clear the value of using specially trained psychologists who are attuned to evaluating the subtleties and complications of developmental dysfunctions, exacerbated by the natural effects of aging in clients who are affected by the consequences of time on their ability to perform and relate to their environment.

16

PASTORAL CARE AND THE ASSESSMENT OF SPIRITUAL NEEDS

Bridget Bearss

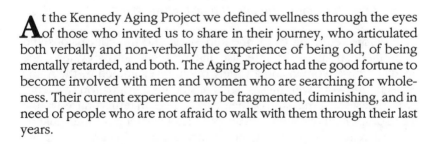

A t the Kennedy Aging Project we defined wellness through the eyes of those who invited us to share in their journey, who articulated both verbally and non-verbally the experience of being old, of being mentally retarded, and both. The Aging Project had the good fortune to become involved with men and women who are searching for wholeness. Their current experience may be fragmented, diminishing, and in need of people who are not afraid to walk with them through their last years.

Joanne and Maria are good examples. They helped us to define the essential role of spirituality in the assessment utilized by the Aging Project. Maria and Joanne had maintained a thirty-nine year relationship. They had seen each other through years of institutionalization, transition into community residence and workshop, and the effects of "retirement" and movement into day programs. When they were referred to the Aging Project, it was noted that Maria had begun to experience a significant decline in ability levels, and staff observed that Joanne was "covering for" and "taking care of" Maria.

Staff suggested that these actions of Joanne's were in response to a deathbed request of Maria's mother, asking Joanne to care for Maria. Joanne felt bound to that commitment and was devoted to her friend. Yet she could recognize that Maria was changing and was unable to perform some of the tasks that had once come easily. She could see that Maria became disoriented more often and for longer periods. Previous evaluation had suggested that it might be necessary to move Maria to a nursing home in the near future. Joanne was asked if she would like to move with Maria or to stay in the community residence. Joanne faced a challenge of self-definition: which was more important, her relationship with Maria, or her reluctance to go to a nursing home, which she associated with the beginning of her own dying process?

Maria and Joanne were referred to the Kennedy Aging Project for an opinion on these questions, with a request to look at the wholeness of each person separately and then at the two friends together. After spending time with the women and their caregivers, it became obvious that this decision was a deeply spiritual issue for Joanne and Maria. It required a decision based on the way their lives had found meaning, their understanding of commitment, their desire to do what was "right," and an unresolvable fear of separation and loss and death and dying.

Before returning to Joanne and Maria and the conclusions and recommendations of the Interdisciplinary Team, let us evaluate the needs of these women and a variety of others examined by the Aging Project. Our work with these clients has defined evaluation of clients' lives in pastoral terms, and of their experiences in terms utilized in the realm of spirituality. Often our clients had not had lengthy, high quality, pastoral relationships that would allow them to integrate their life experiences and to reach in a peaceful way the fulfillment of wisdom in aging. Whether expressed in words or in silence, clients and caregivers were searching fo. ways to make meaning of the experience of aging, both personally and with loved ones.

We could not express this process of meaning-making in purely psychological or medical terminology. It was necessary to give narrative form to the spirituality of aging, based on the client's experience, by means of a spiritual assessment.

Often an interview of faith history, or a personal inventory of those issues that were still unresolved and frequently in need of healing, happened in conjunction with the leisure and recreation assessment. The spiritual assessment was best done in a client's own residence, where the client felt free to identify with the environment and to utilize the self-confidence of being "at home in a place." This assessment often revealed a basic need of the individual to create rituals or structures that reinforced her fundamental values.

This spiritual assessment, then, was created from the needs of the client and reinforced by the caregiver. During the course of the Aging Project, this assessment gradually became more formalized, and the information and resulting pastoral action became a fundamental portion of the change that the Project could set into motion for the client. We began to understand the pastoral care and spiritual assessment of clients in a broader perspective:

- How could we help integrate the client into the life of his church or synagogue?

- How could we assist caregivers in finding transportation for a client to church or synagogue?

- Would it be possible to find someone from a client's church or synagogue to become a "friendly visitor," as a more formalized advocate within the client's worship community?

- Were there activities that took place in the client's worship community (bingo, dinners, arts and crafts) that would allow the client more contact within a non-segregated community?

- And, most importantly, how could we make recommendations that would assist the client to engage in active integration of her life experience? How could we begin to heal the feelings of isolation from family, depression and loneliness, and the lingering anger of those who had not been listened to in their search to understand the world?

As our process developed, we utilized both educational and psychological frameworks to describe pastoral care. It became necessary to formalize our reporting process (see Appendix to this chapter) while maintaining the essential quality of personalization so that, on review of our assessment, caregivers, case managers, and advocates would understand the necessity of providing pastoral care and spiritual companionship for the clients.

This process showed us that the structures of spirituality (meaning-making) often had more to do with clients' perceptions than with the actual chronology of their life experiences. Also, even though each client had a particular story, a generally consistent pattern of responses emerged. As we examined response patterns, we developed criteria for the spiritual assessment and created a tool based on these responses.

Our tool utilized four categories of questions, which were altered according to the needs of individuals. Our primary emphasis was to understand the *individual life of the client.* Then we talked about *important relationships,* explored *hopes and dreams,* and finally discussed *worship history.*

In section one, *life history,* we asked about the client's place of residence, likes and dislikes, number of siblings, recollection of parents and family of origin, recollection of institutionalization, and feelings about moves of residence. These questions were adapted to the needs of the client, his ability to verbalize, and the risks involved for the individual in such self-disclosures.

In section two, *important relationships,* we focused on the concepts of friendships, responsibilities to other people, and the articulation of important others in a client's life. It was impressive that many clients included particular staff members in this area; often the clients, in talking about the departure of a staff member from the residence or workshop, used terminology that is frequently used to describe a death experience. Generally, these clients were seeking meaningful relationships, and they had learned the painful lesson that important relationships are temporal. Still, we found clients who were willing to invest themselves over and over in their search for these relationships.

In section three, *hopes and dreams,* we talked about clients' favorite things, the way they chose to spend time, wish lists, people they wanted to have more time with, and concepts of feeling. It would be a great moment of conversion and growth in the secular service network if caregivers could hear the impact they have on the lives of those with whom they work; self-images, relationships, and ways of defining the quality of work are correlated with the quality of relationships between caregivers and clients. This is a reality that all in the secular service network understand intellectually, but one that sometimes gets clouded in myriad paperwork, Individual Habilitation Plans, and plans for intervention. Clients often invest themselves and take the risk of becoming involved in relationships with caregivers, and it is easy to forget how critical these connections are to them.

In section four, *faith and worship history,* we listened to the clients' stories of meaningful rituals and their hopes for future participation in rituals. By our placement of this category at the end of the list, it is obvious that this is not the sole basis for our evaluation of spirituality. Rather, it is the culmination of encouraging a client to articulate meaning-making. Worship is relevant as it identifies a value for the client. If ritual assists the individual, and if the active practice of a particular faith is important to a client, then we attempt to help make such a desire reality.

In a broad sense, we have come to describe faith as that which identifies a person's center of meaning, commitments, focus of values, and image of power and order. Often, our clients described faith in terms of their image of God. The response-pattern in this area has been a thrilling part of our approach to spiritual assessment. We have seen that, as people become more integrated and are encouraged to explore areas in need of healing, their image of God reflects this newly realized peace.

> One client, whose life-history had been filled with physical abuse and psychological abandonment, described God in these words: "God is very old. Gonna die soon. He has a red face. White hair. Needs to shave. His beard's a mess. God is gonna get all those people who are nasty. God ain't gonna get me, though, 'cause I never gonna get mad, or be sad, or hit."
>
> Realization of and encouragement to talk about her mother's death, her anger at her father for institutionalizing her, and her disappointment in never seeing her brothers, combined with both psychological and pastoral counseling, brought opportunities for new integration for this woman of seventy-one.
>
> Eighteen months later, she described her image of God in these words. "God's pretty. Looks a lot like my mother. Don't yell at me to quit. I guess I like to pray 'cause I just like it. I like feelin' good. So I like prayin'. If you spent time gettin' to know this God of mine, bet you would like the world a whole lot better."

Spirituality in a secular service network is alive and well. Spirituality is not dependent on cognitive functioning or on the ability of a client to verbalize experience. Rather, it is dependent on the individual's search to find an expression of meaning, as a way both to worship and to come to know her own center of meaning. Mental retardation and aging do not prevent spiritual development. Rather we found people who were deeply spiritual and searching for answers, and who wanted to find others who dare to journey with them.

For Joanne and Maria, we were able to make some suggestions to slow down the decision to move either of them to a nursing home. Such a move may indeed happen, but, having explored the way that they want to live their lives, the meaning of God for them, and the quality that they bring to each other's experience of life, both Joanne and Maria can be better prepared to make that decision together. In mutuality, they are utilizing both Maria's Judaic faith and Joanne's Christian faith to put ritual to their experiences of loving deeply and searching for ways to express that emotion. They are two of the many people who have, by their willingness to share their journey, taught us about the quality of life that those who are mentally retarded and old seek to experience.

■ Appendix: Pastoral Care Assessment

Client's Name:

Referred By:

Date of Aging Project Intake:

Case Coordinators:

Date of Pastoral Care Assessment:

Primary Reason for Referral to Pastoral Care:
I. Brief History—Life History—Important Relationships—Hopes and Dreams—Faith and Worship History
II. Presenting Pastoral Problems or Needs:

III. Summary of Pastoral Care Interview

IV. Pastoral Care Recommendations and Further Intervention:

THE ROLE OF THE SOCIAL WORKER

Susan L. Sternfeld

■

In thinking about what role I have played as a social worker on the Kennedy Aging Project Team this year, it has been difficult to separate a *single* role and look at it analytically. The primary reason for this difficulty lies in what I view as the uniqueness of this Team, a uniqueness that can be attributed to the following two factors: (1) the Team was composed of several permanent members, but each year it also incorporated new student members into its body; and (2) although each permanent and student member had a "primary" professional identity—physician, psychologist, minister, nurse practitioner, social worker, leisure therapist, lawyer—almost to a person, each member also had a second professional qualification. How did these factors affect the social work role? In order to answer this question, we need to look at what the ideal social work role would be on any team.

In my view, a social worker's major contribution to an Interdisciplinary Team is the holistic and interactive lens through which he views human problem solving. This particular lens is then applied to both the life of the client being served and the life of the Team as it evaluates the client's needs.

The social worker's viewpoint is particularly useful in the early stages of a Team when a variety of professionals are coming together for the first time, each bringing her own professional expertise. As the Team members begin to talk about a particular client, their professional training often leads them to look at the client with "tunnel vision," that is solely from a single professional perspective. This tendency toward tunnel vision is partially produced by professional expertise and training, and partially elicited by the team process itself, which sometimes creates the need to differentiate from other team members.

Building bridges between people and professions, then, is important if the full benefits of the Team approach are to be realized. The social worker is trained to facilitate this type of interaction and consensus building. At the same time, the social worker's knowledge about individual and group growth, and about systems interaction, is critical to the success of any intervention or suggestion planned by the team. If recommendations are not acceptable to or easy to implement by clients and caregivers, there is a significant risk of creating new problems as well as non-compliance.

On the Kennedy Aging Project Team, the social worker's function was, to a large extent, performed by all the Team members. This was partly attributable to the length of time people worked together and partly due to the dual background each member brought to Team discussions. The broadened viewpoint created by training in two or more fields facilitates understanding and respect among professionals so that traditional areas of conflict or tension related to professional status, terminology, codes of ethics, legal responsibilities, and knowledge base are diminished or eliminated.

However, in spite of the fact that the Kennedy Aging Project Team members had absorbed part of the social work viewpoint, there was still a critical role for the Team social worker. There are three components of the social worker's professional training that offer a continuing and unique contribution to the Team process: (1) the social worker's "eye," or professional viewpoint, (2) the social worker's knowledge base, and (3) the social worker as practitioner.

Ideally, the social worker's "eye" views the world and individuals within it using a broad professional lens. It looks at the human life span and notices that developmental stages are characterized by differing individual needs, potentials, and capabilities. It looks at individual, family, friendship, community, and political systems and assesses how each functions internally as well as in relation to other systems. And finally, it looks at the dynamics of personality, as well as external social factors, and evaluates the "goodness of fit" between person and environment.

These facets of the social worker's "eye" are translated into specific questions posed during a Team evaluation. On the Kennedy Aging Project Team, the social worker might ask: What does the client enjoy doing in his spare time? Does he have a special friend, and how often do they get to see each other? Is there any family contact, and if so, how often do they meet and what is the nature of the relationship? Does the client have access to community events and community services? If not, what might be done to improve accessibility? If yes, is it adequate? Is the client in a work and residential setting that meets his social and emotional capabilities? If not, what might be done to improve the client's own skills, or the characteristics of the setting that cause the client problems?

The social worker's knowledge base is both varied and extensive; it is a rich resource for resolving the many problems, tensions, conflicts, and traumas that occur in the course of human living in all its diversity. It includes the following: knowledge of the psychodynamics of personality development—both normal and dysfunctional; knowledge of normative growth and development from childhood to old age, including such life events as birth, child rearing, entering school, leaving home, starting a family, the "empty nest syndrome," retirement, death, loss, and sexuality from childhood to old age; knowledge of and sensitivity to variations in cultural, racial, and religious values both in oneself and in the clients being served; knowledge of the impact of non-normative events on individuals and families and how to help people develop coping strategies to handle stressful events such as accidental injuries, sudden losses, terminal illness, divorce or separation, birth of a disabled child, and loss of employment; knowledge of legal and ethical rights and responsibilities of both clients and service providers; knowledge of government resources and eligibility requirements; knowledge of strategies for activating community political action when social policy changes seem needed; and knowledge of interpersonal dynamics in natural and therapeutic settings between two individuals, in groups, or in families.

Based on the preceding knowledge base, the Kennedy Aging Project social worker might ask some of the following questions: Does the client enjoy working, or is she looking forward to retirement? Does the client have an opportunity to talk about death and loss? Has she been able to grieve for past losses? Should a seventy-year-old person be moved from her present nursing home to a less restrictive group or foster home? What are the moral and ethical reasons behind either the decision to move or to stay?

And finally, the social worker as practitioner activates this knowledge in response to what his "eye" notices in the dual arenas of concern—the Team and the client. For example, pointing out a client's cultural values to Team members may help the Team frame a recommendation that is syntonic for the client. Or, inquiring about family and neighborhood contacts may reveal that a client is very isolated and therefore will need formal social supports when returning from a hospital stay. Asking each Team member to comment on the specific implications of a course of action from her professional viewpoint often sheds new light on the issue and opens the door to an alternative solution.

The list is endless, but in general, the social worker often assumes the role of facilitating connections within the Team and between the Team and the client. At times this means being an advocate for the client on the Team and at times it involves advocating for the Team to the client.

There is an inherent tension in this process that echoes a central concern of healthy personality growth and development—the ongoing struggle between individuation and attachment. On the one hand, each professional brings a unique contribution to the Team that must be maintained and respected (individuation), and on the other hand, the primary focus of the Team is to bond together (attachment) in a mutually shared purpose and concern for the client.

When it works well, the Team process is unusually creative, often in quite serendipitous ways. Ideas sometimes seem to come magically out of the air, making it impossible to identify a single person as the source. It is like the circle game in which a person starts a story with a single phrase or sentence, whereupon the following person adds whatever she wants and stops at any point to let the next person continue. The end result is a fascinating story production to which each person has added her own creative piece—the parts become blended into the whole. So it is with the Interdisciplinary Team—recommendations and Team decisions are more than a mere compilation of everyone's individual professional ideas. They are the result of a creative, authentic process in which the Team operates and thinks as a living system composed of autonomous yet interdependent parts.

18

MEDICAL ASSESSMENT

Mary C. Howell

■

Evaluation of the client's physical and physiological health and well-being is the responsibility of the physician. In an Interdisciplinary Team setting there will be an overlap of concerns and competencies for the physician and other professionals such as the nurse, social worker, clinical psychologist, and so on. In the interests of effective teamwork, it is important that the physician resist the temptation to "take over" as spokesperson or summarizer of all accumulated information. Two realms of information are the direct and predominant province of the physician: an overview of the client's past medical history and present physical status, and a physical examination.

The degree to which the physician member of an Interdisciplinary Team intervenes directly with the client depends both on the questions brought to the Team by the client's caregivers and on the availability of physicians in the client's geographical residential area. The physician's role is different when there are questions relating specifically to the client's physical well-being than when the caregivers' queries and concerns are directed solely to matters of housing, work, relations with family members, or other problems affecting well-being aside from physical health. In New England, the geographical residential area of the clients of the Kennedy Aging Project, there is no shortage of physicians; there are many physicians (both generalist and specialist) in most communities. Since every client receiving funds from Medicaid must have a yearly physical examination, most clients referred to the Team will have an identified "regular doctor," and the Team will have access to the local physician's recorded health history and physical examination, performed within the past twelve months.

The first questions to be considered by the examining physician on the Interdisciplinary Team, then, are: (1) Do the client and caregivers feel that they have a troubled relationship with their local physician? (2)

Are there specific questions now about the client's physical health status? (3) Are there new symptoms or signs that might represent a recently acquired illness or injury? (4) Are there findings in the recorded annual medical history and physical examination that are puzzling, worrisome, inconsistent, or conflicting, or that otherwise suggest a need for review?

If the answer to any of these questions is "yes," then a formally scheduled appointment for a full medical history and physical examination may be appropriate. Careful review of past records is essential. The presence of a caregiver who has daily contact with the client will facilitate an accurate medical history; the client's trust of the accompanying caregiver will also help make a thorough physical examination possible.

In taking a medical history, the challenge for the interviewing physician is to allow the patient to speak for herself as much as possible, and also to take full advantage of the knowledge of the caregiver. It is obvious that this method of history gathering takes extra time. The physician must also pay attention to the possibility of hearing loss, diminished visual acuity, and arthritic slowness, and the pace of the interview should be suitably adjusted.

Determining the cause of retardation is usually not relevant to the medical care of the aged patient. However, if Down syndrome is suspected, chromosomal analysis should be available for the purpose of family counseling and for prognosis of the telescoped pace of aging that occurs with this syndrome. Laboratory confirmation of the diagnosis of Fragile X syndrome should be sought for every male with unexplained mild to moderate mental retardation, again for the purpose of genetic counseling of the family. The great majority of adults with mild to moderate mental retardation have retardation of unknown etiology. It is important, however, to inquire what the family, caregivers, and perhaps also the patient *believe* to be the cause of the handicap.

Family illness history may be difficult to ascertain. An account of the patient's recent and present stress and loss is essential. Recent changes in functional capabilities may indicate remediable conditions. Immunization status for tetanus, pneumococcus, and influenza are important to record. Current medications can be reported by a reliable informant, usually a nurse; most accurately, medication regimens are reviewed by inspecting physicians' orders or by reviewing medications brought to the appointment with the patient.

As is true of all patients, those with mental retardation are distressed by maneuvers of the physical examination when they are not told what is being done, and why. These patients may not remember previous physical examinations as happy or comfortable occasions. Explanations about the purpose of the examination, and an opportunity to ask questions, should be offered before the patient is undressed. The accompanying family member or caregiver should be allowed to stay in the room if the patient prefers. It is essential that the examiner move slowly and with appreciation for the patient's distress or agitation, and also maintain eye contact with the patient. Many people with mental retardation have difficulty suppressing the urge to protest—in words or actions—treatment that seems to them to be undignified, demeaning, or attacking. The examiner may feel uncomfortable or apprehensive with such a patient. However, many who are retarded are also inclined to be agreeable and do as others want them to do, and this characteristic often works to make the physical examination easier to perform.

If a family member or caregiver is present, it is wise to inquire for information relevant to the procedure before beginning the examination. For example, is there some part of the examination that is likely to be particularly uncomfortable or worrisome for the patient, and is therefore best left for last? What about the ear and rectal examinations? Does the patient mind being partially unclothed? Completely unclothed? Are there special words to use for body parts? Will the caregiver help interpret and translate?

Encouraging the patient to touch, hold, and examine the various instruments of the examination may be reassuring. Physicians should also remember to gauge the most essential parts of the examination so that these can be done with as much dispatch as possible, in the event that a complete examination cannot be performed.

Certain parts of the physical examination are especially important for patients who are old. Blood pressure should be recorded supine, when first standing, and a few minutes after standing; this data is especially important if antihypertensive medication is contemplated. Temples should be palpated for sensitivity or tenderness as a sign of temporal arteritis. Informal observations of visual and auditory acuity should be recorded; formal assessment is always indicated in patients who are both old and mentally retarded, at yearly intervals. The oral tissues must be examined for tumors (with dentures, if any, removed); yearly dental evaluation is also recommended.

Soft aortic systolic murmurs, with a normal aortic second sound and no diminution of pulse upstroke, are common in old age. An electrocardiogram should be performed yearly, and also in response to symptoms of pain or syncope; a 24- hour monitor may be needed to assess the possibility of an arrhythmia, especially when there is a history of falling.

A careful examination of the breasts is essential. Discolored lesions of the skin should be reviewed dermatologically if the history of growth, appearance, or placement indicate the possibility of malignancy.

Rectal and genital examinations should be done to evaluate hemorrhoids, prostatic enlargement, vulvitis, and rectal or genital tumors. A formal gynecologic examination should be done yearly.

For some patients, no formal appointment for history taking and physical examination is needed: if the caregivers report a responsive and respectful relationship with a local generalist physician; if a complete and recent history and physical has been performed and legible records have been forwarded to the Team; and if there are no current signs or symptoms of a change in physical health status.

Even in these instances, however, the physician on the Team may have a special role to fulfill. Many old people wish to have a review of their past medical history, with a concordance of the medical events of a lifetime. Caregivers appreciate a review of currently prescribed medications, with observations about the appropriateness of dosage and the possibility of drug interactions. And communications with the patient's local generalist physician can sometimes be improved with a note or phone call from the Team physician, expressing appreciation for the care given to the patient.

19

ASSESSMENT OF LEGAL NEEDS

Henry A. Beyer and Deborah Lynch

■

For a few clients who came to the Kennedy Aging Project, questions of guardianship or estate planning were included among their presenting problems. But the majority arrived with no legal issues in mind. Nevertheless, an assessment of possible legal needs, which was made for every client, determined that a significant number required some assistance in law-related matters, and that a few were in need of the extended services of an attorney or other advocate.

Questions for the assessing of legal needs were incorporated into the mail, telephone, and face-to-face client questionnaires. They were designed, first, to determine the client's legal and financial status. Clients and their caregivers were asked, for example, whether the client was currently under or had ever been recommended for guardianship or conservatorship; whether he received Supplemental Security Income (SSI) or other disability benefits; whether he had a representative payee to receive and handle such benefits; whether any trust or other financial arrangement had been established or was contemplated by the family or others for the client's benefit; what was the approximate size of the client's assets and income; and whether the client had made a will or might wish to do so.

Another important factor regarding a client's legal status was whether he was a "class client," that is, a member of a class guaranteed special protections by consent decrees entered into by the Common-wealth of Massachusetts in settlement of class actions at five state schools for people with mental retardation.[1] Individuals who were residents of those schools on or after specific dates in the early 1970s have lifelong entitlements, guaranteed by a federal court, to appropriate residential and other services. They thus enjoy a high priority in vying for limited resources. Many other states also have certain citizens in such favored positions, the beneficiaries of similar class actions.[2]

Other intake questions attempted to identify any problems having legal components in those areas of the client's life where such issues often arise: Are the client's residential and day placements considered appropriate? By all those involved? Is the client herself happy with them? Has an Individualized Habilitation Plan (IHP) or Individualized Service Plan (ISP) been developed for the client? Is it appropriate? Is it actually being followed? Does the client ever receive antipsychotic medication and, if so, has it been legally authorized? Is the client considered to have behavior problems? If so, how are they being addressed? Does the client have full control over her own income or other assets? If not, who does, and how are the funds handled?

Based upon the answers to these questions (and, in fact, on all of the information obtained about the client and on the Team's evaluation of that information), a decision was made as to whether particular areas might harbor legal issues that should be explored in greater depth. Specific legal needs discovered and addressed through this process included the following:

■ Estate Planning

About twenty of the Project's clients and their families were given advice concerning estate planning issues. The principles set forth in Chapter 49 were presented,[3] discussed, and applied to the particular circumstances of their individual cases. A plan of action was suggested, and referrals were made to private attorneys knowledgeable in the field for development of appropriate trusts or other estate plans.

■ Will-Writing

If it appeared appropriate for the client to write his own will, referral was made to our own Will-Writing Project (see Chapter 66).

■ Guardianship and Conservatorship

Guardianship and conservatorship are legal mechanisms for substitute decision-making. As discussed more fully in Chapter 23, a guardian or conservator is appointed as the result of a legal determination that a person is incompetent to make decisions in all or certain aspects of his personal or financial affairs. Factors that might be considered in determining the need for one of these legal mechanisms include the client's capacity to understand the basic facts and implications of a decision, for example, that the present discomfort of a medical procedure may be offset by future benefits.

A total (or "plenary") guardian, one authorized by a court to handle practically all of the personal and financial affairs of the "ward," is usually neither required nor desirable. When an individual does need some sort of guardianship service, a conservatorship or a limited and/or temporary guardianship will usually suffice, and is usually preferable. A common example of limited guardianship is a medical guardianship, established when the individual is deemed unable to understand the nature or potential consequences of a proposed treatment involving greater than minimal risk or consequences.

A few clients, already under guardianship when seen by the Project, were considered by the Team to be no longer in need of such protection, if, indeed, they ever were. A guardianship can be removed only by demonstrating to a court that the client is no longer incompetent in those areas covered by the guardianship. (It is rarely advisable to argue that the client was *never* incompetent because it was, after all, the court that had formally found her to be so.) At a court hearing for the removal of guardianship, sufficient evidence must be presented to overcome the legal presumption that persons who are once adjudicated incompetent remain so indefinitely. Although the type and amount of evidence necessary to overcome this presumption will depend on the particular state and on the type of guardianship imposed, it is generally the case that individuals with mental retardation face a difficult task in persuading a court to restore their legal competency and discharge their guardian.[4]

The Team recommended that temporary medical guardianships be sought for several clients for whom diagnostic or therapeutic procedures were recommended, and who were believed to be functionally incompetent of consenting to them. In one such case, follow-up recommendations were provided when those seeking the guardianship were advised that a monetary bond would have to be posted. Because the purpose of a bond is to protect the ward against misuse of his financial assets, we maintained that none was required in this case, since no assets were at risk. Thus, any formal requirement for a bond or for personal corporate sureties should be waived by the judge at the guardianship hearing.[5] We suggested that the client's caregivers consult the legal office of the Department of Mental Retardation for assistance with this matter.

In another case, the Team located a person willing to serve as temporary medical guardian for an 89-year-old woman, dying of cancer in a state institution, with no living family members. After being appointed, the guardian, with the court's approval, had to make decisions regarding the woman's acceptance or refusal of various treatments, none of which would have cured the disease, and some of which would have necessitated her forced removal, under restraint, from the residential building in which she had lived for many years and where she was surrounded by her psychological "family"—caring staff members and other clients.[6]

In one case, there was substantial doubt as to whom a client's guardian actually was, his sister or his father. The father had been appointed guardian many years ago, but the sister now claimed that role. It was unclear, however, whether a court had been involved in this re-designation. In yet another case, it was not even clear whether the client had ever been legally placed under guardianship, although his sister claimed to be his plenary guardian. In both of these cases, the Team advised the concerned caregivers how the client's guardianship status could be clarified by checking county probate court records.[7] They were also advised on how the court could be petitioned to have the guardians re-designated[8] (if this were found desirable) and the guardianships limited to areas in which they were actually needed.

■ An Appropriate Residence

A number of courts have held that individuals with mental retardation are constitutionally entitled to live in the least restrictive environment consistent with their needs and conditions.[9] This common sense rule is an application of the legal doctrine of the "least restrictive alternative"—a judicial recognition that when the state restricts a person's fundamental rights, it must do so in the least restrictive manner consistent with the underlying purpose of the restriction. This principle has been applied to issues of habilitation, treatment, and especially, residential placement.[10] Numerous courts and administrative hearing officers have relied upon the principle (and on its codification in statutes and regulations[11]) to require the community placement of a great many individuals with mental retardation, including a significant number requiring extensive medical services or behavioral programming.[12]

In one least-restrictive-alternative case, the guardian-aunt of an older woman with mental retardation approached the Kennedy Aging Project to request help in preventing her ward from being returned from her community residence to a state school from which she had been transferred years before. The stated reason for the proposed move was that the woman was not capable of self-preservation—could not evacuate the residence within two-and-one-half minutes after the fire alarm sounded. After investigation, however, the Team believed that not all means had been explored for enabling the woman to live safely in the community. A Team attorney, acting in his alternative role as legal aid clinical program attorney-instructor, represented the client at administrative hearings where he successfully used the provisions of a recently enacted state statute to prevent the transfer.[13] Although the new law had been intended primarily to enable families to resist the deinstitutionalization of their mentally retarded family members, in this case it was used on behalf of the aunt to delay reinstitutionalization until all alternatives were thoroughly explored. An opening in another type of community residence, with a higher staff-client ratio (thus obviating the self-preservation requirement) was eventually found, and the client was not reinstitutionalized.

Another client, David, had been transferred, some years previously, from an institution to a couple of community residences and eventually to his own apartment. He had been recently diagnosed as dying of pancreatic cancer. David had lost his residential placement during his diagnostic stay in a general hospital, and was now being threatened with discharge to a nursing home. He had once worked in a nursing home, disliked it intensely, and now vehemently objected to being sent to one. He realized that he was dying, and wished to return to the state institution where he had spent most of his life and where some of his friends still lived. The Team referred him to a law school's legal aid clinical program, which found him capable of retaining their lawyer as counsel. His attorney was negotiating his return to the institution when, sadly, time ran out and he died in a county hospital. (David's case is also discussed in Chapter 52.)

Other clients presented a variety of housing problems, eliciting a variety of recommendations from the Team. As discussed more fully in Chapter 38, because residential services do not meet the demand, many clients were placed on waiting lists and concerned family members and other caregivers were counseled on the necessity for vigorous and persistent advocacy. Several clients and families with access to financial resources were advised of and referred to programs facilitating the establishment of client-owned condominiums (also discussed in Chapter 38).

■ Right to Appropriate Services in a Safe Environment

The U.S. Supreme Court has held that residents of a state institution for people with mental retardation have a constitutional right to safe conditions, freedom from "unreasonable" restraint, and at least "minimally adequate" training in caring for themselves.[14] Many lower courts have gone much further, finding a general right to habilitation or treatment, and extending this right to community as well as institutional settings.[15]

The key element in planning and implementing a program of appropriate services, in either the community or an institution, is an Individualized Habilitation Plan (IHP), in some states called an Individual Service Plan (ISP) or Individual Program Plan (IPP).[16] The IHP should specifically describe the client's long-term habilitation goals and intermediate objectives, with measurable indices of progress. The person with mental retardation, and/or his parent(s), guardian, or other representative, including advocates, have the right to participate in the development of the plan and in its periodic revision.[17]

In determining whether a client is receiving adequate programming, among the factors to be considered are whether an IHP has been developed, whether its goals and objectives are specifically tailored to this individual's needs, whether they are individualized to his particular functional limitations and abilities, whether progress is being made to meet the goals, and whether the IHP is reviewed periodically by the individual and/or his family and his service providers to see if revisions are needed due to changes in the client's condition or in other circumstances. IHPs are thus excellent tools for use in determining whether a client is receiving adequate and appropriate services; they were therefore reviewed carefully by the legal, as well as other, members of the Interdisciplinary Team.

■ Right to Refuse Treatment

The right of individuals with mental impairments to refuse treatment has been recognized primarily in the context of antipsychotic medication. The tranquilizing effects of antipsychotic drugs led to their extensive use in facilities for persons with mental illness and mental retardation.[18] Within the facilities, the drugs were used not only to treat the residents, but also to restrain them. In many institutions, they became a substitute for adequate staffing and programming. These practices have been condemned by courts across the country as violative of both the individuals' constitutional liberty interests and of state and federal statutes.[19] Although the legal and health care professions remain divided over patients' rights to refuse medication administered for treatment purposes, it is becoming firmly established in the majority of states that "medication shall not be used as punishment, for the convenience of staff, as a substitute for a habilitation program, or in quantities that interfere with a resident's habilitation program."[20]

The Massachusetts Supreme Judicial Court has held that individuals possessing the mental capacity to understand the nature and consequences of a decision to accept or reject antipsychotic medication and the capability of comprehending enough relevant information to come to a rational decision have the legal right to make such a decision, even if they are mentally retarded, and even if they have been civilly committed.[21] If found by a court to be *not* competent to make such a decision, the court is to make a "substituted judgment" on their behalf, making the same decision, so far as is humanly possible, that they would make if they were competent to do so. (This process is further discussed in Chapter 23.) Similar (though not identical) rights to refuse antipsychotic medication are being recognized in a growing number of other jurisdictions across the country.[22]

In the Kennedy Aging Project, particular attention was therefore paid by the Team's legally-trained members to whether the client was receiving antipsychotic medication, the reasons for its administration, and whether the use was legally authorized. It was the Team's opinion that, of all the clients seen who were receiving such drugs, probably only one possessed the competence to provide a valid consent, which he had given. Consent for medicating a few others had been given through "substituted judgment" in court hearings (known in Massachusetts as *Rogers* hearings). But, for the majority, there had been no legally valid consent to the drugs. This was not particularly surprising, since it is widely known that the Departments of Mental Health and Mental Retardation have, since 1983, been slowly working their way through the backlog of clients requiring *Rogers* hearings, scheduling first those who are actively refusing drugs. Such refusals tend to come from patients diagnosed as mentally ill, not from the generally more acquiescent individuals with mental retardation.[23] The Team recommended trial reduction or termination of antipsychotic medication for a number of clients, and advised caregivers that the law required that all those believed to be functionally incompetent for the decision, who had not yet had a *Rogers* hearing, must be added to the DMR waiting lists for such hearings, if not already registered there.

■ Other Rights Issues

The Team addressed a wide range of other rights issues presented by clients,[24] some quite successfully, others less so. They included these:

- A man who had fallen twice within two years at his sheltered workshop, each fall resulting in a broken hip, was being required to use a wheelchair by the workshop during his working hours there. Because the Team believed that walking would be physically therapeutic, it viewed the man's confinement to the wheelchair as a physical restraint. Upon the Team's recommendation, an administrative complaint was filed with DMR. The complaint was withdrawn, however, after the Human Rights Committee monitoring the workshop's program found the use of the chair essential to the man's safety. Noting that the man was by that time receiving a regimen of exercises as physical therapy, the committee found no violation of his rights.

- Advice on how to file administrative complaints with DMR, the Massachusetts Commission Against Discrimination, and the U.S. Department of Health and Human Services' Office for Civil Rights was also furnished by the Team to service providers whose clients were excluded from certain community programs for elderly persons because of their mental retardation, and from other programs for mentally retarded persons because of their advanced age.

- Perhaps the most basic question faced by the Team was whether certain clients were, or should be classified as being, "mentally retarded." If the Team's tests should indicate that some clients were not, they might be found legally ineligible for receipt of needed services, unless they qualified under certain "grandfather" provisions. However, a recent administrative decision by a Massachusetts Department of Mental Retardation hearing officer held that a man with a measured full-scale IQ of 82, who experienced seriously impaired functioning as a result of head injuries, did meet the regulatory definition of "mental retardation" and was thus eligible for DMR services. The hearing officer found this to be the case even though, she acknowledged, the man could not be "accurately diagnosed as primarily mentally retarded as the term is used in the context of testing evaluations."[25] This decision was among the materials provided by the Team to the family of one client who might legitimately have been given a primary diagnosis of either mental retardation or mental illness. The family, who had retained a private lawyer to represent the man, desired that he receive the former diagnosis because they believed (with some justification) that the state is providing more and better services to people so labeled.[26]

■ Advocacy

An advocate is someone who actively supports and promotes a client's desires and interests. Advocacy entails more than satisfying the clinical service needs of the individual or assuming some decision-making control over the individual; it involves speaking up for, and on behalf of, the individual's rights and aspirations and helping her to secure those goals.

An advocate need not be, and in most cases is not, a lawyer. It may be a family member, a friend, or an unrelated volunteer who is willing to represent the interests of the individual and provide emotional and practical support. A staff member of the client's service-providing organization may sometimes serve as an advocate, although the conflict of interest inherent in such situations invariably limits such a person's capacity for zealous advocacy when the target of that advocacy is the service provider-employer. There are also advocates who regularly deal with a particular type of need, or set of needs, such as SSI/SSDI.[27]

An individual may need an advocate if she is unable to advocate effectively on her own behalf. This may be due to a lack of communication skills, isolation from the needed service channels, or the vulnerability of the individual's position. The majority of clients seen by the Kennedy Aging Project had some need for advocacy services; for a few the need was critical. In practically all cases, therefore, the Team encouraged family members and other caregivers to persevere[28] in their advocacy work, and provided many of them with informational materials intended to increase their effectiveness.[29] Clients who needed continuing legal services were referred to the Boston University Legal Aid Clinical Program, various legal services agencies throughout the state, or a half-dozen private attorneys who specialize in issues of importance to individuals with disabilities.

20

LEISURE ASSESSMENT

Elizabeth J. DeBrine

■

The purpose of the leisure assessment is to determine if the individual is using her free time to best advantage. I am concerned about how our clients who are old and mentally retarded spend their evenings, weekends, and holidays. The clients' leisure time should include activities that allow mental and physical challenges, present opportunities to see old friends and meet new people, extend freedom of choice, and allow risk-taking.

A leisure assessment is a therapeutic recreation tool that helps a recreation leader inventory leisure interests and skills and determine how those abilities can be best exercised in the client's own community. The leisure assessment developed in the Kennedy Aging Project had to be flexible enough to reflect the wide variety of the clients' abilities. Our clients included people who ranged from severely to mildly mentally retarded; people who were misdiagnosed as mentally retarded; people with no physical impairments and people with several handicaps; people with well-rounded, individualized leisure activities and those who could only do staff-dependent leisure activities; people who had lived at home with their families for most of their lives and clients who had spent their whole lives in institutions for the "feeble minded."

■ Four Goals of Leisure Assessment

Our leisure assessment has four goals: to educate staff, to empower staff to effect change, to search for ways in which clients can initiate independent action, and to consider the benefits and the possibilities of the client having an unpaid friend.

The education of both professional and direct care staff is the primary goal. This is the most effective means of advocating for a client's leisure. We teach staff that they should be concerned not only about the medical, employment, and housing needs of clients, but also about their recreational needs. Clients have a right to experience leisure in the form of participating in or attending sporting events, exploring nature, taking trips, enjoying club membership, or participating in the activities of personal life development that we all take for granted. Discussions with clients and caregivers can help them develop an appreciation of the value and benefits of leisure for clients.

Empowering staff to effect change in a residence and in a client's life is the second goal of the leisure assessment. Another person's perspective on a client's behavior can influence the way the client perceives herself and interacts with others. Focusing on a client's assets rather than on her liabilities can radically change the way staff members perceive clients. For example, a client's playfulness can be turned into a game; staff can channel the client's high energy after work into an active game of follow-the-leader or catch. Viewing these actions in a positive manner can help staff to see clients as individuals who have the ability to be spontaneous and engaging. Taken one step further, these actions can be specifically incorporated into an activity.

Not only are we concerned about what a client's assets and liabilities are, but we also need to know what staff concerns and needs are (for instance, staffing patterns, supervision, and transportation). Then we are able to brainstorm together at least one idea, one way to create a new leisure opportunity for a client. If I can help to plant one firm idea on how to make an activity possible for a client, then I feel that the interview has been successful.

Why spend so much time with staff? Because it would be foolish for me to develop an elaborate ideal recreation plan without understanding what is truly possible within a particular setting. Staff usually know the client best and are the client's greatest asset; this is especially true for those clients who do not have involved family members or an unpaid friend. Direct care staff are the caregivers least likely to receive inservice training or formal education, but spend the most time with the clients and, as a result, have tremendous influence over the clients' lives.

The third goal of the leisure assessment process is to find ways in which independent action for a client can be made possible. The ideal situation would be for every client to initiate a project, hobby, or activity and complete it without staff help.

For most of the clients I have seen, this is not entirely possible. Clients need assistance with transportation, purchasing materials, set-up, clean-up, and introduction to new activities. But our goal remains to minimize staff involvement so that the progress and quality of the activity is fueled by the clients' initiative and not by staff coercion or good intentions.

Bob, one of our clients, was very bored at the workshop and was losing skills as a result. He appeared to be severely mentally retarded due to his lack of expressive skills, but rated much higher on psychological testing. His residence staff came up with the idea of horseback riding lessons for him.

This was an activity in which Bob could excel, and it was totally unrelated to his work and residence. His riding teacher was not a mental retardation specialist, but an ordinary person who really liked him. It is possible now that Bob can spend even more time with horses and have a leisure interest develop into a part-time volunteer position. Bob is making new community friends and is able to be close to animals, who are unaware of any handicaps he might have.

Of course, not all of our clients are as physically able as Bob. Staff members expressed concerns about Lena, who was depressed. She did not have any hobbies and her sister's weekly visits caused more agitation than pleasure. While talking with Lena and her caregivers, I pulled out a box of crafts. Lena immediately threaded a needle and started to sew a piece of fabric. Obviously, this was a skill that she had not forgotten, although her present staff was unaware of her ability. Lena rediscovered an activity that requires little staff supervision and will be a source of satisfaction in the future.

The fourth goal of the leisure assessment is to consider how the client could benefit from a friendship with an unpaid friend. This is one objective deinstitutionalization was meant to bring about, by placing former state school clients into group homes and other community residences. Unfortunately, very few of the clients I have interviewed have an unpaid friend.

Clients have many people who are paid to spend time with them. Staff may move to higher levels of responsibility within the agency, or leave the agency entirely for another job, and thereby lose the day-to-day contact. This is a very unsatisfactory way to develop relationships. Everyone needs people who are involved in their lives because they like them as individuals, and not because it's their job.

Unpaid friends are most likely to be found in volunteer organizations such as churches, service organizations, or other community collaborations. Friends of family members are another source. These friendships work best when there is a common leisure interest that the potential friends can share, such as religious worship, hobbies (love of trains, baseball cards, or doll collecting), service to the community by helping others, or love of music, dance, or sports.

One of our clients has a father who is an active member of a church. His son, Tom, attended all of the fund-raising dinners of the church with his parents. I suggested that, instead of just attending the church suppers as a paid guest, Tom could volunteer his service by clearing the tables, taking tickets, and pouring coffee. This would give Tom a chance to express social responsibility, as his parents do, and also provide opportunities to meet new people who share the same interests: faith, service, and good food. Tom is more likely to be seen as an individual when he attends those functions with his family, as opposed to when he participates in a large group outing from his residence or workshop and is accompanied by staff. This will provide him with more opportunities to meet potential friends and cultivate new relationships.

■ Leisure Assessment Process

I use *free time* as my definition of leisure when I assess my clients. Free time means all of the time left over after working, commuting, running errands, and taking care of household responsibilities. Most

Americans define their leisure in this way. For many clients, there are three hours each evening on workdays, plus half of Saturday and all of Sunday for leisure.

Our leisure assessment interviews are divided into two parts: information gathering and brainstorming. First, the client and caregiver describe a typical week of activities performed outside of work. The list should include activities that have been performed in the past, and also activities in which the client is currently engaged. The client and caregiver both give opinions as to their satisfaction with the present activity level.

We discuss the client's understanding of leisure through simple questions such as "What do you do for fun?" and "What are three things you wish you could do?" The answers give us an indication of the client's value system: his appreciation of leisure, the value given to work, his preference for individual versus group activities, and his current opportunities for exercising freedom of choice.

One gentleman, Fred, disliked some activities because he thought they were not very "manly." He liked performing chores like sweeping and clearing the table, watching sports on television, and looking at sports magazines, but he considered coloring, crafts, and music to be "sissy stuff." He valued his job at the workshop and put forth his best effort there; he came home tired with little interest in the house activities.

We thought perhaps Fred would enjoy collecting baseball cards. In Fred's community, there is a sportscard shop where the cards are sold; it also serves as a meeting place for a card collectors' club. Perhaps Fred could become involved with this group and meet new people? Staff were very interested in taking Fred to the shop on a weekend to see if Fred would be interested in this hobby. Meanwhile, at the residence, Fred would increase the number of chores he is responsible for around the house, since he enjoys them so much. Staff would help Fred fill out a subscription form to a sports magazine and take him to sporting events.

Clients may refuse to attend activities for reasons other than their value system. Some clients say "no" because it is the only opportunity they have to refuse an offer made by staff. Others decline because they are withdrawn or depressed. Some clients refuse to spend their paychecks because it is the first time they have ever had money to save. Perhaps the most frustrating people to work with are those who accept an invitation, but then get cold feet at the last minute. In these instances a more thorough assessment may be required, which might include a home visit, Team consultation, or psychological evaluation.

We ask, "In what community activities is the client participating?" The client may be involved in a weekly or monthly group run by the local Association for Retarded Citizens, Special Olympics, or Elks. We also want to know if the client is participating in group home or nursing home activities. If a client attends a workshop and resides in a nursing home, she will have missed all of the home's activities that are scheduled during the day and will have lots of free time in the evening and weekends, with little or no stimulation.

Next we want to know what kinds of support the client has from family and friends. We learn who the client considers to be the most important people in her life. What are some of the activities they do together? Are staff members considered to be the client's family? Are there any unpaid friends now? What resources might be drawn on to foster a relationship with an unpaid friend?

■ Four Components of Leisure

During the interview, the present and future activities listed by the client and caregivers are placed into four activity categories: physical, social, mental, and spiritual.[1]

Most of our clients have little or no regular physical activity during the week. They are often overweight and sedentary. As a result, they are placed on calorie reduction diets by staff. Since they would lose weight faster if they increased their activity level, we then design a physical activity program in which they should be engaged at least three times a week for at least one half-hour on each occasion.

One of the many benefits of exercise is that it works well as a mood elevator. Also, the ability to maintain physical endurance and flexibility can play a major role in determining housing and care needs in later years of life. An activity program may include dancing to music in the living room at the group home, taking long walks in the neighborhood, swimming at the local YMCA, participating in a weekend sports competition with Special Olympics, playing Nerf sports (golf, table hockey, volleyball), or any combination of the above.

Many clients also need programs that challenge their mental skills. This is the area most often overlooked by caregivers, because it is supposed to be covered by the work program or through chores at the residence. Mental challenges commonly come from activities like hobbies, games, and puzzles. We can use these interests to increase our clients' skills and opportunities for community access. For example, clients can increase their independence at restaurants by practicing basic picture identification on menus so they can order for themselves. Also, they can learn what topics are appropriate for dinner-table conversations while out in company.

Another activity that involves many mental skills is planning a vacation by choosing a location and mode of transportation, planning for clothing needs, and keeping a budget. A vacation is a prime motivator to everyone. In fact, for most people, planning and dreaming about the trip is the best part of the vacation.

Vacations can be used to ameliorate anniversary depressions due to loss and separation; the dislike of cold weather and dark days of winter that induce winter "blues" can also be helped by vacations. I recommend that every client take at least two vacations, one in summer and one in midwinter.

For the social component, clients need to have friends and family regularly involved in their lives. We encourage staff to help clients reconnect with estranged family members, either through phone calls or cards, on a weekly or monthly basis. After several months, perhaps, the family member could have a short visit, with the staff helping with initial greetings, conversation, perhaps an activity, and then goodbyes.

Every client would benefit from having unpaid friends. These friendships can be supported with staff help: encouraging restraint with regard to frequency of phone calls to the friend, answering the friend's questions about the client's needs and relevant past history, and helping to find resources so the client can pay her share of the monetary costs of their activities.

The clients who most need friends are just those who can overwhelm a potential friend with their neediness. Staff can really help by listening to the friend's concerns and by helping to set limits to the friend's availability and responsibility for the client. The friend may feel that the client's needs are so insatiable that the relationship is of little use. Staff can endorse the relationship and the benefits the client receives through the friend's time and effort. Eventually, the friend and client will establish a sound friendship based on mutual trust and common interests.[2]

The spiritual component is often overlooked because there may be a lack of weekend staff. Also, clients may not have openly expressed a desire to be part of a local church or synagogue community. Organized church or synagogue communities are, in our experience, the best resource for a sense of spiritual belonging for a client in a group home. Nowhere else is there the wide variety of activity (worship, social action groups, fund-raising activities, political action, recreational and social activities, service and educational opportunities, witnessing of "The Word," and opportunities to meet new friends), and also the premise that *all* are welcome and accepted as God's own. Rarely does a client not wish to re-establish ties with a church or synagogue. Almost all clients express a desire to attend worship services regularly and would enjoy a friendly visitor from a religious community.

In the second part of the interview, the caregiver, client, and I brainstorm the best way to put the client's leisure needs into action. We take into consideration staffing patterns for the evening and weekends. Is there someone who can run an exercise group after supper, be it for relaxation or for developing strength or flexibility? We determine if the agency has funding to support leisure activities through extra staff. Can they afford to have a recreational therapist come in once a week for individual consultations? Are there residence-sponsored picnics or weekend trips? We also assess staff knowledge of the community resources for activities and unpaid friends. Is the residence hooked up to the local YMCA, Parks Department, and Special Olympics? Are they connected to a church, Elks Club, Women's League, and local schools?

■ Summary

The leisure assessment has four ultimate goals. I have placed a strong emphasis on (1) staff education and (2) empowerment of staff as the best route to advocacy for the client. Independent action in recreation activities (3), and (4) an unpaid friend who shares common leisure interests are ways to foster community involvement, normalization, and client independence.

The leisure assessment interview consists of two parts: information gathering and brainstorming. The past, present, and future leisure interests are placed into the four categories of leisure: physical, mental, social, and spiritual. The gaps within these headings are discussed as we plot together a way to make the best use of the client's skills.

The leisure assessment used at the Kennedy Aging Project was designed to reflect the wide variety of client abilities and interests. The tool is flexible enough to treat each client as an individual, living in narrowly-defined and often somewhat inflexible living circumstances.

Type of residence and employment, family, friend and staff contact, and community resources are all taken into account.

This assessment is accomplished in one hour. Skill assessment and direct observation of the client in individual or group activities would be helpful, but are rarely possible in a project such as ours because of time constraints. There is an almost total reliance on caregivers as reporters of the client's present and past leisure interests and abilities. Despite these liabilities, the leisure assessment process has helped individual clients, caregivers, and other Interdisciplinary Team members to realize the value and benefits of leisure for clients. The ability to experience leisure is a fundamental right of all our clients.

21

ASSESSMENT BY
REHABILITATION MEDICINE

Keith M. Robinson

■

Rehabilitation medicine is a philosophy of care as well as a specialty of medical practice. It is an approach that induces, facilitates, and maintains the control that an individual has in everyday life. Quality of life can be defined as such control.

This control is achieved by striving for optimal performance of a hierarchy of survival skills in three broad areas: activities of daily living (ADLs), mobility, and communication. Activities of daily living are categorized as basic or higher level; basic mobility being bathing, feeding, dressing, and toileting, and higher level mobility being shopping, preparing meals, choosing clothing, doing laundry, cleaning house, and managing finances. Mobility can also be basic or higher level; basic mobility is getting out of bed, transferring from bed to chair or from wheelchair to toilet, wheelchair ambulation, and walking with or without assistive devices such as a cane or walker; higher level mobility is climbing stairs, negotiating ramps or curbs, taking public transportation, and driving. Successful communication assumes an ability to pay attention, remember, and organize environmental stimuli, and then to organize or solve problems conceptually, in order to be able to express oneself vocally or nonvocally through gestures, communication boards, or more sophisticated computerized communication devices.

For people with mental retardation, these survival skills may never have been performed, may be currently performed at lower levels than the individual's potential capability would allow, or may have diminished because of illness, injury, or processes associated with normal aging. Rehabilitation medicine focuses on helping to bring about maximum skill performance, thus maintaining or increasing the control that the individual can exercise over her immediate environment, thereby maintaining or increasing her quality of life.

Rehabilitation begins with assessment of skill performance, an assessment of function. One area of expertise of the rehabilitation physician is the coordination and integration of specific assessment information from a variety of related disciplines, including but not limited to physical therapy, occupational therapy, communication (speech) therapy, therapeutic recreation, vocational counseling, psychology, neurology, psychiatry, and other medical specialties such as geriatrics, cardiology, and so on.

Functional assessment views the individual not just in terms of anatomic or physiological disease or impairment, but more importantly in terms of disabilities and handicaps. Disabilities are the consequences of the disease or impairment in compromise of survival skills, resulting in less than optimal control of the environment. Handicaps are the consequences of disease or impairment and disabilities; they result in compromised performance of skills at work, at leisure, or in interpersonal relationships.

Functional assessments must consider all of the significant environments for the client, including home, work (or day program), play, and various contexts of social and spiritual relationships. For clients who are old, it is important to separate functional losses that appear to be the result of recent illness (such as stroke, heart attack, or infection that has required confinement to bed) and injury (such as a fall, burn, or damage to a joint) Successful rehabilitation measures usually follow closely on the client's healing, and on her ability to participate in active measures designed especially to facilitate return to former levels of activity and skills. For some clients with mental retardation, a level of function that *surpasses* the client's previous accomplishments may be attained by intensive rehabilitation measures.

On the other hand, functional deficits that are the consequence of physiological aging may be halted and to some degree compensated for, but it is rare that the effects of slowly developing arthritis, loss of tissue elasticity, diminishment of cardiac and pulmonary reserve and response, loss of muscle mass, and decreased sensory acuity can be entirely overcome by rehabilitative measures. But with these kinds of functional loss it is still important to conceive of goals of maintenance. And always it is imperative to understand that very small gains may have large effects on the client's quality of life.

The utility of this rehabilitative philosophy in caring for people who are old and mentally retarded is illustrated when trying to match optimal function with the least restrictive living situation that is realistically available. We must question our basic assumptions about the ability of people with cognitive impairments to learn in practical and structured therapy situations. We must come to understand how changes in both behavior and cognition affect function in everyday life, and affect the likelihood of living successfully in a specific environment. Many of our clients have been living in institutions and have developed behavioral responses to the conditions of the institution, especially dependent patterns that induce indifference to the possibility of being more in control, less dependent, and higher functioning.

> *At 64, Harold lives in a nursing home. He is mildly mentally retarded and has a lifelong behavior problem of rapidly accelerating temper tantrums; sometimes he hits other people with his fists.*
>
> *Harold lived in a state residence for 47 years, from the age of 12 until he was 59. When he was 17 he broke his pelvis in a fall; since that time he has had a severe left-sided limp. When he was 32 he was burned in a fire, and after that accident his right arm had limited range of motion because of scar tissue. Despite all these disabilities, Harold always worked at janitorial jobs, first in the state residence and later, after he moved to the community, in a nearby factory.*
>
> *A year ago Harold suffered a cerebrovascular accident, a right-sided "stroke," which left his left arm weak but not entirely*

paralyzed. His gait problem worsened and he was required to use a wheelchair. He was discharged from the acute-care hospital to a nursing home. A staff member from his community residence who had undertaken the role of advocate for Harold referred him for a rehabilitation evaluation.

As a result of this evaluation and subsequent therapy services, Harold has learned how to walk again, now using Canadian crutches. His burn scars have been released through a surgical operation so that he has much greater range of motion in his right arm. With the use of adaptive devices he has learned enough self-care skills that he has been able to leave the nursing home and move to a new community residence where his disabilities are accepted by staff and his fellow residents.

Through an "unpaid friend" from a community church, Harold has volunteered to work at the church two afternoons a week. He folds announcements and stuffs envelopes; on most days there is also photocopying work saved for him to do.

Through the use of rehabilitation services Harold has been able to achieve remarkably good recovery from his stroke. In some respects his current level of functioning is better than it has been for several decades.

With a thorough and multi-disciplinary functional assessment, the rehabilitation physician can be instrumental in devising the optimal plan for helping the client learn new skills, recover skills previously held but now lost, and maintain performance level of the skills she now has. Some of the tools of this planning are a knowledge of community resources for rehabilitative therapies; a knowledge of and inventive interest in assistive devices, both those commercially available and those that might be especially designed, tailored, and made for this particular client; a knowledge of self-help techniques, including those for conserving energy expenditure, compensating for losses of endurance, strength, and dexterity, and avoiding accidents and injuries.

The rehabilitation philosophy invites us to realign our thinking and values regarding people with mental retardation who are also old. This philosophy demands that we think practically and in an expansive manner to encourage our clients to develop optimal control of the environment, thus sustaining an optimal quality of life in the least restrictive environment that is realistically available.

Those of us who work with people who are mentally retarded and old need to be aware that the rehabilitation world has services that can help the client perform skills at the highest levels of which he is capable. We need to know that people who live with the client are regularly in communication with therapists and other care providers who work with the client in structured therapy and vocational settings. We need to make sure that whatever the client is learning in the structured setting is being carried over into other settings in a consistent manner.

PART 4
INTERDISCIPLINARY
ISSUES AND THEMES

■

ORIENTATION

■

22

SERVING THE UNDERSERVED

Mary C. Howell

■

In our society, people who are both mentally retarded and old tend to be poor, helpless, and unpopular. The intent of the Kennedy Aging Project was to pay attention—elegant, sophisticated, and also caring and empathetic attention—to the health and well-being of this relatively small but socially important group of people.

The World Health Organization proposes that health "is both a fundamental human right and a sound social investment...Ensuring access to the essentials for a healthy and satisfying life is a basic principle of social justice...Closing the health gap between the socially and educationally disadvantaged and the more advantaged in society necessitates a policy that improves access to health-enhancing goods and services, and creates supportive environments. Such a policy would assign high priority to underprivileged and vulnerable groups.[1]

We regard this small group of citizens as socially significant precisely because it is doubly underserved: the mental retardation service system has only recently begun to consider the needs of clients who are old, and the "generic" geriatric service system has been inclined to exclude people who are labeled as mentally retarded. Thus, coming to know people who are both old and mentally retarded, understanding and broadcasting their service needs, and providing exemplary services (albeit on a very small scale) can be seen as responding to the call to provide well for citizens who are needy and underserved, and who can represent *all* who are needy and underserved in society at large.

People with mental retardation who are old are a diverse group. In any group of old people there is an expected diversity that derives from the broadening differences of their various experiences. It is a truism that "we grow more like ourselves" as we mature into old age.

In addition, the various intellectual deficits and physical impairments of those who are labeled as mentally retarded expand the diversity of the group. A 1987 study from the U.S. Department of Health and Human Services proposes three functional sub-groups. The first is composed of people who have only mild or moderate mental retardation and physical handicap, who have been mostly independent in their adult lives, and who require services in old age only because of additional impairments associated with normal aging. The second sub-group is composed of people whose mental and physical handicaps are moderate, who have as adults had a need for supervision and special training, and who will become more dependent on specialized services as they age. The final sub-group is composed of those with severe or profound mental and physical handicaps, who have always required long-term care and habilitation services and other specialized therapies, and whose needs will likely increase as they approach old age.[2]

In approaching the service needs of people with mental retardation who are also old, people in the field of geriatrics can learn from the disciplines traditionally associated with mental retardation, and likewise the perspectives of the geriatric disciplines can be a source of enrichment to the study of mental retardation. For instance, geriatrics has learned from Down syndrome as a genetically determined syndrome of telescoped aging. It appears that many or most of the changes associated with normal biological aging—changes like loss of elastic tissue, decrements in cardiovascular and renal function, greying of hair, testicular and ovarian atrophy and marked reduction of the function of these glands, degenerative joint changes, osteoporosis, and diminished sensory function—proceed in a telescoped and premature fashion in people who have Down syndrome. From a study of this group, those who work in the field of geriatrics can gain new insights into the aging process.

Those who are caregivers to old people (especially in the geriatric institutions we call nursing homes) could also learn about making the most of institutional life by examining the assumptions that direct the care now given in most institutions and community residences for people with mental retardation. This care is driven by an educational (not a medical) focus, and works on the assumption that everyone can learn something, every day of her life. This focus is both hopeful and mastery-oriented, and is a far more positive approach to caregiving than the waiting and resignation typical of nursing homes.

From the other side, the disciplines of mental retardation can look to geriatrics for an understanding of the approach to death that is a normal goal of the aging process. Among families and caregivers of people who are mentally retarded there is, for good reason, a desperate lifelong struggle to locate and provide services that will enhance and extend life. The gradual transition to an affirmation of impending, rightful, and accepted death in old age is not always an easy perspective to learn.

The best of geriatrics works from an acceptance, even a celebration, of the physical, mental, social-emotional, and spiritual changes attendant to old age. Instead of a state to be avoided and ignored, old age is seen in geriatric study as a developmental process to be honored. We all can learn from this perspective.

The Kennedy Aging Project entered the arena of teaching about and providing services to people who are both old and mentally retarded at a time when widespread interest in this work was just beginning. (This, of course, was due to the forward-looking vision of both the Kennedy Foundation and the Massachusetts Department of Mental Retardation.) At the point of our entry, there was some general agreement that service systems needed to make more appropriate, fuller, and more individualized offerings to this needy group of clients.

These deficiencies in service systems nominally responsible for caring for people who are both old and mentally retarded were recognized by stories of disappointments, puzzlement, and sometimes even anger. For instance, we heard about clients who were removed from their workshops because of suspicion of cognitive decline, later refuted; when caregivers asked on their clients' behalf for reinstatement, they were told that the empty places had already been filled—it was too late. We heard about clients who were urged to retire, with talk about how "everybody retires," and "you're tired of working, aren't you?" When the clients discovered that they had been assigned to day programs that provided mostly sitting, with a few crafts and short van trips, they said that, on second thought, they would rather stay at work. In general, vacant workshop places are usually filled immediately from a waiting list and there is no return for a client when a "mistake" has been made. Discontent was often expressed and dismissal threatened when a workshop client's productivity fell or was irregular; this would occur in a work situation where workers performed the most menial and uninteresting of tasks for minimal wages. It seemed little enough to expect that a worker could be kept on the rolls even when high rates of productivity began to fall off.

In similar situations, people were said to have lost residential places unnecessarily for a variety of small and rather easily met needs.

For instance, one man began to fall down frequently and although both the staff and his peers at his community residence wanted him to stay with them (and were willing to modify his environment to decrease the likelihood of his falling), it was decided that he must be moved to a different residence for clients with "high medical needs." Other clients were placed in nursing homes as administratively facile solutions to their residential needs, when other solutions would clearly have been more individualized and less restrictive.

We heard stories about staff members burning out, quitting, taking sick days, even suffering industrial accidents. The problems go beyond too much heavy lifting; there is pain and distress experienced in not having enough time to talk with clients, or to help them walk, or to allow them to feed themselves slowly with a palsied hand.

We also heard stories about medical care that was provided too late, too slowly (so the time for cure was past), or in a manner that was too uncaring. Clients went to emergency rooms with lacerations and returned not sutured because the client—normally rational and easy to console—was said to be "unmanageable." Or clients were hospitalized and held in four-point restraints to contain their anger and terror. Sometimes, in contrast, too much medical care was given—to an old person dying, for instance, or to a person with advanced cancer. (These mishaps of medical care can happen to anyone, of course, but people who are mentally retarded and old seem to be especially vulnerable.)

These instances of perceived deficiencies in the service system reflect systemic difficulties: ageism (bias against the old), too little money, too few staff, and staff too poorly paid or otherwise honored. Sometimes the problems reported were more subtle: a tendency to treat people who are old and mentally retarded just like other old people are treated in our society—which is not very well at all; a planning process that excluded staff or clients from the effort to solve new problems in creative ways; the restrictions of categorical imperatives such as "elderly housing," reflecting a funding arrangement that forcibly segregates old people from others of a variety of ages; a reluctance to apply available legal remedies, such as suing for due process in the dismissal of a client from a workshop position. Finally, there are the old prejudices against people with mental retardation that say that they are all incompetent, that only guardians or professionals know what is best for them, that they do not know that their work is boring, or that they could not or would not enjoy learning new ways to participate in community life.

The remedies to improve services for people with mental retardation who are old are neither brand-new nor surprising. One is to seek better funding: by lobbying, by supporting specific bills in the legislature, and by encouraging verbal and assertive client advocates to speak up on behalf of their clients' needs. Demonstration or model projects are good beginnings, but in the long run money is needed to supplement available programs so they can meet the needs of increasingly frail and dependent people who are growing old.

More staff is needed, staff who enjoy working with old people and who have some special training so they understand the individual needs of their clients. Better working conditions for staff will encourage longevity on the job and give the message that society regards this work as important and valuable. Inventive planning, and the funding and encouragement to try new and good ideas on a small scale, will convince staff and clients that their concerns are taken seriously. And, as the Kennedy Aging Project attempted to do at every turn, treating clients who are old and mentally retarded as honored elders, as valuable citizens, deserving of the most welcoming office and the friendliest and most respectful staff, sends a message to these clients, their caregivers, and all other observers that these are people of great worth.

The manifesto of the Aging Project included these principles: maintain function; work for the least restrictive placement; examine "normalization" carefully, with regard to treatment of elders, and demand better treatment for our clients; support valorization, or the assignment of value and honor, to our clients and their caregivers; decrease overprotection as demeaning and unduly restricting; recognize the hard physical and emotional work of caregivers, and reward it; restrain the tendency to transfer caregiving to professionals, and remember how much of good caregiving is plain common sense and love; and see the client-caregiver-family triad *as a system,* and endeavor always to treat the entire system.

Our assumption was that we as a society cannot afford to abuse or neglect people with mental retardation who are old, nor their caregivers. We especially need to believe that things can be better, in big ways and small ways. Our Project was small. All changes begin small. Caring changes and endures.

23

DECISION MAKING BY AND FOR INDIVIDUALS OF QUESTIONABLE COMPETENCE

Henry A. Beyer and Mary C. Howell

■

When a person's capacity to make decisions is in doubt because of mental retardation, dementia, or mental illness, a number of questions arise: Should someone else make decisions for him? Who should this be? What standard should the proxy decision maker use? Are there some decisions that can still be made by the person whose competence is in question? What are they? Who should decide if a proxy decision maker is needed and what will be the scope of her powers?

We will discuss these and related questions in this chapter. We will not provide definitive answers to all of them, in part because the current rapid evolution of law in this area creates considerable uncertainty about many of the answers. However, we will try to reduce this uncertainty by setting forth some general principles and benchmarks to provide guidance for caregivers and families who are faced with these questions.

■ Decisions by the Client

"Competency" is a term used to refer to a person's decision-making capacity. The word should properly be pluralized—competencies—because there are several types. Two main types are *legal competency,* the legal right to make decisions and speak for oneself, and *functional competency,* the psychological capacity to make decisions. Furthermore, both legal and functional competencies can be divided into a huge number of specific competencies relating to the particular decisions to be made.

Whether an individual is functionally competent to make a particular decision depends upon the abilities of the person, the nature of the decision to be made, and the likely consequences of the decision for the person. Ideally, legal competencies should be closely matched with functional competencies, so that an individual is legally empowered to make those decisions she has the functional capacity to make, but enjoys the services of a surrogate or proxy decision maker for those decisions (and only those decisions) that are beyond her capacity.

In discussing decision making, we begin with the premise that every person should make his own decisions, whenever possible. This makes sense not only psychologically, socially, and humanely, but also legally. In law, we begin with a "presumption of competence." All persons eighteen years of age or older are legally competent to make decisions about their own personal and financial matters unless they have been found by a court to be incompetent. That is the common law in all states, and in some states it is reinforced by a statute passed by the legislature.[1] Even if individuals are mentally retarded or mentally ill, they are still presumed to be legally competent. In many states, this presumption of competence remains even if the person has been admitted to a state school or has been civilly committed to a state hospital.[2] The rationale is that, at least in these states, no competency determination is required before admission or commitment to such an institution.[3]

Of course, most people with mental retardation are capable of making a great many routine, everyday decisions: which dress or shirt to wear, whether to have cereal or an English muffin for breakfast, whether to spend their money for a magazine or a rock music tape, whether to go out to eat or stay home and watch TV, whether to go to church or to a movie, and so forth. And most can also make more important, more difficult decisions that have more serious consequences, especially if they have concerned and loving family, friends, advocates, or caregivers to advise them and to discuss their options with them. It is good to remember that, for all people, making small decisions gives the confidence, experience, and self-esteem that promote the ability to make larger, more difficult decisions.

Different types of training, in areas such as money management and independent living skills, can also be very important in increasing someone's decision-making abilities. Other aids to decision making are useful in reducing the number of decisions to be made, by assisting individuals with mental retardation in structuring their lives so that some processes occur automatically. Banking arrangements that allow for direct deposit of benefit checks and wages into the person's account and automatic payment from that account, through a "permanent withdrawal order," of rent, telephone, or other regularly recurring bills, are often helpful.

■ Decisions by Caregivers

If the decision is a very important one (because it involves a significant risk to the person's health, safety, or finance, or it involves a serious irreversible step or touches on a sensitive topic, such as sexual issues) and if there is some doubt about the individual's ability to understand the question and make an informed decision (perhaps because the person's Individual Habilitation Plan indicates that she may not be functionally competent, not "capable in fact"), then consideration should be given to the possibility that a proxy decision-maker may be needed.

One common situation in which decision-making is required is in the provision of routine medical care to a non-objecting client of the state's Department of Mental Retardation (or equivalent agency). The basic legal rule regarding medical services is that they may not be administered without the informed, competent, voluntary consent of the patient. If the person who needs the services is incapable of giving such a consent, who can provide it? In many states, if the person is a client of a state agency and does not object to the proposed services, state regulations authorize the head of the client's program to give a proxy consent for standard medical examinations, clinical tests, immunizations, and treatment for minor illnesses and injuries, when such services are recommended by a treating physician.[4] Such regulations, however, usually apply only to standard treatments for minor problems. If the recommended treatment is more serious (an appendectomy, for instance), or if the client objects, we have to look elsewhere for authorization for someone to provide proxy consent.[5] (In a real emergency, when a person's life or health will be endangered if treatment is not given immediately and it is impossible to obtain a competent consent in time, doctors in all states have what is termed a "privilege" to administer treatment until a valid consent or refusal can be obtained.[6])

■ Four Useful Legal Devices

What if none of the decision-making approaches we have mentioned so far is applicable to the situation? Legal guardianship may then be necessary. Before resorting to that, however, there are a number of less drastic alternatives that should first be considered. If the required decision involves financial matters, consideration should be given to whether a representative payee, a joint bank account, a trust, or a durable power of attorney might help.

A *representative payee* is someone appointed by the Social Security Administration or the Veterans Administration to handle benefit checks (SSI, SSDI, or Veterans benefits) for a person deemed incapable of doing so.[7] The representative payee has authority over only the funds from the particular source for which he is payee, and he must manage them for the benefit of the beneficiary. The Social Security Administration has the authority to decide if a representative payee should be appointed and who it should be. The procedure for being appointed is much less cumbersome than guardianship or conservatorship, and certainly infringes much less on the autonomy of the person with mental retardation.

Another mechanism of possible value in handling financial decisions is a joint bank account, an account requiring two signatures to permit withdrawals (one by the person with mental retardation and the other by a trusted family member or friend). Such an account may be useful to prevent rash expenditures.

Trusts are yet another possibility in the area of finances. A trust is a legal plan for placing funds under the control of one person, the trustee, who manages them for the benefit of another person, the beneficiary. There are a number of different types of trusts that are suited to a variety of situations. Some are very useful in addressing the problem of how assets of a significant amount can be managed for someone who cannot manage them for herself, without making that person ineligible for state or federal benefits.[8] (See Chapter 49 for a further discussion of possible trust arrangements.)

Another mechanism for decision-making in the financial area is probably not applicable to many people with mental retardation, but it may be useful for a few. That is a *durable power of attorney,* which is now authorized by statute in many states.[9] This is a mechanism by which you may designate in writing another person to be your "attorney in fact," giving that person the authority to make decisions for you in whatever areas you specify in the writing. These frequently include financial affairs, but may sometimes also pertain to medical or other matters.[10] The designated person, the "attorney in fact," does not need to be an attorney, and in most cases is not. She should be a trusted friend or relative, someone to whom you would entrust such power. The term "durable" means that her power of attorney (her proxy decision-making authority) will endure if you become incompetent—if you lapse into a coma, for instance. In fact, the durable power of attorney can be written in such a way that it does not go into effect unless and until you do become incompetent.

This mechanism does not apply to many of the clients we are concerned with here because, in order to create a power of attorney (durable or otherwise), you must be competent to begin with.[11] People with mental retardation can designate someone to be their "attorney in fact," their decision-maker, only if they are competent to do the designating. This device can be useful, however, in states where it is statutorily authorized, for high-functioning people with mental retardation who are at risk of becoming incompetent due to advancing age or some other cause of deterioration of the mental processes.[12]

■ Incompetency Determinations, Conservatorship, and Guardianship

But what if none of these alternatives is a workable possibility for the situation at hand? What if a major medical procedure has been recommended (e.g., surgery requiring a general anesthesia) for a person who does not seem capable either of understanding the proposed procedure and its risks or of making the required decision? Or, what if the person adamantly refuses a procedure that caregivers believe is very important to his well-being? What if the decision concerns the possible expenditure of a substantial amount of the funds of a person of questionable competence, or involves sensitive areas of personal privacy, such as birth control? In such cases, the caregiver may have to turn to a court, usually a probate or family court, for a judge's determination of whether the person is competent to decide the question.[13]

Although there is no formal test, and no agreed-upon standard for determining competencies,[14] one formulation is that the individual should have "sufficiently stable and developed personal values and goals, an ability to communicate and understand information adequately, and an ability to reason and deliberate sufficiently well" about the particular choices to be made.[15]

We have said that competence should, if possible, correspond to functional competence. When a judge hears a case in which she is asked to rule on whether or not someone is competent—whether or not that person needs to have a guardian (or conservator) appointed—several kinds of considerations are relevant. Out of respect for the autonomy of the person under consideration, every effort should be made to allow that person to make decisions for himself. In respect to safeguarding the rights of a person who is of a class of people who have, in recent history, been treated with less than full consideration and deference, every effort should be made to protect the person against exploitation, neglect, abuse, and other forms of denigration.

The judge who makes such a decision can be assisted by expert opinions about the functional competencies of the person. In the past (and, unfortunately, even today), opinions like these were sometimes given on the basis of scant information; it was assumed that competence was reserved for people who appeared and acted "normal," and that anyone who was significantly handicapped in intellectual performance would, of course, also be incompetent. Recently, more serious efforts to define and measure functional competencies have been made.[16,17,18,19] Therefore, the opinions offered to the judge for use in her adjudication can be based on objective information—at least, information as objective as one could hope to gather in response to such a question.

The process and standards for determining competency and establishing guardianship or conservatorship differ in each jurisdiction. In some states, judges have practically unfettered discretion to impose guardianship on whomever they believe is in need of it. Other state legislatures have attempted to express in more explicit statutory language some of the principles discussed previously. The Massachusetts guardianship statute,[20] for example, requires that the court find:

- that the person is mentally retarded to the degree that he is incapable of making informed decisions with respect to the conduct of his personal and financial affairs;

- that failure to appoint a guardian would create an unreasonable risk to his health, welfare, and property; and

- that appointment of a conservator would not eliminate such risk.

In many states there are now rules of procedure that direct the assembly of "expert opinions" to assist a judge in making a decision about competency and the need for a guardian.[21] In Massachusetts, for instance, a report is made by a clinical team consisting of a social worker, a psychologist, and a physician (specialty qualifications unspecified).[22] The expertise of the team's physician and psychologist is usually most useful in addressing the first part of the standard, the person's decision-making ability (sometimes called the standard's "clinical" component). The social worker on the team usually focuses on the second part of the standard, the degree of risk the person faces without guardianship, a factor that is highly dependent on the social and environmental context in which the person is living.

The third part of the standard, which suggests the possibility of conservatorship, introduces the idea of least restrictive alternative. Ideally, it should also require that the court consider the possibility of limiting the guardianship, but the Massachusetts legislature has not yet seen fit to include such language. As discussed below, the state courts have ruled that limited guardianships can be instituted despite this absence of explicit statutory authority. Not all judges in the state are aware of the possibilities or desirability of limited guardianships, however, and it is frequently up to the members of the family seeking guardianship, their attorney, or (most commonly) the professionals who conduct the assessment, to educate them as to this option.[23] The clinical team report is an ideal place to accomplish much of this education. As Gunnar Dybwad has said, "even judges are educable."

Probably anyone who knows how to discuss such delicate matters with people who are old and mentally retarded could give a valuable opinion concerning the person's competency. An exception must be made when there is a question of early dementia with failing short-term memory and consequent impairment in learning ability; the matter then should be considered by a psychologist with experience in assessing clients with these problems. What is essential for the competency adjudication is that time be invested in amassing information to support the opinion, and that a detailed and specific written account of the questions and answers of the interview be supplied to the court, along with the considered summary opinion of the expert.

The dimensions of an assessment of functional competence are these:

1) Define narrowly the situation in which the competence in question would be exercised. Is this about spending money? How much money? What kind of purchases are foreseen? What kinds of recommended procedures are anticipated?

2) Consider whether the person in question can accept and learn the information that must be dealt with in order to make the decisions in question. If there is a question of failing capacity to learn (failing short-term memory capabilities, or early Senile Dementia of the Alzheimer's Type) then challenges to short-term memory and learning must be made. (See Chapter 15) The examiner must decide at what level of complexity the information needs to be learned; for instance, how intricate and complicated a description of "the operation" needs to be understood by the prospective patient? To be most helpful, the expert opinion on this question of the person's ability to accept and learn relevant information should be discursive, giving specific and detailed examples from conversations with the person being examined.

3) Consider whether the person can apply this newly acquired information to make decisions; this is another way of asking whether emotional considerations might overwhelm the person's capacity to deal with cognitive information. If she has had frightening experiences with doctors in the past, she may be unable to agree that she needs to go to the hospital to get care for what appears to be a broken leg.

4) Consider whether the person can contemplate the possible outcomes of deciding affirmatively in the proposed situation. What are the possible risks and possible outcomes? This problem is one of holding several kinds of information at one time and balancing probabilities—not an easy cognitive task, but one that we all do in one form or another all the time. Again, there will be an arbitrary level set for complexity of information, and complexity in the balancing process. Different individuals among these undoubtedly competent deal with very complex information (for instance, information about medical procedures) at different levels of detail. The expert examiner will need to decide what level of complexity is "enough," and make this decision explicit in advising the court.

5) Finally, consider whether the person being examined is able to understand and accept the possible consequences of deciding to make a "wrong choice," that is, a choice that results in a "bad outcome." None of us can predict with certainty which choices will have good outcomes: for instance, just being a patient in a hospital brings risks of infection, medication errors, and discharge before adequate recuperation. If a person is adjudged to be competent, and to be able to make decisions about her own life, then she will have to cope with the consequences of her decisions, which may on some occasions have bad outcomes. Her caregivers (which in the larger context include family,

paid staff, and even in a sense the judge who is deciding her case) will also have to deal with the possibility that she will make some decisions that have "bad" outcomes. Recognition of this likelihood—in this very uncertain and unperfectible universe—is an important part of the competency adjudication process. Among the questions to be asked of the interviewee are questions in the form of "If you do not go to the hospital and have your leg put in a cast, what would happen to your leg? How would you feel about that?"

It is apparent from this outline that for most people with mental retardation it is difficult to conduct an investigation of competence in the abstract, and much more possible when there is a specific, concrete situation to discuss—a proposed surgical procedure, a broken leg, a series of appointments for dental repair, making arrangements to deal with spending and investing a recent inheritance, or other specific circumstances. This is only to emphasize that plenary guardianships that are adjudicated in the absence of some specific decision-making situation probably do clients a disservice.

If the court finds the person competent, then that person's decision must be respected, even if it appears to be wrong to you, the medical people, and society as a whole. Under our system, each of us who is legally competent has the right to make foolish decisions about our own best interests.

If, on the other hand, the court finds the person incompetent to make the decision, then a proxy decision-maker, called a guardian or conservator,[24] will be appointed by the court. This is done, of course, to help the person, and to protect his interests and welfare. However, we should recognize that this legal mechanism for exercising society's paternalistic instincts and responsibilities also imposes restrictions on the individual and deprives him of some measure of autonomy by permitting someone else to overrule his wishes and reverse his decisions. For psycho-social reasons, as well as for considerations of human kindness and decency, we should resort to legal guardianship or conservatorship only when absolutely necessary, and even then we should impose the minimum level of restrictions that will suffice to protect the person's well-being.[25] In legal jargon, we say that we should use the "least restrictive alternative."

What are some of these alternatives, in order of increasing restrictiveness? The least restrictive is called, in many states, "conservatorship."[26] If the court finds that the person with mental retardation is incapable of making decisions about financial matters, but is able to handle his or her own personal affairs, the court may, after a finding of incompetency, appoint a "conservator," a person authorized to manage the incompetent person's financial affairs, but not his other affairs. To be even less restrictive, in some states the conservatorship may be further limited by the court. In Massachusetts, for example, if the "ward" (the term used for a person who has a conservator or guardian) is capable of handling modest amounts of money, the court may order that up to $300 per month be exempted from the conservatorship and left to the ward to use independently.[27]

If a proxy decision maker is required for personal affairs as well as financial matters, a *guardian* (sometimes called a "guardian of the person and the estate") may be required. But, again, in keeping with the principle of the least restrictive alternative, it is usually preferable to make this a *limited guardianship* rather than a total guardianship.[28] A number of states have, in the past two decades, enacted statutes explicitly authorizing limited guardianship.[29] In some other states, although the guardianship statutes may still be phrased so as to imply that all guardianships are total or "plenary," courts have found that judges have the inherent equity power to create limited guardianships.[30] That is, they can tailor a guardianship as needed, limiting it to only those areas in which the ward is incapable of making his or her own decisions, such as where to live, where to work, what school or day program to attend, or whether to accept certain medical or dental treatment. Depending upon the jurisdiction, the guardian's area of responsibility may be delineated either inclusively (by listing each type of decision under the guardian's authority) or exclusively (by specifying the decision areas excluded from the guardian's authority). It is also possible in many states for the court to set specific dates (months or years in the future) at which time the guardianship will be reviewed by the court, so that it may be modified or terminated, to fit the ward's changing capacities or needs.

Another common type of limited guardianship is *temporary guardianship*. In many states, it is specifically authorized by statute,[31] and is frequently used when immediate decisions are required concerning the use of a recommended medical procedure. A typical temporary guardianship lasts two or three months, but usually may be renewed by the court for an additional few months.[32] Its advantage, other than the limitation of its duration, is that it can usually be obtained very quickly, in a matter of hours or days, rather than in the month or two frequently required for a permanent guardianship. This expediting is possible because the usual requirements of providing notice to the prospective ward's relatives are greatly reduced or eliminated. However, a temporary guardianship will ordinarily be granted only if the judge is persuaded of the emergency nature of the situation. Another advantage is that it is frequently much easier to find a person willing to serve as temporary guardian than to find one willing to take on permanent guardianship responsibilities.

If none of the mechanisms discussed thus far is sufficient to safeguard the individual's welfare, it may sometimes be necessary for the court to appoint a *plenary* (or total) *guardian,* a person authorized to make all decisions for the ward, in both personal and financial matters. Aside from a few limited exceptions in some states (discussed later), full guardians are authorized to make *all* of their ward's decisions.[33] In doing this, guardians must act to protect the welfare of their ward and must always make the decision they think is in the ward's best interest.

It is the responsibility of the person seeking the guardianship to find someone willing to serve as guardian. This is often not an easy task. The best guardian is usually a family member, relative, or friend.[34] Occasionally it is someone on the staff of the service-providing agency who has formed an attachment to the individual. The latter possibility is ordinarily not a good idea, however, because of the potential for conflicts of interest. After a person is nominated to be guardian, it is up to the court to decide whether he or she is suitable for the role and, if so, to make the appointment. In a growing number of states, certain public agencies or private corporations may also serve as guardian.[35] Some state and local chapters of the Association for Retarded Citizens have established corporate guardianship programs.[36] In rare cases, if the need is truly urgent and no suitable person is available, the court itself has been known to serve as guardian.

■ Decisions by a Court

In the last few years, courts and legislatures in several states have concluded that some decisions (most of which involve medical treatment that is characterized as "extraordinary") are too intrusive, irreversible, or risky for even a legal guardian to make on behalf of his ward, These decisions include those involving sexual sterilization[37]; electroconvulsive therapy and psychosurgery[38]; the administration of antipsychotic medication[39]; the withholding of life-sustaining treatment[40]; and admission to a mental health or mental retardation institution.[41] Courts have also indicated that there may be yet other treatment procedures in this class that they have not yet had occasion to consider.[42] Proxy decisions involving these extraordinary procedures must be made in these states by the judge of an appropriate state court.

The initial judicial proceedings in such cases are identical to those already described. The court must first decide whether the person with mental retardation is truly incompetent to decide upon the recommended treatment. If not incompetent, the person must, of course, be permitted to decide for herself. If the person is found to be incompetent, however, the court will then make the decision on her behalf.

In making such a proxy decision, some courts apply the same standard that is used by guardians: What decision is in the best interests of the incompetent person?[43] In other states, however, the courts have decided that the individual's right of privacy requires that they not decide on the basis of the person's "best interests," but rather that they make a "substituted judgment."[44] In making a substituted judgment, the court tries to put itself into the shoes of the person (or, as courts sometimes say, tries to "don the mental mantle of the incompetent") and make the decision that person would make if she were competent, taking into account in the decision-making process the present and future incompetency of the individual.[45]

In making a substituted judgment, the court is to consider all factors that might help it to know the actual values and preferences of the incompetent individual. Foremost among these are any expressed preferences of the person regarding treatment. Even preferences expressed by an incompetent person must be given great weight.[46] The court should also consider: the individual's religious beliefs, if known, and any effect they might have on her decision; the impact of the decision on the person's family, insofar as she would have considered this in making the decision; the probability of adverse side effects; the prognosis with and without treatment; and any other relevant factors.[47]

When the court determines what the individual would have decided, that decision must be respected, even if it will not achieve the restoration of the person's health, or will result in longer hospitalization. The incompetent individual "has the right to be wrong in the choice of treatment."[48]

■ Decisions That No One May Make

We have said that individuals of questionable Competence may make most everyday decisions for themselves; their caregivers may make other low-risk decisions; legal conservators or guardians are required in order to make other choices with greater consequences when the individuals lack the competence to make them themselves; and, in at least some jurisdictions, only courts may make, for incompetent individuals, those decisions involving extraordinary medical treatment with even graver consequences. One might ask whether there are yet other decisions so personal, or having possible consequences so severe, that only a competent individual may make them on his own behalf. Are there some decisions that no one may make on behalf of another person?

There do appear to be at least a few such decisions. They probably include, for example, voting, entering into a contract of marriage, enlisting in the armed services, and volunteering to be a research subject in a dangerous experiment that can be of no conceivable benefit to the volunteer.[49] In addition, the Massachusetts Supreme Judicial Court decided in 1986 that no one, not even a legal guardian or a court, may enter into a plea bargain on behalf of a permanently incompetent, mentally retarded criminal defendant.[50]

We should note that the result of not deciding is, in fact, equivalent to making a negative decision on the person's behalf—a decision not to vote,[51] marry, enlist, volunteer, or plea bargain. Thus, it is probably more accurate to say that there are some questions about which no one may make an *affirmative* decision on behalf of an incompetent person.

These are some principles and benchmarks relating to decision making by and for clients of questionable competencies. Although they do not specifically answer the myriad questions that arise, we hope they will provide some guidance and a general framework for analyzing such questions.

24

CONFIDENTIALITY

Eric Harris

■

It is said that the notion of a "right" to privacy is a peculiarly American convention. In our society, information is important. If information gets into the wrong hands it can be damaging. We all value our privacy.

As is the case with so many of the interests of people with mental retardation, their rights to privacy and confidentiality may not be carefully protected. In part this is because they are often looked upon as perpetual children, surely an inappropriate designation for people who are chronologically adult. It is also true that we tend to think of people with mental retardation as "incompetent," a designation that can in fact be made only by a judge; all adults are competent until a judge rules otherwise. (See Chapter 23)

Beyond this legal convention, however, lies a confusion about what rights are owed to all citizens, competent or incompetent. This is not only a question of laws but also a question of values and ethics; we must each decide whether we think that privacy and confidentiality are due to every citizen, even a citizen who may in some respects not be competent. Finally, the privacy and confidentiality rights of a person with mental retardation might be ignored because that person needs to be cared for by others, and those who give care may feel *they* have a right (as a return for caretaking) to talk about the person in their care in a way that violates her privacy.

In the mental health field, the nature of client information is exceptionally sensitive. In fact, the therapeutic endeavor cannot take place unless people are encouraged to reveal the most sensitive and important information about themselves. If a client does not feel safe to talk about what is bothering her (and this is often confidential information), then it is most difficult to have effective therapy.

Confidentiality is an important issue for mental health professionals. Discussions of legal issues in mental health care always consider confidentiality in detail. This is not equally true, however, about work in mental retardation. There are no books that deal with confidentiality with respect to the rights of people with mental retardation. There are two reasons for this difference.

The first is that mental health professionals are interested in confidentiality for therapy patients because they are at risk of being sued for malpractice. The second reason is that in this society we do not value, and in fact we discriminate against, people who have mental retardation. Thus, the kind of damage that can be done by dissemination of information about a person with mental retardation is not seen as being potentially damaging. But the dignity of all people is very important, and people with mental retardation have—or ought to have—the same kind of rights to confidentiality as people who are not mentally retarded.

We must define the terms *privacy, confidentiality, privilege,* and *duty to warn. Privacy* is the right of individuals to choose the time and place of disclosure of facts about themselves. It is the right of every individual in our society (including a person with mental retardation) to keep information about himself secret, unless he chooses to reveal it. In Massachusetts, a statute[1] establishes that every citizen of the Commonwealth has the right to privacy; in fact, it sets up a procedure whereby one may sue for damages if one's privacy is violated. There is also a constitutional right to privacy, which has been used by federal courts to support important decisions such as the right of a woman to get an abortion and the right of a couple to use contraceptives.

Confidentiality is a duty that is placed on a professional who is doing mental health work with a client. This confidentiality usually stems from the professional ethics of the individual's profession. The distinction between professional and paraprofessional workers is determined by whether or not the state requires the mental health worker to be licensed. Professionals are licensed by the state and thus required to abide by ethical codes through the state's regulatory power. Paraprofessionals are unlicensed and thus unregulated. Licensing or certification by the state gives an individual status as a professional, which results in certain privileges and responsibilities. Paraprofessionals and professionals are treated differently with regard to confidentiality, and have different responsibilities with regard to court testimony. If you are not a member of a profession, then you are not required to follow professional ethics.

Privilege concerns court testimony only. When a psychiatrist, psychologist, or social worker says, "I have privilege in court," what she means is, "I am legally obligated to maintain confidentiality on behalf of my client." When a professional worker is asked to testify, her client can say, "I choose not to have this person reveal information about me." That worker then is required *not* to give testimony, and the court cannot override that refusal. Anyone who is not in those defined professional categories can be subpoenaed into court and asked to testify. There might be no protection for a nonprofessional from having to testify. On the other hand, it is important to note that all privilege statutes have exceptions.

Sometimes there is also a *duty to report* when required by law to give information, to breach confidentiality. There are only two duties to report that are likely to concern those who work with people who are mentally retarded: the statutorily-imposed duty to report abuse of children, elderly individuals, or disabled persons to appropriate state agencies, and the court-imposed responsibility to protect an identifiable victim of one's professional clients by warning or other appropriate actions.

The basic premise of the latter duty is that certain mental health professionals are responsible for protecting identifiable victims of their client from potentially dangerous behavior. This "Tarasoff" duty is named after a California case[2] where a man who was being seen by a psychologist at the University of California at Berkeley threatened to kill a young woman. There was an effort to have him arrested, and also to have him committed to a hospital, but he was let back out on the street. He did, in fact, kill the young woman he had threatened to kill, and the woman's parents sued the mental health professionals for failure to warn them that this dangerous person was a threat to their daughter.

The court decided in favor of the parents, holding that the mental health professionals had a duty to the parents; it created that duty out of a series of quarantine cases (doctors who have information about contagious disease having a responsibility to protect the public health). The court decided that this was a similar case, saying that professionals who have information about their clients have to take some steps to protect endangered people.

This case has been extended to different circumstances in different states, although so far it has only been applied to professionals. The ruling concerns professional malpractice; if the professional doesn't protect the victim, the victim can sue for damages. The ruling has also been associated with cases applying to *institutions* that fail to protect victims from potentially dangerous clients. It might work in the following way: if a community program admits a potentially dangerous person, and that person actually does something dangerous in the community, then it is possible that the state could be sued. It is also possible that the individuals who work for that institution may be sued for not having taken sufficient steps to protect the individuals in the neighborhood.

People who are employed by a program that is either run or funded by, and also regulated by, the state Department of Mental Retardation (or whatever department of your state government has the responsibility of overseeing the care of people who have mental retardation) must consider two types of confidentiality in these relationships: confidentiality of communication and confidentiality of formal records. Communication with clients involves a lot of information, only some of which is written down. These communications are important, and if you were subpoenaed to testify in a court case you would be asked to relate specific communications that took place between you and your client. To refresh your memory, you would probably refer to your notes for specific facts.

The second type of information is in formal records. Formal records include some records of conversations, but they also contain other information dictated by Department of Mental Retardation regulations with regard to citizens with mental retardation. These regulations for record-keeping are stringent; the records of citizens who have mental retardation are probably more complete than those of other citizens.

Information about people with mental retardation that is kept in formal records must be accessible both to regulating authorities and to third-party payers. So, for example, information about a client is subject to review by both government and private payers who want to make sure that you are providing the services you say you are providing; they also want to investigate the quality of the services. Regulating agencies also have a right to look at these records; if you are a contractor for DMR, then DMR has a right to look at your records.

There are important distinctions between communications and records. With regard to your involvement in counseling or any similar kind of relationship with one of your clients, the difference between privacy and confidentiality, or privilege and duty to report, pertains to knowledge that you have from observing the day-to-day life of the individual and from the relationship you have with him; it also includes information that you obtain from someone else.

Although there is no law other than professional regulation that dictates the confidentiality of communication, there are a lot of regulations that affect the confidentiality of treatment records. These vary considerably from state to state. Some states have enacted a "patients' and residents' rights" law that assures general hospital patients and DMH and DMR clients confidentiality of their records, control over release of records to third parties, and records access for themselves and their advocates.[3] Some states, however, also have other more specific statutes that may limit the right of mental health or mental retardation clients to see their records unless such access is ordered by a court or is found by their service-providing agency to be in their best interest.[4] Federal and state regulations governing research involving human subjects, and state regulations governing Individual Habilitation Plans (IHPs) or Individual Service Plans (ISPs) also contain provisions on records access. Furthermore, human rights committees, licensing agencies, and others monitoring the quality of service have certain rights to see at least some client records.

In summary, there are three reasons why information about clients should not be discussed except with people who are authorized by the Department of Mental Retardation to hear that information:

1) The client has a citizen's right to privacy, just like every other citizen.

2) Your work with the client may be considered to be therapeutic in its effect on her mental health, in which case you may be bound by a special obligation of confidentiality.

3) In most states, the Department of Mental Retardation (or a similar regulating agency) enforces the client's right to privacy.

The cardinal point of this discussion is that a citizen who is mentally retarded has rights to privacy, and rights to be regarded and treated with dignity and respect. "Damage is done to a patient, client, friend, or colleague more often as the result of a careless or boastful revelation than from…evil design or the demands of others…"[5] Awareness of these rights, and of the dangers of thoughtless and unnecessary breaches of privacy, can help us become more sensitive to our obligations in giving good care.

25

WHAT IS FUNCTION?
HOW CAN IT BE MAINTAINED?

Mary C. Howell

■

The word *function* is derived from an Old French word that means "to perform." We use it to denote a human ability or capability—a process that is defined by the effect it causes. This means that we determine the presence of a function by looking for its effect: the function of the sense of sight allows vision, the function of the immune system overcomes infection, the function of eating with utensils results in food being consumed in a certain way, and the function of manual dexterity permits a variety of instrumental activities such as dialing a telephone. Because of this assessment of demonstrable effect, the measurement of function differs from other kinds of measurement (like tests for IQ) in which conclusions are often drawn that go far beyond what is actually observed. The measurement of function is usually direct, simple, and commonsensical.

There is an interesting history to the emphasis on function. Initially, this sort of measurement was proposed in relation to the needs of those who were injured—at the workplace or in war—and who needed assistance, especially in the form of compensation. It was clearly more useful to know that the injured person could not walk, than to know just that there had been a spinal cord injury. The diagnosis told what had happened to or inside the body; the functional assessment told what the whole person could and could not do.

From these beginnings, functional assessment has moved in two directions that are important for those who are both old and mentally retarded. The first direction is a focus on rehabilitation, bringing back lost functions. Assessment in this instance is aimed at specifying all functions (relevant to the discipline or disciplines available for rehabilitation services) that are now impaired or absent, and for which specific services are needed.

We are going to consider function from another perspective; we want to look at functions that are now present and that we wish to provide assistance in maintaining. This perspective demands that we place primary emphasis on what exists (and not on what is missing), and also that we accept as a goal the continuation of the *status quo*. It is an axiom of aging that many if not all functions, both those essential to survival and those related to pleasure, sociability, and a richness of variety in everyday activities, are likely to decline with advancing age.

Now it is true that many functions are sustained, or may even improve, well into old age. It is not entirely a downhill slide after age twenty! But it is the nature of the process of dying—which often goes on for many months or years—that reserves diminish, flexibility of pathways is lost, and capabilities dwindle one by one or even in clusters.

The other relevant axiom of aging is that once a function is lost, it may not be possible to regain it. A thirty-year-old who is bedridden while a fracture begins to heal can then get up and quickly return to full activity; an eighty-year-old may never walk again after a hip fracture, not because the fracture has not healed but because in the interval of bedrest she lost her ability to walk. With advancing age, the likelihood diminishes that impaired functions will return. For this reason alone there is some urgency in investing our energies in *preserving* functions that are still vigorous, when our clients are old and getting older.

There are differences between the capabilities that we are referring to as "functions" in the terminology of the very useful handbook called the *International Classification of Impairments, Disabilities, and Handicaps.*[1] First we should notice that this handbook from the World Health Organization is subtitled "A Manual of Classifications Relating to the Consequences of Disease." Here we are intentionally focusing on the consequences of *aging,* which are emphatically not those of disease. Getting old is not, in and of itself, a sickness. In the course of getting old, someone may develop a disease and lose function as a consequence, but this process is different from that of normal aging.

By the World Health Organization definitions, an *impairment* is a loss or abnormality of psychological or physiological function. (Examples are amputation, mental retardation, arthritis, or dementia.) A disability is a restriction or lack of ability to perform an activity in the manner or within the range considered normal for a human being, which is the result of an impairment. (Examples are reading, playing goalie in ice hockey, or putting on one's clothes.) A *handicap* is a disadvantage for an individual, resulting from an impairment or disability, that limits or prevents the fulfillment of a role that is normal (depending on age, sex, and social and cultural factors) for that individual. (Examples are holding a job, caring for one's self, or taking public transportation.) Impairments do not always lead to disabilities or handicaps.

While impaired functions are usually relatively easy to define and measure, the concepts of disability and handicap are both more difficult to define and certainly more imprecise to measure. Terms like "within the range considered normal (depending on age, sex, and social and cultural factors) for that individual" move far away from directly measurable effects that we can easily agree on. Note also that the hierarchy of impairment, disability, and handicap is used to describe the *absence* of function and its consequences; by contrast, we here are considering functions, ranging from the elemental to the complex, that are present.

There is a taxonomy of human functions. The figure entitled "Domains of Function" is useful because it is broadly inclusive. There are many proposed catalogues of human functions, each compilation different from the others. It would be a waste of time to struggle to compose the perfect, all-inclusive list. Sometimes, in fact, we only focus on those functions that we have the *means* to try to maintain; this is an entirely reasonable and practical approach.

The proposed domains of function start with the simplest and purest capabilities: those contained within the person. We refer here to physiological functions, such as the capabilities of individual organ systems (heart, lungs, and skin) and the capabilities of the sensory apparatus for vision, hearing, balance, touch, and so on. The functions of the person also include those capabilities of the *whole* organism in which there is no essential interchange with the environment, like walking, stair-climbing, and other forms of ambulation, taking in and digesting a variety of foods, differentiating emotions like anger and fear, and maintaining a cycle of sleep and wakefulness.

In the next layer of functions there are capabilities that enable interactions with an environment of objects, activities, and persons, such as holding a conversation, shopping for food and preparing meals, participating in group activities, and traveling to a destination.

Beyond these, there are more complex capabilities that have to do with sustaining relationships with family and non-family caregivers, notably with regard to dependency. Chapter 26 considers the functions related to these relationships in more detail.

Figure 1
Domains of Function

The functions required to negotiate within the system of community resources—being able to use the facilities of the neighborhood senior center; putting together a financial package of Medicaid, Supplementary Security Income earnings, and family support to make some degree of independent living possible; or attending both formal religious services and midweek activities at church—are still more complex.

Finally, the outermost ring indicates functions that allow participation in those aspects of society that are the most demanding, intricate, and interconnected. Examples are the various competencies for which evidence is sought when one contemplates the need for appointment of a guardian, such as the competence to understand a proposed medical treatment and to give or refuse consent for the execution of that treatment.

Two general comments are necessary at this point. The first is a reminder that, for any individual who is labeled as mentally retarded, there is the potential for intact functions at *every* level. Only for those who are most profoundly retarded does the circle of capabilities narrow to the innermost rings. The second observation is that, with increasing age and frailty, functions in both the outermost and innermost levels are likely to be lost first, those at the outermost level because they are the most complex, and those at the innermost level because they are the most vulnerable to the consequences of the physiological and physical changes of aging.

We can summarize the means to maintain function very succinctly: they are *practice,* and *instruction,* reinforced by *reward.* There is nothing very startling here. However, we can attain a radical change in the way we think about and approach the clients we care for, as well as our goals for our work with them, by keeping in mind the need to maintain function by every possible means.

A function is lost, when one is old, if it is not practiced. Put a seventy-five-year-old into a wheelchair for a month and he may not be able to walk again. Take away human companionship from someone who is very old and she may withdraw to the extent that she never regains her sociability. Tell a person with Down syndrome who is fifty (the equivalent of seventy or so for someone who has normal chromosomes) that he is no longer allowed to dress independently and must submit to having his clothing put on him by an attendant, and he is likely to forget, and not to care, in a matter of a few weeks.

In contrast, maintaining a function requires consistent and repeated practice. Caregivers can create opportunities for practice, must resist the temptation to "do for" the client who is getting slow or even mildly confused, and should reinforce the practice with rewards of approval, companionship, and special treats.

Instruction can occur by modeling, verbal direction, and hand-over-hand assistance. It serves both as a form of reward (all that attention, touching, and talk) and as an intermediate means of improving component bits of the activity, in an effort to keep the whole coming off smoothly, without interruption or confusion, and with the desired effect.

Having broken down the categories of function in this greatly subdivided analysis, it is important to put Humpty Dumpty back together again and remember that any given activity probably serves to offer practice in maintaining more than one function. Take, for example, a group of residents who are going for a walk with two staff members. The walk reinforces some personal functions such as muscular strength, cardiovascular endurance, mineralization and strengthening of the long bones, and a positive emotional outlook. At the same time, some functions related to interactions with the environment are practiced and taught on this walk, functions like observations of the weather and the approach of spring in the budding trees and bushes, conversations about the walk's destination and purpose, the practice of prudence at street-crossings and intersections, and building an awareness of the need to adjust the pace so all walkers can stay together as a group. Relations between individual residents and staff can be exercised (favorite conversations continued or jokes exchanged) and complex exchanges that explore issues of mutuality in relationship can be experimented with. If the walk's destination is a neighborhood store, functions related to the use of money and the exercise of both choice and a restraint in making purchases can be practiced. All of this can happen on one walk!

I want to make two observations about the exercise of choice by people who are old. The first is that, in this ageist society, if we do not actually ignore or overlook the presence of old people, we are inclined to overprotect them. We discourage ambulation and even tie them down in their chairs, because they might fall and break bones. We restrict their opportunities to socialize or do productive work because they might tire. We limit what they can see, hear, and observe as spectators or join in as participants, because they might be confused. I am not suggesting that it is never appropriate to simplify the environment of those who are old, or to protect them from imprudent exposures to injury. I am only urging all of us to consider, when we suggest or implement restrictions, what functions we are limiting, what opportunities for practice we are curtailing, whether our apprehensions arise from evidence or from our own inner needs, and whether some compromise is possible that permits maintenance of function while safeguarding the client who is truly frail and vulnerable.

Another comment about choice arises from an opposite concern. Although we believe that we know what is best for our clients, we do not have any right to override their choices. One hopes that their choices are as informed as they can be. For instance, the woman with osteoarthritis that causes aching ankles, knees, and hips, and an inefficiency of veins and leg muscles that causes pronounced ankle edema, may decide that she wants to take to a wheelchair and give up walking. We know that in a matter of just a few weeks she will probably lose her capacity to walk again. Ideally, we would like to be assured that this outcome is explained to her in language she can understand, so she knows what her choices are in dimensions that are real and comprehensible to her. But surely we will all agree that the choice is hers to make; just because we are staff and understand how quickly she will lose her functional ability to walk, and have set goals for *ourselves* for maintenance of function, does not justify overriding her choice.

Finally, a word about goals. I believe that bureaucracies sometimes challenge goals that are set for "nothing more" than maintenance of *status quo*. In this, as in many other areas, we are experiencing the effects of being on the forefront of caring for those who are retarded and growing old. Whole new areas of policy need to be set. Maintenance of function (status quo) is not only a reasonable goal for people who are reaching old age, it is also a central and essential goal.

In previous decades, rehabilitation specialists sometimes turned away from working with old people because they could not be returned to full—which is to say, youthful—function. We want to strive to maintain function even if that aspiration is not widely considered an acceptable goal for the Individual Habilitation Plan. We want to maintain function because it is life-enhancing as old age approaches.

26

THE FUNCTION OF RELATIONSHIPS

Mary C. Howell

In order to enter into and sustain relationships with other people, we need certain capabilities. By *relationship,* I mean a connection or affinity between two people that exists over time and is valued by both parties. The capacity for relationship allows us to engage in relationships with other individuals. Relationships are of great importance to all of us.

I want to suggest, as a focus, a set of functions that allow relationship to flourish. The set is not finite, nor is this the only possible compilation or organization. It is useful to think about the *functions* that relationship draws on, so we are more aware of how we can help clients by encouraging and promoting the maintenance of these functions.

Some functions that promote relationship are physical: vision and hearing, the ability to smell and taste, mobility for ambulation and embrace. Some are cognitive: memory and recognition, language skills, and the ability to anticipate and make plans. Some are creative: imaginative playfulness, intuitive leaps of humor, discernment of faces, and the ability to link intense experience to feelings or emotion. And some functions are social: making and holding eye contact, the ability to trust, the ability to speak to another person about matters of intimate importance to one's self, and the ability to participate in a mutual exchange of control. Note that the emphasis here, with reference to the circular diagram (Figure 1) is on functions in the inner three domains, those of the person, interactions with the environment, and relations with family and caregivers.

No single function is essential to relationship. Remember, however, that we are considering people who are old and getting older, people whose continued existence is defined, in one sense, by declining functions. For instance, although poor or absent vision is in no sense a barrier to full participation in relationship, for a person who has always been sighted a diminution or loss of eyesight can mark a major change in the nature, number, and quality of the social connections that can be made.

All functions are sustained by practice and by instruction. Sometimes manufactured aids, like eyeglasses or a wheelchair, can be used to extend the utility of a given function. But if we live long enough, we can assume that some of our capabilities will diminish, and some will ultimately be lost. We are looking for ways to maintain function both preventively (before we are aware that the process of loss has begun) and also in counterpoint to perceived decrements, as age advances.

Before we look at specific functions, we need to consider three special aspects of the *context* of relationship for a person who is both mentally retarded and old: the range of people involved, the amount of reciprocality that is feasible, and the intersection of numbers of people and time.

Figure 1
Domains of Function

First, we usually think about the range of people with whom we can be in relationship as belonging to rather simply defined groups: kin (the people we consider to be "family"), neighbors (the people we are geographically close to), and communities (people with whom we share interests, activities, beliefs, or rituals). For those who are handicapped in their ability to care for themselves in this complex world, there is another group of people to enter into relationship with: caregivers. (For all children—also "handicapped in their ability to care for themselves"—teachers function as caregivers.)

Families in which one member is both retarded and old have borne a burden of "chronic sorrow" for a long time. Usually one or both parents are either incapacitated to some degree by extreme old age, or they are already dead. The responsibilities of caring for, supervising, and relating to the retarded family member commonly fall to the sibling generation, or even to nephews and nieces. The mainstay of care for the old in this culture—one's children—is almost never present in the family assembly of the person who is mentally retarded and old.

As someone who is mentally retarded begins to show the changes of advancing age (with increasing frailty and the acquisition of chronic limitations to well-being), the family may undergo a crisis, not unlike the crisis experienced when the family as a group first realized that one of their number was mentally retarded. Death always raises questions about meaning, and the death of someone who is significantly retarded, and perhaps also disfigured, is no exception. This search for meaning can push family members apart as they seek to cope with the problem by avoidance or denial, or it can draw them closer together. The person who is mentally retarded and also old may have either a number of kin who share the responsibility of relating to her, or there may only be rare and infrequent contacts with a small and dwindling number of family relations.

Neighbors are the great anomaly among those who might form ongoing relationships with someone who is mentally retarded. Ordinarily, we can assume that if we share geographic space and have enough encounters to get to know each other, neighbors will become, perhaps not exactly friends, but at least reliable supports in time of need. In some instances neighbors become partners in feud rather than positive relations—but relations, nonetheless. For the person who is mentally retarded, there are usually two groups of neighbors. There are those with whom one shares living space (in a staffed apartment, group home, or residential school) and with whom one usually develops a relationship more reminiscent of siblings than of neighbors; for each person, however, there is or was a real family, with perhaps real siblings, off in the wings. There is also a second group of neighbors, who are neither mentally retarded nor particularly interested in the day-to-day happenings of the person who is mentally retarded. These true (geographical) neighbors can, in some instances, live next door and never allow any sort of relationship to be created with the person who is mentally retarded. That is to say, they may regard the retarded person with mental retardation as a *non*-person. Some neighbors, of course, do establish neighborly relations with people who are mentally retarded.

Relationships in community are, by contrast, not particularly different for the person with mental retardation than for the person who is not retarded. The same reasons—shared activities, interests, beliefs, and rituals—bring about opportunities for relationship to be created. The principal difference is that the person with mental retardation, whose location and time are often managed by caregivers, may have circumscribed opportunities to try out relationship in community. Some people with mental retardation, for instance, have never had a chance to become part of the community life of a church or synagogue.

Finally, there are relationships with caregivers, a group somewhat like family members—involved in the most intimate awareness of the everyday life of the person who is mentally retarded—but different in certain very important respects. Caregivers cannot be claimed as permanent relationships, although that may come about as a matter of voluntary choice. Caregivers may not engage in a relationship of mutuality. And caregivers are *paid* for their connection with the retarded person.

The second aspect of the context of relationship for someone who is both mentally retarded and old arises from limitations of control and has to do with reciprocality. Because the label of retardation confers a status of both handicap and dependency, a person who is considered to be mentally retarded is often not allowed independent opportunities to initiate, deepen, and sustain relationships. The person with mental retardation usually must wait to be called or visited, wait for opportunities for mutuality in intimate conversations, and wait for displays of trust and trustworthiness. Part of the habitual agreeableness that is exhibited by most people with mental retardation is a reflection of their hunger for opportunities for relationship.

The last aspect of the context of relationships to consider is the intersection of numbers of people and time. It is difficult for a family alone to care for a mentally retarded person. Whether through an extended kin network or through a Department of Mental Retardation, large numbers of people can often be mobilized to help with the family member who is mentally retarded. Almost all find some deep personal value in the relationship.

What this means, then, is that there is a potentially large field of interested persons with whom the person who is mentally retarded and also old might reunite and create relationship. Remember that for most people who are old—at least in our society—the steady shrinking of the pool of friends and acquaintances is the foremost reason for social isolation. For many who are mentally retarded, in contrast, because there is a history of multiple caregivers, there is at least a possibility of sustaining an ample roster of relationships.

The functions that make relationship possible, then, need to be taught, practiced, and reinforced by reward. Some of these functions have already been discussed. I'd like to focus on three examples of functions that contribute to complexity and richness of relationship.

As a first example, consider *imaginative playfulness,* an ability to go "beyond the information given." We often believe that this sort of playfulness depends on cleverness with words for its development and display; we tend to emphasize activities like punning, telling stories, or writing poetry. Our culture's focus on verbal capabilities and on left-brain analytic skills makes it difficult for us to recognize other kinds of imaginative playfulness, just as it encourages us to think about "mental retardation" as a monolithic lack of some essential and central ingredient of humanity.

In fact, there are many forms of imaginative playfulness that are not derived from word play. For instance, any one of us, or any one of our clients, may have a rich capability for improvised dancing, for the kind of repetitive and trance-inducing singing we call a drone or chant, for subtle variation in the arrangement of a pattern of pebbles, for improvised musical rhythms with voice or bells or a drum, or for a game of hide-and-seek. Each one of these capabilities is a function that affects the capacity to form and elaborate on human relationship. We might even say that one definition of a relationship is that it is a set of improvised variations on a few interpersonal themes, repeated over and over again as a source of pleasure and interesting effect.

Another function that is important for relationship is *trust.* As Eric Erikson reminds us in his discussion of old age, trust is not only a very early challenge, task, and milestone, but also a recurrent theme throughout every human lifetime.

We might posit that trust is an especially important recurrent theme for those who are labeled as mentally retarded. This function is important because of the circularity of its practice and exercise; that is, trust is learned and relearned, rehearsed and reinforced, in the context of relationship, and at the same time trust is an important, perhaps even an essential, precondition for relationship. This perspective serves as a reminder to those of us who work directly with retarded clients that our personal trustworthiness is always on the line. It is also an example of a function that can be taught in part by verbal exchange, by small and recurrent comments about constancy, consistency, and fidelity. I believe that this sort of instruction is greatly reinforced by sharing with clients the critical fact that we all struggle recurrently with the issue of trust in our most intimate relationships. Crises of trust are not unique to those who are labeled "retarded."

The third example of a function whose maintenance supports participation in relationship is that of *exchange of mutuality*. This is important because it forces us as caregivers to ask ourselves whether we can be both credentialed staff conforming to professional standards, and at the same time genuinely human in our regard for our clients and in the conduct of our relationships with them. I think that the model of psychotherapy is an appropriate ideal: that is, being genuinely one's self and participating in an exemplary relationship in such a way that the client practices and is instructed—and, of course, rewarded—in the dance of relationship. This is a large demand for staff energies, caring, and attention. It may not be in the job description. (It might, though, be identified as "being fully human.") It should be explained and discussed in staff orientation.

Opportunities for the practice of the functions of relationship can be promoted every day. Old age means that death is approaching and that opportunities lost may not present themselves again. Many who have been treated by society as mentally retarded are fortunate, in their old age, to have a wide range of people—caregiving staff, peers, family, neighbors, and members of a variety of communities—with whom relationships could potentially be sustained or recreated. For the most part, however, this won't happen unless someone makes it possible. We want to remember that gentle introductions, modeling, and repeated opportunities for brief contact go a long way toward bringing long-lost kin and other relations back into contact with the person who is mentally retarded and old.

An essential key to our activity as caregivers is the understanding that, here, as in all other functions that survive into old age, the rubric is "use it or lose it." We often forget how easy it is for someone who is old to give up on social contacts, withdraw, and retreat. And while this may be appropriate as death approaches, we do not want to see that withdrawal come about because relationships have been abandoned for reasons of lost function.

This opportunity to participate in, teach, and enjoy fully elaborated relationships with our clients is a reward of the work we do. And it is hardly a one-way street. What we gain from these relationships is rich and immensely valuable. "Every encounter between persons is an exchange of gifts."

27

A CONCEPTUAL FRAMEWORK
FOR POLICY AND SERVICE DESIGN

Bruce Blaney

■

In the development of an aging policy in the field of mental retardation, one overarching reality must be kept in mind: the norms that govern our society's perception and treatment of its citizens who are old are rooted in powerfully negative stereotypes that have created "the old" as a devalued group.[1] In this process, the norms associated with old age have been particularly decisive: (1) The presumption that an older chronological age entails departure from major societal roles—especially from occupational roles, but also from central participation in family and community life[2,3]; and (2) the belief that the needs of people who are old, both emotional and practical, are most effectively addressed outside the social mainstream and in congregate settings with others who are old.[4]

At the core of the modern experience of aging is the assumption that a certain chronological age is synonymous with biological decline.[5] The "old" have been defined as a biologically bonded peer group, who have quite naturally come together in their shared fate.[6] The impact of these norms is the nearly universal belief that it is acceptable for a person to lose most of his valued roles and to be socially segregated on reaching a certain age. As Alex Comfort observed:

"Oldness" is a political institution and a social convention based on a system which expels people...[It] is a political transformation which is laid upon you after a set number of years, and the ways of dealing with it are political and attitudinal.[7]

The fact that our culture experiences it as typical for those who are old to be viewed and treated as a marginal group poses a major dilemma for the field of mental retardation, as attempts are made to formulate a policy on aging. Policy makers encounter this dilemma in seeking to apply the principle of normalization to service recipients who are old. Because role exclusion and age segregation are regarded as normative for those who are old, applications of the principle of normalization would seem to call for a duplication of these patterns for adults with mental retardation who are defined as old. Such efforts to "normalize" the lives of people with mental retardation who are old include the proliferation of retirement programming, age-segregated groupings, and institutionalism.

■ The Proliferation of Retirement Programming

Retirement programming is now a national pattern in mental retardation services.[8] "Retirement" in this context seldom refers to an actual role exit, because most of these service consumers have not yet occupied occupational roles. One can, however, describe such programming as an exit from the expectation that one will ever have a job, in effect eliminating individuals from any consideration for a job role. The more global presumption, introduced by this use of the term "retirement," may be described as the withdrawal of the expectation that one will ever enter any adult roles, such as owner, friend, spouse, community member, or job holder.[9] The resulting role is apparent from its title, "retired client."

■ Age-Segregated Groupings

The tendency to create oldness groupings is almost irresistible, so strong is the belief that chronological age should be the major criterion for prescribing one's peer group, once one has been defined as old. Indeed, this tendency derives from the very core of social policy toward people over the age of 60: "America's social policies for the aged are structurally segregated, particularistic policies that tend to separate the old from others in society."[10]

In service delivery systems for people with mental retardation, this predisposition frequently takes the form of the development of an age-segregated subsystem of services for those identified as the "elderly mentally retarded." Or it may be a kind of pseudo-integration, manifested by placing people with mental retardation who are old in age-segregated spaces for people who are old and not mentally retarded.[11] In either event, the individual remains isolated from the valued mainstream of her community and in separate social spaces that daily reinforce the perception that she is very different from the rest of us.

Judy Heumann of the World Institute on Disability has cogently articulated this issue:

> The same type of segregated service delivery system has been created for the elderly that younger disabled people and their supporters have been fighting for years to disassemble. I do not want to see myself or other disabled people who have fought so hard for integration being relegated back into segregated programs when they grow old.[12]

■ Institutionalism: Re-entering and Remaining

A survey of residential settings for developmentally disabled adults over the age of 60 in New York, California, and Massachusetts revealed that 58 percent were living in public institutions not including nursing homes.[13] Institutionalism is a long-standing norm engulfing older citizens—the belief, not yet significantly challenged (especially in the area of service patterns) that total institutions are appropriate for the "old."

In this century, there have been at least two major deinstitutionalization movements. The first, in the period during and after World War I, replaced the scandal-ridden poorhouse with a system of so-called outdoor relief for welfare payments. It is crucial to note that, although every other category of poorhouse inmate was provided an alternative, people who were old were left to languish in these institutions. People who were old were not deinstitutionalized because, alone among the classes of the poor, they were viewed as having no rehabilitative potential.[14] Beginning in the 1920s, the functions of the poorhouse devolved to the state mental hospital, which by the mid-1930s was predominantly inhabited by people over 60 who lacked both income and family support.[15]

In the second major movement for deinstitutionalization, beginning in the late 1950s, both mental institutions and institutions for people with mental retardation were decried as anti-habilitative. For people who were old, however, the institution continued to be viewed as an appropriate setting. As the preceding survey illustrates, people who were old remained in the state school.

People who were old were also, in John O'Brien's phrase, "trans-institutionalized" to nursing homes. The size of the nursing home population more than doubled during the high tide of deinstitutionalization in the late 1960s and early 1970s. There exists in our society, then, an unbroken historical connection between service patterns toward people who are old and the total institution.

During the 1980s, institutions for people with mental retardation have been reconceptualizing their rationale in terms of old age. The "new" institution defines its model as a high technology hospital, and sometimes also as a hospice, for people who are old.[16]

There is likely a kind of organizational preservation instinct at work here. Proponents of the total institution for people with mental retardation, a field in which institutionalism has perhaps been more thoroughly challenged than in any other, are focusing on the one area of ideology and social policy where the institution is alive and well—in services to people who are old. In its practice and its norms, our society continues to believe that the total institution is relevant to people who are old. And it is in that norm that those invested in the perpetuation of the total institution have found their very reason for being. "Of course, we must have state schools, because people who are old need institutions."

The preceding patterns of "retired" clienthood, age segregation and congregation, and institutionalization are currently the predominant programmatic directions for adults with mental retardation. All of these should serve to underscore the unique predicament of policy makers regarding adults with mental retardation who are defined as old. What does one do in a situation in which the replication of social norms is in its essence also a process of devaluation?[17]

The principle of normalization, as defined by Wolfensberger, provides some guidelines toward resolving this dilemma:

> As much as possible, the use of cultural valuation means to enable, establish and/or maintain valued social roles for people.[18]

Normalization as a theory of policy and service design has always distinguished the culturally valued from the typical or normative. The implicit corollary, bearing directly on the problem described here, is that in a situation in which cultural norms are themselves devaluing, human services must reject the norm and seek instead to accomplish the valued both in the means employed as well as in the outcomes achieved.

Obviously, normalization was never intended to promote role exclusion, wholesale segregation, or institutionalization. How then should we conceptualize our mission regarding people who are both mentally retarded and old?

The answer to this question is at once both straightforward and complex. Straightforward, because our mission toward people with mental retardation who are old should not diverge at all from our mission to all adults with mental retardation: to support entry into valued adult roles and relationships in one's community. Complex, because once identified as old, one falls under the shadow of a virtually unchallenged stereotype. The message of that stereotype is that this mission is not relevant to the "old." For people who are old, we speak of exits, not entries; segregation, not integration; and institutions, not communities. This widely accepted message has shown its ability, nationally, to confuse the principle of normalization and, in certain instances, to replace it with an exclusionary, segregative, and custodial content. So there must be an addendum to our mission, to prevent people who are old with mental retardation from being defined by ideas and practices that derive from age-based stereotypes.

We can speak of this two-fold mission as (1) entry and (2) destereotyping/positive imaging. One action implication is the expeditious creation of very visible demonstrations that will send resounding messages of competency, membership, growth, and entry, such as targeting people with mental retardation who are old for job opportunities. Another action implication is a major educational effort aimed toward giving mental retardation policy makers, planners, and providers an understanding that the current vision of community and entry into valued adult roles is relevant and vital to adults who are mentally retarded and old. This educational effort should provide an analysis of the profoundly undermining impact of age-based stereotyping on this vision, and should emphasize the guiding principles of integration and community living to counter the several emergent rationales for segregation and institutionalization inherent in age-based stereotyping.

"We do not first see, then define, we define first and then see."[19] This is a critical time for people with mental retardation who have also come to be seen as "old." We are in the midst of a period of definition. Where we should be seeing individuals poised for entry into our society, we are instead defining a new, devalued, categorical identity: "the elderly retarded." We are not seeing the individual, but "one of them," in fact, a new "them," who are not poised for entry, but are tottering out of the mainstream.

The process of defining the "elderly retarded" is a recent one, beginning within the past five years. So this is an especially crucial period, what Schur calls a "stigma contest," a struggle over social definition in which the outcome has not yet been determined.[20] In one scenario, human services would impose a new stereotypic identity on people with mental retardation. In another scenario, human services would be instrumental in preventing the imposition of that stereotype, and would at the same time demonstrate the relevance of full adulthood and community membership for all members of our society who are old. At the heart of this contest will be the capacity of the field of mental retardation to affirm the relevance of its vision for people labeled "old." If we decide as a field that the old are outside our vision, the consequences are particularly unsettling. For the major aspect of this group is their universality; they are indisputably us who have merely lived longer.

We do, however, know better. As a field, we have perhaps the most thorough understanding of the process of devaluation of all the human services. It is imperative that we mobilize our experience to prevent the devaluation of still others of our citizens. In this effort our bywords might well be to *teach* and to *demonstrate*.

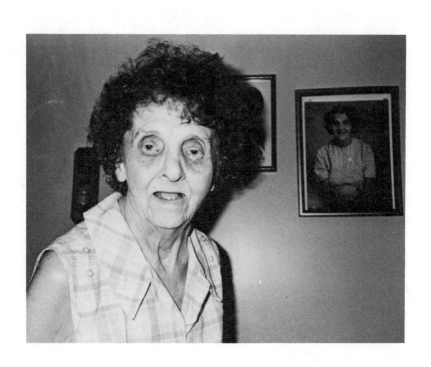

HEALTH AND WELL-BEING

28

THE PERSPECTIVE OF HOLISTIC HEALTH AND WELL-BEING

Mary C. Howell

■

Contemporary medicine can be criticized for its emphasis on physiological disease caused by known, identifiable agents. It is argued that people are more than just their physical processes, and good health is more than just freedom from illness and injury. Further, many experts in health believe that most human maladies and afflictions have multiple causes and multiple consequences in the life of an individual.

In the Kennedy Aging Project we were charged to teach "health professionals." We were fortunate to be able to work with faculty members who were knowledgeable about aspects of well-being that are important to health but are not always considered in assessments of health. These aspects included leisure, law (the individual's relationship with society and public policy), and spirituality, in addition to more conventional areas of health professionalism like nursing, medicine, and social work.

In order to move away from a narrow view of health as a negative state, the absence of illness and injury, we needed to challenge conventional habits of thinking about health and well-being. One conventional habit, a simplistic outgrowth of the science of medicine, is to think in dichotomies. We think: this is either a physical disease or it is a psychosomatic disease. We think: this patient either needs attention from a doctor or from a spiritual counselor. We think: we must find a diagnostic "litmus test" for Alzheimer's disease so we can know whether that particular form of dementia is present or not. Clean, clear, dichotomous answers are actually rare in the art of medicine; more commonly we have to deal with multiple causation, probabilities, and ambiguity.

We health professionals have also let ourselves be drawn into more and more narrow fields of specialization. First there was specialization in mental retardation, then specialization in geriatric mental retardation. On the Interdisciplinary Team of the Project we have had specialists in the medical problems, the legal problems, the leisure and recreational problems, and so on, of people who are both mentally retarded and old. We live in a time of information explosion, and it is difficult to manage an area of professional knowledge except by narrowing and limiting. In addition, the structure of professional work dictates restricted specialization ("claiming a turf"), as necessary for employment advancement.

At the same time, anyone who works with people in such a way as *really* to look at and listen to them, to come to know them, is struck by the indivisibility of human existence. A legal problem has psychological ramifications. Distance and disorder in one's spiritual life cause stress and thus can precipitate an acute infectious illness. And surely every significant physical affliction affects one's cognitive, emotional, and spiritual state. Subdividing human existence into "areas of specialization" may make sense in the world of professional employment, but it is a fiction, and not always a helpful one, to the person whose existence is being examined.

In recent years an old idea has reappeared to address this problem. That idea is subsumed under the rubric of "holistic health," and it has three central aspects. The first is that physical health and well-being must always be seen as intertwined with health and well-being in the realms of the cognitive, emotional, and spiritual. The second is that the process of giving help and advice with regard to health must, in order to be of maximum usefulness, be coordinated by taking an overview of all realms of well-being; many specialists are not enough, there must also be a generalist who serves as advocate and interpreter for the *whole* person. The third central tenet of holism is that the patient is not passive, but active in understanding and striving for her own improved well-being. Not only do these three tenets contrast with current professional assumptions about complexity and control, they are also not always utilized in working with clients who are labeled as "mentally retarded."

The Kennedy Aging Project was primarily a teaching venture. Among our basic assumptions, guiding both the process and the content of our teaching, were the tenets of holistic health. We assumed that it was important that we bring together the perspectives of a variety of different disciplines. We assumed that we each needed to learn, in a rudimentary way, the language of all the disciplines, the different ways of identifying and describing problems, the universe of possible solutions. This perspective helped us to see the client as a fully-rounded person of many dimensions.

We stressed, also, two creative and common-sense ways to consider the whole of a client's life. One focus was to take a present-moment portrait, as clearly detailed a picture as we could discern, of the most important elements of the client's life at that very moment in time. The other focus was to seek a sense of the trajectory of the client's life, past, present, and future, in order to try to understand the specific and individual flavor of existence for this one person.

As an example of this kind of approach, think about including a spiritual component in an Interdisciplinary Team established to assess health and well-being. It seems transparently evident that an individual's spiritual life is an essential matter to understand if one wants to look not only at the trajectory of a whole life but also at a detailed portrait of what is important at the present moment. By *spiritual* we refer to the person's sense of relationship in a universe of beings and places of various levels of *grandeur*. For many of us that sense of relationship takes special reference to a Supreme Being, or God. For others our relationship to other creatures, large and small, human and non-human, or to the world of nature, water, trees, and rocks, forms the primary core of spirituality. That sense of relationship is a point of reference, and over a lifetime it deepens, takes on a multitude of new meanings and referents, and calls us to contemplation. Toward the end of life one's sense of spiritual relationship comes more and more into central focus.

If we mean to understand the client's life as a rounded whole, and to comprehend present problems in a fashion that enables us to be of help, then we must learn about the client's spiritual history and present circumstances. We know that illness, pain, and disability can powerfully affect one's faith, religious practice, and sense of membership in a spiritual community. So can the awareness of advancing age: increasing frailty and the anticipated approach of the death of family members, friends, peers, and one's self compound the depth of one's spiritual experience and awareness.

On the other side of the evaluation, it is clear that an exploration of the client's spiritual life can lead to resources of care. For instance, a reunion with family members on the occasion of religious holidays can be the beginning of a broader family reintegration, centered in a shared faith, important to all family members as old age proceeds and death is anticipated. For instance, regular attendance at community church or temple services can validate spiritual preoccupations and provide rituals through which to express religious fervor. For instance, a worship community can be the source of an unpaid friend who will sponsor the client in various activities of community integration.

In the perspective of clinical medicine, when we work with people who are old we are confronted with many chronic diseases and disabilities that are not caused by any disease, but are frailties that result from the aging process. Often clinical medicine has no specific remedy for these afflictions. But that does not mean that help can not be offered. To be able to offer substantive help we need to look beyond the narrow limits of the medical specialties and consider the patient's whole existence.

In the past there has been rather strong resistance on the part of "scientific" professionals to taking account of a patient's spiritual history, present status, and needs. That resistance arises from many places. One is the supposed opposition of science and religion, and the supposed exclusive attachment of clinical caretaking services to science. I believe that this line of resistance is weakening and that practitioners of the clinical caretaking services are more and more open to the need for a spiritual perspective.

Another level of resistance is expressed as a "respect for privacy," a reflection of an inward-looking individuality with respect to spiritual beliefs. In our history-taking, we have been reluctant to ask about spiritual matters, and we express this reluctance as an unwillingness to violate the patient's privacy. There is, of course, a good deal of logical inconsistency in this, as we do not hesitate to inquire about the most private details of the patient's *physical* existence, including eating, bowel habits, and sexual practices.

Still another level of resistance arises in the intuitive sense that we hold our spiritual beliefs with such profound faith, passion, and intensity that we do not want to invalidate the other person's beliefs, to foist our package on the other person. It is as if we discounted the passion and strength of any spiritual beliefs other than our own.

Finally, there is our traditional separation of "church and state," the state being represented in human services by public funding sources. We have all been indoctrinated from early grade-school years on the necessity of separating firmly those activities that can be promoted or received through public monies, and those that can only be pursued with private resources, and we have allowed this warning to keep us from acknowledging the importance of the patient's private spiritual life.

For these reasons and others, the secular service network has tended to ignore or overlook spirituality in the client's life. This means that people who work in pastoral care have not been members of clinical assessment and treatment teams, that a formal spiritual assessment has not routinely been done for each patient, and that solutions to problems and caregiving options have not been sought in the realm of the spiritual. We sought, in the Aging Project, to change this focus by including the spiritual dimension in our approach to our clients.

We sought, also, to fulfill the other tenets of a holistic perspective by providing each client with a generalist case manager (actually two case managers, a faculty member and a student, acting in harmony) and by empowering the client to speak for herself in telling her history, what was going well in her life and what was a problem, and what her hopes were for the future. Our goal was as broad and comprehensive a sense of health and well-being as we could muster.

29

PRIMARY HEALTH CARE NEEDS OF ADULTS WITH MENTAL RETARDATION

Frances Wiltsie

■

Ninety percent of adults who are mentally retarded are only mildly to moderately retarded, and most are not institutionalized. For approximately 75 percent, the cause of retardation is unknown; Down syndrome is the most common *known* cause. Thus, in considering the health care needs of adults who are mentally retarded, one is typically looking at people who do not have unusual syndromes and who are not severely retarded. Their health care problems are usually not exotic, but rather similar to those of their families, staff persons, case managers, and health care providers. Adults who are mentally retarded may have other disabilities, such as cerebral palsy or hemiplegia, and they have a high incidence of seizure disorders. However, what they have in common with average adults receiving health care is more important than how they differ.

For all adults, there is a need for health promotion aimed at reducing the risk of heart disease, stroke, cancer, and accidental injury or death. Those of us who live or work with people who are mentally retarded have a responsibility to help them reduce their risk of these ailments. Sensible management of minor acute illnesses (most of which are self-limiting), basic infectious disease control, and consistent follow-up for chronic medical problems (such as seizure disorders, thyroid problems, or congenital heart disease) constitute the other major health care needs of adults, including people with mental retardation. More serious acute illnesses and accidents will also occur to a minority of individuals, but this reality should not overshadow the other central issues, particularly risk reduction.

The possibility of acute illness reinforces the need for a good primary health care provider who knows the client and his history, is accessible, and is well connected to local acute-care facilities. This will often be the same person who manages chronic medical problems. Some clients may be well served by a community "family doctor," internist, or nurse practitioner, and one or more specialists (such as a cardiologist or neurologist), who may be local or affiliated with a large medical center. Some clients have no chronic medical problems and may rarely see a doctor or nurse. However, each client should have an identified primary care provider for health promotion as well as for management of acute problems.

Family and staff play an important role in providing needed history and feedback, promoting compliance with treatment, and ensuring follow-up. Adults with mental retardation obviously vary in how much self-advocacy they can perform. However, these tasks are important ingredients in a positive relationship with a doctor or nurse practitioner. In return, family, staff, and client should expect the extra time and patience that the client may require of the provider. Often it is necessary to "shop around" for a doctor; even more than other adults, the adult with mental retardation *needs* to establish a consistent relationship with a primary provider. This is the key to the management of chronic medical problems, as well as episodic ones.

As recent reports of the U.S. Surgeon General[1] have pointed out, heart disease, stroke, cancer, and accidental injury are the major causes of illness, disability, and death for American adults, and there are ways in which we can reduce our risk. Often changing one behavior, such as quitting smoking, will reduce the risk of several diseases. Relatively modest lifestyle changes, such as increasing exercise, can have significant positive effects on health. I suggest that we need to help our clients with mental retardation reduce their risks by promoting the same behavioral changes we need, or are working to accomplish, for ourselves.

Many of these changes cluster in the area of diet and exercise. A sedentary lifestyle is typical for many adults, but it is even more problematic for the adult with mental retardation who may need supervision to go for a walk, be afraid to go out, lack active leisure skills, or have physical mobility limitations. Exercise is a critical ingredient of good health and it should be valued for more than its recreational rewards.

Adults with mental retardation are not exempt from the U.S. problem of obesity, which contributes to heart disease and stroke. Obesity also puts extra stress on weight-bearing joints in the hips and legs, which becomes a particular problem for people with abnormal gaits. People who use their hips and knees in unusual ways, as with cerebral palsy or one-sided weakness, have special "wear and tear" problems, which are made worse by the extra load of obesity. It may be difficult to help a client appreciate the need to lose weight, understand a reduced-calorie diet, and stick with it, but it is extremely beneficial. The goal is not to reach some advertising ideal of the perfectly built person, but to attain a moderate weight and maintain it.

Successful long-term weight loss is a slow process and requires significant changes in eating patterns. Special diets can be confusing to the adult with mental retardation and maintaining motivation is always a challenge. Families and staff may be reluctant to restrict what they perceive as a major (or sole) source of enjoyment; they may also be using food to "buy" compliant behavior. It is often difficult to carry a diet over into the day program, workshop, or job site, where breaks and lunch may be minimally supervised and "junk food" is readily available. Some money management programs are based on using vending machines or purchasing coffee shop "treats"; nutritious, low-calorie choices in these situations are very limited. Thus, any diet change needs to be carefully worked out with day program or workshop staff, and with the families of people who live at home or regularly spend time with relatives. Adults with mental retardation who work in competitive employment or who eat out independently will need special support in dieting.

In addition to the frequent need for weight loss, there are other diet modifications that will reduce the risk of heart disease, stroke, and cancer. The Surgeon General's 1979 Report specifically recommends "moderate dietary changes to reduce intake of excess calories, fat, salt, and sugar."[2]

The fat that is particularly hazardous to health—because it tends to increase our cholesterol level—is saturated fat; this includes animal fats found in butter, cream, whole milk, eggs, cheese, fatty meat, cold cuts, and bacon. It also includes some vegetable fats, such as palm oil, coconut oil, and cocoa butter, which are frequently found in candy bars, crackers, and other baked goods. Intake of saturated fat can be reduced by substituting low-fat milk, low-fat cheese, poultry, and fish; by limiting the frequency with which one eats red meat, cold cuts, eggs, and bacon; by choosing baked goods made with unsaturated oils (corn, soy, safflower); and by choosing snacks that are low in fat (fruit, vegetables, and rice cakes).

Reducing salt in one's diet involves not only table salt but also salty foods such as crackers, salted nuts, and potato chips. Many "convenience foods," like frozen dinners, canned or "instant" soup, or pre-packaged noodles with sauce include additives, flavorings, and preservatives that contain very high levels of sodium. Ham, bacon, sausage, and cold cuts are well-known sources of concentrated sodium. Soy sauce (Chinese food) and some canned vegetables are also high in sodium. Unfortunately, canned food and cold cuts are staples in many group homes for adults with mental retardation; convenience foods are often heavily relied on by adults with mental retardation who cook for themselves. Like calorie and fat reduction, sodium reduction should be a goal for all of us. The adult with mental retardation or inexperienced staff person cooking in a group home may need help in exploring foods that are new to him, and he may need instruction in cooking, This is a particular challenge for the adult with mental retardation who cooks for himself—certainly frozen or processed foods are easier—but the benefits are life-long and considerable.

The fourth dietary change recommended by the Surgeon General's Report is a reduction in sugar intake. Identifying sources of sugar is not difficult, but reducing it is a challenge. The use of

Nutrasweet by people with seizures is controversial; some believe it contributes to headaches, while other authorities are concerned about as yet undiscovered long term-health hazards from this and similar manufactured chemicals added to food. However, one can use fruit as a snack, reduce the sugar in favorite recipes, explore different iced teas in place of soft drinks, and generally reduce reliance on desserts.

There are additional dietary changes that contribute to better health. Increasing fiber will reduce risk of cancer and bowel disease. Fiber is found in whole grains, fruits, and vegetables. Reducing caffeine intake (cola, chocolate, and non-herb tea, as well as coffee) is also recommended. For women, it is advisable to review calcium intake, and, if necessary, consider a supplement; adequate calcium intake, particularly just before menopause, reduces osteoporosis (brittle bones). High levels of dietary calcium are found in milk and milk products (low-fat), and in dark green leafy vegetables.

Taken together, these dietary changes are ambitious but have real potential for affecting both short- and long-term health in positive ways. They need to be a major point in any consideration of the health care needs of adults who are mentally retarded. The keys are gradual change, persistence, modeling, and reinforcement. (For a further discussion of healthful eating, see chapter 31.)

Another major risk factor is smoking. Many Americans continue to smoke in spite of awareness of its serious consequences. However, if we are trying to promote the health of adults with mental retardation, we need to encourage the smokers to stop. Some residences enforce strict rules about smoking, such as only allowing people to smoke outdoors in the company of a staff person. Other residences ration cigarettes, and reduce the number rationed on a pre-set schedule that is agreed to by family or guardian. Strong incentives such as a special vacation can be offered for quitting for a specific period of time. However, the competent client who wants to continue to smoke has the right to do so; we can only try to convince him otherwise, enforce reasonable safety rules, and set aside a non-smoking area, to protect non-smokers' rights to clean air. Of course, staff working with clients must not smoke in their presence; if the "no smoking" message is to be well received, staff should also stop smoking.

People with mental retardation are not exempt from other common problems of addiction, although their opportunities to develop full-blown alcoholism or drug abuse may be limited. When alcohol or drugs are readily available, the possibility of abuse should be considered. Teaching about appropriate "social" drinking or abstinence is important. People with seizures or psychotropic medications should not drink alcohol. There are some instances in which a detox center, drug and alcohol treatment program, and/or Alcoholics Anonymous group may be indicated and useful. This is true for staff and families as well. The effect of addiction on others, especially people depending on care, can be very negative.

Accidents, including motor vehicle accidents, are a major source of injury, disability, and death. Safety is addressed elsewhere in this book, but is mentioned again here because of its importance.

Minor acute illnesses, such as the "flu," are usually self-limiting; one gets better sooner or later, regardless of what one does. Likewise, minor injuries usually heal. However, all staff in residential programs and all people with mental retardation (to the extent of their ability), need to learn basic first aid, such as how to take a temperature and when to call the nurse or doctor. Basic management of minor viral illnesses, including colds, should include rest, aspirin or acetaminophen for aches or fever, and increased intake of fluids. "Clear liquids" (no milk products, no fat, and no solid food) for a day or two will allow the body to recover from an episode of diarrhea. It is appropriate to call the doctor or nurse if a client is sick for more than two days, has a fever of 103 degrees or higher, seems unusually sick, does not stop throwing up, has seizures while sick, or cannot keep medications and liquids down. It is also good to call or see the doctor if someone starts to get better but then develops new symptoms, such as a bad cough, and feels worse. A question of a fracture should be evaluated that day, as should a cut that might need stitches. If staff have limited experience with minor illnesses and injuries, in-service education by a nurse would be helpful.

Infectious disease control for adults with mental retardation centers on hygiene, particularly handwashing. For those who are capable, it should also include covering one's mouth when coughing or sneezing, and appropriately disposing of used tissues. People who drool heavily need to learn to wipe their secretions and dispose of the tissues, if they are able. Dishes and silverware need to be adequately washed; used cups and silverware, like razors and toothbrushes, should not be shared. Open cuts or abrasions should be covered with bandaids.

Annual flu shots are indicated for people with chronic health problems such as asthma, bronchitis, emphysema, heart disease, and diabetes, as well as for people with limited mobility who are at higher risk for respiratory infection. Flu shots can also be considered for anyone who lives with or works closely with others whose hygiene, as discussed above, is marginal. Pneumovax (pneumonia vaccine) should be considered for people who have respiratory problems or who are over age 45. It is administered once in a lifetime. Periodic testing for tuberculosis (PPD) is a good idea, particularly in urban areas; the previous history of testing should be checked to avoid testing people who are already known to be positive.

Heptavax (hepatitis B vaccine) may be appropriate for those who live with, or are intimate with, a hepatitis B carrier. The vaccine is given as a series of three shots at set intervals. There are precautions that the hepatitis B carrier should take to reduce the risk of spreading infection to others; this issue should be discussed with the doctor or nurse. Adults with mental retardation who are potentially sexually active also need information about other sexually transmitted diseases, and may need additional followup, such as periodic testing for gonorrhea. This education should include basic facts about AIDS and "safer-sex" guidelines. This will be a real cognitive challenge for some sexually active people with mental retardation. Motivation and compliance are also potential problems, as in the population at large. Help may be needed in considering whether or not to be sexually active and in learning how to discuss sexual behavior with a partner. Some people with fine motor coordination problems may have particular trouble in learning to use a condom. All teaching about AIDS with people with mental retardation should be simple, concrete, and graphic; particular care should be taken to verify that the vocabulary used is understood.

A tetanus shot (TD or tetanus toxoid) is needed every ten years; it may be repeated earlier in the event of a large, "dirty" wound. Knowing when a person's last tetanus shot was given may prevent unnecessary revaccination for smaller wounds.

An annual physical exam is a Title XIX requirement for people in federally funded programs and a DMR/DMH requirement for people in state-funded programs in Massachusetts and many other states. It should include a breast exam for women and a testicular exam for men. A test for blood in the stool ("guaiac test") should be performed. Often blood work is done at this time, including a complete blood count, serum chemistry including electrolytes and other measures of liver and kidney function, and anti-convulsant levels for those on seizure medications. A urinalysis should also be obtained. At some point after age 40 a baseline EKG (cardiogram) should be obtained.

Women should have periodic pelvic (GYN) exams; often they are mandated to be performed yearly, but may not be truly necessary if three previous PAP smears have been negative (Pap smears should then be done at least every five years, and all women should probably be examined every two to three years). A monthly breast exam is desirable, but it presents a practical problem unless the client can learn self-examination; a partial solution is to schedule the annual physical and the annual GYN visit at different times of the year, as both include a breast exam. A baseline mammogram should be obtained between ages 35 and 40, and then repeated every three years until age 50. After age 50 it is recommended yearly. Women with a family history of premeno- pausal breast cancer should have annual mammograms after age 40, and more frequent breast exams. The need for birth control should also be considered.

Regular hearing and vision testing should also occur; frequency of testing will depend upon individual results or problems. Some clients will need to be under the care of an ophthalmologist.

Dental care is very important. This includes regular cleaning and scaling (ideally every four to six months, although payment may be a problem), as well as good toothbrushing at home. Many adults with mental retardation have poor oral hygiene, gum disease, and missing teeth—these are preventable problems for most people.

People with Down syndrome are at higher risk for a number of health problems. Their poor resistance to infectious disease is well known. Recent attention has been given to a high incidence of Alzheimer's disease, which is discussed elsewhere in this book. Clinical experience and limited research suggest that they are also more likely than other people to have thyroid disease, cervical subluxation (an abnormality of the vertebrae in the neck), cataracts, hearing loss, ear infections (because of an anatomical difference, as well as low resistance to infection), hip problems, congenital heart disease, skin problems, and problems with esophageal motility. This is quite a list; consequently the person with Down syndrome has a particular need for a good primary care provider and a few extra evaluations (such as periodic thyroid tests and at least one set of neck X-rays). She should also have hearing and vision followed more closely. Nonetheless, most people with Down syndrome do very well, even into old age.

All people share the risk of heart disease, stroke, and cancer. We all catch infectious diseases in the same ways. We benefit from the same immunizations and screening tests. Our major role as families, staff, and health care providers for people with mental retardation is to assist them in adopting healthier lifestyles, as we try to do so ourselves, and to facilitate their use of routine preventative health services.

30

EXERCISE

Elizabeth J. DeBrine and Mary C. Howell

■ Attitudes Toward Physical Activity

More attitudinal than physical barriers keep people who are mentally retarded and old from attaining physical fitness. Most of us perceive people who are old as passive, sedentary, and incapable of performing vigorous activity.

A prejudice expressed by both society and program leaders is that people who are old cannot learn new skills or habits. This sentiment is especially strong when the old person has been institutionalized for most of his life. Program leaders are also afraid of working with people who are old because health risks are greater for the clients, and liability risks are greater for program leaders, than if they worked with young people. Many programs for people who are old only offer activities that are nonaerobic and, for those reasons, have little challenge or variety.

The person with mental retardation who is old and sedentary may take longer to train and may achieve less dramatic results. He may have negative attitudes or misunderstandings about physical exercise. Conrad[1] has characterized older adults' attitudes toward physical fitness as follows:

- As they grow older, adults believe their need for physical activity decreases and eventually disappears.

- After reaching middle age, adults overstate the risks involved in a vigorous exercise program.

- Older adults overestimate the benefits of light physical activity.

- Older adults underestimate their own physical capabilities.

These are "cultural wisdoms," and we should assume that people who are old and also mentally retarded are likely to share them. Sidney and Shepard[2] found that society's expectations reinforce these misconceptions regarding physical activity. The researchers concluded that, since people who are old overrated the benefits of their present activity level as being above average, they supported the common belief that even light activity is unusual for most people who are old.

■ Stress Tests

At the Kennedy Aging Project, we advised that each client be screened by a nurse or nurse practitioner before joining a fitness or sport training program. If there are any special conditions such as osteoporosis, cardiac condition, fractures, Down syndrome, seizure disorder, or abnormal thyroid, then the person should be seen by her physician or a specialist to clear her for the exercise program.

Each adult should also fill out a physical activity profile, with the help of a caregiver who knows the client's daily routine. The profile assesses the level of physical activity the client performs at the workshop, in the home, and during leisure time. We are particularly interested in aerobic activity performed for more than fifteen to twenty minutes, three times a week. This amount of activity would indicate that the person has a higher level of fitness than a sedentary adult.

The third component of the screening is an exercise tolerance test that challenges both the cardiorespiratory system and the endurance of the lower extremities. Most people who do research in this area prefer the treadmill or stationary bike for the stress test. The subject's pulse is monitored by electrocardiograms and blood pressure measurements.

Both of these types of stress tests have their advantages and disadvantages.[3] The stationary bike has handlebars to help maintain balance. But exercise on the bike is not weight-bearing, and the seat is considered to be very uncomfortable; some adults find it difficult to maintain an even pace. For others, the quadriceps muscles tire quickly and do not allow sufficient time for an accurate test.

The treadmill works well for most adults, since walking is a natural activity. Some people need to hang onto the handrails for balance, and this changes the reliability of the test values.

If the equipment and professional staff for the bicycle or treadmill are not available, we recommend using Cooper's 12-minute walk/run stress test.[4] This test is modified, in order to meet the abilities of athletes who are less physically fit, by having the athletes walk as fast as possible for twelve minutes. The distance covered on a track is then correlated to the oxygen-consumption level of various sports, thereby giving the coach a range of sports that an athlete can safely participate in.

The term MET (the acronym comes from "metabolic") refers to a multiple of the resting rate of oxygen consumption. A person who is sitting still is using one MET. With a MET level of two, a person is working twice as hard and is consuming twice as much oxygen. A person who walks 30 minutes per mile is using a MET level of two. A jogger who runs ten minutes per mile is using a MET level of ten. Various activities can be ranked according to the rate of oxygen consumption needed for their performance.

Last fall, 19 athletes out of 172 participants were tested at the Massachusetts Special Olympics (MSO) Senior Master Sports Festival held on Cape Cod. The purpose of the testing was to find a range of physical fitness for each age group. Although a very small number of athletes were tested, the results are interesting.

Athletes aged 30 to 39 years had MET levels of 3.0 to 4.6, which suggests they were getting some regular exercise. The 40 to 49-year-old athletes had MET levels in a lower range, 1.5 to 3.5. The MET range was higher for the 50 to 59-year-old athletes; they had levels of 3.0 to 4.6, the same as the 30 to 39-year-olds. Athletes of 60 to 69-years had MET's of 3.0; those 70 to 73-years used METs of 2.0.

Sixty percent of the athletes' pulses were lower than the desirable "target heart rate" for aerobic exercise, for their age group, at the end of their Walking Stress Test; a pulse within the "target heart rate" indicates that the athlete is working hard enough to get maximum benefit from the exercise, but not so hard as to stress the cardiovascular system unduly. We can interpret this to mean that they should be encouraged to walk faster because they were not "trying" as hard as they might; their MET-level results would be increased if they did so. Thirteen percent of the athletes were within their target heart rates. The coaches of the athletes who were exercising above their target heart rates were cautioned to instruct their clients to slow down and thus to decrease the level of stress on their hearts.

Eighteen percent of the 19 athletes tested were actively involved in regular physical activity at least three times a week for at least 30

---

minutes. This time commitment is considered by exercise physiologists to be the minimum for physical maintenance. Therefore, a majority (82 percent) are not regularly involved in physical activity or exercise.

The athletes who participated in this testing really enjoyed the Senior/Masters Sports Festival. Some remarked that they had never walked so fast for such a long time. One man stated after he finished, "Boy, I feel good!" and pounded on his chest. These athletes' coaches now know at what level their clients could start training; they can also recommend particular sports the athletes are eligible to participate in.

The question of whether exercise tolerance tests should be stopped due to symptoms of fatigue, or when the target heart rate has been reached, is still undecided by researchers.[5] Since we did not have special monitoring devices run by professionally trained staff, we chose to let the athletes stop exercising either on their own initiative or on signs of shortness of breath, even though the target heart rate might not have been reached. Smith[6] recommends that the exercise tolerance test be stopped when any of the following signs are noted: dizziness, chest pain, nausea, cyanosis, marked shortness of breath, pain, unsteadiness, mental confusion, facial expression signifying severe distress, loss of sustained vigor or palpable pulse, or lack of rapid return of skin color after brief and firm compression.

■ Training

At the present time there is little information on optimum training regimens for people who are mentally retarded and old, although there are numerous booklets that illustrate different exercises. There are no data to indicate what variables facilitate either new skill acquisition or the relearning of old skills.[7] There are currently no diagnostic tools to assess motor development in people who are. As a result, the programmer has to rely heavily on her intuition and experience to develop a progressive regimen for each adult.

The risks for sedentary older adults who engage in vigorous exercise are higher than those for active people both young and old. For this reason, we must consider both the welfare and safety of the athlete who is old and the legal welfare of the exercise director. All of the programs reviewed advise, for the clients' safety, that the heart rate be monitored during exercise—that is, testing pulse, exercise pulse, and recovery pulse.

Shepard[8] recognizes the value of medical supervision but also realizes that if every program were to be medically supervised the cost to the client would be prohibitive; he recommends that the role of the physician be "restricted to (a) development of exercise guidelines, (b) encouragement of exercise, and (c) identification of subgroups in whom exercise is contraindicated or requires close supervision."[9]

He also suggests the following simple rules to prevent both injuries and emergencies: (i) outdoor exercise is avoided in extremes of heat and cold and under icy conditions (ii) prescribed exercise is advanced gently; (iii) activity never leaves the athlete more than pleasantly tired the next day; (iv) activity is halted for chest pain, or excessive breathlessness; (v) warm-up and warm-down are adequate; (vi) sudden twisting movements are avoided, along with forms of exercise that threaten balance; and (vii) vigorous activity is prohibited during acute infections.

■ Program Components

In one good type of aerobic program, an instructor leads one or more people through a series of exercises, frequently to the accompaniment of phonograph music. There are three general components that are crucial to any exercise program, whether developed for an individual or a group. They are the warm-up period, aerobic activity, and the cool-down period.[10] In the fifteen minute warm-up period, stretching muscles reduces the risks of both musculoskeletal injuries and cardiac dysrhythmias.

For the aerobic activity the individual can walk, jog, swim, cycle, or ski cross-country. Training intensity for an aerobic activity is generally estimated in one of three ways; METs, exercise heart rate in beats per minute, or rating of perceived exertion.[11]

The researchers agree that aerobic exercise must be performed three to four times a week for a duration of 20 to 30 minutes. Some advise that the intensity be between 40 and 73 percent of the individual's MET capacity; others recommend between 60 and 80 percent. The starting level of intensity should be determined both by the general fitness of the individual and by how long she has been active in an aerobic program. For athletes with METs of 2, the aerobic activity should be five to ten minutes in duration until her body adjusts to the new stress level.

The third component of the exercise program is the cool-down period, which consists of stretching for approximately fifteen minutes to decrease the heart's workload slowly.

Since most everyone can start in the same program, the exercise prescription is divided into three stages: starter, progression, and maintenance.[12] The starter program is the initial stage of training, which can last from two to six weeks depending on the initial fitness level of the individual. The exercise intensity is low and includes lots of stretching and calisthenics. There is a low-to-moderate intensity aerobic period included in this program. The starter program introduces the client to exercise and allows time for proper adaptation to the training. For sedentary adults who are mentally retarded and old and who have not exercised for many years, the starter program could last as long as sixteen weeks.

In the progression program, the participant progresses at a more rapid rate. The intensity and duration of activity is increased every one to three weeks. How well an individual adapts to the current level determines the frequency and magnitude of progression.

After six months to one year of training, an individual is ready for the maintenance stage. The client will have reached a satisfactory level of cardiorespiratory fitness and will continue the same workout schedule to maintain fitness.

■ Program Guidelines

A program leader must take into account the sensory deprivation experienced by many older adults with mental retardation. Loss of sight or hearing requires special consideration. The leader must also understand that the central nervous system is unable to process some kinds of information as quickly in old age; this will result in a slower reaction time and less movement during exercise.

To ensure that the program is successful, the leader should use well-lit rooms where he faces the sun. The verbal instructions must be given slowly and repeated when necessary. The instructions should be given before the record player is turned on; otherwise the information will be lost in the music. Visual cues should be used as much as possible and physical barriers should be removed to avoid falls.

Many people who are old underestimate their abilities to perform. They overrate the risks of exercise and hold back on the energy they exert. Others may feel more fit than they are. They may set a walking pace that is too rapid to maintain, or they may set themselves up to be defeated in competition.

The leader should exercise good counseling practices to deal with the reminiscing that people who are old engage in while in a group setting. It is important to know when to stop and listen, and when to suggest that the matter be discussed at another time. For many people who are old (as for all people), an exercise class is a good time to make new friends. A program leader should encourage this since it will help maintain regular attendance.

Clark[13] suggests that the following criteria be met to improve participation:

- Program variety that meets the needs and interests of those involved, such as dance, tai chi, yoga, and weight lifting.

- A pleasant, convenient, safe setting with qualified, caring staff. Transportation is still the biggest barrier for most adults.

- A challenging yet individualized progression within the capability of all.

- Adequate rewards and social support to help coalesce the group. Regular feedback on performance and support from significant others have been proven to be very important actors in someone's continued participation.

- An educational base to promote understanding of principles. Give information on proper attire, nutrition, sleep, and contraindications to exercise.

Ostrow[14] states that continued participation depends on perceived increased health and fitness, social contacts, achievement of well-being, improvement of self-image, fun and enjoyment, and feedback on achievement.

Mobily[15] found that the needs and motivations of people who are mentally retarded and old and live in institutions are different from those who live in the community. The physical activity program must help them to vent feelings of frustration and anger, while at the same time it should increase socialization and promote feelings of well-being. The programs must also help them to maintain or increase their present levels physically, psychologically, and cognitively. Finally, the program must increase clients' awareness of the importance of remaining active in order to increase or maintain their independence.

People who are mentally retarded and old need to share in the responsibility of increasing or maintaining their present level of health. One way they can exercise their freedom of choice is through a physical activity program, either in a group setting or on their own. It is up to caregivers, service providers, and program leaders to increase awareness of the many benefits of physical activity among people who are mentally retarded and old.

31

DIET AND NUTRITION

Elizabeth J. DeBrine and Mary C. Howell

■

We are concerned about nutrition for three reasons. First, nutrition, along with physical activity, can help a client maintain or increase her present level of functioning, which in turn can affect where she works, lives, and recreates. A healthy diet combined with a safe exercise routine can increase self-esteem, life satisfaction, and opportunities for community interaction.

Second, food is one area where clients have opportunities to make choices that directly affect how they feel about themselves. To provide choice, a variety of fresh foods has to be readily available. There is no sense in teaching older adults about nutrition if all that is available are snacks high in sugar from vending machines, and overcooked, highly processed institutional food.

Third, we are what we eat. This is true not only in terms of the types and quantities of food that we choose but also in terms of the impact that growing and processing foods have on the environment. Healthy eating promotes sustainable agriculture; sustainable agriculture is a policy that supports local food production while decreasing the wasteful use of water, soil, and fossil fuels. Fresh local foods are best.

They are most nutritious, and their use promotes a healthy local economy. Fresh locally grown foods have not been processed or shipped semi-ripened from corporate farms thousands of miles away. Choosing fresh, locally grown foods whenever possible allows us to participate in efforts to take good care of our planet, Earth.

Almost every day, new studies provide conflicting information regarding obesity, cholesterol, vitamins, and so on. Some of these studies are about small details of physiology that do not actually have much to do with how we choose the foods we eat. One of our main goals in this paper is to demystify nutrition. We focus on physical exercise and athletic performance to highlight the nutritional needs of the active body, and as a way of encouraging people with mental retardation who are old to increase their activity, even to participate in Special Olympics.

■ Diet Misconceptions

Myth: Athletes need to increase their intake of protein to prepare for strenuous physical activity.

Fact: Strenuous physical activity involves no increased use of protein, but does require an increase in calories, usually as carbohydrates. The average adult needs two small servings (2 ounces each) of protein-rich food every day. For example, a serving could consist of two meatballs with spaghetti and sauce, or two eggs with toast, or one cup of beans and rice.

Myth: Steak is the best source of protein.

Fact: Steak is no better as a source of protein than cheese, eggs, poultry, fish, or balanced combinations of vegetable proteins. In fact, steak provides a relatively large amount of fat—which is not good for health—along with its protein.

Myth: An athlete's body does not require extra fluids during practice and competition.

Fact: A major cause of poor athletic performance, exhaustion, and sickness during vigorous activity is inadequate fluid intake. Water regulates body temperature through perspiration, rids toxic wastes through urination, and helps maintain a proper volume of blood supply, which feeds oxygen and nutrition to muscles and organs.

Myth: Athletes should increase their salt intake by taking salt tablets while exercising.

Fact: Athletes lose less sodium than water while exercising in the heat. It is unnecessary to replace the sodium lost because the amount of sodium in your blood actually increases with heavy sweating. You need to increase the intake of water, not salt, during heavy exercise. Besides, salt tablets can be dangerous because they draw more water away from the bloodstream into the stomach. Diluted juice, herbal tea, and water are good drinks.

Myth: It is too late for athletes who are old to change dietary habits.

Fact: Even small changes in an athlete's diet can make a difference in how he performs at work or in competition. Decreasing fat, salt, and sugar will have long-range effects on an individual's ability to function in sports and other independent activities.

Myth: It is better to change all of one's eating habits at one time.

Fact: Nothing could be further from the truth. We recommend making small changes over a long period of time to incorporate better eating habits. Making too many changes at once usually results in frustration, and then changing back to the old habits. We recommend one change a month. (See section at the end of this chapter entitled "A Healthful New Year.")

Myth: Beer is a good source of fluids, the B vitamins, and carbohydrates for athletes.

Fact: Do not drink beer before competition because alcohol depresses the nervous system. The brain and muscles will function less skillfully and quickly. Drinking beer immediately after an event will decrease, instead of increase, the water in the body through increased urination. Athletes should drink several glasses of water before having that celebratory beer. Also, beer has fewer B vitamins than a slice of bread, and less carbohydrates than a glass of orange juice.

Myth: Athletes should take vitamins to supplement the vitamins they get from food because of the heavy demands of strenuous exercise.

Fact: Vitamin supplements are unnecessary for most athletes because the nutrients needed by the body are supplied by eating a well-balanced diet. Research shows that athletes do not need an increased intake of vitamins. Vitamin supplements will not prevent injuries, build muscle, or increase strength, endurance, energy, or performance.

■ Healthy Eating for Everyone

Our daily food intake should consist mostly of "staple" foods in the freshest, healthiest form we can find. The following are staple foods:

Fresh Fruits and Vegetables

The best ones are locally grown, recently picked (not sitting in a store for a long time), and grown with a minimum of, or no, chemicals such as pesticides and herbicides. In the summertime we can buy fresh locally grown fruits and vegetables at farm stands or farmers' markets. We can also ask the produce workers in the neighborhood grocery store to tell us which fruits and vegetables are locally grown, recently picked, and grown without chemicals. Fruits and vegetables are among our best sources of vitamins and minerals; they also give us carbohydrates, including natural sugars and fiber.

Grains Such As Wheat, Rice, Oats, and Barley

Again, we can look for grains that have been grown without chemicals. Grains give us carbohydrates, fiber, some protein, and some vitamins and minerals.

Proteins

Eggs, low-fat dairy products, legumes (peas and beans), poultry, fish, and meat should be consumed in small amounts.

Fresh, Clean Water

Eight to ten glasses should be drunk each day.

Certain food habits are less than healthful. We want to try, slowly and patiently, to overcome the following eating habits:

Eating Sweet Foods

White sugar has no food value except calories. Artificial sweeteners are chemicals, not natural foods; we cannot be sure whether they might be harmful. Recent studies suggest that artificial sweeteners are associated with weight gain. Other sweeteners (such as honey and maple syrup) are less objectionable, partly because we tend to use them only in small amounts. But we need to train ourselves to choose foods that are not super-sweet because sweetness is never very healthful. Some authorities think that craving sweets is an addiction, very much like a drug addiction.

Eating Salty Foods

Most of us eat more salt (sodium chloride) than we need. Our bodies need only a little salt each day and we can get this from our food without adding extra salt.

Eating Fat

Chips, red meat, and some kinds of chicken and fish, many baked goods (cookies, pies, and cakes), ice cream, and dressings, dips, and sauces are common sources of fat. Oil is just another form of fat. Many of the worst chemicals from pollution can dissolve in fat, so when we eat fat we also risk eating these chemicals, which then tend to be stored in the fat in our bodies. Fat (or oil) is probably the single most dangerous food we eat. The amount of fat we need can be obtained from a balanced diet; we never "need" pure fats (like butter or margarine) or very fatty foods (like chips or muffins).

Eating Red Meat in Large Quantities

Red meat (like beef, pork, lamb, and veal) is a good source of protein, but many of us eat more red meat than we need. This is a health problem because red meat also tends to have a lot of fat. Much of the red meat that is in our grocery stores comes from animals that were treated with chemicals (like hormones and antibiotics) when they were being raised; the chemicals are still in the meat when we eat it. (See the section on Vegetarian Athletes later in this chapter)

Eating "Convenience" Foods

These foods are prepared with chemicals that have no food value. Chemicals are added to make the food keep while it sits in the store for a long time, to change the color or texture of the food, or for other reasons that have to do with the manufacturing and packaging processes. Many of these chemicals are suspected of causing harm to our bodies when we eat them repeatedly over long periods of time.

There are positive rules we can follow to promote a healthful diet—it is not just a matter of doing without! Here are some diet guidelines that will tend to make us healthier people and better athletes:

Eat more legumes (dried peas and beans).

Cooked into stews and casseroles—like beans and rice, New England baked beans, and bean dip—these foods are tasty and excellent sources of protein, without fat and usually with fewer harmful chemicals than are found in meats.

Eat more raw foods.

Although this new healthful diet will sometimes seem like a lot of work (without unhealthful "convenience" foods to fall back on), we can save some work by eating foods more simply; fruits and vegetables are almost no work at all if we eat them raw.

Eat a good variety of foods.

Explore new vegetables that you have never tried before. Try new recipes. If you get stuck eating a few "favorite" foods for several days, make a real effort to switch over to other kinds of foods now and then. In this way you will be most likely to get all the nutrients you need.

Eat in moderation.

Eating excessive amounts of any single food probably creates stress for your body. If it tastes good to you, have some more tomorrow, do not overeat today.

Choose fresh foods whenever you can.

Do not buy too much at the store or cook too much at one time (unless you can freeze the leftovers). Food values are highest in foods that are fresh.

■ Special Considerations for Older Athletes

A nutritious diet helps us to become more fit and healthy, whatever our age. Diet suggestions for older athletes are the same as for younger athletes, and for people of all ages. While some changes of old age cannot be reversed—like knees that sometimes are stiff or creak or ache—we can take positive steps to slow the aging process. Getting regular physical exercise is one of the best known ways to do this. And eating the best, most healthful foods will help our bodies to be strong enough to get that exercise. A very good diet helps us to cope with stress and to repair minor injuries from hard training, falls, and similar problems.

Here are some rules of eating that are especially important to remember after we pass middle age:

• A steady intake of potassium tends to prevent stroke and heart attack; potassium is found especially in green vegetables.

- A daily intake of protein-rich foods (two servings of 2-ounces, an amount that would fit in the palm of a small adult hand) is required because tissues might need to be repaired; when you are injured or ill, two additional small servings each day will help bring full recovery.

- Dietary fiber—found in pits and peels and skins and seeds—is especially needed as age increases, to help protect against bowel disorders like appendicitis, diverticulitis, bowel cancer, and constipation.

- Calcium is needed for strong bones; extra calcium is needed as bones start to weaken in old age. Calcium is found in low-fat dairy products and in green leafy vegetables. (Weight-bearing exercise will put the calcium into your bones; walking is great for this.)

When an athlete starts training, it is important to pay attention and improve the diet. That is not the time to break a lot of the good-eating rules. Eating at a "training table"—a special table where athletes eat together— is a good way to be sure that you remember how important it is to have a good diet.

The advantages of getting regular physical exercise are helped by a good diet. They include: putting more calcium into your bones so they are stronger and less likely to break; building up your muscles; and becoming stronger, having more lasting-power (endurance), and more grace and flexibility. Diet and exercise work together for athletes of all ages.

■ Obesity

Although nutritionists and physicians are unable to determine an individual's exact ideal weight, they agree that obesity is the storage of large amounts of fat tissue that results from an excess of food intake over energy output. An individual's weight usually remains the same for long periods of time, despite the fluctuation of food intake that takes place during holidays or short periods of illness. Since weight remains fairly constant, energy output and food intake must be approximately the same.

Obese people do not eat much more per unit of lean body mass than do non-obese people. Obese people usually have a lower caloric requirement for weight maintenance than do people who have never been obese. This makes weight loss by dieting very difficult for someone who is obese. Another factor that adds to the frustration and low success rate of dieting is that the obese person's metabolic rate decreases while dieting, making it more difficult to lose weight.

Exercise increases the body's metabolic rate, which helps the body to lose weight. The increased metabolic rate may even continue for several hours after exercise, burning still more calories. And the more one weighs, the more energy is used during physical activity; as a result, more calories are burned.

Many scientists believe that each of us has a biological set point that determines the amount of fat in the body, and therefore the body weight. This is still a controversial theory, but it may help explain why some people are naturally fat, while others are lean. This theory helps us focus on our eating habits rather than on trying to achieve a specific numerical weight.

If you still feel that you need a specific "ideal weight" as a guide, then we suggest that you use the Body Mass Index (BMI) recommended by the National Institutes of Health. BMI compares weight with body height. It does not require any special laboratory tests or equipment.

■ Calculating Body Mass Index

Body mass is obtained by dividing your weight in kilograms by the square of your height in meters.

To convert weight to kilograms, measure weight (without clothes) in pounds, then divide by 2.2. (This is your first number.)

To convert height into meters, measure height (without shoes) in inches, then divide by 39.4. Then multiply this number by itself. (This is your second number.)

Divide your weight in kilograms (your first number) by the square of your height in meters (your second number).

For women, desirable body mass is 21 to 23. Obesity (20 percent above the desirable range) begins at 27.5. Serious obesity (40 percent above the desirable range) begins at 31.5. For men, desirable body mass is 22 to 24. Obesity begins at 28.5 and serious obesity begins at 33. The experts at the National Institutes of Health urge those whose BMI is higher than the desirable range to lose weight.

■ How to Lose Weight

"Diet fads" are based on unsound nutrition and just do not work. If they did all that they promised, why would there be a new fad diet in the news every month?

Diet fads are supported by our society's obsession with thinness. American women are especially targeted by advertising, camps for weight loss, spas, fat farms, weight loss clinics, and diet books. Women are urged to believe that being thin will make them happier, more confident, more loved, and more successful at work and at home.

Some people are very obese. However, millions of other Americans just *perceive* themselves as being seriously overweight, and as a result do not feel comfortable with their bodies.

Diets that recommend eating just one food or group of foods are not only unhealthful but potentially dangerous, both physically and emotionally. High-protein diets contain far too much protein and fat. Diets that restrict eating to just, for instance, grapefruit and eggs, become very boring and do not supply the necessary nutrients.

Many diets promote quick weight loss—more than three pounds a week. But those pounds are almost always regained. In fact, 98 percent of people who lose weight by dieting regain the weight they lost, and 90 percent of those gain *more* weight than they lost.

The old basic principles of dieting (counting calories, weighing in, restricting carbohydrates) are for many people a sure way to *gain* pounds. The new message, according to nutrition experts, is to cut down on fat, increase complex carbohydrates, stop counting calories, and have a regular exercise program.

Calorie counting does not work because not all calories are created equal—what foods the calories are in is more important than a caloric number. Calories come in the form of fats, proteins, and carbohydrates. We burn most of the carbohydrates as we eat. Carbohydrates are found in fruits, vegetables, breads, cereals, and grains. Fat, on the other hand, tends to be stored by the body for future use, in case a time comes when food is not readily available. Protein is used by the body to repair or rebuild tissues that are damaged or used up. Adults need only small amounts of protein.

More importantly, we need to give up the concept of dieting as something that we do now and then. Instead, we should develop an eating plan that will last a lifetime.

■ Recommendations for Losing Weight

1. Forget calorie counting and concentrate instead on a low fat, high-carbohydrate eating plan.

2. Eat a wide variety of foods.

3. Make dietary changes over a long period of time instead of making many changes at once. (See "A Healthful New Year" later in this chapter.)

4. Change the quality of your diet by decreasing your intake of fats, salts, and sweets. (See "A Healthful New Year.")

5. Change the quantity of your eating plan by eating smaller portions and eating small meals frequently to satisfy your appetite.(See "Great Snacks" later in this chapter.)

6. If you cannot give up sweets entirely, then cut down on the number and size of servings and incorporate them into your eating plan.

7. Choose a plan that allows you to cheat once in a while. Eat slowly and enjoy your food more.

8. Start an exercise program. For example, try walking, dancing, swimming, or volleyball. For more information, see the videotape and booklet, It's Never Too Late, available from Massachusetts Special Olympics, P.0. Box 303, Hathorne, MA 01937, Tel. (508) 774-1501.

■ Precompetition Meals

Precompetition meals give muscles the energy that they need to perform efficiently. The pre-event meal must also help maintain body hydration, especially during strenuous physical activity and excessive heat. A meal that includes some fat keeps the athlete from feeling hungry while competing.

What an athlete eats before competition can help discourage stomach or intestinal upset during competition. Athletes should avoid nuts, beans, cabbage, cauliflower, cucumbers, raw fruits (except oranges, bananas, peeled apples), raw vegetables (except lettuce), and bran. But many athletes believe a particular food is a winner; if it has not caused stomach upset in the past, then go for it.

Precompetition meals should be eaten three or four hours before the event. Some easy-to-digest pre-game meal suggestions include: cereal with skim milk and banana; poached egg on dry toast; peaches with low-fat cottage cheese; yogurt with unsweetened applesauce and cinnamon; sliced turkey on whole wheat bread, without mayonnaise;

vegetable soup with crackers; baked potato and broiled chicken; pasta with low-fat sauce and cooked carrots.

Avoid eating meat (hamburgers or steak) because it is hard to digest and will overtax the body during the event. Heavily salted foods (chips, pretzels, and salted nuts) will deprive the body of liquids that are needed to cool the body down through perspiration.

Athletes should drink two to three glasses of fluids three hours before the event, and then two glasses one and-a-half hours before the event. Water and unsweetened diluted juice are fine. DON'T WAIT TO BE THIRSTY!!

■ Vegetarian Athletes

Many athletes are concerned that their protein needs will not be met if they become vegetarians. These fears are unfounded because grains, legumes, and dairy products are excellent sources of protein. Besides, athletes do not require more protein than the average adult because muscles use carbohydrates from food for fuel. Vegetarians have the benefit of a diet that eliminates the excess fat found in animal protein.

There are several reasons why people choose to become vegetarians. Many religions promote the benefits of a vegetarian diet as a means of becoming closer to God. Two eastern faiths, Buddhism and Hinduism, and two expressions of the Christian faith, Trappist monks of the Roman Catholic Church and Seventh Day Adventists, all favor a vegetarian eating plan. Others may feel a moral or ethical mandate not to kill animals for food or to imprison animals in order to take their eggs and milk.

Many authorities are becoming more aware and concerned about animal protein as a source of unhealthful chemicals and infectious organisms. By eating only plants, an individual consumes fewer toxins by eating lower on the food chain. Animal protein has had many opportunities to accumulate toxins, as animals often eat grains and field grasses sprayed with pesticides and herbicides. (Animal flesh that has a high fat content concentrates these poisons.) Many animals commercially raised to become food are also treated with hormones and antibiotics to speed their growth. Infection with antibiotic-resistant organisms sometimes results.

Another reason some people become vegetarians is their concern about the wasteful use of the Earth's resources. Animals are fed a great deal of grain so that the desire of people in wealthy countries to eat meat can be satisfied. Eating the plants directly would mean more protein to share with people in less wealthy countries; it would be less expensive to feed the world.

Among the benefits of becoming a vegetarian are a decreased risk of coronary heart disease, atherosclerosis (hardening of the arteries), and cancers of the colon, breast, and uterus. Many scientists believe that environmental chemicals and radiation work together with a diet rich in animal fat to produce cancer.

Osteoporosis, diabetes, high blood pressure, and obesity can be prevented or improved by the transition to vegetarianism. More importantly, a vegetarian eating plan may contribute to longevity as well as to feelings of increased health and vigor.

There are three different kinds of vegetarians:

1. Strict vegetarians: all protein is derived from plant foods; no animal foods, including milk or eggs, are consumed.

2. Lactovegetarians: No meat, fish, poultry, or eggs are eaten, but milk, cheese and other daily products are acceptable.

3. Ovolactovegetarians: Eggs and dairy products are eaten, but not meat, fish, or poultry.

Here are some general guidelines to consider when becoming a vegetarian:

1. Vegetarians must know how to combine protein elements from different foods to make complete proteins to meet the daily dietary requirements. For example, combine legumes (dried peas, beans, or peanuts) with grains (beans and rice, or a peanut butter sandwich). Combine legumes with nuts and seeds (a snack of peanuts and walnuts, or sesame seeds with baked beans. Combine dairy products with any vegetable protein (add a glass of milk or some yogurt dressing to any meal).

2. The body must have enough calories to support the "ideal" weight while meeting the protein needs.

3. A vegetarian diet must include foods that will meet the body's needs for vitamins and minerals. Nutrients that have in the past come primarily from eating meat must now come from other sources, for instance iron (found in green leafy vegetables and dried fruits) and vitamin B-12 (found in eggs, milk, and in smaller amounts in many vegetables).

■ Great Snacks

It is better to eat small meals frequently rather than three large meals every day. One way to decrease a ravenous appetite is to eat healthful snacks mid-morning, late afternoon, and before bedtime. The following snacks are low in fat, salt, and sugar, and high in protein and carbohydrates: apple wedges with natural peanut butter (without sugar or other additives); low-fat plain yogurt with fresh fruit; low-fat cottage cheese on toasted whole wheat bread with cinnamon; banana and a glass of skim milk; vegetable salad; peanut butter and banana on whole wheat bread; unsweetened dry cereal, raisins and nuts; pizza made with whole wheat english muffins, tomato sauce, and grated cheese, baked in toaster oven.

What should you drink? Water, water, water!! And also herbal teas and diluted fruit juices. Beware of so-called fruit sodas and drinks. They often have a lot of sugar, artificial flavorings, and artificial sweeteners.

■ A Healthful New Year

Beginning one small change each month for a year can make a big difference in how you look, feel and perform.

January: Take the salt shaker off your table. Cut the amount of salt in half in recipes.

February: Eat a bran muffin instead of a jelly donut at break time.

March: Drink only one cup of coffee in the morning. Drink tea or fruit juice the rest of the day.

April: Bring a jar of old fashioned peanut butter (without additives) and a box of wheat crackers to work so that you will have a readily accessible alternative to the candy machine.

May: Drink at least eight glasses of water every day.

June: Substitute a vegetarian meal for one red meat meal each week.

July: Cut your use of butter or margarine in half.

August: Drink low-fat milk instead of whole milk. Eat only low-fat cheese, yogurt, cottage cheese, and milk.

September: Eat raisins, unsalted peanuts, and dry cereal for snacks instead of cookies, cake, or pie.

October: Drink unsweetened diluted fruit juices or water instead of sodas.

November: Eat raw carrots, celery, or broccoli for an afternoon snack.

December: Eat a vegetarian meal (with beans or dairy foods for protein) at least once a day.

32

SAFETY FOR ADULTS WITH MENTAL RETARDATION

Frances Wiltsie

■

Accidents are a major cause of disability and death. The Surgeon General's Report ranks motor vehicle accidents third, and "all other accidents" fourth, among causes of death for adults from age 25 to 44; for adults from age 45 to 64, they rank seventh and fifth respectively.[1]

We are all familiar with the pain, suffering, and disability associated with burns, fractures, and knife wounds. Minor injuries result in aggravation and inconvenience—sprained fingers taped together, a twisted ankle that limits dancing, and stiffness, bruising, and soreness. Consider how one person with a leg in a cast might hold back all other residents in a group home who want to go out; at the least, the outing might require extra staffing. Reflect on the political consequences of a preventable fire in a group home, given the tendency of some communities and families to oppose community placement.

Accidents are serious. Even when minor, they can have a significant negative effect on quality of life. Service providers are held to high standards for safety, both by the community and by regulatory agencies. This article will review safety precautions for families and group homes.

People with mental retardation may have difficulty recognizing a safety hazard and determining an appropriate response. Their physical ability to respond may also be impaired or delayed. More anticipation and prevention on the part of families and staff is necessary to compensate for these difficulties. Structured teaching about common hazards on a client-specific basis is also necessary.

Safety hazards here will be categorized as factors related to falls, appliance hazards, poisons, asphyxiation, automobile and street hazards, getting lost, fire, and interpersonal violence.

Numerous factors contribute to *falls*. They include ice, wet floors, highly waxed floors, and small loose rugs—all of which can be avoided. A floor must not be mopped at times when people are actively using the area. Objects, including cords, that could be tripped over should not be left on the floor, and especially not on the stairs. Staircases should have railings, and the railings should be used. Bathrooms, especially tubs and showers, are safer with securely anchored grip bars. If a client has any gait problem, her shoes need to be firmly attached to her feet; no "cute" footwear that can fall off should be permitted.

Attention must also be paid to situations where people could fall off something—a fence, the roof of a shed, a ladder, and so on. Careful thought should be given to who is able to sleep on a top bunk bed, and whether a bed rail is needed. Some physically disabled people will need siderails on a regular bed. Staff and families should be careful not to model unsafe climbing behavior, such as standing on a chair to reach a top shelf. If an object cannot be reached with the help of a step stool, it should be stored elsewhere. Inappropriate climbing by anyone needs to be discouraged. After a ladder is used, it should be put away promptly.

Appliances present multiple potential risks. Evaluate carefully who can use the stove, the garbage disposal, the microwave oven, the iron, and other appliances. Make sure that all cords and electric outlets are in good repair, that outlets are not overloaded, that appliances are grounded if necessary. Minimize the use of extension cords. Do not leave light sockets empty.

Poisons should be clearly labeled, preferably in their original containers, and stored in one place. They must never be put in food containers. In many situations, the storage space for poisons is better locked. For people with mild mental retardation, special pictorial "poison" labels can be used, with appropriate teaching. Extremely toxic substances, such as drain cleaner or pesticides, need to be locked away or not stored in the home. Toxic substances should not be mixed.

The phone number for the local poison control center must be immediately available; the center can also be consulted for questions of potential toxicity before an accident occurs. Syrup of Ipecac, to induce vomiting when advised by the poison control center, belongs in every first aid kit. Medications should also be considered potentially toxic, and given safe, separate storage. In homes where someone might eat house plants, the choice of plants can be guided by the poison control center; many common plants are toxic to humans.

Asphyxiation is a potential hazard in homes where someone might try to ingest inedibles such as small metal objects or game pieces—these small objects need to be carefully watched and stored. Besides the risk of choking, some of these can cause damage to the stomach and intestines. Similarly, caution is necessary with plastic bags if there is a possibility someone might put one over his head, which might cause asphyxiation.

Automobiles and streets are extremely dangerous. Street crossing and automobile awareness in parking lots often merit more attention and formal instruction than is provided. Even those who "don't cross alone" need to learn caution around cars. Staff and families should be careful to model good street crossing; you cannot cross in the middle of the block yourself and expect the person with mental retardation to go up to the crosswalk at the corner. When riding in the car, seatbelts should be used—again, think of yourself as a role model. (It is sometimes argued that staff should not be confined by seatbelts, so they can deal with client problems such as physical assaults. But physical assaults and other extreme behaviors cannot be managed while one is driving; if this is a likely problem, a second staff person or family member, who also wears a seatbelt, is needed in the car.) In some cases, locks on the passenger doors that the passenger cannot unlock may be required. If a wheelchair van is used, check that the wheelchair locks hold the wheels securely; if not, they should be adapted to fit.

Getting lost should never happen to people with mental retardation, but it does happen occasionally. Clients should be taught their addresses and phone numbers, if at all possible, and they should carry accurate identification. Role-playing how to find help may be useful. Staff and families should have a recent photograph available for a search; many Department of Mental Retardation programs are also required to maintain an "emergency fact sheet." For people with mild mental retardation, a plan such as meeting back at the car in case of separation at the park or store is useful.

Fire is another serious threat. Formal programs always have fire drills and "self preservation" tests; this might also be advisable for a family, using smoke detectors. Fire drills should include an established meeting place outside. People with mental retardation need to be taught to get out in case of actual fire, as well as when they hear a fire alarm. Trying to "hide" a fire or to "fix it" could be disastrous. Non-compliance with fire drills should be taken very seriously; some people respond to being paid or otherwise strongly reinforced for getting out in a timely manner. For those who cannot hear an alarm, there are strobes and bed shakers. Smoke detectors should be in place and functional. Opportunities for a fire to start must be reduced; this includes supervision as needed when using the stove. Space heaters should either be avoided or very carefully monitored for the possibility of tipping over, getting too close to drapes, or overloading the electrical circuit. Staff and families should know how to rescue someone whose clothes are on fire. No one should smoke in bed or play with matches or lighters.

Finally, it should be remembered that people with mental retardation may be victims of *interpersonal violence.* Weapons, including guns and non-kitchen knives, do not belong in group homes. Sometimes even kitchen knives should be locked up when not in use, for instance, if one client has been threatening another with the bread knife. Teaching about street safety, including having people travel in pairs, may be desirable.

The importance of good judgment on the part of staff cannot be overemphasized. It is also essential to have a basic emergency plan, i.e., an idea of what to do when you are alone with eight clients and someone cuts her finger badly. At such times, being able to depend on a neighbor, call an administrator on a beeper, or find your sister is crucial. Several options need to be available. One might be able to call an ambulance and send the injured person off alone. Clearly, however, accident prevention is preferable to reacting after the fact.

33

WORKING WITH THE PERSON WHO RESISTS MEDICAL TREATMENT

Alison Boyer and Kathy Wilkie Kossey

∎

Some people are so fearful of doctors, nurses, and other medical technicians that they refuse medical attention. Medical desensitization is an interdisciplinary approach to help the client become more comfortable with a variety of medical procedures. The objective of desensitization is to improve health care. The clinician (nurse practitioner, physician, or nurse) works with a psychologist and other appropriate staff or family members in sessions that are held at regular intervals. Several approaches are used to facilitate these practice sessions, including positive reinforcement, relaxation, distraction, and role playing.

For the past five years we have worked with several women who are mentally retarded to help them tolerate gynecological and physical examinations. First we try to help the client feel comfortable in the examination room. Then we introduce the components of the physical examination step-by-step, beginning with the least intrusive procedures, such as listening to the heart and lung, or examining the eyes or throat. We proceed gradually to the more intrusive portions of the examinations: ear, abdomen, breast, and finally, the pelvic and rectal areas.

The client has the option to terminate any portion of the examination, but the session is always ended with a procedure that the person responds to positively, such as a heart and lung exam. The reinforcers that we use are praise, stickers, food, and other preferred items or interactions, depending upon client preferences.

One woman rarely had gynecological examinations prior to our working with her, and those were only able to be performed under general anesthesia. After a year of weekly sessions, she allowed a full examination by the gynecologist in the nurses' station of her residence, a place that was familiar to her.

Another client was initially very resistant to any medical examination. She would jump off the table and run away, or scream and strike out. Although we have not yet met our goal of her completing an examination with a gynecologist, there have been great improvements in her cooperation with a variety of medical procedures, such as blood drawing, eye examinations, ear irrigations, and more.

We have seen varying degrees of improvement in cooperation take place with all the participants in the program. The clients have grown to look forward to their weekly sessions, and their general response to medical examinations and procedures has been less fearful and more productive.

34

EASING THE TRANSITION
OF HOSPITALIZATION

Sharon B. Roth

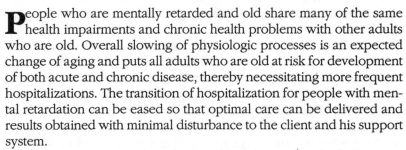

People who are mentally retarded and old share many of the same health impairments and chronic health problems with other adults who are old. Overall slowing of physiologic processes is an expected change of aging and puts all adults who are old at risk for development of both acute and chronic disease, thereby necessitating more frequent hospitalizations. The transition of hospitalization for people with mental retardation can be eased so that optimal care can be delivered and results obtained with minimal disturbance to the client and his support system.

For many people, the thought of being hospitalized is frightening. It is quite disturbing to be placed in a foreign setting with a multitude of people, sights, sounds, and experiences that you have never been exposed to, and then forced to depend on others for functions that you usually manage independently. It is even more disturbing for people who have below average intelligence, a tendency to think concretely, a highly individualized and specialized communication system, and little history with the health care system—people who are old and mentally retarded.

It is better to be proactive than reactive in planning and preparing for the inevitable. In most situations, education helps decrease anxiety about the unknown. It is important that these future patients be exposed to a variety of health care settings so that they will become familiar with various medical and nursing practices. It is never too late to expose people who have mental retardation to books about health care experiences like doctor's appointments and hospitalization. Giving inexpensive—or even pretend—health care instruments to manipulate (stethoscope, syringe, or thermometer) can also be useful. If possible, call the local community hospital to arrange a tour of the facilities, including a patient care unit. This would be extremely helpful prior to a scheduled hospitalization. When feasible, allow clients to accompany parents, siblings, friends, and case workers to health appointments, ensuring that a resource person is available to explain everything in simple, non-threatening terms.

When an acute hospitalization is necessary and no planning has been done, it is of utmost importance that communication from the client's primary caregiver is initiated within the first few hours. Accompanying the client to the emergency room and through all procedures until she is settled in her assigned room will reduce many potential future fears and frustrations, not only for the person with mental retardation but also for the primary caregiver and the health care provider. However, if this is not possible, hourly calls could be made, establishing contact with a specific person (for this, an emergency room nurse would be best) and informing that person of your plan. This initial phase is extremely important since it can determine the nature of the remainder of the hospitalization.

Once the client is settled in his room, make it a priority to familiarize the nursing staff with the special subtleties of his personality. If the hospital utilizes a system of nursing care delivery known as Primary Nursing, find out who will be the client's Primary Nurse. This nurse will be responsible for planning and coordinating the client's care in collaboration with the attending or primary physician. The Primary

Nurse will seek input into the plan of care from the client and his caregivers. In other systems of nursing care delivery, it is best to communicate with the team leader or the head nurse.

In addition to the usual health data, specific information to share with the designated nurse includes: 1) Communication style of the client: How concrete must the staff be when talking to him? What is the best way to explain tests or procedures? How does the client communicate his needs for toileting, relief of pain, and so on? 2) Functional abilities of the client: Does the client bathe himself, feed himself, dress himself, groom himself? Can the client walk? Does the client have bowel or bladder control? What words does the client use to describe bowel movements and urination? 3) Behavioral patterns of the client: How does the client cope with fear, anger, sadness? Are you following any behavioral modification programs? Express any concerns you may have regarding use of restraints (chemical of physical). 4) Legal information: Who is the client's legal guardian? Who will act as spokesperson for the client? All of this information is best delivered verbally, but can be enhanced if a written profile is provided as well.

Throughout the remainder of the hospitalization, daily calls at a pre-arranged time to the designated nurse will further enhance open communication. Other key personnel who may be utilized as resources and supports for the person with mental retardation who is hospitalized are the chaplain, the social worker, and the clinical nurse specialist. In addition, it is important that the client have some sense of continuity with her community environment. Providing the client with a favorite object from home is frequently helpful, as are visits from friends in the community.

Although hospitalization can be traumatic, there are many ways to ease the transition. Through education and communication, the person with mental retardation who is old can have a positive health care experience in the hospital.

35

MENTAL HEALTH PERSPECTIVES

Frank S.G. Wills

■

Psychiatry is usually thought of as a field that attempts to restore lost functions, rather than to preserve existing ones. Most psychiatrists spend a great deal of their time treating existing illness.

However, many of us are strongly concerned to try to keep illnesses from occurring in the first place. This essay will focus on three topics: (1) some common psychiatric problems in people who are old, (2) characteristics of common conditions in people who are mentally retarded and, (3) a piece of psychiatric preventive medicine that can be practiced without a medical license.

Primary prevention, which is the ideal of the field of preventive medicine, is the creation of conditions that will prevent one or more diseases from occurring. Classic examples are sanitation of food and water supplies, pest control, and vaccination programs. Secondary prevention involves early diagnosis and prompt treatment to shorten the duration of illness, reduce its severity, reduce the possibility of contagion, and limit after-effects. Tertiary prevention aims to limit the degree of disability and promote rehabilitation in chronic and irreversible diseases and states. We can include habilitation as an aspect of rehabilitation.

Most people would think that the bulk of work with people who are mentally retarded and old would be tertiary prevention. It is certainly important work, but it need not be and actually is not the *main* work. Most of the work that is being done, which is referred to in other parts of this book, is primary and secondary prevention.

For instance, there are many preventable or treatable conditions that are confused with dementia in people who are old. The most common is the consequence of the side effects of medications the person is taking. Symptoms of physical disease, clinical depression, effects of alcohol, and symptoms of head trauma also can be seen in people who are old and mentally retarded. Good secondary prevention in these cases can prevent the need for tertiary prevention. In other words, good immediate care can often prevent these conditions from dragging on and becoming chronic.

There are opportunities here for primary prevention as well. Keep in mind the possibility of someone getting access to excessive amounts of alcohol and suffering deleterious effects from this. I deliberately say "excessive amounts" because there is no reason why someone who is mentally retarded and old should have to be a total abstainer any more than anyone else; however, there is a big difference between moderation and excessive amounts.

Most psychiatric problems that occur in people with mental retardation of any age are transient, are closely involved with reality issues, and are strongly related to the patient's need to relate and be accepted by someone. The latter deserves special emphasis. Generally, the dynamics of the problems tend to be relatively transparent. In other words, the background of the problem is probably not terribly complicated. It is not necessarily easy to figure out, but once you figure it out, it is usually fairly straightforward. Most patients respond to good secondary prevention and relatively few require the specialized services of a psychiatrist experienced in working with people with mental retardation who are emotionally disabled. Most of those who are severely disturbed are sufficiently obvious that you and your teams will know it and will be able to find appropriate resources for them. Many of the potential candidates for psychiatric problems among people with mental retardation who are old can be helped by good primary prevention techniques.

Maintaining function can be rephrased as preventing the loss of function. The remainder of this essay will address the one way that I feel psychiatry fits most importantly into the role of maintaining function in people who are old and mentally retarded: encouraging and training caregivers to recognize the key importance of relationships in the lives of people who are retarded, people who are old, and therefore people who are old and retarded. This includes social relationships for all, sexual relationships for many, and most important, it includes affectional relationships.

Neither socializing nor sex should ever be underrated for anybody of any age or intellectual level, but I believe that people's needs for affection *are* usually underrated. There is something about our culture and the way we talk about relationships that undervalues pure and simple affection. How often have you heard staff say, "He just does that for attention," whatever "that" may be? Do we ever wonder what is likely to be the real motivation of the behavior? I challenge you to consider that he is doing whatever it is as a way of begging for some affection. Consider also the probability that those who are the most desperate for affection are those who are least appealing, either at that moment in time, or in general.

That would not have to bother us or even concern us if it were not for the fact that we have agreed to be caregivers or supervisors of caregivers to people who are often unappealing. As we know all too well, we get precious little support from society in this effort. This does not mean we have to try to do it all by ourselves. We cannot. It means we have to do all we can and try to mobilize others to help us do it.

One of my early teachers in psychiatry put it very graphically when he said that if we could not go into a back ward and see and smell someone sitting naked on the floor in a pool of his own excrement and feel love for that person, we needed to go back and get more analysis. (That obviously was in the heyday of psychoanalysis, which was then thought to be a panacea by some people.) I would rephrase that and say that if we could not see and smell such a person and feel some compassion and even fondness toward that person, we then need to give extensive thought to why we cannot and what we can do about it. It is easy to jump to the conclusion that no one can instantly feel compassion and even fondness for such a person, and it is easy to excuse ourselves by saying that it is only normal and natural not even to want to try. The fortunate fact of the matter is that there is a large number, maybe not a high percentage, but a large number among caregivers who *do* feel that way, who do feel compassion, fondness, and affection. There could be many more if we would take time and energy to support and groom those who are struggling with their early reactions of revulsion and their tendency to run.

Showing compassion and affection is the kind of thing you have heard or read about so often that it is very easy to take for granted. Taking it for granted is one of the easiest ways not to put it into practice, or to help other people try to put it into practice. I'm sure that even among those with enough interest to read this book, there are some who find this difficult sometimes, as I do. I try to practice what I preach and it does not always come easy. Also there are probably a few of you who feel that you just cannot do it, that it is too much to ask. Most, if not all of us, can do it much of the time. And we can teach others to do it. I am convinced, and it is the reason that I write this, that compassionate, affectionate caregiving is the nearest thing to a key that there is to maintaining a maximum level of functioning in the population we are talking about.

36

THE DOWN SYNDROME ALZHEIMER'S DISEASE CONNECTION

Mary C. Howell

■

Down syndrome is a genetically-determined condition characterized by premature aging. The person with Down syndrome shows typical and usual signs of physical aging, such as greying of hair, loss of efficiency of renal and cardiovascular function, loss of elasticity in a variety of body tissues, and decrements in the acuity of vision and hearing, earlier than are seen in people who do not have Down syndrome. The usual estimate is one to two decades earlier.

Alzheimer's disease is a condition in which some common symptoms of aging in the central nervous system are seen at an earlier age than in most of the population, and in an accelerated and virulent manner. In his original published description, in the first decade of this century, Alzheimer defined the syndrome by the occurrence of certain characteristic markers, called tangles and plaques, found in high concentrations in certain areas of the brain at *post mortem* examination. There are also characteristic behaviors, and a typical clinical course, that we use to make a diagnosis of Alzheimer's disease while the person is still alive.

It has been observed that virtually everyone with Down syndrome, when examined at *post mortem,* shows the concentration and distribution in the brain of tangles and plaques that we consider to be diagnostic of Alzheimer's. Yet only a much smaller proportion of those with Down syndrome ever exhibit the behaviors and the characteristic course of Alzheimer's. Still, the incidence of the typical behavior change called "Alzheimer's disease" is estimated to be about 35 percent in persons with Down syndrome who live to be older than thirty years; this is a much lower frequency than the universally-observed changes in central nervous system structure seen at *post mortem* examination of the brains of people with Down syndrome, but much higher than the estimated 15 percent of the general (non-Down syndrome) population who develop the disease.

The etiology of Alzheimer's disease is not known. The increased incidence of Alzheimer's in people with Down syndrome suggests a genetic predisposition. There are also rare family pedigrees with a notably high incidence of Alzheimer's disease. But there is not enough regularity in the patterns of heritability to lead us to believe that this is the whole story of causation. Probably inheritance establishes a suscep-tibility, and events during life cause or trigger the brain changes. Among the possible causative or triggering events under study are viral infec-tion, loss of efficiency of the immune system, and exposure to various chemical toxins. Of these, the most promising so far is the latter; it seems likely that no single chemical exposure is responsible, and it may be that a broad variety of toxins contribute in an additive manner to the premature degeneration of brain tissue.

The diagnosis of Alzheimer's disease needs to be considered from two perspectives. The original description of the disease established diagnostic criteria that can only be evaluated after death. (Even then, there is not a direct one-to-one correspondence between the distribu-tion and number of plaques and tangles in the brain, and the behavior changes seen during life.) The second diagnostic perspective is the characteristic and typical course of this progressively degenerative disease.

The course of Alzheimer's disease has been better studied in people with normal chromosomes than in people with Down syn-drome, but in general the development of behavior changes in the two groups is parallel. What skills and abilities are lost will depend on the subject's earlier level of function. For instance, increasing forgetfullness in speech is a fairly early symptom that is more obvious in someone whose language skills were very good, compared with someone who had never developed a large vocabulary and an ability to express complex, abstract concepts. In some people with Down syndrome whose cognitive function was always relatively low, the first-noticed symptom of Alzheimer's disease is a change in gait, with unsteadiness, following and holding onto walls, and frequent falling. A description of the typical progression of Alzheimer's symptoms, therefore, must be adjusted according to the prior functional capabilities of the individual client.

The most common early symptoms are related to rapid decrements of short-term memory. Short-term memory regularly and predictably falls off with increasing age, but with Alzheimer's the losses are marked and sudden. Inability to learn names of new acquaintances, loss of favorite and important items of personal use (such as keys or billfold), and stopping in mid-action, unable to remember what project had been started, are commonly observed. Increasing poverty of language, with difficulty finding words to complete an idea or sentence, is also an early symptom. Confusion in the midst of familiar tasks (emptying the dishwasher, making lunch, doing personal laundry) is often a first complaint from caregivers of a person with Down syndrome who is developing Alzheimer's disease. These early changes, which are part of the first stage of the disease, ordinarily develop over a period as short as six months or as long as six years.

The second stage of Alzheimer's disease is marked by more alarming changes. Pacing is common; wandering away from residence or workshop (with or without a specific destination in mind) is worrisome, especially if the person becomes repeatedly lost. There is usually some confusion about the names of familiar people, although the ability visually to distinguish strangers remains for a longer time. Urinary incontinence becomes frequent and fecal incontinence follows. A regular toileting schedule is helpful for a while, then a need for diapers is usual. The same repetitive remarks are made over and over, and the same conversations will be initiated. ("What time is it?" "When is lunch?")

As short-term memory is less and less functional, the ability to learn also is lost; one cannot learn if memory will not sustain the new material. Episodes of hitting or other physical assault can appear in this second stage when the person is confused and overwhelmed by too much stimulation or too high expectations. Simplification of the environment and of expected performance becomes essential to prevent these dangerous "catastrophic reactions."

Abilities to perform activities of self-care—toileting, dressing, bathing, feeding—are lost gradually. There may be episodes of choking on food; early in the second stage choking is usually related to an increased appetite and stuffing food into the mouth (and chewing inefficiently); later the choking is related more to dysfunctions of swallowing, throat clearing, and coughing. An additional common symptom of the second stage is wakefulness at night. Usually the person will go to bed at an ordinary hour and fall asleep without difficulty, only to waken around midnight and not be able to go back to sleep; often the person will arise, dress, and attempt to leave for work or the day program.

This second phase again can go by rather fast—over as short a period as six months—or can be drawn out over six years or so. Caregiving becomes increasingly difficult as there must be enough staff to keep the person from wandering away, from stealing other people's food, from choking, and from being dangerously careless in the night. Extra staff will also be needed for dressing, bathing, toileting, feeding, and for assistance with walking.

The third stage of the disease is marked by loss of the ability to walk; the person becomes chair- and bed-bound. Commonly in the person with Down syndrome (more often than in people with Alzheimer's disease who do not have Down syndrome), episodes of choking will increase and there will be repeated bouts of aspiration pneumonia. In most cases a permanent feeding gastronomy will need to be placed (a hole cut directly into the stomach, through the skin, for tube feedings), as the patient's eating difficulties come at a time when he is still capable of significant social exchange. Eating usually continues to be a pleasure and small amounts of favorite foods (such as ice cream) can still be fed, slowly and cautiously, by mouth: the major nutritional needs are met by tube feedings. As the patient becomes more and more immobile, nursing and direct care needs increase markedly; the patient must be turned and limbs must be moved passively through their ranges of motion, skin care must be meticulous to prevent breakdowns that are difficult to heal, and regular regimens for the bowels must be established and frequently adjusted. A mild seizure disorder, with fairly frequent, brief, limb-jerking seizures, commonly develops during this stage; it is rarely well-controlled by anticonvulsant medication. Urinary and respiratory tract infections are the most common intercurrent illnesses; people afflicted with Alzheimer's disease seem relatively immune to cardiovascular disease and cancer. With good nursing care and no life-threatening accidents (such as wandering into traffic, or getting lost in cold weather with insufficient warm clothing), the third stage of Alzheimer's disease can last for ten or twenty years. Alzheimer's disease, in and of itself, is not life-threatening.

While the diagnosis of Alzheimer's disease during life is best made by observation of this predictable course of behavior changes, there are certain remediable conditions that can mimic Alzheimer's and must be assessed early in the course of the process. They include:

- Drug interactions or toxicity, common for a person who has been taking many medications for a long time.

- Depression (see Chapter 37).

- Metabolic abnormalities (ascertained by blood tests)—deficiencies of Vitamin B-12 or folate, or too much or too little circulating thyroid hormone.

Chronic alcohol intoxication, and small strokes, can also result in behavior that is very like that seen in Alzheimer's disease.

There is no treatment for Alzheimer's disease at this time. Psychoactive drugs are rarely needed to manage hyperaggressive hitting or kicking. Antidepressant medication will sometimes relieve a concomitant depression (see Chapter 37). No drug treatment has been found that will reliably reverse, or even significantly slow, the course of this debilitating disease.

The major route of treatment is environmental. Simplifying, reducing choice and confusion, avoiding over-stimulation, and remembering always the defect of short-term memory, will ease stress and tension. Creating structure and predictable sameness may even slow the progression of the disease; it is probably more accurate to note that confusion and sudden change are often followed by acceleration of symptoms.

Suggest one activity at a time. Don't startle the client. Address her from the front, remind her of your name, and move slowly. Reinforce familiar markers of time and place: whether it's morning, afternoon or evening, summer or winter, breakfast time or teatime, remind her to notice. Say when you are in the kitchen or the living room or the bedroom, and where you are going to be next. Announce that it's time to eat, or to put on a sweater, or to go out-of-doors. Your conversation will become a running commentary on present reality, which is just where the person with Alzheimer's disease lives. Your comments are comforting for her, orienting, and help her to cooperate with you.

Staff who give care to people with Alzheimer's disease share with the families of these clients the sorrow of watching them lose their grip on their former existence, so slowly that there are almost no landmarks. It's important to remember that the person afflicted with Alzheimer's, who may be much less of an active, engaged person than he used to be, is still socially connected, often witty, affectionate, and appreciative of what is done for him. It's a question of looking at a glass half empty, or a glass half full.

37

DEPRESSION

Mary C. Howell

■

Depression among the old is complicated by the natural experiences of loss that characterize old age in our society. Some losses, such as the deaths of kin and friends, are inevitable and age-related; other losses, such as retirement or institutionalization or loss of social status ("ageism"), are culture-related. Grief and mourning, as normal responses to experiences of loss, are both similar to and different from depression, but episodes of significant depression can be triggered by loss. Major physical illness is also associated with depression in about half of those afflicted.

An episode of depression can be especially debilitating for someone who is old. Maintenance of all functional skills—cognitive, physical, emotional, and spiritual—is essential, as functions that fall into disuse rapidly become irretrievable. Depression threatens maintenance of function when withdrawal of interest and attention, physical ("vegetative") slowing, and feelings of hopelessness combine to remove one from active participation, which is the substrate of functional competence.

The principal differences between people who are old and mentally retarded and their non-retarded peers, with regard to depression, are threefold: (1) because of deficits of cognitive abilities, they may perceive, experience, and interpret life events in different ways; (2) a lifetime of exclusion and stigmatization may result in a persistent and significant level of self-denigration; and (3) both mourning and depression may be expressed idiosyncratically in behavior, and therefore be difficult to recognize and diagnose.

The diagnosis of depression is not especially problematic when the experience follows the usual and expected course: a rapid onset of a few hours to a few days (sometimes but not always with triggering environmental circumstances), pronounced sadness and darkness of mood, clear-cut vegetative symptoms such as decrease or increase in appetite, sleeping, and sexual activity, and a tendency toward self-blame and self-denigration. At the other diagnostic extreme, there are instances where mood or behavior, or both, change in puzzling ways, without fulfilling the historical and symptomatic criteria for depression. The diagnosis may be made when the sufferer responds in a dramatic and clear-cut manner to administration of antidepressant medication.

In people with mental retardation who are also old, as in other adults, depression may present with a broad variety of behavior changes; these behavior changes are usually the reason for the referral. In seeking an historical account, specific examples of the patient's recent, observed behavior should be sought. The following information should be requested: the duration of the problem, the course (Did all the symptoms appear simultaneously, or have symptoms developed progressively over a period of time? Has there been improvement since the onset, or are the symptoms now as severe as when they began, or have they gotten worse?), the occurrence of any events that might be interpreted by the client as distressing or stressful, the patient's usual (previous) level of function and any recent changes, current medical problems and all medication dosages, recent changes in vegetative function and behavior (sleep, eating, weight loss or gain, urinary or fecal incontinence, and changes in sexual behavior), and observed changes in the client's experience of pleasure.

Information should be sought from the client, as well. Several brief interviews are more likely to elicit a full array of information than is a single prolonged examination. Brief interviews can be conducted in any setting—the client's residence or workshop, while taking a walk or sharing a cup of coffee. The client may be more comfortable and more revealing in a setting that is familiar to her. The following areas of psychological function should be observed and described: general appearance and behavior, thought processes and language, feeling states, orientation to time and place, and ability to use short-term memory.

Remember that the person with mental retardation often tends to want to please the interviewer, and thus to answer all questions in the affirmative. Consider the likelihood that depression may be revealed more in vegetative symptoms or behavior disturbances than in sadness, guilt, or self-denigration. Be sensitive to limitations of communicative skills that handicap the capacity to interpret, label, and report experiences and emotions. Notice whether there are spillover effects from a depression that further distort both communicative and cognitive performance. Remember that a relatively low level of cognitive, language, and communication skills will impair recognition by the clinician of disorders of *thought processes* to a greater degree than they impair the recognition of disorders of *affect* and *mood.*

The strict diagnostic criteria for a Major Depressive Episode, according to the Diagnostic and Statistical Manual-III, are shown in Table 1. Minor occurrences of depression may be considered to be Adjustment Disorder with Depressed Mood; a reactive component is implied. Reactive episodes of depression, which are preceded or surrounded by trigger events or significant stress, are contrasted with endogenous episodes, which occur with no discernible precipitants. The characteristics of Melancholia (mood variation that is worse in the morning and improves as the day goes on, early morning awakening, severe guilt, and weight loss) are correlated with a satisfactory response to antidepressant medication. The diagnostic category of Bipolar Disorder or Manic-Depressive Disease, with alternating periods of depression and hypomania (both states reaching major proportions), as a recurrent, lifelong, significantly disabling, and often inherited disorder, should also be kept in mind. Bipolar Disorder responds specifically to treatment with lithium salts.

The process of mourning, when uncomplicated and not protracted, is considered to be a normal experience and not a mental disorder, although it is included in DSM-III among conditions not attributable to a mental disorder that are a focus of attention or treatment. Ordinarily it is expected that mourning after a major loss will be an active process for a period of about two years, but that the individual will not become incapacitated in everyday activities and relationships; if incapacitation should occur, a diagnosis of reactive depression would be appropriate.

The fact that depression manifests in so many different forms suggests that the disease entity arises from many different causes. Indeed, incapacitating and enduring feelings of sadness may arise from stressful experiences that are beyond the individual's coping capacity, from profound loss, from innate or early-learned personality tendencies, or from what appear to be physiologic or "chemical" predispositions. In addition, many manufactured chemical medications cause or exacerbate states of depression.

Table 1
From DSM III

1. poor appetite or significant weight loss (when not dieting) or increased appetite or significant weight gain (in children under six, consider failure to make expected weight gains)
2. insomnia or hypersomnia
3. psychomotor agitation or retardation (but not merely subjective feelings of restlessness or being slowed down) (in children under six, hypoactivity)
4. loss of interest or pleasure in usual activities, or decrease in sexual drive not limited to a period when delusional or hallucinating (in children under six, signs of apathy)
5. loss of energy; fatigue
6. feelings of worthlessness, self-reproach, or excessive or inappropriate guilt (either may be delusional)
7. complaints or evidence of diminished ability to think or concentrate, such as slowed thinking, or indecisiveness not associated with marked loosening of associations or incoherence
8. recurrent thoughts of death, suicidal ideation, wishes to be dead or suicide attempt

C. Neither of the following dominate the clinical picture when an affective syndrome (i.e., criteria A and B above) is not present, that is, before it developed or after it has remitted:
1. preoccupation with a mood-incongruent delusion or hallucination (see definition below)
2. bizarre behavior
D. Not superimposed on either Schizophrenia, Schizophreniform Disorder, or a Paranoid Disorder.

As the categories of depression seen in people who are mentally retarded and old are not significantly different from the categories of depression seen in other clients, so treatment possibilities also parallel the gamut of treatments ordinarily recommended for these problems. These treatments are situational adjustment, drugs, and psychotherapy.

Bettering one's immediate personal situation is often much more difficult for the person with mental retardation to do without assistance, compared to a like person without mental retardation. Common situational triggers for depression are losses (of people, status, position, or opportunities) and esteem-diminishing circumstances (failures or disappointments at work, in one's residence, or in one's relationships with kin or friends). It is important to acknowledge with the client that these circumstances exist and are painful, and to assert that efforts will be made to change or adjust the discouraging situation for the better. In actual fact, however, losses and esteem diminishing circumstances are often intransigent. For the person with mental retardation, the personal intransigence of individuals in his world may be layered onto the bureaucratic intransigence so common in the administration of public entitlement programs.

Maneuvers that should be considered include exploring the possibility of a change in workshop or residence placement; restoring lost opportunities for recreational or leisure enjoyments; and creating bridges for communication with people who have "gone away" (moved, taken other jobs, made other friends). Relations with kin may have decayed slowly over many decades, but their absence can seem freshly painful to the person with mental retardation who is growing old. Sometimes an encouraging communication from a therapist or caregiver will remind family members that, as they, too, are growing old, time for reconciliation is finite. Although family members may react with guilt and irritation or passive disinterest at first, we have seen genuine reunions accomplished, sometimes after decades of distance.

Psychoactive drug treatment, which we are ordinarily inclined to use only after all "less restrictive" avenues of treatment are explored, should be considered early when there is a question of depression in a person who is both old and mentally retarded. A therapeutic drug trial can be used as a diagnostic maneuver. Although the antidepressant medications are not without possible undesired side-effects, they are on balance relatively safe drugs when used with prudence and caution.

There are many possible drug choices. For example, amitriptyline (Elavil) and imipramine (Tofranil) are essentially interchangeable for most patients. At dosages beginning at 10 milligrams three times a day and progressing by 10-milligram increases every five days (increasing preferentially the last dose of the day), to a maximum of 30 milligrams three times a day, side effects are few and rare; excessive drowsiness and increased appetite are the most common. For patients in whom there is a question of a dementing process, the preferred antidepressant drug is trazodone (Deseryl), which has the least tendency to worsen the symptoms of dementia; the initial dosage is 50 milligrams twice a day (after eating), with increases of 50 milligrams every five days to a maximum of 200 milligrams a day.

Lithium is the drug of choice for a person with manic depressive (bipolar) disorder. Unlike the antidepressant medications, this drug has many possible side effects, including suppression of thyroid function and compromise of renal function. Occasionally lithium is given in conjunction with an antidepressant medication. A daily dose of 900 milligrams is usually appropriate, but serum levels and other functional blood values must be followed.

A full six weeks should be allowed for a drug trial, unless the occurrence of significant side effects forces discontinuance of the drug. Often there will be no definitive response until the client has taken the maximum dosage for three weeks. Assessing blood drug levels is essential when lithium is given, but less informative for the other antidepressants.

Because of the undesired side effects that are always possible with drug treatment, it is essential to make a systematic approach to evaluation of the effectiveness of the medication. A baseline account of observed relevant behaviors, reassessed in three weeks and again when the maximum dosage has been given for three weeks, allows a relatively objective estimate of the effectiveness of the medication. After an appropriate interval there should be a trial off the drug. That interval will verify if it appears that the drug has no effect, the trial off the drug (with observation and recording of relevant behaviors) will occur at the end of an eight-week period of treatment. If the drug appears to have relieved the symptoms, a trial off the drug should be postponed for at least three months but no longer than six months. While in most cases of successful drug treatment there will be no rebound when the drug is discontinued, occasionally the initially disturbing symptoms will recur. Even more likely, once a client has been successfully treated with an antidepressant medication for symptoms that appear to be those of depression, there can be recurrence of similar symptoms and repeated successful treatments with the same medication. Most who suffer from manic-depressive disorder are severely disturbed by the symptoms of their disease unless they take lithium steadily; appropriate intervalic measurements of blood, serum, and urine must be made to monitor the possibility of significant physiologic side effects.

The remedy of verbal psychotherapy requires that the client have an ability to speak in mutually responsive conversation, and this is usually limited to clients who have only mild or moderate retardation. In actual fact this remedy is far more significantly limited by the failure of helping professionals to recommend and try it with clients who are mentally retarded.

Even among those who are not mentally retarded, psychotherapy is often overlooked for people who are old, on the assumption that "old" means rigid and unchanging, and that there are few options for life change in old age. In fact, however, one of life's greatest changes, death, looms with more and more presence for those who are old. The very concept of "old," which is much disdained in our society, forces those of advanced age to deny their oldness. This denial generates powerful feelings of rejection, lack of worth, and hopelessness. And for people with mental retardation these feelings are layered onto a lifetime of social ostracism, non-attainment of many of the usual and strongly-desired milestones of adulthood (independence, self-support, marriage, parenthood, and so on), and social instruction about personal inadequacies. For this reason, many or even most clients with mental retardation who are old can benefit from psychotherapy.

Psychotherapy can be given in either an individual or group setting. In either case the therapist will want to be relatively directive, setting the goals for therapy both in the long run and, to a lesser extent, from session to session, and utilizing more of the externally-focused techniques (such as modeling, role-playing, therapist self-disclosure, and psycho-drama) and less of internally-focused maneuvers (such as silence and reserved therapist privacy).

The experience of depression, for a person with mental retardation who is old, cannot but be fueled by a lifetime of social exclusion, lost opportunities, and impoverished self-esteem. Even a depressive episode that appears to be strictly "chemical" and quickly responsive to treatment with antidepressive medication should be considered as an opportunity for a beneficial experience of psychotherapy. The goals would include the attainment of some understanding of what triggered and underlay the depression, and how these life experiences that predispose to depression might be coped with in the future.

LIVING IN COMMUNITY

38

COMMUNITY HOUSING

Henry A. Beyer

■

■ Legal Issues

A right that practically all Americans will support, at least in the abstract, is that, economic factors permitting, citizens should live wherever they choose. Yet considerable advocacy efforts have been required over the past two decades to ensure the recognition of that right for citizens with mental retardation, particularly those who are attempting to move from large institutions to community arrangements.

The major legal impediment to the establishment of community residences has been exclusionary zoning.[1] In a typical case, a city or town board refuses permission to locate a residence in a preferred location because it would violate the "single family" zoning ordinance applicable to that neighborhood. In the great majority of cases in which such bans have been subject to judicial challenge, however, courts have ruled in favor of those establishing the home.[2]

Some courts have reasoned that the home's prospective residents, even though not related by blood or marriage, should be considered a "family" for purposes of interpreting the ordinance, since they will share kitchen and dining facilities as a single housekeeping unit.[3] Other courts have ruled that a state policy of deinstitutionalization and communitization overrode local exclusionary ordinances[4] or restrictive covenants.[5] Yet others have held that community residences constitute "public educational" facilities, and are therefore exempt from local zoning ordinances under the laws of some states.[6] In this last set of cases, the judges recognized that "education" is a broad, comprehensive term for developing and training all capabilities of human beings and thus encompasses such instruction in activities of daily living as meal preparation, personal hygiene and grooming, travel, budgeting and banking, and care and cleaning of the home.[7]

On the other hand, courts have generally upheld restrictions that regulate the density of group homes in a geographic area or the number of residents per home, or rules that impose "reasonable dimensional controls," including the mandating of sufficient on-site parking spaces for staff and visitors.[8]

The only time the U.S. Supreme Court directly considered this issue was in 1985, in a case involving a Cleburne, Texas zoning ordinance. The court's opinion in Cleburne was a mixed blessing for people with mental retardation.[9] On the positive side, the Court struck down the Cleburne ordinance as unconstitutional. It violated the Equal Protection Clause by requiring a special permit for the establishment of a group home for thirteen adults with mental retardation, while requiring no such permit for apartment houses, hospitals, sanitariums, convalescent nursing homes, or fraternity or sorority houses. The Court noted that "[m]ere negative attitudes or fears...are not permissible bases for treating a home for the mentally retarded differently"[10] from those other uses, and concluded that the city's requirement "appear[ed] to rest on an irrational prejudice against the mentally retarded."[11]

However, the Court refused to grant people with mental retardation the status of a "suspect" or "quasi-suspect" class, a class entitled to the higher level of constitutional protection that courts afford to racial and other minority groups that have historically been subjected to discrimination. Also, the Court mentioned, but failed to delineate, the "wide range of decisions" in which governments may legitimately take into account the "characteristic" of mental retardation.[12] In the long run, therefore, the decision may prove to be of limited (or even negative) value to individuals with mental retardation in arguing zoning or other issues.

■ Some Housing Alternatives

In this section, we shall discuss a few of the possible options available when seeking an appropriate residential placement for a family member or client with mental retardation.

Publicly Provided Residences

In all states, the responsible state agency (Department of Mental Retardation, Office of Developmental Disabilities, or similar service agency) probably controls the largest number and widest range of residential resources. They are usually ranked in order of the types and amounts of services provided. An "Intermediate Care Facility for the Mentally Retarded" (ICF/MR), which was established under the federal Social Security program and enjoys both a high staff-client ratio and ready access to a range of medical services, is often the type of facility most appropriate for a client who has substantial health care needs.[13] Admission to an ICF requires that the client be eligible for Medicaid. The "Type A" ICF/MR is typically designed to house eight individuals who are not capable of climbing stairs and are not capable of "self-preservation" (i.e., evacuating the facility rapidly in case of fire). A "Type B" facility may house from eight to fifteen clients who are capable of self-preservation, and only the first floor needs to be accessible to wheelchairs.

Other types of living arrangements that may be operated or funded by the state service-providing agency include:

• group residences, which typically house six to twelve residents capable of self-preservation and have staff-client ratios of about 1 to 8;

• limited group residences, which house clients who are not capable of self-preservation and have both higher staff-client ratios and fire sprinkler systems;

• staffed apartments, which house one to four clients and have a staff presence ranging from continuous to a few hours per day;

• independent living apartments, which have staff visiting only weekly or at some other periodic interval.

Other living arrangements include home care in a foster home or with the client's biological family, with the state service agency providing training, respite, and possibly other support services. The most appropriate placements for individual clients are those that satisfy their particular needs and safeguard their welfare, while imposing the fewest restrictions and providing the greatest opportunities for the exercise of individual autonomy and for personal growth and development.

It is a truism that there are never enough appropriate residential living arrangements for all who need them. Waiting lists are ubiquitous and lengthy. Nevertheless, vacancies do periodically occur as new facilities are established and as clients leave current placements either by moving to other programs or through death. It is, therefore, essential that clients and their advocates apply for residential services as early as possible, with the advocates monitoring as closely as possible the clients' progress through the system of processing and waiting lists. A caring, informed, assertive advocate, who documents a client's residential needs and brings them repeatedly to the attention of the key decisionmaker(s), is probably the greatest aid a client can have for obtaining an appropriate placement in a reasonable length of time. When in doubt as to the proper balance to strike between (1) irritating the state agency through repetitive communications and (2) refraining from frequent contacts so as not to try the decisionmaker's patience, we recommend that an advocate err on the side of being a polite, but persistent, pest.

Apart from the state service-provision system, certain private residential possibilities may be well-suited to the needs and situations of certain clients. Of the wide variety of alternatives that exist across the country, only three will be described here. Some inquiries to your state's public service-providing agency and Association for Retarded Citizens may help determine whether similar projects, or even more imaginative privately-sponsored alternatives, exist in your state.

Client-Owned Condos

Several thriving client-owned condominiums have been organized in Massachusetts, in a project called Specialized Housing Incorporated, by parents of adults with mental retardation.[14] There is no inherent reason why such projects should not be equally successful elsewhere. Admittedly, condos present a viable housing alternative only if clients or their families have the financial resources required for the purchase of the condominium building. After the initial start-up, however, because one's "principal residence" is not counted as an asset by the Social Security Administration in determining one's eligibility for Supplemental Security Income (SSI),[15] individuals with mental retardation may continue to receive SSI while living in their very own condos. Their SSI benefit checks can then help to pay living expenses, real estate taxes, and fees of the condominium association, including salaries for staff members hired by the association to assist residents. Because of the monetary resources required, client-owned condos are not an option open to all clients. But if the funds are available, they should definitely be considered.

L'Arche

In 1964, Jean Vanier, a Canadian priest, established a home in a small French town for people with mental disabilities. This home, which he called L'Arche (The Ark), has served as the model for other L'Arche homes around the world.[16] These are religiously based, non-sectarian communities of people, some of whom have mental disabilities and others of whom do not, who live together as families, sharing work and responsibilities. The L'Arche philosophy is that God communicates through people's hearts more than through their heads. Since all people are equal in their hearts, each person has as much capacity to give as to receive; thus all contribute equally to the community. There are now approximately eighty L'Arche communities in sixteen countries world-wide, including several in the United States with others currently being planned.[17]

The Camphill Communities

The first Camphill Community began in 1937, following the principles of education and group living proposed by Rudolf Steiner, an Austrian philosopher, scientist, and educator. There are now seventy communities in Europe, Africa, South America, and the United States. "Within each center, life is shared by people with and without mental handicaps in an integrated residential community setting."[18] Each community is as self-sufficient as possible. There are three Camphill Villages for adults with mental handicaps in North America.

39

COMMUNITY-BUILDING
IN GROUP HOMES

Bridget Bearss

■

There are four stages that the people who live in a community residence or an institutional building go through to develop a community that seeks to meet the needs of each individual, as well as to allow growth for both individuals and the community as a whole. In the case of a community residence, it is often the role of the staff and service providers to create a climate in which such development can occur.

The first stage is *pseudo-community*.[1] At that time, all things seem to be going well. Everyone has his "best foot forward" and everyone is completing both the tasks and the personal responsibilities that make for a smoothly running living environment. The members attempt to be an instant community by being extremely pleasant to each other and avoiding all disagreement. This is the honeymoon period; it is often accompanied by a recent transition or a major change that makes the community a new experience.

Gradually, this tranquil community becomes more real, as the members begin to feel more secure and individuals behave more normally. Once individual differences are not only allowed, but encouraged to surface in some way, the group almost immediately moves to the second stage of community: *chaos*. At this stage, instead of trying to confront and cope with differences, the group is attempting to erase them. Ordinarily, there is one staff member, or possibly even a client, who attempts to smooth over the surface and ignore the uncomfortable feeling that exists with conflict. This usually does not help matters, but instead creates more tension. This stage is very difficult, and, in community residences, this is the time when staff members begin crying for help. "Why has everything fallen apart?" In reality, this stage can produce real and meaningful change and growth. We have to remember that fighting and disagreement are far better than pretending that everything is all right. It is infinitely more hopeful than if everyone is afraid to express a feeling. But it is an uncomfortable time and will take some work.

A stage described as *transition* follows the time of chaos. There are two ways to solve the problem of a pseudo-community. One is to move back into the stage where everyone is performing, but few are entirely authentic. The other way is through transition. It is a time to empty oneself of the barriers to communication and assist others in dropping expectations and judgments about how someone else will participate or communicate. The moment at hand should be the focus. As caregivers, it is the moment when we help clients to learn to listen to one another; we also really begin to listen to clients themselves. It is the time to recognize unconscious prejudice. We are forced to look at why we cannot deal with this client or that staff member. It implies knowing why we do what we do, and most importantly, it is the moment when we can make a critical choice. Either we continue to think that we can solve or fix all the problems within the community, or we choose not to solve but to embrace, listen to, and become immersed in the lives of people as they are, not as we would like them to be. At this stage, we notice clients beginning to let defenses down and let others in. Clients may not have experienced this before, and therefore, they are liable to make mistakes. They may become overly attached to one person, let someone dominate, or be vulnerable at the wrong moment.

Building a community of strength and honesty does not imply that a residence becomes a 24-hour-a-day therapy session. It implies honesty: with caregivers, with clients, and with ourselves. This is the moment when clients choose the people with whom they will become intimate, even if it is a subconscious choice. We must all realize the responsibilities of being both a person chosen and a member of the community in which such a choice is happening. Again, it is messy, unpredictable, and without simple solutions.

Slowly and gradually (and sometimes it does not happen), a group of people choose to form a community of communicators. They recognize that they are people who have their own needs and want to, or need to, live together. A community that has reached this stage is more a feeling than a set of words. It begins with a feeling that all are "at home in this place" and is characterized by an environment in which people are free to make mistakes and know they will be loved anyway. It is a place where people are able to argue and to reconcile. Each person is valued, and there is a sense that everyone is both listened to and encouraged to speak. Manipulation is kept at a minimum and potentials are put at a maximum.

It sounds like a wonderful place, doesn't it? It sounds like the kind of place we would all like to see our favorite clients involved in, but it is not that easy. Any community takes energy, commitment, and the courage to sustain on days when the vision of what is ahead gets clouded by the challenges of what now exists. I have seen it work, in a few cases. And yet I hold the ideal as one we can all continue to work toward. When it does work, people flourish, tap into new skills, and abound in growth.

I believe that building community is a matter of justice. I wonder how we hope to create world peace if we cannot also choose to become builders of peace in this present moment. I have chosen to engage in the building of community by my lifestyle. I have learned about living in community by assisting clients in learning about living in community. For those of us involved in the social services, understanding community-building can be a very useful tool in helping clients choose to be people who are open and intimate, and who engage in relationships and take the risk of choosing to become alive.

40

WORK AND RETIREMENT

Elizabeth J. DeBrine and Mary C. Howell

In our culture, the ability and opportunity to work for pay is very important to one's self-esteem. This importance of work is no less salient for citizens who are mentally retarded. In fact, because the citizen with mental retardation views the world rather directly and without sophisticated and abstract elaboration, it is likely that for him the value

---

of work is concrete, direct, and very powerful.

This is indeed what our clients tell us. They value work because it makes them feel productive and important, because "it's what everyone does." They value work because it provides social contacts and a respectable occupation five days a week. They value work because the money earned allows them a degree of independence, choice, and pleasure.

Giving up work—retiring—is regarded by many clients with some puzzlement. On the one hand, retirement (like work itself) is seen as something that everyone does. On the other hand, work is so highly valued that the idea of giving it up can be worrisome, threatening, even frightening.

In addition, our culture views retirement with ambivalence, an ambivalence that citizens who are mentally retarded cannot help but share. Retirement, as respite from the onerous responsibilities of work, is regarded as an earned privilege. At the same time many of us intuit that work—almost any work, except the most degrading—offers values that *cannot* be found in any other program of activities. Further, we see retirement as a symbolic kind of "end of the road," a marker that foretells senility and death.

Our own reluctance to rejoice in turning away from work should spur us to evolve new arrangements that allow aging workers to stay on the job as long as they want to. Until such changes in our employment arrangements have been devised and put into place, we should be very cautious about assuming that forced universal retirement at a predetermined age is a good plan for citizens who are mentally retarded. A brief history of retirement can serve to remind us why forced universal retirement is less than felicitous for society as a whole.

Carole Haber, in *Beyond Sixty-Five,* traces society's treatment of elderly citizens in America from colonial times to the twentieth century. Her discussion of early public policy in America helps us to understand how and why industries embraced retirement as a cure for business ills in the late 1800s.

In colonial America, most people died before the age of forty. The median age was not far from sixteen. In fact, only 5 percent of the population lived beyond sixty [1]. In colonial New England, religious and civic leaders lectured on the glories of reaching old age. Old age was seen as an expression of God's benevolent order and not just the last segment of the life cycle.

In colonial times, people could retain their family and work roles until death. Women married in their early twenties and bore children for the next twenty years; the last child would not leave home until the parents were in their sixties. Thus, aging parents could be both grandparents and parents of young children at the same time. This blurred the distinctions between the generations and the stages of life. Fathers were responsible for the financial needs of a family regardless of their age or state of health. Parents were responsible for their children's care until they left home.

Old people who were poor were considered to be part of God's plan in colonial America. "The poor will always be with you." They were part of a group that was destined to be dependent on others for charity; other groups included people with handicaps, sickness, or insanity. There was no need to single out those who were poor and old as being a special group, or to question the legitimacy of their need for care.

All of this changed in the 1800s By their sheer increase in numbers, old people came to be categorized as a serious and growing welfare problem. This was based on two factors: first, the changing social and economic conditions faced by a large number of adults through the increased urban and industrial growth resulted in decreased control over family, wealth, and possessions; second, people who were old were perceived as needing special consideration by newly professionalized charity workers and social scientists.[2]

The philosophy and methodology of research performed on the aging process in the new industrial society led professionals to believe that people who were old were not able to change, and were different from the rest of the socially dependent population. In 1864, twenty-six percent of the population in Massachusetts' poorhouses were old; in 1904, it was forty-eight percent.[3] This change was largely caused by the discharge of individuals with handicaps to separate institutions for people who were deaf, blind, or feeble-minded.

The aged were now segregated into a separate class of needy persons who required total assistance by society. The medical profession also supported the philosophy that people who were old needed special care. In fact, the medical field predicted that eventually all people who were old would need constant medical care.

It was believed at the turn of the century that an individual was born with a certain amount of energy that was not renewable. The energy was decreased by working in factories, in transportation, and in the fields. The worker who was old was defined by the medical field as one who had used up a "considerable amount of his alloted nervous force."[4]

In *A History of Retirement,* William Graebner investigates the economic, political, and social pressures behind retirement. In the nineteenth century, most businesses were too small to support mandatory retirement. The close personal relationship between employer and employee made it difficult for most employers to fire workers who were old. Most of the time, special jobs or areas were set aside for these workers, and many kept their jobs until they died.

The growth of our capitalistic economy changed many small cottage industries into large bureaucracies. Industry developed into large corporations with hundreds or thousands of laborers; separated from their homes, they spent their days in factories and office buildings. Mandatory retirement was feasible in these settings. Retirement made it possible to transfer work from one generation to another when there was a large labor supply.

In the late 1880s, agitation for a shorter work week led directly to age discrimination. This caused high unemployment of workers who were old and eventually led to retirement pensions. At that time a typical work day was ten hours long and people worked six days a week.

The shorter work day was supported by labor because it would mean more time for recreation, leisure, and education. However, an underlying reason was the fear of widespread, technology-induced unemployment. The shorter day was a work-sharing program that was supported by many.

The large number of unemployed older workers and industry's drive for efficiency led large corporations to offer pensions in the 1880s.[5] The pension was used as a tool to control the younger employees (who could strike or leave for better pay) while laying off the more costly older worker.

Pensions were administered by the company. Workers were unable to control the monies or make direct payment to the funds. Thus, the pension became a gift, rather than a right. Workers had to follow regulations closely in order to qualify for their pensions. The worker's widow also was rated on her conduct and could be denied her deceased husband's pension based on her behavior.

One of the benefits of retirement for labor was the seniority system. Management began to base employment practices on years of service, thereby ridding the system of favoritism and nepotism. Labor exercised control over hiring, firing, and promotions. Management, on the other hand, gained further stability in the work force. Management was able to limit the drawback of high pay for workers who had worked a long time through a mandatory retirement age.

Laborers were automatically pensioned at age sixty-five or seventy. This system was strongly supported by the new drive for efficiency in the new industrial era. All workers who were old were seen as weak and inefficient. "These employees," efficiency experts cautioned, "were just as much a threat to high production as the totally disabled."[6] Once industry established that senescence began at age sixty or sixty-five, charity organizations adopted a similar system of classification. Many groups found it more efficient to set criteria based on age rather that to deal with people on an individual basis. Mandatory retirement created a separate class of citizens over the age of 65. The policies were designed to help the poor and sick, but instead they ensured the dependence of a large population of adults who are old.

Although retirement is now often considered to be a normal process of the life cycle, we need to re-evaluate our assumptions about retirement as a process, program, and policy for people who are old and mentally retarded. Retirement forces the retiree to take on an "oldness" role. This role encourages dependence on others in all aspects of daily life because the adult who is old is often seen as being nonproductive, incompetent, and expendable. The great majority of people who are both old and mentally retarded have never been allowed to become adults. They have moved from adolescence to old age, missing opportunities for competitive employment, stable relationships with unpaid friends, marriage and parenthood, and other signal experiences of adulthood.

Most people who are mentally retarded and old have never held competitive jobs. Retirement as a policy usually removes them from low-paying, highly repetitive, structured work, and places them in non-paying, age-segregated, activity-centered day programs. The result of these programs is even more isolation from the community than was previously experienced. Most people who are mentally retarded and old do not have financial resources to fund a successful retirement, as some who are not retarded are able to do, because they have neither savings nor pensions. They are often unable to pay for travel, to support hobbies like woodworking, collecting, or restaurant exploring, or to join clubs in the community.

Stanley lived at home with his family until he was 17. As a boy he had done odd jobs in the neighborhood to earn pocket money, and he was proud of his reputation as a good and trustworthy worker. At the age of 17 he was admitted to a state residential school. He was considered to be moderately mentally retarded.

After 44 years of institutionalization in the state residence Stanley moved to a group home, where he has now lived for six years. During those six years his daytime occupation has been at a sheltered workshop, where he has done assembly benchwork.

Each time Stanley came to our Geriatric Clinic he would look around and ask if we couldn't get him a job at "this place." He told us that he was a good worker, that he could sweep and mop and wash windows. He told us that his work was "boring." His case manager said that Stanley was restless, that it was difficult for him to sit still at work for so many hours.

Several months ago an opportunity for competitive employment became available for Stanley, after nearly two years on a waiting list. With supportive guidance, Stanley has taken a position as Assistant Janitor in a large commercial building. He sweeps and mops floors, washes windows, empties trash, and performs a variety of other similar tasks. He takes direction well and is extraordinarily proud of his new work, which he finds quite suitable to his abilities and aspirations. At 67, Stanley has "come home" to work that seems right to him.

In a survey conducted by Elizabeth DeBrine of the Kennedy Aging Project on 23 April 1987, eighteen adults were asked what retirement meant to them. Those questioned were from two group homes and a group residence at a state institution. Here are some of their responses:

1. *What is retirement?* We're not retired yet! I don't want to be retired! Sit in a rocking chair. Go out and see the world before I go. Relax doing things you want to do.

2. *When do people retire?* When you retire is when you retire. I'm not ready. When I get old. No particular age. Don't want to work anymore. Damn sick of it. When I get to be 65.

3. *Why do people retire from work?* To get a rest. Sick of work. Too old. In my place, they want you to work until you drop. Lose your pay. Sick, take pills.

4. *What do people do with their extra free time after they retire?* Nothing. Go out and sell potholders. Day trips. Go places. Get retire-

ment checks. Railroad trips. Go where they can relax. Work in the house to keep busy. Go home and sit down.

5. *Where do people live after they retire?* Same place. Different place. Old folks' home. Get married and find a home. Special kind of apartment.

6. *Who do you know has retired from work?* Sister. Brother. Two girls from cottage 8. I'm retiring next year. I'm retiring pretty soon. Nobody. My mother, she's 84.

7. *How would you like to retire from work?* Part-time (3 respondents). Full-time (5 respondents). Not at all (7 respondents). Won't get paid. Don't get much now, everything is high.

8. *When would you like to retire?* In two years when I'm 62. In three years when I'm 65. I'd like to retire right now. Pretty soon. Work as long as I can. May 5, 1987. Never. July 5, 1987.

9. *Where would you like to live?* Apartment with other retired people. Stay here. In my own home. Where retirement people are.

10. *What would you like to do in your free time after retirement?* Dancing. Live with my sister in Waltham. Anything is possible. Travel. Help my family, someone has to take over after they are gone.

11. *Describe a typical day after you retire from work.* Beautiful day. Don't know. I could participate at the Activity Center. Go for a walk. Go to town. Feed pigeons. Watch the ducks. Nothing. Smoke a pipe, cigar, watch T.V. Sleep till 9. Have breakfast. Plan my day, not rushing. Have a good day as each day comes along.

■ Recommendations

1) Expect the workplace to accommodate to the worker who is old and whose productivity is falling. Sheltered workshops should not be held to the politics of profit-making businesses. Workers who are mentally retarded have typically given long, faithful hours to boring, repetitive work and have received almost no fringe benefits—paid vacations, retirement funds, choice of health insurance, paid sick leave, and so on. When their capacities for efficient work begin to fail, the workplace should be expected to be forgiving and flexible, so the worker can continue to work, if only on a modified schedule, as long as she wants to.

2) Don't take away a worker's right to work without offering something better as a daytime occupation. For most workers who are mentally retarded, "something better" can be found in a program of true

community integration: consider opportunities like photocopying at the church, setting up tables and chairs for weekly bingo games, handing out towels at the YMCA, gardening in the "community gardens" space, and volunteering at the local re-cycling center.

3) When a worker's productivity appears to be falling, investigate possible causes—consider depression, remediable illness, interpersonal conflict, boredom, or lack of challenge. Don't be too quick to assume that it's time for retirement; wait to see whether the failing capacities for work might not pick up again.

4) Discuss with the worker the values that he finds in work. If it really is time to retire, some of the values of work (a weekly source of pocket money, opportunities to be with friends, a chance to get out of the house during the day, opportunities to be productive) may be replaced in post-retirement activities or arrangements.

5) Keep in mind the possibility that the worker may not have the breadth of vision or personal experience to enable her to imagine what retirement would be like. This may be true even if a specific program is planned and described to her. We have known clients who enthusiastically agreed to retire, only to find after the event that the post-retirement program was boring and work was sorely missed—and then it was too late to reclaim the position at the workplace.

6) Make the transition from work to post-retirement program slowly and deliberately. Allow the client to be part-time in both occupations for a while. Don't close the door on work too soon.

7) Remember that leaving work is always a loss, a cause for mourning. Help the client to recognize, name, and honor the emotions of grief.

8) Don't allow arrangements for forced universal retirement to become institutionalized. Insist that arrangements for each worker be individualized.

41

RETIREMENT PROGRAMS

Linda S. Corman, Thomas V. Barbera, Jr., Stephanie Bowen, Deborah Jennings, and Lucille Sanford

∎

Two programs now functioning at the Fernald State School in Massachusetts will be described in this chapter. The Senior Enrichment Program is a retirement program that provides a variety of life enrichment activities for individuals whose skills are at a prevocational level, people who are sometimes called "severely" retarded. The Health Focus Program is for individuals who now have Alzheimer's disease, who previously functioned at a variety of levels of cognitive competence. The age of clients in these two programs ranges from 53 to 83 with an average age of 68.

Many of the individuals in our two programs have physical limitations. They have visual and hearing difficulties, and other losses of function, that are part of normal aging. Some have heart disease, arthritis, hypertension, pulmonary disease, anemia, Parkinson's disease, osteoporosis, stroke, seizures, or tardive dyskinesia.

Most of the people in these two programs have spent a good part of their lives in institutions. Some of these individuals were not specifically diagnosed with mental retardation when they entered an institution 50, 60, or 70 years ago. Some were clumsy or disruptive, could not hear or see well, and perhaps had emotional problems. Because of the nature of life in institutions, many people did not receive appropriate training.

Our rationale in dealing with the needs of people with mental retardation who are old begins by recognizing that our first and foremost responsibility is to develop a normalized setting. Many in our programs have had limitations of choice due to their history in the institution. We recognize that the most important skill for many of these individuals is to develop an ability to make choices. Choice can be as simple as a decision to use red paint instead of blue paint to make a picture. Choice could also be more complex, for instance, choosing the type of music one would like to have at one's own funeral.

We want a program that meets the specific physical needs of our clients, in recognition of their frailties. Further, clients need to have access to information about the specific types of physical changes that they are experiencing.

We recognize that these clients are not very different from others in the same age range. They have the same categories of needs as the general population of people who are old: leisure needs, physical activity needs, needs for social and emotional support, and needs for intellectual stimulation.

The Senior Enrichment Program was developed to provide a variety of life-enriching activities and experiences for clients who are mentally retarded and old. The program offers to prevocational clients at the "basic skills" level a socialization and leisure base, working towards the maintenance of function. The program was started because workshops and day programs at Fernald were not able to meet the changing social, cognitive, motoric, and emotional needs of clients at this functional level who were growing old.

The Senior Enrichment Program offers group social interactions and community outings. Goals developed for the program include: (1) provision of satisfying ways of occupying increased leisure time, (2) fostering friendships, (3) provision of opportunities to achieve recognition as an individual, (4) promotion of opportunities for self-satisfaction and a sense of achievement, (5) promotion of good health through nutrition and physical activity, and (6) provision of experiences for suitable mental stimulation.[1] Individual client goals are developed through the client's interdisciplinary team. There are quarterly reviews of clients' progress, maintenance, or changing needs, and of the program itself to ensure that program activities are flexible and will not stagnate.

The skill deficits exhibited by clients in the program include limited attention span, decreased tolerance for structured activities, and limited abilities in peer/staff interactions. Historically, these clients did not do well in full-time or part-time structured workshops or day programs.

Due to the nature of the Senior Enrichment Program and its shortened hours, routine structure, and small group settings, clients began to ask and look for certain familiar and preferred activities, especially cooking. Over time, clients also began initiating small gestures of peer interaction. They exhibited an increased tolerance for structured activities, and an increase in peer socialization. Furthermore, many began to experience a sense of accomplishment, as evidenced by their showing their completed art work to peers, staff, and family.

The program runs five days a week for three hours each day, two hours in the morning and one hour in the afternoon. This allows extended time for activities of daily living, such as meals. The schedule also allows for afternoon naps and individually pursued leisure activities; one client watches her favorite TV show ("General Hospital") every day at 3 p.m. The sessions start out with a greeting, followed by reality orientation, a main activity, shared prepared snack, and a closing. The morning and afternoon programs follow the same routine; only the main activity changes daily.

The Senior Enrichment Program is interdisciplinary, with staff bringing their interests, expertise, and backgrounds to the activity sessions. The staff involved include professionals from the fields of Adult Education, Occupational Therapy, Physical Therapy, Speech Therapy, Music and Recreational Therapy, and Psychology. There is a core person and a direct-care staff person assigned to the group, plus one of the aforementioned professional staff. This rotation of staff has allowed many different professionals to become involved in geriatric programming; the time commitment for each professional staff person is approximately two hours a week.

As we grow older, the pace, quantity, frequency, and variety of our activities change. However, activity at some level remains important in our lives. Pace of the Senior Enrichment Program is based on the tempo at which particular clients complete an activity or task. Frequency is based upon the clients' own choice. Quantity is based upon the clients' interests and physical stamina. And variety is determined by clients' choice and experience and on staff creativity.

Another part of the Senior Enrichment Program provides clients with the opportunity to conduct a personal life review. Most people, as they grow older, would like to spend some time recalling and evaluating the major events, accomplishments, and disappointments of their lives. This can be difficult for our clients, due to their limited cognitive abilities and their years in a structured institutional setting. However, some clients, with help, are able to remember parts of their past, and to talk about some of their joys and sorrows. Staff assist clients by looking at archival records, reviewing their early experiences prior to admission, and talking to staff who have known individual clients for as long as 25 years. From this review, program staff learned that one client speaks and understands a little Yiddish, another Greek; one talks about living in Boston's South End and remembers going to Revere Beach. One client can tell you she's lived in one particular building for twenty years and before that in another building for ten years.

These past and present experiences, part of the clients' histories, are used by staff to develop and personalize clients' individual programs. The program attempts to put clients in touch with their pasts through activities such as the celebration of ethnic days, complete with authentic food, music, and dance. The program also includes daily discussion of who is in the group (staff and peers); who is missing and why; the day, the time, the place; and what will be taking place in the program today. When clients travel from one building to another on the way to the program, there is a van orientation that includes a discussion of where they live, where they're going, who they're picking up next, what buildings they're passing on the way, and what takes place in these buildings. There are expressive arts and cooking activities to maintain fine motor, gross motor, and receptive and expressive language skills, and to provide creative outlets. There are sing-a-longs and community outings. One set of activities, referred to as the aging socialization program, deals with body awareness, physical changes, life issues, death and dying, family, and friends.

The Senior Enrichment Program was developed to provide a variety of life-enriching activities and experiences for people who are old and mentally retarded. It represents a holistic approach that allows staff to adapt to the changing needs of these clients.

The Health Focus Program is designed to meet the needs of clients who have been diagnosed with Senile Dementia of the Alzheimer's type in the later stages. It was founded in 1984 by Mary DeRosia, OTR and Deborah Jennings, OTA because they recognized a need for specialized programming. These clients have a special set of needs; certain treatment approaches have been found to be effective in handling these needs.

Currently all of the clients treated in the Health Focus Program were born with Down syndrome. They range in age from 53 to 63, are in the late second or third stage of Alzheimer's, and are all totally dependent on staff for the performance of Activities of Daily Living. They are prone to a variety of preventable and nonpreventable illnesses and health-related problems.

The staff-client ratio in this program is 2:1. The number of clients in the program averages 10-11. The professional staff includes an occupational therapist, physical therapist, direct care staff, and a music therapist. The morning session runs from 9:30 to 12:00 noon, the afternoon session from 2:00 to 3:00 p.m. Equipment includes standing tables, bolsters and other positioning devices, weights, hot-pack equipment, a suctioning machine, mat tables, counter balance slings, and various splints.

A variety of preventable problems are addressed in the Health Focus Program. Pneumonia can be prevented through mobility, change of position, and chest physical therapy at the first sign of congestion. Aspiration can be prevented by proper feeding techniques and proper positioning. Bed sores can be prevented by frequent position changes and proper wheelchair positioning. Contractures and poor circulation can be prevented by heat treatments, passive range of motion, and change of position. Osteoporosis and urinary tract infections can be partly prevented by daily sessions at a standing table; weight bearing will help prevent calcium loss from bones, and urinary tract infections are prevented by emptying the bladder while standing as well as by hydration. Constipation can be prevented through rotation exercises at the trunk (constipation is caused in part by immobility) and through use of the standing table to take advantage of gravity and a change of position. Infections in general also tend to be treated earlier when clients are being seen in program all day, rather than lying in bed.

Our treatment goals are maintenance of health through motoric intervention. Being engaged in disciplines that thrive on objective and measurable goals, we define health as maintenance of range of motion, skin integrity, and clear respiratory function. We also try to maintain good circulation, bone integrity, and good wheelchair positioning. And above any physical and emotional cures, we strive to maintain our clients' dignity and the quality of their lives.

42

SPIRITUAL AND RELIGIOUS CONCERNS

Henry A. Marquardt

■

For many people with mental retardation, it is difficult to sort out feelings, emotions, and needs, and to give expression to them. Also, the means and opportunities to satisfy their concerns are not always easily available. It is important to understand these two factors in relation to the history of this population with regard to their religious education and faith development, and the status of the Church today with regard to its ministry to people with disabilities.

For those who were raised in the Catholic tradition, this age group was served by a Church whose primary ministry was a sacramental ministry to people with handicaps. They received Baptism, Penance, First Communion, and Confirmation. Matrimony and Priesthood were ruled out because of the presence of disability. People with mental retardation were given basic education for reception of the sacraments, but there really was no follow-up or ongoing challenge to grow in their faith commitment. Mental retardation automatically conferred saint-hood. Their goal was achieved. The Church could breathe easy. Also, this group was sheltered from knowledge and awareness of bereavement process and from education about human sexuality—both means of continued personal growth. Religion stressed offering up one's handicap as a means of bearing the cross.

The focus of the Church has changed significantly in recent times. It now takes a holistic approach with its parishioners. The major concern is not just the soul, but the total person. Development of personhood is vital for salvation. Religion should assist a person in discovering her identity, and the goodness, talent, and beauty that God has given to her. Preaching "love your neighbor as yourself" takes on a whole new meaning. It is important to know that one is lovable and has an inner gift to share with others. Thus, liturgy, services, and religious education become experiences of personal growth. The Church calls its people into a meaningful and sharing relationship, not just with God, but also with neighbors.

In old age there may be withdrawal from activity, pressure, and responsibilities. In the area of religion, however, there need be no retreat since growth is ongoing. For people with mental retardation, faith in God can be the one stable and pervading element in their lives. Administrations, staff, family, volunteers, and programs all come and go. No matter the age or disability, the person can still, through religion, contribute, feel needed, be worthwhile, and continue to discover more about himself.

I will cite a few cases to show what faith can provide for people with mental retardation.

> *One woman, ninety-two years old and moderately handicapped, possessed a deep religious faith. She took great pride in reciting her prayers and used her talent of spelling to profess her belief in the teachings of the church. Although she had slowed down physically, she increased her personal prayer life. She had a world map and each day she selected a nation to be the object of her prayer; this made her feel needed and worthwhile.*
>
> *When her health failed, she thought it was time to die, but hoped God would be good to her since she had not committed too many sins. Religion was able to assist this woman through a focus on integrity, looking at the dignity of her own lifestyle. We spent time considering her spiritual and material accomplishments. She learned that it was more important to focus on what one had achieved than on one's sins, which had already been forgiven. From that moment on, she seemed to take control of her life and death. Her desire was to die in her cottage with her friends. Having been transferred to local hospitals and then to the clinical unit, she persuaded the medical staff to allow her to return to the cottage one more time. Two evenings later she died quietly and peacefully.*

Reaching a state of readiness and acceptance and waiting for death—while living each day to the fullest—is a great gift of maturity, whether one is mentally retarded or not.

> *A moderately retarded, sixty-four-year-old woman was a full-time employee of the state. The staff began to talk to her about retirement. They drew up a list of possible activities, programs, and*

involvements. The woman selected some that interested her, but said that she really wanted to spend her time working at the Chapel. I met with her and set up a schedule of four mornings a week to work in the sacristy, Chapel, and my quarters. I also asked her to assist as Eucharistic minister, serving at funerals, special liturgies, and memorial services.

Working in a faith environment, she has in a year's time blossomed, matured, and grown more self-confident and self-assured. She says that she feels like a new person and has never felt so alive.

Churches and temples are now having senior citizens fulfill the role of server or assistant at religious services. A potential negative response might be, "But the person has never done this before." Offer it as a challenge and the person with mental retardation will accept and achieve it.

Another client was eighty years old, moderately retarded, and in failing health. He had not been attending Chapel because of an unstable gait. I began visiting him at his residence and bringing him Communion. Each time he would offer his artwork to hang in the Chapel. One day, I told him I would rather have him at the Chapel. He could be an example and inspiration to the other members of the community. It was up to him to ask one of the Chapel volunteers who went to his building to assist him on Sunday. He took the initiative and has been coming ever since. From time to time, he serves Mass or is in the Offertory Procession.

I think the Church has enabled this man to enter into and complete the stage of generativity, guiding the next generation. I have never seen this gentleman with such self- esteem. He has said he hopes when the others get to be his age they will continue to be at Chapel and feel as though they are doing something good for the younger clients.

Do not hesitate to ask that the client's pastor or rabbi make a home visit. This is part of the ministry. If the client has not been attending services, it does not matter. It might take several calls before the clergyperson comes, either because of commitments or because she might feel uncomfortable with people with handicaps. If the latter is so,

---

offer some in-service assistance, or include the person in a team meeting.

Another client was an eighty-year-old woman who is not mentally retarded, a widow with five children. She was in the advanced stages of Alzheimer's disease when I began bringing her Communion and praying with her. Even on my last visit she seemed to be able to live in the present moment, knowing who I was and what I was there for. After praying, she said to me, "I did a pretty good job, didn't I?" The family said she remained calm and serene for a few hours after my visits. I suggested that they pray with her a few times a week, especially if she seemed agitated.I know this would require more study, but there just might be a spiritual component that will enable a person with this disease to experience the present a little more deeply.

Let's be honest in what we are saying and doing. We claim we are taking a holistic approach with service to the client. However, in many cases, we fail to include the spiritual and religious needs of the client, claiming there is no place on the Individual Service Plan form, or that Church and state must be kept separate. Yet how often at a review are activities, services, and programs that the client would not personally think of or verbalize, suggested by staff?

Clients have a right to service in this area of their lives. By not providing this service, the client is being deprived of a special means for ongoing growth and a vital aid in coping with aging. The client might be missing opportunities both to feel needed and to continue to contribute to the larger community.

Remember that religious faith is a means of giving the client who is old psychosocial strength all the way to the completion of his life.

43

MODIFYING RELIGIOUS SERVICES FOR PEOPLE WHO ARE OLD AND MENTALLY RETARDED

Henry A. Marquardt

■

I would like to offer some ideas about modifying religious services for people who are both old and mentally retarded. You might think a topic such as this should be addressed to clergypersons, rabbis, seminarians, and deacons. However, many of you presently have or will have important roles to play, especially since the Massachusetts Department of Mental Retardation (like corresponding agencies in many other states) subscribes to a holistic approach in the provision of services to clients. The Individual Service Plan (called an Individual Habilitation Plan in some states) assesses the needs of clients in all areas of their lives—psychological, physical, emotional, sexual, recreational, and religious. I hope the following ideas will assist you as you strive to seek resources to fulfill the spiritual needs of your clients with mental retardation who are old.

First, a word about religious services. A religious service, whether it be in a church, temple, or community residence, always has a twofold focus, a communal aspect and an individual aspect.

The communal aspect of a religious service enables members of a particular faith community to gather together in prayer, worship, and a prescribed ritual to express their common belief, to strengthen one another in their shared faith, and to give a sign to the larger community of their belief in a God who is present to them and making His presence felt in their lives.

The individual, or personal, aspect of a religious service enables believers to deepen and intensify their faith commitment, to be nurtured in religious teachings, and to be supported and sustained by fellow believers. Most important, a religious service should afford individuals opportunities to discover more about themselves, and time to discover the goodness, beauty, uniqueness, talent, and abilities God has given them. The poster "God doesn't make junk—only good things" is a wonderful way of getting this point across.

As you search for religious services to meet the needs of your clients, keep in mind that there are two main types of services. This is based on Glasser's theory that there are two predominant cultures in America, a goal-oriented culture and an identity culture.[1] There are religious services pertinent to each culture.

The goal-oriented religious service has as its focus the assistance of the congregation in their ultimate goal of eternal salvation. This goal is to be sought after at any cost; no consideration is given to the personal cost. This type of service proclaims lists of do's and don'ts, rules and regulations, and commandments and precepts. Individual needs, conditions, situations, and conscience are inconsequential. Personal submission to power, control, and authority of the institutional body is more important because this is the only way to attain the goal. Religious services of this nature flourished prior to the 1960s and still do exist.

With the advent of the identity culture—"I've got to be me," "Who am I?"—a new religious service has developed. The Second Vatican Council, convened from 1962 to 1965, also advocated this new approach. The new Catholic liturgy focused on the person as being unique, individual, and beautiful. Heaven is still the goal, the content of faith is the same, and the call to grow in one's relationship with God remains. However, the institutional body is a guide or shepherd that enables each person to achieve these goals according to his conscience. Power, authority, and control give way to freedom, trust, and risk-taking. Sin and guilt are overshadowed by redemption and resurrection. A chief objective of this new religious service is to afford its congregation opportunities to discover more about themselves, and to grow and develop in their personhood.

Since there are two very different emphases in religious services, it is imperative to understand your client's spiritual history and current needs, as well as where you can find religious services that will meet those needs.

There may be occasions when you will be called upon to assist in designing religious services for those who are both old and mentally retarded. The following suggestions might be helpful, but I would like to preface my remarks by saying that the clergyperson does not have sole claim on the religious service. If your clients are participating in a special service, in a church, temple, or community residence, you should take the initiative to discuss with the clergyperson your clients' situations and needs, and what you think they are capable of handling.

When planning services for people who are old and mentally retarded, consider not only their age but also their level of cognitive function, their declining physical vigor, other handicaps, and whether there might be dementia (Alzheimer's disease).

There should only be one theme or topic for the service. However, the leader of the service should be prepared with two to three approaches, depending on the needs of the congregation. It is important to observe and understand the congregation. One cannot simply bow one's head in prayer and then raise it at the conclusion of the service.

The purpose and tone of the service should be established at the beginning. Let the group know where the service is going, and that it is an integral part of it.

You should always get the clients involved in the service. When a service is held in the chapel, be sure the aged clients participate, even those with walkers and wheelchairs. They can still carry out roles of servers, gift givers, ministers of the Eucharist, or lectors. When the service takes place in the clients' building, have the clients set up the altar, arrange the chairs, and assist other clients in coming to the service. You can occasionally have them select the location for the service. While setting up for the service, encourage the clergyperson to recognize each client by telling them how nice they look and how much they are needed for the service.

Music is essential to the service. It is good to use live music in chapel services. The music should consist of familiar hymns and not childish songs. Also, an effort should be made to have a choir composed of clients. I suggest taped music for services in the buildings. It enables the clergyperson to have greater control over the tone and length of songs. Also, you can involve clients with the turning on and off of the recorder. With people with more severe infirmities, especially those with hearing impairments, you can carry the recorder around the area, allowing the clients to hold it to their ears for better listening. For clients with Alzheimer's disease, I suggest familiar songs and hymns from their earliest years.

Every service usually has a homily or a sermon. This is one of the most important elements of the service. In the homily one can respond to the needs, worries, and concerns of the clients; it is a time of praise, support, challenge, and response. In all cases, the homily should be a dialogue. The clergyperson can present what the topic means to her and then ask the clients for their thoughts on the subject.

It should be kept in mind that people with mental retardation do not want a theological explanation of a doctrine as much as they want to know how it will affect them personally; they do not want proof of resurrection but they want to know what it will mean for them. The homily for individuals with more severe impairments will rely on many more visual aids, symbols, signs, hand actions, and body movements. It is important to walk among the clients during the homily, to be close to them, and to touch them.

A religious service should not be used to fill the aged clients' time, but rather to make use of their talents and resources. The religious service is a time to reaffirm the good that clients have contributed to the church, temple, and society. It is also an opportunity to enable the clients to continue to contribute, in ways such as "the sign of peace." Rather than extend it to one another, they can send it silently to some particular area or group in need.

Worshippers who are mentally retarded have much to give to the wider faith community: energy, attention, love, and good wishes. Always include in the service an act (being silent, touching hands, or holding one's hands prayerfully) intended to send peace, hope, and healing to others who are in need. For instance, congregations have directed healing thoughts to people who are hungry, homeless, or ill in hospitals. Healing intentions can also be focused on individuals in need, such as a client's sick brother.

For a group of people who are suffering from dementia, the service should be very brief. The prayers, readings, music, visual aids, and symbols should be those that were familiar to them in their younger days—things that are still in their long-term memory.

Be supportive and encouraging to the clergyperson conducting the service. It can be very easy for him to become discouraged. Point out how necessary it is for the clients to have ample opportunity to get to know the clergyperson and to gain trust.

The end result of each religious service should be that the clients have deepened their relationship with their God; that they leave feeling better about themselves; that each person has discovered something new about herself; and that each person feels she has contributed in some way to the larger community.

44

PARTICIPATION IN RELIGIOUS OBSERVANCES

Marjorie Rucker

■

There are six areas that are important aspects of participation in religious observances. They are:

• a concept of God and the purpose of the church

• opportunities for socialization

• ritual and holiday celebrations

• an understanding of death and dying

• a means of equality

• a special relationship between staff and clients

Most of us believe in a power greater than ourselves; this is something people with mental retardation are also able to do. If only in the most basic of terms, they know about God, heaven, and hell. Some clients have been taught about this in a very punitive manner: "God only loves you when you are good," or "if you do this or that God will be angry or you will go to hell for being bad." Others have had more formal training either from their families of from their clergy; they have quite a different idea of God. They understand that God can be a friend, companion, and someone or something in whom they can believe, trust, and hope. This is expressed by their attachments to pictures, statues, Bibles, or prayer books.

Some clients have learned about prayer. They say grace before meals and are able to understand that they are giving thanks for the food they are about to eat. Others know the Lord's Prayer or other songs and prayers that they have learned at church or synagogue, and they have some understanding of them.

Attendance at synagogue or church is very important to many clients. It gives them an opportunity to share their understanding of God with others, which gives them a sense of pride, dignity, and self-acceptance. I am reminded of a client in the community, who is Jewish; she does not live near a temple so she attends an interdenominational church nearby where she has found full acceptance and encouragement. She is able to talk about her experiences there by explaining that she is Jewish and understands what that means, and that she is not able to attend temple because there is not one close by. She wants, however, to worship with others and is able to verbalize the fact that the church she goes to is attended by people of all faiths and that they all have something to share.

There are other clients in an institution who know when Sunday comes and understand that on that day they dress up and behave in a manner that is different from the other days of the week. Staff reinforce this, but you know a client really understands why she is doing this when she says to you, "I prayed for you at church today." Another example is a client who was approached by someone at church who wanted to say hello; the client responded in a very different way than he would in the building, on the campus, or at workshop. He knew that at church you are supposed to be quiet and behave differently. This is also shown by the clients who are able to sit quietly for forty-five minutes to an hour at church or synagogue when they are unable to do this for other functions.

Clients realize that attending church or synagogue enables them to socialize with others for a very different reason than when they are at work, at home (in the residential building or with family), or at the Activity Center, a social gathering place on the grounds. I have experienced this when attending church with clients both at a state school and out in the community. They put on their best manners. Clients are truly able to understand the concepts of God and church or synagogue; this is shown by their willing attendance, by their vocal participation during community prayer, responses, and songs, and by the disappointment they express when they are not able to attend.

I believe religious holidays have a very different meaning for those clients who are exposed to spirituality through church or synagogue ritual than for those who lack this opportunity for development. The client who is spiritual knows and understands that there is something more to Thanksgiving, Channukah, Christmas, New Year's, Rosh Hashona, Easter, and Passover than merely receiving presents, having good times, and eating good food. If asked, clients can tell you the reasons why these times are different. Christian clients are able to talk about Christmas as the time of Jesus' birth and describe Him as God's gift to us.

Spiritual involvement enables clients to have a better understanding of death and a hereafter. Clients who attend church or synagogue are able to attend funerals or memorial services of deceased family members, staff, and peers. They are not afraid or confused about where these individuals are and are more apt to talk about their loss in a very straightforward manner. They realize and can verbalize "she died and now she's in heaven with God" or "I lost my best buddy and I'm feeling very sad."

The expression of worship and the outward manifestations of spirituality offer a rare opportunity for equality for the person with mental retardation. Their needs for acceptance and caring are no different from those of anyone else. The realization that they are children of God and loved for who they are offers our clients the same consolation and self-esteem that religion has provided people for centuries. Being encouraged to express his spirituality, a client is able to feel equal with family members, friends, staff, and society at large.

For those staff members who appreciate spiritual aspects of experience, there is nothing more touching than being able to attend church or synagogue with clients and realize the enormous amount of strength they get from believing in God. The closest I have come to observing the true expression of the spiritual teachings of all faiths is to experience the love that these clients have for themselves and others. Our clients are really no different from ourselves, in that this love is enhanced by the depth of their spirituality. Our role in offering opportunities for spiritual growth and development is as important as any other service we might offer.

45

INTIMACY ISSUES OF CLIENTS AND CAREGIVERS

Bridget Bearss

■

In the Kennedy Aging Project I had the good fortune of working with clients, caregivers, service coordinators, program managers, and family members—the people who participate in the web known as the human service network. This term describes people who have chosen either directly or by the circumstances of their lives to work to create an environment that allows people to reach maximum wellness, and that encourages the development of an individual's full potential.

In my two years of listening, looking, and seeking to understand this secular service network, some patterns have come to seem relatively consistent. I have seen how relationships between caregivers and clients can make a difference. I have examined the stories from caregivers and clients, and the theoretical bases of relationships, and have come to understand how community forms because of relationships that encourage growth. Community is built and growth is encouraged when a connection of quality has been made between client and caregiver.

■ Intimacy

After listening to the stories of clients and caregivers, and observing the difference between community residences in which clients thrive and those that are less successful, I look upon the most positive situations as those achieving balance between communication and recognition of individual needs.

Communication in community residence is a process that must be rooted in honesty, openness, and dialogue. Communication between clients and caregivers creates an environment that fosters growth and intimacy when it is honest and when it encourages responses from both sides. It is not one-sided, and not dependent on roles.

The *individual needs* of both the clients and the caregivers are complex. Not to encourage individuals to know themselves well enough to know what will assist them in maintaining their own wellness is to foster a breakdown in the relationship. This is particularly important for caregivers. Understanding the needs of the direct service provider is an essential piece of information in the examination of a client's quality of life. We cannot serve effectively unless we are willing to recognize our own needs and allow both supervisors and peers to support us in those areas.

Clients also have particular needs, specifically in the area of intimacy. It is frequently a part of their lives that has not been developed. Underdeveloped areas can look unfinished, much like a car that has an efficient engine but looks unsightly. Clients need the chance to make the same kinds of mistakes in relationships that we have all made and continue to make. To protect them from such growth is to perpetuate further disability.

Intimacy occurs where these two areas converge—where both are receiving attention and are allowed to coexist. Where there is true intimacy, there is often the birth of what I have come to understand as a deeply spiritual experience. Spirituality is about truth—trusting in it, searching for it, recognizing when it is discovered, and having our experience verified.

There is a tendency within the secular service network to want to avoid things that are messy and complicated. Both spirituality and intimacy are messy and complicated, and yet integral to the experience of the human condition. We are all involved in relationships, and therefore come into contact with the challenges and gifts of such involvement. Let us direct our attention now to the relationships between clients and caregivers, those that are challenges and those that are gifts.

Consider Fran, a forty-seven year old woman, the youngest of six from a working-class family. By the time she was eleven she had failed in school, experienced alienation from the neighborhood, and come to view herself as a problem to her family. Hardly realizing what was happening, Fran found herself at the age of eleven in a state school where she would spend the next thirty years of her life. The days were not all bad, but she never stopped believing that soon she would be going home. She spent most of her time longing to see her family and wondering what would happen when she did. When she received a card or a visit, she was so excited she almost felt paralyzed. She found it hard to talk when she saw her favorite brother, and recalls vividly the day he came to tell her that her mother had died. It all seems like a blur to her now, but she remembers incidents rather than a whole chronology of events. Fran made some good friends in those years. The staff were the most important people in her life. She created an identity by listening to the staff tell her who she was.

Things are not too different now. She lives in a community residence, goes to workshop, has learned new skills, and can read and take a bus independently She is doing things that she never dreamed she would do. But she still describes a feeling of emptiness, of utter loneliness. She wants to be loved by someone.

She marks her days by the staff work calendar. There is a particular staff person that she is very attached to, and the relationship is marked by authenticity and mutuality. Fran spends a lot of time worrying about what will happen when this particular staff member, Mike, leaves the residence.

Fran knows Mike's family and is concerned about his children. She loves to hear about what he does on weekends, and how he goes to visit his mother on holidays. Fran is creating a world of intimacy for herself and responding to the world as she was conditioned to respond within the institution, through the staff.

Mike genuinely cares about Fran and his wife does also. Sometimes Fran even spends a weekend with them. Fran is very fortunate. Mike can hardly comprehend the importance of the relationship for Fran. Mike had never really thought about the implications of this relationship prior to our discussion about it. He had never considered that Fran is creating an identity for herself in that relationship.

Fran is a practicing Catholic. She both fears and seeks God. She has become attached to her use of meditation tapes, and likes "church music." Her image of God reflects Mike, and her understanding of relationship is strongly connected to her relationship with Mike. It is easy to question the relationship, and yet it is important for both individuals. Intimacy between clients and caregivers is very real and happens often. We can understand the reality of this relationship by seeing that Fran meets a need of

Mike's, and that Mike provides Fran with a "vicarious" life. By sharing his life, Mike has extended the walls of Fran's world. Hopefully, good people, decent and honest people, will be available when Fran and Mike loosen the bond of their relationship. It will be a death experience for Fran, and, at best, it will be stressful for Mike.

In the case of Fran and Mike and the many other caregivers and clients who are "in relationship" either directly or indirectly, we are talking about intimacy as it relates to the sphere of human growth and spirituality. The spiritual is the ultimate ground of all of our questions, hopes, fears, and loves. It is the basis of our efforts to deal with life and to find a purpose in life beyond our "doing." To spiritualize life means to immerse ourselves in the present moment, appreciating the ordinary things around us as extraordinarily important. We spiritualize the unspoken, the gesture, and the way that we are with one another. We enter the spiritual realm when we recall the words of Antoine de Saint Exupery, "What is most essential is invisible to the eye; it is only with the heart that one can see clearly."[1] Relationships with our clients take this form of companionship when we no longer define individuals in terms of disability, and when we begin to see ability. These are relationships between people who are unique, compelling beings. Such companionship is at once both a great risk and a great opportunity.

I define relationships that take on this spiritual quality as "pastoral." I would describe most caregivers who have truly invested themselves in the lives of the clients as pastoral. Therefore, I understand the relationship of intimacy between clients and caregivers in the terms used by Gerald Calhoun; this relationship is called "pastoral companionship."[2] Perhaps this sounds too strong a term for the caregiver who drives the van or who works as a service coordinator; these people see the client only briefly. But then, consider Joe.

Joe is a fifty-one year old man with a thirty-nine year institutional history. He has lived in the community for twelve years; the last seven years have been spent in the same community residence. About six months ago, Joe seemed depressed. He began regressing and refused to complete household tasks that were once simple operations for him. He frequently went to sleep as soon as he returned home from his workshop. He also cried about his father's death, which had occurred twenty-two years ago. He spoke about how much he loved his father, how much he missed him, and his anger at not having gone to his father's funeral—a typical experience for a person with mental retardation.

Staff were bewildered. They liked Joe very much and wanted to understand the nature of his problem. Medical and psychological evaluations revealed no drastic changes; medications for depression seemed inadvisable. After several weeks of this behavior, an alert staff person looked back to see what might have precipitated these changes and found only one change, a critical one. Joe's longstanding cab driver had moved on to a better job. No one perceived this as a major change. No one, that is, but Joe. Tom, Joe's cab driver, had shared six years of his life with him. Joe had come to treasure his time of hearing about Tom's life. Joe was doing what many of our clients do; he was living through, and having his intimacy needs met by, a "pastoral companion," a friend with whom he shared brief but important moments of time. For Joe, the absence of this consistent force was a death experience, and his silence was a signal of the anger he felt.

Certainly, Joe's cab driver should not be criticized for having taking a new job. Rather, he should be affirmed for having entered into a meaningful relationship with Joe. But if Tom had helped Joe prepare for his departure, it could have been a moment of progression, rather than regression, for Joe.

One of the most important experiences we can give to our clients is that of authenticity. If our commitment to a client has been deep-rooted, then our grieving and detachment from companionship will be painful. Saying goodbye well involves a willingness to review the relationship and remember the mutual caring. It communicates to the client, to colleagues, and to those around us what it means to care. It is the challenge of bringing our experience into narrative form.

I am not advocating that we not become invested in the lives of clients. Rather, it is critical to know what investment means in the life of the client, and it is essential to so value the client that we allow him the painful, yet growth-filled step of saying goodbye. Joe was grieving. Perhaps his cab driver was doing the same. If they had shared the experience, it could have been a time for Joe's primary caregivers to encourage Joe's development, rather than to use valuable time and energy seeking solutions to a "problem."

■ Needs of the Caregiver

As caregivers and service providers and as pastoral companions and friends, we have needs that relate directly to the quality of life of our clients. Caregivers have needs that encompass seven areas. The most positive relationships between clients and caregivers take place when these needs are met, and when caregivers recall that they are best equipped to provide services to their clients when they themselves are continuing to develop.

The best relationships between caregivers and clients exist in the situation where each experiences an independent, supportive relationships. It is especially important that the caregiver feels he is not alone in his work: isolation reaps bitterness; bitterness and overwork reap burnout; and clients cannot be helped by burned out staff. Thus, the first need of the caregiver is to feel support *from other staff.*[3]

We are a culture of specialists. As much as I have come to believe in the value of being a generalist, I am also a specialist. We are each dependent on other professionals for information and services. In order for quality relationships to exist within the context of a client and service provider, the caregiver must be able to trust the information received from other professionals, We must be able to *cooperate and trust other professionals.* Without mutual trust, we run the risk of spreading ourselves too thin and attempting to do too many people's jobs.

We continue our own journey toward wholeness and integration by recalling the process of learning: having information, receiving new information, experiencing cognitive dissonance when new information does not fit into old categories, and, finally, equilibration. If we close off ourselves or those we supervise from new information and education, we run the risk of reducing our ability to provide services, and we forget the process that our clients must utilize to gain new information and skills. We become the best companions and educators when we realize that the process of learning does not change, only the techniques and materials learned. Thus, as caregivers, we must continue to *pursue further education.*

Caregivers talk with me about their frustration in advocating for a person, and frequently they talk about the close relationship they have with a particular client. They may say, "She is my best friend. I forget that she is depressed. I forget that she is mentally retarded." These statements indicate that roles have been dropped, and that there is a mutuality that indicates there are more likenesses than differences. Such an attitude can be a very positive one, unless it is carried to an extreme.

When we completely lose objectivity, it is time to step back and recall that individuals have special needs. When objectivity is lost, it is time to evaluate whether or not this relationship is benefitting the client *and* the caregiver, or one over the other. Again, it is important both to be invested and to maintain some distance; one over the other leads to an imbalance that is not growth-filled for either party. It is important, then, that the caregiver *recognize the special needs of each client.*

We are positive and helpful companions and caregivers to the extent that we also continue to find ways of having our own needs met. It is important for caregivers to have lives outside of the place of caring. Whether it is in the family home, the institution, or the community residence, we all need to have lives outside our lives as caregivers.

We are best equipped to be pastoral companions when we are willing to be both ministered to and to minister. Without one side of this scale, the imbalance is immobilizing, and it will be only a matter of time before the energy of the caregiver will be so completely drained that continuation in the setting will be impossible. Frequently, it is this imbalance that results in a precipitous departure of a staff member, without appropriate separation time, and that causes unnecessary stress in the life of the client. Sadness at the departure of a friend is not an emotion that we seek to protect our clients from. Rather, we seek to enable them to grieve and mourn in the company of those who realize the quality of the relationship they have lost.

We are responsible for our clients, and therefore, we must be responsible for maintaining our own personal wellness. We can only share resources that we are able to replenish. A significant need of caregivers is to *recognize their own journey,* and to continue to pursue it with integrity.

The quality of life of a caregiver (and of a client) can sometimes be measured by his ability to share the gift of health, which is laughter. It is important that caregivers do not begin to take themselves so seriously that they forget how to laugh and live life to the fullest. This modeling will be helpful to the client, and will significantly alter the environment in which caregiver and client interact. It is very important that the caregiver continue to be able to *enjoy life.*

It is critical that we become so attached to the lives of our clients that we can hold them with "open hands." We cannot "protect" them from either the system they are in or the world at large. The best that we can hope to do is to provide them with a strong relationship and an environment in which they can achieve their potential. As pastoral companions, it is important that we remember that while this is part of the need of the caregiver, it is also a need of the client. We become empowered to give services to our clients when we realize that we cannot change everything; however, we can enter into the moment at hand. It is a challenge to *use the time we have well,* while still realizing that time is not without limitations. It is the stage of pastoral companionship that I find most difficult, for in it we must recognize our own powerlessness, and yet we must convey reasons to be hopeful to our clients. It is at these moments of powerlessness, when we try to create a vision of courage for ourselves and our clients, that we are most able to be companions.

I learned this lesson the hard way. I came to the Aging Project after having spent ten years as a special and elementary educator and administrator. I looked forward to the possibilities that existed for changing the lives of my clients. In my interactions with clients, I heard the stories of painful lives of oppression that had been transformed by caring relationships with staff and direct-care providers. I was convinced that we could make a dramatic difference and felt an urgency to work unceasingly to provide justice for those who could not advocate for themselves.

In December of my first year with the Aging Project, I found myself at the bedside of a 65-year-old man who had experienced a major heart attack and had undergone emergency quadruple bypass surgery. With my best pastoral care tools, I began a conversation that I was sure would be helpful. But what I experienced was the utter powerlessness to change the events of nature. I found that the only companionship I could offer was the quality of my silence. At that moment, at the bedside of my father, I became a different kind of pastoral companion. I left that experience with a deeper understanding of what it means to journey with others and to realize my own limitations.

"A pastoral companion can be hindered from ministering because of anxiety, and excessive need for affirmation, experiences of over-identification, a desire to save our unfulfilled needs for friendship."[4] We must see our own limitations and know our own motivations. We are most able to give when the needs of our clients, and our ability to meet those needs, exist in the shadow of our own inability to cure or save. Recognizing that, we are finally able to sink into the present moment and appreciate the ordinary things around us. We can then experience the depth of time as well as its duration, and not attempt to reshape experiences to match our need to control the events of our clients' lives.

It seems that, with each new client, I find a new challenge and reshape the way I have previously viewed pastoral companionship, education, and the issues of intimacy between clients and caregivers.

> One of my clients, Robert, provided a great deal of "category-clashing." Robert is a 51-year-old man who currently resides in a nursing home. He spent some time in a state school, but primarily has lived at home or in private institutions. Robert identifies those who are in the nursing home as being "old" and understands the use of the word "geriatric" to describe the other residents with whom he lives. Robert is very clear about what he wants to experience within his life and how he wants to live. He is extremely verbal and can describe the anxiety of "waiting" for appropriate placement. He has had strong affiliations with several religious groups, and finds utilizing rituals and images within the context of the Catholic Church to be most helpful. It is difficult for him to understand why he cannot attend church with more regularity, and why all churches are not wheelchair accessible. He wonders what God expects of him.
>
> In the course of our initial interview, Robert said to me, "God just expects too much of me. God expects me to do all my exercises and not complain. God put me in this wheelchair, and now God expects me to work to not be in it." In the course of the interview, we investigated Robert's image of God, the experiences that had helped form it, and the kind of emotional responses that Robert supposed God expected. We examined such questions as "Is it all right to be angry?" "Is it all right to be sad?" "Does God get sad?" I asked Robert to suppose for a minute that God was in a wheelchair. What did he think God would do in a wheelchair? Suppose Robert looks more like God than those of us who are not in wheelchairs? Suppose that God likes him just as he is?

Often, as caregivers become invested in a client's life, they find that they can identify five strong emotions or stages of reaching the ability to really serve people well.[5] These categories are protest, silence and distancing, memories, gratitude, and deep trust, and inclusion.

Protest

As we become involved with a client, really listen to her, and encourage her to reach for her potential, we find ourselves ringing the familiar chorus, "It isn't fair." We are right, it isn't. It isn't fair that some clients have no family involvement, have to wait for placements, are forced to leave their workshops because of their age, or have to bear uncomfortable stares in a grocery store. We're right. It isn't fair. We have to continue to work for change, but we also must try to give our clients reasons to hope. We must recognize our own protest against injustice and the frustration of working within a structure, but we must also continue to be people of hope.

Silence and Distancing

Sometimes caregivers want not to be so closely involved, we begin to believe that the personal costs are too high. We wish that we could bag groceries or be a receptionist for a while. Hopefully, that won't last too long. It probably means that the caregiver needs to replenish his resources: take a course, have a day off, do something to revive the spirit and encourage the soul. It is important for caregivers to recognize that at times they need to silence and distance themselves, to replenish what has been given.

Memories

Occasionally, working with a particular client brings to mind an experience from our past. It is in memory, in remembering both times of hardship and joy, that we can become free to enter completely into the present moment.

Gratitude

We often find ourselves grateful for the privilege of working with our clients or grateful for the gift of life. Sometimes this gratitude can lead us toward realizing how temporal life is; we become aware of our own limitedness.

Trust and Inclusion

Finally, there are moments when we can rejoice in the lives of the clients, recognize the quality of the staff with whom we work, and enjoy life deeply. It is these moments of intimacy, as both clients and caregivers work together and become involved in each other's lives, that most hope to experience.

We have looked at the needs of clients and their caregivers. I understand this as an articulation of the things within the secular service network that are deeply spiritual; they can just as easily be described in theological terms as in psychological terms.

There are no barriers to spirituality. We are all spiritual people, just by the fact that we walk this Earth. To be a person with mental retardation does not stop that from happening. Also, to be old is not to stop being spiritual; it is merely to describe it in another way.

To be part of this secular service network is both a great opportunity and a great risk. It is a great risk because it is difficult to do without caring. It is a great opportunity because of the growth that can happen both inside and outside of boundaries. It is the challenge of seeing with the heart, for it is only with the heart that one can see clearly.

46

DYSFUNCTIONAL BEHAVIOR AND INTERVENTIONS

Arianna Fucini

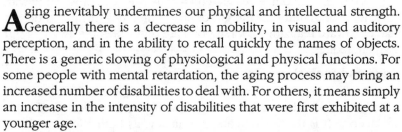

Aging inevitably undermines our physical and intellectual strength. Generally there is a decrease in mobility, in visual and auditory perception, and in the ability to recall quickly the names of objects. There is a generic slowing of physiological and physical functions. For some people with mental retardation, the aging process may bring an increased number of disabilities to deal with. For others, it means simply an increase in the intensity of disabilities that were first exhibited at a younger age.

What is the response of the aging person to the experience of the physical decline? The most common one is refusal to accept the inevitable reality. In people with mental retardation such refusals often manifest themselves behaviorally, i.e., refusal to wear dentures, a hearing aid or glasses; resistance to using a wheelchair at some social events; or denial of lapses of memory.

The cognitive impairments of aging take many forms, ranging from the impairment of cognitive functioning associated with depression to the impairment characteristic of organic brain syndrome. In people with mental retardation the range of impairments is more limited and depends on the client's prior level of function; the behavioral expression can be disorientation, misplacement of personal items or objects, hoarding behavior, or general confusion.

The conflict between the experience of physical and cognitive decline and the refusal to accept and adapt to it frames one psychological component of aging. The expression of this conflict in people with mental retardation often takes the form of non-compliant or oppositional behavior, verbal and sometimes physical aggression, and outbursts of tantruming.

In clients who have been diagnosed as having Senile Dementia of the Alzheimer's Type, the above-mentioned behaviors have an influence on the client's ability to manage his day-to-day affairs such as performing household chores, satisfying self-care needs, and enjoying self-paced leisure activities. There may also be other troublesome behaviors like wandering, pacing, withdrawal, and repetitive questioning.

The problem of growing old for a person with mental retardation is not limited to physical and cognitive decline; there are also the requirements of the environment to deal with. For example, rules at the workshop may be inflexible (production quotas, etc.), and so may be the rules about residing in a "least restrictive " environment (self-preservation, etc.). The client who is growing old may not make a consistent one-hundred-percent correct performance during testing trials for self-preservation. Consequently, clients who might intermittently satisfy the standard are sometimes forced out of the workshop or out of the house.

There is a wide range of dysfunctional behaviors exhibited by people with mental retardation who are growing old. What is the best thing to do in order to decrease these dysfunctional behaviors? The first step is to require a cognitive assessment of the client. It is important to know if the client is aging, is depressed, or is exhibiting early symptoms of Senile Dementia of the Alzheimer Type.

The second step, also important, is data collection to establish a baseline for the dysfunctional behaviors. In order to evaluate effectiveness, any intervention requires prior documentation of the frequency, duration, and intensity of the behavior in question. Further, the functional analysis of the target behavior is the keystone for appropriate intervention. For example, if the client's inappropriate behavior functions as an attention-getting device, any intervention, verbal or otherwise, will be ineffective if it provides the client with social and physical contact. A good behavior analysis identifies the event that precedes the behavior and the reinforcement that maintains it.

Certain interventions were frequently recommended by the staff of the Kennedy Aging Project. In the majority of cases, if the client was simply aging, the treatment approach was to adapt the environment to the aging individual. Interventions for people with mental retardation who are old have been aimed mainly at creating an environment more adaptable to their deficiencies. Such a modified environment is intended to minimize frustration and consequent dysfunctional behavior. For example, in some cases workshop staff were instructed to lower quotas or other performance requirements, or to offer tasks with fewer steps for the same production quotas. At other times they were instructed to use a different method of communication that was more functional for the individual. In all these cases, the functional analysis of the behavior was very helpful because the intervention targeted the antecedents to the behavior in question.

Behavioral and psychopharmacological interventions were used for depressed clients. Clients were referred to their own doctor or to a psychiatrist for possible pharmacological intervention. In the majority of the cases an increase of the density of reinforcement was the suggested behavioral intervention. The functional analysis of the behavior was also very important for these clients because the intervention targeted the consequences that maintained the behavior.

For clients exhibiting the first symptoms of Alzheimer's disease, staff training was the most successful intervention. As mentioned in Chapter 15, the initial training involved information about the disease. The majority of the staff did not know much about the disease or its inevitable progression.

Staff were also encouraged to express their frustration and anger with the client's behavior and to participate in support groups in the area. The major aim of this training was to teach staff to accept the client's decline and to change their own expectations and demands. Other important purposes of the training were:

• to have staff establish less demanding goals for clients

• to have caregivers be very consistent across settings in order to limit confusion and feelings of failure

• to have staff minimize criticism of the client and to inform the client's peers about the client's inability to accomplish some tasks

Staff were also urged to see the disease from the client's point of view, to imagine the fear, doubt, defeat, and self-blame of the client who finds herself unable to complete tasks that were previously familiar to her, and who cannot understand why she can no longer perform as she once did. In a considerable number of cases, data collection and a behavioral analysis were helpful in providing an understanding of client behavior and the staff's reaction to their own beliefs.

It is gratifying to be able to report that a number of the interventions that were recommended proved to be very effective. Staff and service coordinators were kind enough to volunteer feedback about the value of the suggestions that were offered. These unsolicited testimonials were much appreciated reinforcements for the members of our Team.

47

SEXUALITY

Gerard A. Cabrera

Sexuality is a part of life, a part of our whole being. To ignore our sexuality is to ignore and deny that synthesis of ourselves.

When we see someone who is old, we usually do not think of her as being sexual, or even having a sexuality. In our culture, sex appeal belongs to the young and to the "beautiful people." Our prejudice tells us that old people "can't" have sex, that their bodies are no longer pretty, that their drive is lowered, and that their passion is dimmed by decreasing health. And when we see people with mental retardation, cast out of the "normal" world in many cases, we project our fears onto them.

The mentally and physically handicapped figure personifies uncontrolled sexuality or total lack of it in the Western imagination. Thus, in many cases their sexuality has been repressed by our society. Fortunately, these attitudes are changing. With the increasing population of people who are old in this society, and the increasing longevity of people with mental retardation, we need to examine issues of sexuality for the person who is both retarded and old. We should know that age and mental status do not preclude sexual activity.

For the person who is mentally retarded and also old, sexuality is a topic fraught with conflict. Historically speaking, many of our clients have spent long years in institutions where there was little opportunity for healthy sexual expression. In many of our institutionalized clients' lives, how sex has been taught and experienced has left emotional, psychological, or physical scars. The caregiver must take this into account when discussing sexuality with the client who is old and mentally retarded.

When talking with clients about sexuality, caregivers should consider the client's history. If a client lived or lives in an institution, we should remember that many times clients expressed themselves sexually in a furtive manner, perhaps without approval of staff and in an atmosphere of fear. In this way, many relationships may have been formed with a "seige mentality," where secrecy was seen as necessary for protection. We should be sensitive and respectful of a client's desire for privacy.

We should also be aware, however, that comfortable discussion of sexuality can be very helpful for clients with concerns about relationships and practical matters. After the Consent Decrees of the 1970s and the restructuring of the mental retardation system in Massachusetts, many opportunities were created to begin addressing sexuality more openly and to begin integrating it into the rest of our clients' lives.

What should caregivers know about clients' sexuality? The most important thing to remember for anyone involved in a caretaking relationship is respect for that person's dignity, worth, and right to a love relationship, whether that be homosexual or heterosexual.

Practical matters are of extreme importance when discussion arises about sexuality. We have been taught that sexual matters are private and not to be openly discussed. Caregivers should be able to listen and respond to questions regarding topics such as intercourse, contraception, masturbation, sexual abuse, marriage, incest, and sexually transmitted diseases (STDs). Although many of our female clients may be post-menopausal, the use of condoms is still important as a way to prevent STDs such as herpes, hepatitis, yeast (candida), gonorrhea, syphilis, chlamydia, and most particularly AIDS.

AIDS has become an epidemic. It is no longer solely the bane of certain social groups. As caregivers we must be aware of the risks involved for our clients. In addition, we need constantly to reaffirm the benefits and inherent good of intimate sexual relationships. We must educate ourselves and our clients as a way to diffuse fear and ignorance about AIDS. If one practices safer sex, and remains knowledgeable about current safer sex information, a full and satisfying sexual life can be continued for clients. Abstinence is a rather poor way of coping with the current crisis.

Another practical matter is mechanical. As a client ages, elasticity of the joints decreases, and so sexual positions that may have been comfortable before are now uncomfortable. Clients with a limited knowledge of sexual expression may need counseling or sex therapy regarding masturbation or new, more comfortable positions for both partners. A prosthetic device such as a dildo may also be helpful as a way to get around physical disability or impaired mobility and increase pleasure in a way that does not infringe on the rights of others. Innovation is desirable and very helpful.

Genital sexuality should not, however, be the only focus for caregivers concerned with issues of sexuality and its expression. There are many ways to express affection besides the specifically genital. Hugs, holding hands, massage, kissing, and other intimacies may be very satisfying to clients who wish to express affection. The full range of pleasuring should be considered and should never be taken for granted. Physical touch can be both satisfying and liberating. The benefits of touch should not be underestimated.

Attitudes must always be taken into account when it comes to sexuality. Older clients have the values of their generation, which should be respected, as should the moral values of clients from different religious and cultural backgrounds.

In summary, the person who is both mentally retarded and old carries a double burden of discrimination. She may be looked on as asexual or as hypersexual. We must conquer our fear of difference and see the fullness of sexual expression within mental and physical limitations.

Caregivers should put aside their own prejudices and help facilitate a full life for their clients. A spirit of support and openness should prevail. Questions should be answered directly and honestly. Autonomy should be encouraged and respected in sexual matters. Information about sexuality and sexual matters should be easily available in a non-threatening atmosphere for clients. Finally, we should always think of how we would like to lead our own lives as fully as possible, and how that includes our sexuality, our senses, our bodies, our spirits, and our imaginations. Remember that the most important sexual organ is between one's ears!

48

SENIOR/MASTERS GAMES IN SPECIAL OLYMPICS

Elizabeth J. DeBrine

■

Established in 1968 by the Joseph P. Kennedy, Jr. Foundation, and chaired by Eunice Kennedy Shriver, Special Olympics is the world's largest sports training and athletic competition program for people with mental retardation. Special Olympics offers athletes opportunities to compete in a wide variety of year-round sports from aquatics to floor hockey.

Massachusetts Special Olympics (MSO) started its program in 1970. Like most state programs, it was initially geared toward children and young adults. In 1982, MSO responded to the growing number of adult athletes by pioneering an innovative program called the Senior/Masters Games. Over the years, the Senior/Masters Games have become an important component of the MSO schedule of sports events.

MSO decided to form a separate event for older athletes because their coaches and families felt that these athletes were unable to compete fairly with athletes who were children or young adults. Also, coaches felt that these athletes were more interested in improved physical fitness and increased skills than in heavy competition. As a result, they combined a sports event with a weekend get-away that provided fitness information, sports competition, and opportunities for socializing and sightseeing.

The Senior/Masters Games take place on Cape Cod at a seaside resort in late September. The athletes, coaches, and volunteers are housed in luxurious condos for the weekend.

In 1986, the opening ceremonies took place beside the outdoor pool at the resort. There was a wonderful atmosphere, full of anticipation. The bagpipe band was thrilling to listen to and helped to dramatize the event. The speech-making was kept short and to the point. After the opening ceremonies, there was a dinner and party with a Hawaiian theme held in three large tents for the athletes, coaches, and guests.

Since there were not enough tables and chairs for everyone, people made themselves comfortable sitting on the grass. The weather was very cooperative. The night was cool and dry.

There was a disk jockey in another tent who was playing zippy, good music. The volume was just right—not too loud—and there were lots of people dancing. The best part was seeing athletes of all ages dancing with each other and with their coaches. I saw one young female coach teasing and coaxing one of the older male athletes to "get down." He loved it. The party was a big success because being outdoors felt so special. It was a sophisticated party with no barriers of age or handicap. This was Special Olympics at its best.

In the sports competition, MSO requires each athlete to participate in one aerobic sport, either racewalking or swimming, to increase cardiovascular fitness. Also, athletes participate in one of the leisure skill sports. The leisure sports comprise a separate category of sports that, except for bowling, are not presently sanctioned by Special Olympics. The category includes bowling, croquet, horseshoes, golf, and fresh water fishing. MSO coaches and trainers felt that they needed to include a variety of sports in order to meet the athletes' wide range of abilities and interests.

To increase competition, the athletes were divided into two age groups: masters (30-49 years) and grandmasters (50 years and up). Athletes are placed in the appropriate age group and ability level for each event.

MSO and the Kennedy Aging Project experienced several problems in developing this special program for older athletes. First, we found that there is an overwhelming prejudice against athletes who are

---

old competing in sports events. Most people perceive athletes who are old as passive, sedentary, and incapable of performing vigorous activity.

Society in general and program leaders in particular believe that it is too late for athletes who are old to become proficient at a given sport. Also, there is a fear of working with athletes who are old because the health risks are greater for them, and liability risks are greater for the program leader, than when working with young people.

At the Senior/Masters Games we saw some of our older athletes make remarkable progress. One athlete, Sally, led a very secluded life when she lived with her parents. Sally was obese, fearful, and almost nonverbal. When her mother died, Sally's sister started to become more involved in her life. Sally moved into a group home and joined the local MSO program when she was almost fifty years old.

As a result of the MSO swimming and racewalking training, she lost more than fifty pounds, started talking more, became more confident, and made many new friends. The first time I tested Sally, I was afraid she would not be able to walk around the track because she was so obese and unfit. The next year, after losing weight, Sally worked so diligently to win in the racewalking event that she had to be reminded several times to walk, not run.

Our second concern is that Senior/Masters Games must offer sports that provide the right level of competition to meet the wide range of athletes' talents and skills. Within this group of more the 200 athletes, there are thirty-year-old athletes who have been in MSO training programs for many years, and sixty-year-old athletes who have had little experience or training. Also, we have a wide range of fitness, from overweight young people to hale and hearty oldsters who could easily run half a mile.

To take some of the mystery out of what an athlete is able to do, the Kennedy Aging Project designed a stress test based on Cooper's twelve-minute walk/run stress test. The results of the cardiovascular fitness test can be used to determine which sports are appropriate for each athlete. For a booklet explaining how to administer a walk stress test, contact Massachusetts Special Olympics, P.O. 303, Hathorne, MA 01937, Tel. (508) 774-1501. (See Chapter 30)

Third, there is much discussion about age-appropriate sports. We at the Kennedy Aging Project do not feel that one sport is more age-appropriate than another. However, we do advocate that participation in sports be based on the athlete's interests, aerobic capacity, and skill level. We support a system that would offer a variety of sports, challenging the athlete in a manner that affirms the athlete's adulthood.

We have also recommended that each sport have more levels of competition to attract both the frail and the high-endurance athlete. The more fit athlete should enter into a 400-meter run; we have seen instances where athletes, young or old, have had a difficult time refraining from running during a racewalking event. More competitive events will become an important part of the Senior/Masters Games in the future because younger athletes will be more fit and will already have spent many years in Special Olympics training and competition.

Coaches recommend changing sports from year to year within the leisure skills area to increase the choice and skill level. Some suggestions are badminton, bocci ball, shuffleboard, and billiards. This past year, MSO offered fresh water fishing for the first time.

The Senior/Masters Games lends itself to blending sports competition with social events and physical education. Two years ago, the Kennedy Aging Project offered to give stress tests to all athletes at the Games. Since coaches are required to walk the track with their athletes in order to monitor their progress by pulse and appearance, we offered to test them as well. Everyone seemed to enjoy finding out about her present level of fitness.

Special Olympics is not just for young people. Now there is a sports competition for athletes who are old that teaches fitness and provides competition and opportunities for socialization. We at the Kennedy Aging Project have found physical exercise to be the greatest deterrent of, and at the same time the greatest remedy for, the frailties of old age. The Senior/Masters Games of Special Olympics is one of the best ways to provide the adult athlete with a structure for good health and a sense of well-being.

49

ESTATE PLANNING: PROVIDING FOR YOUR CHILD'S FUTURE

Henry A. Beyer

■

A question frequently asked by the parents of older, disabled individuals is how they can best provide for their offspring after their own deaths. This is a question faced by all parents, but it assumes special importance for parents with a child who is unlikely ever to be independent.

What happens to your property after your death? If you have a will, your property will be distributed according to your instructions given in the will A court, called the probate court, is the agency that insures that this is done. The probate court first determines if the will is valid, and then takes steps to put it into effect. This is called probating the will, and the gifts that are made through the will are called bequests.

What happens to your property if you die without a will—or, as lawyers say, if you die intestate? Your estate is then disposed of according to a formula set down in a statute enacted by the state legislature. If you have a spouse and children, your spouse typically gets a specific portion, usually one-half or one-third, and the children get the remainder of all of your real and personal property. If you have no spouse but only children, they typically receive all of your property.

When property passes to children in this manner, it is divided equally among all of the children, whether or not they need it, and whether or not they are competent and able to manage it. Thus, many parents, but especially parents of a child with disabilities, might wish some different form of distribution. These parents should have a will.

■ Creating a Will

In a will, parents can provide for the distribution they wish, and also can do other things. They can suggest to the probate court the name of someone they think would be a good guardian, or limited guardian, or conservator, for their child, if they think such a person will be needed to assist the child after their death. Only the court can appoint a guardian, but a parent's nomination will be given very strong consideration by the court and, in most cases, will be accepted. In a will, the parents of a person with mental retardation can also express other preferences, relating to, for example, the individual's care, training, living arrangement, or religious practices.

In every will the testator should also name the executor of the estate. The testator is the person who makes the will; the executor is the person who has the responsibility of collecting, maintaining, and distributing the assets of the estate in accordance with the terms of the will. The executor need not be an attorney. In most cases, a family member or close friend is named as executor. She can hire an attorney, using funds from the estate, if one is needed to carry out the terms of the will.

Through their will, parents can divide up their property however they think best, perhaps giving a larger share to the most needy child, who may be the one with a disability. There are several significant problems with this approach, however: (1) The disabled son or daughter may not have the capacity to manage property left to him outright. (2) Property left outright to disabled people will be counted as their assets and thus may make them ineligible for certain government benefits in which eligibility is based on need. A person is ineligible for Supplemental Security Income (SSI), for example, if her assets exceed $1800, and if an individual is not eligible for SSI, she is also usually ineligible for Medicaid, which may be an even more serious problem. (3) With the additional assets counted as their own, disabled people receiving government services may be subject to charges for care.

Thus, in many ways, leaving substantial assets directly to a person with mental retardation who would otherwise be eligible for government benefits is very much like making a contribution to the government—something that some parents might wish to do,[1] but many others would not.

■ Leaving No Money

What alternatives do parents have if their offspring will lose benefits if she has an inheritance? They might disinherit their disabled child. This approach of leaving no money directly to the child has advantages: the parents' assets can be left to their other children, who might put them to good use, whereas, if left directly to the disabled child, they might have been dissipated rapidly.

Disinheritance, however, also has disadvantages: if at some future time after the parents' death, government programs are eliminated or benefits reduced or discontinued, the retarded child may be in great need of the resources the parents could have left him. But then it will be too late. Also, it is extremely difficult emotionally for most parents to disinherit a child. Even when they believe it is rationally the best thing to do, the act often produces strong feelings of guilt. Nevertheless, if the parents' estate is very small, disinheritance is a possibility that should be seriously considered.

■ Morally Obligated Gift

Another alternative to leaving property directly to a person with mental retardation is leaving what is called a "morally obligated gift" to someone else, such as a brother, sister, cousin, or friend of the individual who is mentally retarded. The gift, or bequest, is accompanied by a request that the recipient use the gift for the benefit of the child with the disability.

The principal advantage of such a gift is its simplicity. It also has significant disadvantages, however, which arise from the fact that the recipient becomes the owner of the property. If the property draws interest or otherwise generates income, the recipient is liable for any taxes due. Also, the recipient's creditors might be able to take the property in any number of ways—in a divorce settlement, for example, or if the recipient suffers business reversals, or has any other uninsured liability.

Furthermore, a morally obligated gift imposes only a moral obligation on the recipient to use it for the person with mental retardation, not a legal obligation. If times become difficult, the recipient may experience an irresistible temptation to use the gift for her own family. Conversely, if the inheritance is exhausted, the recipient may feel obligated to use her own assets to continue supplying assistance to the retarded individual. This may impose a significant hardship on the recipient's own family; it can cause a result that the testator would never intend.

Finally, if the recipient of a morally obligated gift dies before the person who is mentally retarded, the remaining assets will be considered part of the recipient's estate and will be passed on to others by whatever manner the estate is distributed, with a substantial risk that the moral obligation will be lost in the process.

■ Joint Property and Life Insurance

Another option open to parents is the creation of jointly owned property. The parents may decide to make their adult child with mental retardation, during their lifetime, a joint owner of some of their property, subject to a right of survivorship. Then, if they die, their child (the survivor) automatically becomes the sole owner of that property. This approach has the same effect as if that portion of their estate had passed to the child through a will and is subject to the same disadvantages, including possible incapacity to manage, ineligibility for benefits, and charges for care. Nevertheless, parents should consider the possible usefulness of a small joint bank account, possibly of the type requiring two signatures for withdrawals, in teaching their son or daughter money management skills.

Life insurance is one more option parents should consider in planning their estate. Life insurance is a contract made with the insurance company and is not affected by the parents' will unless the beneficiary of the policy is the parents' estate. Making the estate the beneficiary has the disadvantage of possibly increasing the cost of probating the estate, as well as possible undesirable tax consequences. Naming the child with a disability as beneficiary, however, creates the same problems as a direct bequest, and naming another individual as beneficiary, with a request that the funds be used for the benefit of the person with mental retardation, entails the same disadvantages as a morally obligated gift.

■ Trusts

Another solution is for parents to name, as the beneficiary of the insurance policy, a trust for the disabled child. Trusts can avoid many of the disadvantages of the various approaches considered so far.

A trust is a legal relationship created by one person, called the "settlor," in which another individual, the "trustee," owns and manages property for the benefit of a third person, the "beneficiary." In the situation we have been considering, the settlor will usually be a parent, the beneficiary will be the person with mental retardation, and the trustee might be a brother or sister of the person with mental retardation, or perhaps a cousin or close family friend. The trustee should not ordinarily be much older than the retarded person, because the hope is that the trustee will live to manage the trust funds up until the death of the beneficiary. (A successor trustee should be appointed to assume the role if the first trustee should die during the life of the trust.) Because the trustee owns the trust property, lawyers say that she has legal title, but because the trustee must use the property only for the benefit of the beneficiary, the beneficiary is said to have "equitable title" to the property.

A trust is created by a document called a "trust instrument." If properly worded, a trust instrument establishes a relationship with the following advantages:

- The beneficiary is not considered the owner of the trust property. Thus, his eligibility for government programs based on means is not endangered, and the trust assets cannot be taken by the government as payment for services rendered.

- The trust funds can be used by the trustee to buy goods and services for the beneficiary, to pay bills on behalf of the beneficiary, to give spending money to the beneficiary, etc.

- The trustee has great flexibility in managing the trust assets. He can use them to buy and sell stocks, bonds, property (in some states, the trustee must obtain authorization from the probate court before selling any real estate), or other investments; the trustee can deposit trust funds in a bank account or can withdraw them; the trustee can tailor the payments she makes to or for the retarded individual to suit that individual's needs as they change over time (i.e., as the individual with mental retardation grows more or less disabled, or as government programs change).

- If the trust is very large, the trustee can use trust funds to hire financial experts to manage it. The trustee can hire an attorney if one is needed.

A trust is an extremely flexible mechanism that overcomes most of the disadvantages of the other estate-planning approaches.

Trusts may be established in the settlors' (parents') will and take effect upon the parents' death. This is called a testamentary trust; the will specifies what portion of the parents' estate is being left to the trust. Or, the trust may take effect during the parents' lifetime; this is called an *inter vivos* trust. The parents can make gifts of real or personal property to the trust while they are still alive. They can also suggest that others, such as aunts, uncles, and grandparents who might be inclined to make gifts to the person with mental retardation, do so by having the assets go to the trust rather than directly to the individual. The relatives can do this either by a gift during their lifetime or through a bequest made in their wills.

The trust instrument, in addition to naming the beneficiary and the trustee, should state the purpose of the trust. In most cases, the purpose will be to provide a higher quality of life to the beneficiary, a quality beyond that which would be possible using only the benefits provided by government programs. A higher quality of life might include extra education, training, recreation, vacations, habilitation, treatment, etc. It should be stated very clearly that the trust's purpose is to supplement, not replace, government aid. Because of this stipulation, this type of trust is sometimes referred to as a luxuries trust. On the other hand, the trust instrument should not state that the trust may not be used for the support of the beneficiary; the day might possibly come when no government programs are available to provide support, and the trustee must then be able to use trust funds for that purpose.

The instrument should describe the powers of the trustee. He has only powers that: (1) are stated in the instrument, (2) are required to carry out the purpose of the trust, or (3) are conferred by statute or court order. (In Massachusetts, for example, a trustee may invest and reinvest trust assets, buy and sell assets, deposit and withdraw funds in banks, distribute funds to and buy goods and services for the beneficiary.)

The instrument may require the trustee to act in certain ways. The trustee is then said to have "imperative" powers. The instrument could, for example, say that the trustee shall pay to the beneficiary $100 on the first day of every month. Including such mandatory provisions, however, is usually not a good idea, The settlor cannot know what the distant future holds, what needs the beneficiary will have, or what the status of government programs will be. If, for instance, an outstanding government program were established at some future time, open only to people whose income was below $90 per month, the beneficiary receiving $100 each month would be ineligible, and the trustee would not have the power to reduce the mandated monthly $100 payment.

Therefore, it is usually advisable to give the trustee mostly discretionary powers. In a discretionary trust, the trustee can adapt the benefits paid to the beneficiary according to the situation, adjusting them to meet the changing condition and needs of the individual with mental retardation, and the changing status of government programs.

The trust instrument created by the settlor (parent) should name the "remainderman," that is the person or persons who will receive any assets remaining in the trust at its termination. Another provision should state when that termination will occur. In the type of trust we have been considering, the instrument normally provides that it will terminate upon the death of the beneficiary.

The instrument should also contain a "spendthrift clause." This provision ensures that the beneficiary may not pledge or encumber the assets of the trust. This will prevent any creditor, including state government, from acquiring the trust funds.

■ Choosing a Trustee

Clearly, the trustee plays a central role in the operation of a successful trust. Great care must therefore be taken by the settlor in selecting a trustee. The trustee should be someone who knows the person with mental retardation, understands her needs, and in whom the parents have considerable confidence. A sibling of the retarded person or a family friend is often a good choice. If the person whom the parents wish to name as trustee is inexperienced in investments or for any other reason is unable to manage a trust as large as the one being created, the parents might name a bank or other financial institution as "co-trustee," with the trust instrument specifying the powers and duties of each. For example, the financial trustee might be responsible for investing and managing the trust's assets, and the personal trustee responsible for distributing funds to the beneficiary and buying goods and services for him. Before naming a corporate trustee, the settlor should determine what fees will be charged; fees vary widely between institutions. Some local chapters of the Association for Retarded Citizens are also willing to serve as trustee or co-trustee.

Resources

Because considerable care is required to develop an estate plan that will fill the specific needs of particular parents and their particular child with mental retardation, it is essential that the family considering estate planning consult a good lawyer, preferably one experienced in planning for parents in their situation.

A booklet, "Estate Planning for Parents of Persons with Developmental Disabilities" (revised, December 1986) is available from the Disability Law Center of Massachusetts (DLC), 11 Beacon Street, Suite 925, Boston, MA 02108; (617) 723-8455 (Voice or TDD). (DLC requests a small contribution for each booklet.) The booklet is written in clear, non-technical language and should be useful to parents, service providers, and also lawyers who have knowledge and experience in estate planning and trusts but are not familiar with the special considerations that apply to families where one member has mental retardation.

Glossary of Terms

Beneficiary: the person for whose benefit a trust has been created.

Bequest: a gift made through a will.

Co-trustee: one who shares in managing a trust.

Discretionary powers: powers that provide a trustee many options in managing a trust's assets and in adapting the benefits furnished to the beneficiary in order to accommodate varying situations.

Disinherit: to exclude from inheritance.

Equitable title: In a trust, the beneficiary has equitable title but no legal title, meaning that he does not own the trust but is legally entitled to all benefits flowing from the trust.

Estate: all property, both real and personal, that a person owns at the time of her death.

Executor: the person responsible for collecting, maintaining, and distributing the assets of an estate in accordance with the terms of the will.

Inter vivos trust: a trust that takes effect during the settlor's lifetime.

Intestate: dying without leaving a will.

Jointly owned property: When two or more people jointly own property, and one of the owners dies, the remaining owner(s) becomes the sole owner of the property. This is the right of survivorship.

Legal title: ownership.

Life insurance: a contract with a life insurance company under which the company agrees to pay a specified sum of money to a designated beneficiary upon the death of the insured person.

Luxuries trust: a trust that supplements rather than replaces government aid.

Mandatory provisions: statements contained in a trust that require the trustee to act in certain ways.

Morally obligated gift: a gift or bequest given to someone with a request that the gift be used only for the benefit of a third party.

Personal property: everything other than real property, including cars, jewelry, clothing.

Precatory language: instructions accompanying a morally obligated gift that state the uses to which the gift should be put. Precatory instructions are not legally binding.

Probate court: the court that determines the validity of a will and then ensures that the will's instructions are carried out.

Real property: real estate, land.

Remainderman: the person(s) who receives the remaining assets of a trust at the trust's termination.

Settlor: a person who establishes a trust.

Spendthrift clause: a provision in a trust ensuring that the beneficiary does not pledge or encumber the assets of the trust.

Survivor: the remaining owner of jointly owned property after the death of the other owner(s).

Testamentary trust: a trust established in the settlor's will that takes effect upon the settlor's death.

Testator: the person making the will.

Trust: a legal relationship created by one person, called the "settlor," in which another individual, the "trustee," owns and manages property for the benefit of a third person, the "beneficiary."

Trust instrument: the document that creates a trust.

Will: a legal document providing instructions for how an estate will be distributed upon death.

50

BURNOUT AMONG FAMILY CAREGIVERS

Edith Finaly-Neumann

■

The concept of *burnout* emerged in the early 1970s. Its heritage is embedded in the ideas of Herbert Freudenberg, Christina Maslach, and Ayala Pines. Since then, the term "burned out" has been used to describe a condition of staff and administrators in positions that have a high degree of people contact.[1] I would like to extend this concept of burnout to family caregivers as well.

Burnout may be a widespread consequence of caregiving. A definition of burnout as a response to chronic emotional stress contains three components: emotional and/or physical exhaustion, lowered job productivity, and depersonalization. There is a general consensus that the symptoms of burnout include attitudinal, emotional, and physical components.[2]

Staff who work with people who are mentally retarded and old often need to make decisions on behalf of their clients. (See Chapter 23) One important type of recommendation made by our Interdisciplinary Team had to do with placement out of an institutional residential setting. Sometimes this recommendation resulted in the person with mental retardation being placed either in a foster home or in the care of a family member. Financial assistance, services, and emotional support are needed to provide an alternative to institutional care of people who are old. This sort of residential placement also links the older person with mental retardation to the formal community resources that he needs.

The results of a decision to have a family care for a person with mental retardation who is old are not without possible adverse consequences to the parties involved. One of the major consequences of this care is the family burnout response. The process of burnout is more often the result not of stress *per se,* but of unmediated stress: being stressed and having no "out," no buffer, and no support system.[3]

Stress occurs when there is a substantial imbalance (perceived or real) between the environmental demands and the response capability of the individual. As the environmental demands increase or the response capability of the individual decreases, the likelihood that stress will become a negative experience—ultimately effecting a burned out state—becomes higher.

As mentioned earlier, the term *burnout* is usually reserved for human service work. I believe that as family caregivers are basically exposed to the same risks of exhaustion and burnout as formal human service providers. In particular, the family caregiver shared the emotional burden of the developmental problems of the care receiver and channels large amounts of cognitive and emotional energy into the care receiver's struggles to cope. Typically, there is little return flow of understanding and support from the care receiver to the provider. This asymmetry in the emotional "balance of trade" is one of the major causes of burnout.[4]

But close contact with the problems, and the emotional asymmetry, are not by themselves sufficient cause for burnout. Another level of the relationship that causes burnout *is* symmetrical: as the care receiver depends on the care provider's help in her functioning, so too does the provider depend upon the care receiver's milestones of growth for a needed sense of efficacy. It is not just the heavy emotional investment that drains the provider; it is the fact that it is an investment that has insufficient dividends. The most highly valued dividends are the developmental gains of the care receiver, not her expressions of appreciation for those gains. Clients or family members who do not progress deprive their providers of an essential psychological nutrient. Once it becomes obvious that efforts on behalf of the client are partly ineffective, in that they do not result in significant developmental gains, the emotional withdrawal of the caregiving provider is almost inevitable. The care receiver becomes a painful reminder of the caregiver's ineffectiveness.

Despite mounting evidence that informal care providers are often subject to excessive burdens that can result in burnout, the informal care system is still chosen by professionals in health and social service systems as the best solution. The legal system has also turned to informal care providers as guardians.

The family has been viewed as the last line of defense in caring for people with mental retardation who are old. Adult foster care homes have been recommended as a way to create family units for the care of these clients.

It is important to assess informal care providers carefully to determine the appropriateness of placement for a person with mental retardation who is old. Carefully planned intervention may relieve some of the burden caregivers experience. Support groups and programs that focus on improving coping with everyday problems, that provide opportunities for respite, and that give special attention to early intervention with family caretakers, may have considerable impact on the family's burden of caring for an person with mental retardation who is old. When an assessment team recommends placement of a client in an informal (family) caregiving system, it is essential that external supports be sought in order to prevent burnout.

51

TOM: THE STORY OF A FRIENDSHIP

Elizabeth J. DeBrine

■

Last winter I requested that my minister, Joanne, match me with a member of my church who was mentally retarded. Joanne responded, "God is gracious." Then she proceeded to tell me about Tom.

Tom is in his late forties. He is the oldest of three sons. Tom's parents died several years ago, and Joanne officiated at their funeral services. Joanne continued her contact with Tom by visiting him once or twice a month.

Tom has had some schooling. He can read and write fairly well. He used to work in a furniture store. He is an excellent housekeeper and a meticulous dresser, sometimes even a little flashy. Tom was living with his brother Fred in the apartment that they had shared with their parents. A third brother is married and has had little contact with the family in recent years.

I met Tom after church one Sunday. His brother Fred brought him to church just to meet me. Things did not go well at that first meeting. Tom was very nervous and only made eye contact with Joanne. Joanne had to repeat my questions to Tom, and then he would direct his answers back to her. Joanne tried to wrap things up as neatly as possible by explaining to Tom that I would visit or phone him a couple of times a month in order to develop a friendship. Tom panicked. He thought Joanne was leaving him and didn't want to be his friend any more. Eventually I got up to leave while Tom was still talking to Joanne. He was trying very hard to hold her by telling her how much he loved her and what a good friend she was.

After that disastrous introduction I decided Tom was far too needy for me and that this friendship idea just wasn't going to work. I spoke to Joanne, citing all of my reasons for not continuing this relationship: my 9-month-old son, Andrew, my impending move to the North Shore—Tom lived on the South Shore—and my lack of access to a car and public transportation. It was to no avail. Joanne was not going to let me off the hook.

The church could give me money so I could rent a car. Joanne would accompany Andrew and me, so I could get driving experience, and she would babysit for me. I could see that there was no way out. Joanne would not let me say no.

I decided to call Tom. What could I lose? Most of the conversation was spent explaining who I was and why I hadn't called earlier (it had taken me at least two weeks to get up the nerve), and why I couldn't come out and visit him the next week. I decided to try to develop trust with Tom by giving him my phone number, which he repeated back to me several times to make sure he had it right. Well, of course he did just what I, as a professional, expected him to do: he called me the next night. After being called several evenings in a row, I decided to "set some limits." Tom and I would negotiate just what night we would talk together and who would do the dialing. We decided to talk on Mondays, Wednesdays, and Fridays at 7:30 p.m. for twenty to thirty minutes. Another part of the agreement was that Tom would let me hang up any time there was an emergency at my house, because Tom had a very difficult time letting me go.

What did we talk about? Everything. The stars, God, our families, trips we had taken, things we liked to eat, cold remedies, wallpapering, and gardening. I found myself sharing with Tom things from my childhood that I hadn't ever told my husband—things like stars at night and pet snakes.

I was amazed. I was beginning to feel less like a counselor and more like a friend. I guess I really didn't believe Tom was capable of friendship because he was mentally retarded. I had never before had a relationship with someone who was judged to be much less intelligent than I.

Meanwhile, Tom's family life was becoming more complicated and stressful. In the late winter Tom's brother Fred married Marie, a woman who came from Korea with her four-year-old daughter, Susan. Awareness of the prearranged marriage was one of the primary reasons that Joanne felt Tom needed more friends. At first Tom was happy to have Marie living at the apartment, because she fulfilled Tom's need to be mothered. But this was short-lived. Tom quickly realized that Marie was Fred's wife; she focused her attention on Fred and her daughter.

My phone conversations with Tom continued as usual, but I began to hear complaints about Marie. Tom was very secretive about our friendship and didn't want me to give my name to Marie when she answered the phone.

The hostility between Tom and Fred increased. It appeared that Tom was being rude to Marie. He was calling her names while talking to me on the phone. He was angry that she was unable to understand him. English is a second language for Marie, and Tom stutters.

Also, the fact that Marie was using the household items that were left by his parents was almost too much for Tom to bear. Fred was gone for long periods of time during the week, because he was working two jobs; he spent weekends with his wife and child, building a family. There appeared to be little or no interaction between Tom and Fred.

In the late spring, Joanne, our minister, announced that she would be leaving the church by the end of the summer. I wasn't in contact with Tom for a week because of my family's move to the North Shore. When I did call Tom's apartment, Marie told me that Tom had blown up over the weekend and was in a psychiatric hospital. She was unable to give me the exact name of the hospital or phone number. Marie said Tom was "crazy."

I decided not to wait until Fred came home from work to get the number; I started calling mental health centers and institutions. I realized that I had finally found the right center when the nurse told me, "If we have a patient by the name of Tom, we will give him the message to call you." Two minutes later the phone rang, and it was Tom. I was so glad to hear his voice. It was during that conversation that Tom and I acknowledged that we loved each other very much.

I still don't know the whole story, but it seems that Tom lost control while at home with Marie. Fred called the church to see if someone there could try to calm Tom down. The situation deteriorated quickly, and Tom was taken by the police to jail, where he was "pink-slipped" (determined to be potentially harmful) and taken to the mental health center.

The mental health center staff didn't know what to make of me. I introduced myself to the case manager as Tom's friend and advocate and therapist. They wanted to know what part of the system I belonged to: the Department of Mental Health, the church, the family, or the Kennedy Aging Project. I didn't fit into their system, and I quickly discovered that they were not used to dealing with someone who was labeled as a friend.

The mental health team decided that Tom was not psychotic and, in fact, was barely mentally retarded with an IQ of 69. They acknowledged that Tom had rigid behaviors and loved routine, but they could find no grounds to keep him locked up. In fact, the therapist told me that their center did not know how to handle cases like these.

Unfortunately, Tom's family had had enough. They could no longer tolerate Tom's rigid behaviors, overwhelming anger, and loneliness. Fred had taken responsibility for Tom for years with no help from the system. He refused to let Tom come home. Since it had taken weeks for the mental health team to assess Tom's needs, and the center placement was to be only for twenty-one days, the time to find Tom a residence was running out. At this point the choices were nursing homes and the state psychiatric hospital. The case manager and therapist requested that I use my influence to find Tom a better placement. My contacts told me there were no group home openings, and Tom was too young for the nursing home. I was ready to concede and agree to the state hospital placement when Tom said to me, "I'm not crazy. Don't let them do this to me. I know how to do things. I'm not stupid, and I 'm not crazy!"

I called our lawyers at the Kennedy Aging Project. They advised me that Tom could not be committed to a state institution without an examination to establish that he was psychotic.

A big meeting was scheduled to discuss Tom's placement. The case manager suggested that I attend, but there was resistance from the therapist's supervisor, who felt that a friend's attendance was not appropriate. Tom's needs were supposed to be addressed by the mental health center's staff. However, if I wanted to attend as a professional there would be no problem. I finally convinced her that I would not interfere, but that I could help explain to Tom why he couldn't go home.

I was determined to attend because I felt no one was representing Tom. The case manager and therapist represented the agency that wanted Tom discharged as soon as possible. Tom's family were insisting they did not want Tom to return home; they felt they could not negotiate on this.

Tom was being seen by other ministers from the church who did not know him well. The ministers were rotating vacations during the summer, so I spoke to a different one each week. Despite these problems, the ministers were very supportive of Tom and me. However, due to time constraints and a lack of familiarity with Tom's situation, they couldn't go to bat for Tom. That left only me.

The day of the big meeting arrived with everyone feeling nervous because no one knew how Tom was going to react to Fred's decision. The case manager, the therapist, Fred, Tom, Marie, and her daughter were there. Fred explained to Tom that he couldn't move back home. Fred was upset, but managed to keep calm and state his reasons with love. Marie spoke about her anger toward Tom when Tom tried to deny that anything had ever happened between them. I felt deeply for both Fred and Marie. There is no question in my mind that they both loved Tom very much and found it very difficult to break the news to him.

Tom was panicking and was no longer listening. He just kept trying to patch things up between Fred and himself. Then the subject changed, and we talked about where Tom was going to live. The state hospital was brought up as being the only option, although it was a distasteful solution.

Then I spoke up. I thanked the professionals for all their hard work, but said that the state hospital was not an acceptable answer. I threatened to get a lawyer from our Project to keep Tom from being admitted to the state institution. I told them that I would not allow Tom to be admitted, and that I had important people who would back me up. The meeting ended shortly thereafter. Before I left I was able to speak to Fred and Marie about their decision, and I agreed that it was best for everyone.

About two weeks later Tom moved into a boarding house for men. No one knew if he could live with other roommates, get up early to catch a taxi to the mental health center three times a week, or adjust to living in a new town. In fact, Tom did all of this very well.

After about six weeks, Tom, Fred, the minister, the boarding house owner, the new case manager, and I sat down to review the situation and to define who was responsible for what. The church agreed to donate over $200 a month to meet room, board, and personal expenses; Supplemental Security Income covered only a small part of Tom's expenses. Fred turned the SSI check over to the boarding house owner, who would now be Tom's representative payee.

I promised I would call Tom at least two times a week, send cards, and visit once a month. Fred promised to visit two or three times a month. There seemed to be no hard feelings between the two brothers, although Fred appeared to experience some feelings of guilt.

Because of the church's support, Tom was to receive twenty-five dollars a week. It was the first time in years that Tom had access to his own money. There were no strings attached to the church's money. Tom could join a local church while maintaining his ties with his old church and not jeopardize his funding.

One of the nicest outcomes was that Tom's other brother, who had previously had no contact with the family, started seeing Tom twice a month, on Saturdays. Joe picks Tom up and takes him to his house, where Tom helps Joe with outdoor tasks. On one of the visits Tom treated his brother to a pizza. His brother was embarrassed, but Tom was very pleased.

Tom recently found a job at a local supermarket as a bagger. The sheltered workshop that Tom had been attending for several months helped him to fill out the forms and gave him a reference. Tom is very happy at the supermarket and is very proud of his work. His co-workers really like him and think he is a hard worker.

I learned many lessons from this experience. Most important was the fact that the results were worth the fight. Tom is successfully living in a boarding house with two roommates and is working at least 20 hours every week at the supermarket .

I have some doubts about the professionals and the system that is supposed to help people, mainly because the professionals never really *saw* Tom or his assets. Some tried to be helpful, but most were stuck within the system. I learned to look at a worker as an individual and not to be impressed by the title or degree.

I gained some insight into what it is like to be a parent or sibling of a person with special needs who requires services. Parents and siblings have to fight every step of the way for programs and services. It takes a tremendous amount of time and energy.

I learned that I could be three times more effective acting as a friend than as a professional representing an agency. In fact, the mental health professionals encouraged me to advocate for Tom because I could push harder than they could. I was unable to be an advocate for clients at the Kennedy Aging Project because of our time constraints and my unfamiliarity with clients.

I never could have taken on this relationship and all of its responsibilities without the church's emotional support. The ministers were very responsive to my anger and helped me to focus it in a constructive manner. Also, the church's ability to help support Tom financially made the boarding house placement possible.

At the Kennedy Aging Project we have found that churches in general are among our best resources for people seeking community. Churches offer a wide variety of social and educational activities and opportunities for service for their formal members, communities at large, and people who are undervalued.

When performing leisure assessments for Kennedy Aging Project clients, I usually recommend that staff try to find an unpaid friend for their client. However, I had no idea how much work it would entail. I strongly recommend that staff actively support the friend in the beginning stages of the relationship in order to help set realistic limits in terms of time and commitment.

Discussion of clients' finances has new meaning for me. An SSI check of $350 per month is very little money for housing, food, and personal expenses. It would have been very difficult for Tom to find a residence without the church's support. Also, it is degrading for clients to have to ask family or friends for pocket money.

I learned that friendship is a very powerful relationship, at times even stronger than familial ties. During his stay at the mental health center Tom often would not listen to the therapist, to the case manager, to family's advice and recommendations. But Tom would listen to me. Whenever the professionals could not convince Tom to try something new, they would call me. This gave me a great sense of responsibility because I knew Tom trusted me implicitly.

The final and best result is that Tom and I are now just friends. We no longer negotiate phone calls. I no longer counsel him, pigeonhole him, or mother him. He's just Tom, a very good friend.

ETHICS

52

ETHICAL DILEMMAS

Mary C. Howell

■

Elmer is a seventy-five year-old man who tends horses at a state farm. He is aware that people who are "old" are required to retire. He is so worried that this might happen to him that he conceals injuries that he sustains at work. When a horse stepped on his foot last month he did not report the accident, and his blue, swollen foot was noticed only while he was being helped in the shower. What retirement options should be available for Elmer? What is the value of his work for him, compared to the value of safety from risk of injury? What is the responsibility of the institution? What rights to self-determination does Elmer have?

Annie is a fifty-seven year-old woman, recently discharged from a state school, who lives in a community residence. At the age of twenty-three she had a tubal ligation at the time of a therapeutic abortion; apparently she had neither a part in the decision for sterilization, nor any education or counseling after the fact. What services should she now be entitled to, with respect to this prior experience? Is she due some compensation?

John learned to smoke cigarettes while residing at a state school; the cigarettes were given to him as reward for good behavior. Now, at sixty-eight, he refuses to stop smoking. His community residence and workshop both require him to smoke only outside the building. He has been exposed to a great deal of information about the health hazards of smoking. He is developing some shortness of breath after exercise. He is mildly retarded, presumed competent, and has no guardian. Should he be allowed to continue smoking cigarettes? Should caregiving staff take his cigarettes away, or force him to cut down? What are John's rights to autonomy? What should staff do on his behalf, "for his own good?"

We provide care for a special group of clients. Some with Down syndrome are old at the age of forty; others live on into their eighties or nineties, many of them in robustly good health. But their problems of well-being are many. These problems stem mostly from the fact that they are and have been isolated and excluded from a society that prizes intellectual capacity over other human qualities—such as friendliness, gentleness, and loyalty—a society that makes stigmata of degrees of individual differences that are perceived as alien, distasteful, even threatening. In short, most people with mental retardation, especially those who are now old, have been excluded from participation in the ordinary, everyday events of ordinary, everyday life.

Certain ethical dilemmas arise over and over again in the care of these clients. A dilemma is a situation that requires one to choose between two apparently equal alternatives. An ethical dilemma is a situation in which the two alternatives are defined or limited by opposed ethical principles. The preceding examples illustrate the kind of dilemmas we encounter; these are dilemmas that must be resolved by action and are not hypothetical.

In the Aging Project we taught about ethics in a variety of ways. In our day-to-day work with clients we sought and emphasized ethical dilemmas of care. In addition, we held a formal "Ethics Conference" twice a month; at these conferences a case was presented for debate by a broad range of interested attendants, both professional and from the lay community.

Before looking in detail at an additional instance of a representative dilemma, it is useful to consider a categorical analysis of certain typical themes and conflicts. This analysis proceeds from our experience in the Aging Project.

There are many ethical principles that can fall into opposition to each other to result in dilemmas of caregiving. Two opposing pairs are recognized over and over again. This first is the conflict, or dialogue, between *beneficence* and *respect for autonomy*.

The principle of beneficence is an ancient underpinning for professionalism and also for the more simple, less pretentious, and more primitive activity of taking care of another human being. Whether care is given freely, as a familial responsibility, or as work done for pay, there is an underlying assumption that what is being done ought to promote the well-being of the recipient. And whether the caregiving is performed directly—as by a mother for a child—or indirectly—as by nurses and aides under the orders of a physician—it is assumed that the recipient will benefit, on balance, from the care. Sometimes the principle is given as "first, do no harm."

The opposed principle, that of respect for autonomy, has only recently come into the foreground of these debates. It was not long ago, for instance, that one tended to assume that extreme old age or mental retardation was synonymous with legal incompetence, and that anyone cared for in a residential institution gave up all rights to make his own decisions. In our common law, however, every adult is presumed competent unless a judge decides, on the basis of evidence, that incompetence should be declared. And today there is increasing acceptance of the notion of legal incompetencies—situation-specific assessments that serve to ensure that an individual loses as few of his rights to self-determination as are necessary for the circumscribed need to make delimited decisions. (See Chapter 23) For instance, someone who has a condition for which surgery has been recommended may be found not to be competent to learn new information about the illness condition, about the proposed intervention, and about the comparative risks and benefits of having the surgery; that person might then be adjudicated as in need of a temporary guardian for medical purposes only, thus preserving all other rights to autonomy.

It should be clear that sometimes—often—there is a conflict between respect for someone's autonomy and the intent to do good for that person. For instance, a competent individual has the right to refuse any recommended medical treatment, even if that refusal is presumed to have a detrimental effect on the person's health and well-being. Our assumptions about the need to "take good care" make this a potential dilemma.

A second common opposition between ethical principles is the conflict between the requirements that *we protect the vulnerable,* on the one hand, *and make equitable distribution of scarce resources,* on the other. In the ethical traditions of government and society, and of our dominant religious and philosophical traditions, we take pride in our determination to protect, care for, and cherish those among us who are old, weak, poor, or in need. At the same time, we are told, now more than ever, that there are not enough resources to go around—that all of our national budget could be spent, for instance, on medical care alone—and that we must abandon the notion that everyone deserves to have every possible benefit. It is easy to see how these opposing principles lead to dilemmas of care.

These contrasting principles reappear again and again, in one real-life dilemma after another. Most of the dilemmas we encountered fell into one of the following four domains.

1) Dilemmas arise with regard to the definition, discovery, and defense of the rights of individuals. Do people who are old or disabled or mentally retarded have a right to live in a community, integrated with other people who are not old, disabled, or retarded? A right to compete for paid work, insofar as they are able to master work skills? A right to confidentiality in their dealings with caregivers? Many of these questions can be formulated by attorneys so they can be argued in courts of law.

2) Dilemmas arise with regard to competence to make decisions and consequent needs for protection by a conservator or guardian. What criteria can be used to make a confident assessment of a person's decision-making capacities? Is informed consent primarily a safeguard for the patient or for the professional? What requirements of character and knowledge should be expected of a guardian? Standardized protocols for examination of competency, drawing on experience from medicine, clinical psychology, social work, and law, need to be developed.

3) Dilemmas arise with regard to the process by which decisions can be made on behalf of the person who is deemed to be incompetent. What weight should be given to the person's own expressed wishes, such as a past occasion of apparent terror and rage in response to hospitalization? What elements of care are we obliged to give because a community of opinion believes that care is warranted? When, if ever, does a person's wish for immediate bodily comfort outweigh a professional's recommendation for a painful procedure that will probably extend life? One standard, usually called a "substituted judgment" standard, may deprive the person of, or allow the person to refuse, certain kinds of care that would be given under the second standard, usually called the "best interest" standard. (See Chapter 23) By what process do we try to find the space between "too little" care and "too much" care?

4) Dilemmas arise with regard to defining and measuring past wrongs and deprivations imposed by social policy, government action, and discrimination, and with regard to questions of restitution or recompense. Who is responsible for the existence of large, crowded, isolated public institutions where people with mental retardation (and

many others who were "misfits" but not retarded) were housed, treated sometimes with abuse and often with neglect, and were kept, bored with inactivity and lack of opportunity and education, out of the general view? Who now acknowledges the injustice of years of hard labor, for little or no pay, with no employment benefits? What is owed to an old man who has survived this sort of life and wishes only for a little pension so he can travel before he dies? Our public policy will not embrace these questions unless someone makes the effort to ask them, and to vouch for their importance.

There is a reason for this recent, burgeoning concern about the ethics of taking care of one another. It is, at least in part, because we are moving more and more in the direction of a service economy: a society in which much that we used to do for each other out of love, responsibility, guilt, or a sense of obligation, we now do for money, as a job. From day care for children to nursing homes for old people; from household maintenance to leisure and sports activities; from personal financial advice to the decoration of our homes and bodies. We are a society of "professional experts" selling services to each other, hoarding our knowledge and skills as commodities of the marketplace. In a service economy, accountability is both more exposed and more examined. The buyer is wary. And as a consequence we are increasingly thoughtful about how many-sided and qualified are the human needs we are proposing to meet.

For our clients who are both old and mentally retarded, ethical dilemmas are most likely to arise in four realms of choice and decision. The first has to do with housing: it is a provision of the federal Developmental Disabilities Act that people with mental retardation should live in the *least restrictive* environment compatible with security and safety. Large, isolated institutions are almost never least restrictive environments. Neither are nursing homes in most communities. There are not enough of the kind of residential opportunities that work best: foster homes, group homes, neighborhoods, and supervised apartments.

In a second realm of choices and decision, people with mental retardation are entitled to take part in daytime activities that make use of their acquired skills, promote sociability and bonding with friends, offer risks and challenges, provide opportunities for mastery and achievement, and promote self-esteem. Forced mandatory retirement is resisted by most workers who are mentally retarded; they do not want to leave their workshop positions—however dull, boring, repetitive, underpaid, and exploitative they might be—except for the opportunity to do something more challenging and more interesting.

Third, there are difficult choices to be made with regard to social supports, including paid caregivers, professional services, access to friends, and relations with family members. As in every other realm, it is clear that mental retardation does not disqualify an individual from needs for and rights to services, both paid and unpaid. At the same time, a close look at the services that can be found and sustained reminds us how fortunate we are when we can avoid cataclysms of *exceptional* need in our lives.

Kin, for instance, may avoid the adult family member with mental retardation because they feel they cannot afford to be drawn into a position of personal and financial responsibility; because they have already made large sacrifices for this person's well-being and care; or because they are burdened by feelings of worried guilt. At the same time that these pressures keep family members apart, there is also a great yearning for reunion and forgiveness, especially as old age proceeds and death becomes a foreseeable reality. Paid social supports are often given in a manner that is demeaning. Unpaid friends are difficult to locate and make arrangements with, but can be treasures of genuine respect and affection.

Finally, there are the twin hazards of having access to too little, or too disrespectful, services for health care, or having access to too much, in the form of medical protocols that value prolongation of life over quality of life and cannot allow dignified death to come in its own time. Who, for instance, should be entitled to organ transplants? To advanced reproductive technologies? What relevance do the principles of hospice care have for those who are mentally retarded? Who should make decisions about medical care on behalf of the person with mental retardation who is dying?

As illustration of the context in which these sorts of ethical dilemmas are played out in real life, we present another story:

> *David is seventy-five. He was the youngest of five children and lived at home with his parents until he was fourteen, when first his mother and then his father died. David was a poor student and a discipline problem, and soon after his father's death he was placed in a state residential school, where he lived for forty-nine years.*

When David was sixty-four he left the state school to live in a community residence, first in a group home and then later, by progressive steps, in a staffed apartment, and finally in his own apartment. He was visited on a daily basis by a variety of paid caregivers who provided minimal assistance to him in managing his affairs. David is illiterate and mildly retarded; both before his discharge from the state school and after, he worked diligently and successfully at a number of paid jobs; for several years he was a porter in a nursing home. His wages were always minimal, and he has no savings, retirement benefits, or pension.

For the past year David has complained of mild abdominal discomforts, and also of indigestion; he has lost thirty pounds. No cause for these complaints was identified until recently, when cancer of the pancreas was diagnosed. As David has become weaker and less able to take care of himself in his apartment, transfer to a nursing home was suggested. David, who has a poor opinion of nursing homes from his personal work experience, reacted very strongly and negatively. He would never, he said, go to a nursing home.

The solution proposed by David is that he be readmitted to the state school that he left eleven years ago, the only place that he now identifies as his "home." His readmission would, of course, go against current state policy that the large state residential institutions accept no more admissions. David, who has always been considered competent and whose competence is not now challenged, insists that he wants to go home—where there are familiar buildings and grounds, and even some old friends among staff and residents—to die.

Should an exception to state policy be made for David, on grounds of his great need? On grounds that no less restrictive environment can be found for him? On grounds that he is entitled to some recompense for his years of involuntary institutionalization, and his unpaid and ill-paid labor? (David's case is also discussed in Chapter 19.)

53

INSTITUTIONAL ETHICS COMMITTEES

Mary C. Howell

■

W herever ethical dilemmas of caretaking arise, an Institutional Ethics Committee can help clarify ethical principles and issues and inform the decisions that must be made. Although Institutional Ethics Committees are ordinarily committees of hospitals, any residential institution where people who are dependent are cared for, and where numbers and disciplinary orientations of staff members (or consultant members) are broad enough to provide depth and variety of perspective, could consider the establishment of such a standing committee.

The notion of the Institutional Ethics Committee, or IEC, first came to prominence as a consequence of three landmark events in the late 1970s and early 1980s. In 1976, in the case of Karen Ann Quinlan (whose parents wished that she be disconnected from a mechanical respirator, as she was diagnosed as being in an "irreversible coma"), the Supreme Court of New Jersey recommended that a family should be able to consult an "ethics committee" in order to make this sort of decision.[1] In 1983, the President's Commission for the Study of Ethical Problems in Medicine and Biomedical and Behavioral Research, in the document "Deciding to Forego Life-Sustaining Treatment," recommended that appropriate procedures be used for decision-making, that ethics committees might improve decision-making, and that the courts should be involved only as a last resort.[2] Also in 1983, the federal Department of Health and Human Services promulgated the so-called Baby Doe regulations, which encourage but do not mandate that hospitals caring for newborns establish infant care review committees, analogues of what we call IECs.[3]

The functions of the generic IEC are to develop policies and guidelines for limitations of treatment; to monitor problematic cases by record review; to review specific cases in progress; to enhance patient (and family) competence by education; to provide for designation of surrogates to make decisions, in appropriate cases; to overcome the influence of dominant institutional biases; to provide review of the processes of decision-making; and to refer to the courts, when this is appropriate.

Ronald Cranford and Edward Doudera gave us this definition for an IEC: "a multidisciplinary group of health care professionals within a health care institution that has been specifically established to address the ethical dilemmas that occur within the institution."[4] One ongoing question with various answers is the matter of the authority of the committee, that is, whether it has enforcing or only advisory powers; this question can be answered by local custom, by the courts, or by the administration of the institution.

The idea of the IEC has evolved with striking rapidity. In 1983 there were seventeen committees in a survey of four hundred hospitals of more than two hundred beds. By 1986 nearly two-thirds of hospitals of this size had IECs.[5]

The IEC at the Fernald State School was an outgrowth of the Ethics Conferences begun by the Kennedy Aging Project soon after the start of the Project in 1985. Ethics Conferences were held bimonthly and were open to anyone who wanted to attend; at times during the tenure of the Project, Ethics Conferences were attended by caregiving staff and administrative personnel from the Fernald School, by caregiving staff from the community, by administrative personnel of various levels from the state Department of Mental Retardation, and by family members of the person who was central to the ethical dilemma being considered. On no occasion did a client attend the conference, but this would not have been counter to the purpose of the conference. A primary reason for deferring the explanation of the proceedings of the conference to the involved client until a later occasion was the constraint of time; the conference met for ninety minutes, and much of that time would have been spent introducing the attendees to the client and confirming that the discussion was understood as it proceeded.

Ethical dilemmas were brought to the Ethics Conference by members of a steering committee who were interested volunteers from the Aging Project and the Fernald professional community; while the members of the steering committee prepared the cases for presentation, anyone could recommend a case for review. Dilemmas discussed at conferences included such matters as the request by a group of parents of Fernald residents that adults be bathed only by same-sex staff; the question of retribution for a client who had been sterilized without her knowledge twenty years earlier; and continued residence at the Fernald School of a woman in her late sixties who was eligible to move to a community residence, but who considered Fernald to be her home and did not want to be required to leave (to be "deinstitutionalized"). In addition, more traditional dilemmas that recurrently confront medical caregivers for people with mental retardation, including questions of access to expensive or scarce procedures and questions of limitation of treatment at the end of life, were addressed. The purpose of the Conference was not to resolve dilemmas or make recommendations, but to educate about the ethical issues involved and to serve as an open forum to sensitize those who attended about the frequency of ethical dilemmas in caregiving, and about possible routes to the analysis and resolution of such dilemmas.

Out of this forum an interest developed in starting a formal IEC, with full cooperation of the administration of the school. Members of our IEC have always included a physician, a nurse practitioner, a nurse, a social worker, a member of the pastoral care staff, the Human Rights Officer, the legal counsel of the school, an administrator as delegated representative of the Superintendent, a member of the paraprofessional direct-care staff, an outside ethicist (from the Department of Philosophy of Boston College), a family representative (a layperson), and the Director of the Kennedy Aging Project as chair. The committee meets regularly on the second Tuesday of each month, and on an impromptu schedule as requested by anyone (professional or paraprofessional caregiving staff, administrative staff, family members, or a client) seeking consultation with regard to an ethical dilemma. In contrast to the Ethics Conferences, the IEC meetings are not open to the public. However, all who are involved in the case at hand are encouraged to attend, and on many occasions entire families attend to consider a problem of care for their family member.

We believe that the Institutional Ethics Committee at the Fernald School was the first such committee at a state residential school for adults with mental retardation. In several respects this presents the committee with circumstances that are different from those of the usual hospital-based IEC. For instance, medical care is provided at the school, but the institutional staff also provides total care for residents; the school is a self-contained community for the residents, although the staff come and go and do not live on grounds; the institution is funded by an arm of the state Department of Mental Retardation and is subject to the rules and regulations of that Department; an Office of Human Rights at the school has historically worked to resolve the kinds of dilemmas that were presented to the IEC; and all of the residents of the school shared the experience of institutionalization without culpability, a possible history of neglect or abuse from past experiences in institutions, and a label of mental retardation with some presumed level of being incapable.

The purposes of our IEC are those that similar committees in hospitals identify: (1) education of committee members, the community of the school, and the broader community concerned with the care of adults with mental retardation; (2) development of policies and procedures, both at the level of the school and for the central administrative office of DMR, with regard to the resolution of ethical dilemmas arising in the course of caregiving; and (3) consultation on dilemmas arising in particular cases brought to the committee by any member of the school community. Recommendations by the IEC are noted in the client's record; on occasion a letter has been written to the client's family, reviewing the committee's deliberations and recommendations.

Our Committee has no authoritative force, either according to law in our state, by local custom, or by administrative ruling; however, the recommendations of the committee have always been received with respect and have often been followed.

Certain pitfalls are common to IECs. One is the tendency to "groupthink" in committee decision-making, such that individual opinions are held back in the interests of reaching quick consensus. A second is the apprehension, within the institution, that the IEC wishes to oversee and judge; it is important to be sensitive to these concerns and to seek permission for IEC involvement in a particular case by emphasizing the educational focus of the committee's work. A third arises from the pressures of time: membership on the IEC obligates an individual to a substantial amount of reading, writing, discussion, scheduled and impromptu meetings, and outreach to both the institutional community and the broader community of reference. Otherwise the IEC is only a shadow committee and will be neither effective nor trusted. Probably no IEC can function efficiently unless it is staffed by an enthusiastic, competent, and energetic administrative assistant; we were fortunate to be able to provide this service for our IEC as a contribution of the Kennedy Aging Project.[6]

Bernard Lo suggests that one criteria for the effectiveness of an IEC is whether "parties in disagreements [about decision outcomes are]...satisfied with the process of review and with the recommendations of the ethics committee."[7] The next chapter considers the experience of the Institutional Ethics Committee at the Fernald School.

54

IMPACT OF AN
INSTITUTIONAL ETHICS COMMITTEE

Carolyn Nock

■

The functions of the Institutional Ethics Committee at the Fernald School were clearly stated from the beginning. The first was education of Committee members, of Fernald staff (both direct care and professionals from various disciplines), of families, and of a wider audience of professional and laypeople. The second function was the development of policies and guidelines to be promulgated to those who would have a role in recommending procedures and treatments. The third function was consultation and case review, of cases in progress as well as of cases no longer active.

Members of the Committee included physicians, a nurse practitioner, nurses, an ethicist, a priest, a social worker, a lawyer, a member of the direct care staff, the Human Rights Officer, a member of the Fernald administration, and a layperson who was also a relative of a resident of the school.

Early on the Committee recognized that there were no other state schools with ethics committees. The Committee at Fernald thus began work with the bare structure of a stated function and purpose. The lack of precedent is reflected in the early minutes; members raised many questions as to procedure and jurisdiction. Early discussion centered on how decisions made in the context of a hospital might be applicable at a state school for people with mental retardation.

Self-education began at the early meetings. The ethicist on the Committee offered a list of relevant journals for reference. Individual members attended conferences on ethics and shared information at meetings. Articles were distributed, read, and discussed. Terms with legal definitions—such as "best interest," "substituted judgment," and "competence"—were drawn from the readings and discussed as to their relevance to the special circumstances at Fernald.

Progress in developing as a functioning Committee was not linear; nor was self-education sought to the exclusion of other goals. Discussion of articles and terminology led inevitably to debate on issues and policy-making. For example, consideration of the ethical dilemmas posed by Do Not Resuscitate (DNR) orders led to discussion of how death and dying are dealt with at Fernald, and when and how a Do Not Resuscitate order might be written.

DNR orders became a major focus during the early meetings. There was already an active Death and Dying Committee on grounds. Members of the Kennedy Aging Project, in conjunction with that other Committee, had written a handbook on death and dying as a guide for staff serving developmentally disabled adults. It soon became evident that however well thought out a plan of care might be, implementation of this plan meant that caregivers had to grapple with the ethical questions involved. And so while discussion continued in Committee, practical aspects came more clearly into focus, particularly for those who were in clinical practice at Fernald.

A competent individual choosing to die at home is permitted to do just that; indeed, our society has sanctioned this in statutes and in the courts and also in a type of care—hospice care—that is now widely available. (See Chapter 60) Such sanction is less clear when the individual is mentally retarded. Is the person competent to decide for herself how much care she wants and how extensive treatment should be? If not, who decides and what factors are taken in consideration?

Out of a need to provide those who are mentally retarded with the same options as are available to other citizens, the Committee consciously decided to help create and support guidelines to enable people at Fernald to remain in their residence even if gravely ill and dying. The guidelines that were eventually published recognize the positive value of being in familiar surroundings with familiar staff and peers. (See Chapter 65) At the same time they define who would be eligible to be considered for remaining in residence, who should be part of the decision-making process, and what to do in the event of disagreements. As part of these guidelines, the IEC offered its services in consultation.

As an adjunct to the concept of remaining in residence, the Committee assisted in developing a Do Not Resuscitate policy. (See also Chapter 65) The ramifications of this seemed more serious—after all, not to resuscitate means making a life or death decision. It must be very clear that a decision not to resuscitate is never to be equated with abandonment of active medical treatment, and is consistent with the highest quality of medical care. Such an order is not carved in stone but may be rescinded at any time, should the prognosis or other factors change. The Committee agreed that a DNR order is appropriate only when the client suffers from a terminal and irreversible illness. In July 1986, a DNR policy was officially adopted by the Walter E. Fernald State School. In the policy is the statement: "Questions regarding the implementation of this policy should be referred to the IEC and to facility administration."

A case may be illustrative. Mr. C, a 61-year-old man, had a very serious heart condition. For years he had lived in a residence with a group of men who were his peers. He had many friends among both his peers and the staff. But the most important people in his life were his sisters, both of whom visited frequently. He went home with them often on weekends.

His heart condition worsened; there was no surgical treatment that could cure this. Aggressive medical therapy was instituted, but this too became less and less effective as time went on.

The primary care physician, nurse practitioner, and nurse met with the sisters in February; the doctor explained to the sisters about the worsening heart condition. As Mr. C's legal guardians, did they want him to be resuscitated if it should happen that he stopped breathing, or his heart stopped beating? A lengthy and sometimes difficult discussion ensued. The sisters were assured their brother would receive full and aggressive medical care, that a Do Not Resuscitate order meant only that cardiopulmonary resuscitation would not be started. Although the sisters felt fairly certain on that day that a DNR order was what they would want, the medical team respectfully declined their immediate decision, asking that they reflect on their answer over the weekend. They did so and decided that a DNR order was appropriate for their brother. The physician, relying on the policy, complied with the family's wish and wrote the order.

Gradually Mr. C's condition grew worse. Although he usually did better as warmer weather approached, the arrival of spring did not help. Adjusting his medications would alleviate his symptoms briefly, but then he would once again become sick.

As each setback occurred, the staff who worked with Mr. C grew apprehensive. The nurse practitioner attended a caregivers' team meeting to talk about some of the issues. The team voiced their commitment to Mr. C while telling of their concern that he receive the best care. As a result of the meeting, the nurse practitioner wrote a straightforward procedure for the staff to use. It was agreed that if any staff had a question or concern about Mr. C's physical well-being, the nursing staff would be called. The physician stated that a cure was unlikely and that some potentially helpful treatments also carried the possibility of pain and discomfort; he also agreed that for Mr. C, familiar surroundings and familiar people were an important condition of treatment.

The medical and nursing members of the caregiver team, as well as other team members, made daily reevaluations and reassessments of Mr. C's needs. On a good day he would go for a ride with his sisters. On a Thursday in May he had a particularly comfortable day and went home with his sisters for a visit.

The following Sunday, as he was getting dressed, he told staff he felt tired and wished to rest. He lay down on his bed. The staff, uncertain as to his physical condition, called the nurse. Mr. C had stopped breathing. When the nurse arrived she called the physician and Mr. C was pronounced dead.

The scenario could have been much different, obviously, if Mr. C had deteriorated in such a fashion as to require hospitalization for specific therapy. The point is that the DNR policy was in place, as were the "remain-in-residence" guidelines. Mr. C, his sisters, the medical staff, and the caregivers could rely on them.

The case was never presented to the IEC for consultation. It did not need to be; the policies and guidelines established by the committee were adequate guidance.

As the Committee developed and was publicized, people began to refer cases. Sometimes team members would raise questions about a resident's changing physical condition and how they could continue to provide quality care. One team presented a case of an elderly man, Mr. L, once ambulatory, now increasingly confined to a wheelchair; staff members and other residents were anxious to keep Mr. L in his current residence, protecting his safety as much as possible with the least possible restriction. The Committee members were able to help the team frame their questions in an ethical context. As the team worked through the problem they decided that they *could* adapt the environment; more importantly, they concluded that Mr. L's right to remain with familiar people in a familiar setting outweighed the risks inherent in his staying there.

Use of artificial feeding is as conflicted at Fernald as it is generally. In one case the Committee and the family concluded that no artificial feeding tubes or intravenous feedings would be used for a retarded gentleman with recurrent aspiration pneumonia, urinary tract infections, and seizures who was now suffering from Alzheimer's disease. In the shadow of the *Brophy* Case,[1] the administrators of the institution and the Medical Director were uncomfortable with the decision and sought review in the Probate court. The court's decision differed from the decision of the family and the IEC. Unfortunately, this led to an appeal that was lengthy, tiring, and expensive for the family; on appeal the family's wishes were affirmed, although the patient had by then died.

The most telling illustration of the effect of this gradual process of education, policy-making and promulgation, and case review occurred when a team coordinator approached a member of the Committee. He had thought through a case, isolated the ethical issues and asked the IEC member, "Can you help us? Can you do one of those ethical things to help answer this?" At the administrative level, also, division directors have begun to request case presentations.

This is only a beginning. The Committee must begin to reflect on its accomplishments and plan its future existence and goals.

55

A CASE FOR EQUAL ACCESS TO HEALTH CARE

Richard J. Pitch

■

Equal access to health care is a basic human right. It is not a privilege that must be earned by being productive in society, or by inheriting gifts of intelligence, beauty, wealth, race, or social class. When resources are limited, however (and they usually are), health care is delivered according to a priority list. Those who write that list generally place people who are mentally retarded near the bottom. I believe they do so not maliciously, but because they have little experience with people who are mentally retarded. With a long history of being hidden in closets (literally) and stowed away in institutions, people with mental retardation are among the most misunderstood of people.

The following discussion, which is based on an actual recent case,[1] illustrates some of the difficulties involved in maintaining equal access when a bureaucracy as large as an academic medical institution subscribes to the myth that people who are mentally retarded are less valuable than others.

> *Mr. R. was a 58-year-old man with moderate mental retardation who lived in a staffed community residence. Although nonverbal, he could make his needs known through sounds and gestures; in fact, he expressed a well-developed sense of humor. His receptive language skills were very good. Mr. R. was employed part-time doing table-top tasks at a sheltered workshop, and he helped prepare meals at home. He also enjoyed a number of social activities and had numerous friends. Mr. R. had no family contacts since he had been brought to a state institution when he was very young, and family members did not visit him. He moved to his community home when he was 47 years old.*

Mr. R. began to develop symptoms of fatigue and shortness of breath. At a university teaching hospital he was diagnosed as having aortic stenosis, a pathologic narrowing of the aortic valve in the heart. Although medicinal treatment can bring temporary relief of symptoms, open-heart surgery—a replacement of the aortic valve with a prosthetic one—is the only corrective procedure. The staff from Mr. R.'s residence advocated for the surgery, but the medical staff at the hospital decided, for a number of reasons, that Mr. R. would not be a good candidate and should not have the surgery.

One reason the hospital team decided against the surgery was that the post-operative care would require a great deal of compliance on the part of the patient. He would be on a breathing machine for a while. Then there would be breathing and ambulation exercises. Poor cooperation could lead to serious complications, such as pneumonia and other infections.

It is likely that the hospital staff assumed that because Mr. R. was not only retarded but also nonverbal, he would be unable to understand what was expected of him and would thus not comply with the necessary procedures. However, they did not know his capabilities. They were also unable to see the valuable resource they had in Mr. R.'s advocates—an interdisciplinary clinical team of professionals who knew Mr. R. well and were willing to be a reliable support system.

The rationale that was given, that Mr. R.'s condition could worsen if the surgery were done and he did not comply with post-operative care, did not seem to be a valid one. The complications from poor compliance were not as potentially severe as those from withholding surgery. Without surgery, Mr. R. would inevitably degenerate progressively; there would be increasing fatigue and pain, and he would eventually be confined to bed. He would die in one to three years. The rationale for not doing the surgery was probably based on concern about scarcity of resources; patients who seemed most likely to have a successful outcome were given the first priority of care. However, since the hospital team did not make an accurate assessment of Mr. R.'s ability to comply with procedures, Mr. R. was denied access to health care that he should have received.

Mr. R. was, in fact, capable of following instructions. The staff at his residence knew that he complied with medical procedures *when they were explained to him beforehand and when familiar people were present for support. Physicians know this is generally true for most patients, but they often do not take the time to explain procedures. It is also well-documented that the less educated the patient, the less likely the doctor is to allow the patient to have an active role in decision-making. In this case, as the patient was both mentally retarded and nonverbal, he was written off as so marginal as not to be capable (or deserving) of the procedure.*

One physician at the hospital explicitly stated that he felt Mr. R. did not have a quality of life worth preserving by open-heart surgery. This physician thus revealed that he felt that people with mental retardation are unfortunate and perhaps not even fully human. Further, he masked this prejudice as a concern for Mr. R.'s best interest: he implicitly welcomed Mr. R.'s impending death as a release from a unfortunate state of being. Since most physicians have had little exposure to people who are mentally retarded, and even less training as to their special needs, I would venture to say that this is a relatively common perception among physicians. Uninformed pity, however, can cause much harm.

This physician was also unwilling to listen to the evaluations of Mr. R.'s advocates, who would have liked to explain that Mr. R. was indeed a valuable person with a quality of life "worth preserving." They would have liked to tell the physician what Mr. R. was like when he was not sick, but the physician was not interested, and neither were most of the staff involved at the hospital.

What, in fact, defines a "quality of life worth preserving?" What disqualifies a person from the right to a medical procedure? Does intense physical pain make a life too terrible to save? Does emotional pain? Would a severely depressed person be denied open-heart surgery? How depressed would he have to be? Perhaps we define the quality of someone's life on the basis of his functional level. Therefore, the man with mental retardation must be miserable, as must the woman with paraplegia, the individual who is blind, and the recluse who knows no social relationships. Since each human experiences both pain and joy in life, perhaps we should construct a scale by which to rank the quality of each life, so we could know whether or not to save it if it is in danger.

Another way we can rank our relative value is by our contribution to society. One man is unemployed, he'll fall near the bottom. That woman is old, she has few years left anyway, so an investment in her care is not efficient. Those people own large businesses, they can pay for expensive medical care. In fact, they have already bought a share in the copyright for the scale we just proposed.

Unfortunately, this is the kind of scale that is constructed when we have only limited resources to provide services to many people. We are forced to decide whom to help first. (Who are "we?" Who has the right or the burden of making such decisions?) Under these conditions, the ethic of providing equal access is tested and often falls apart. Actually, there are many principles that outline, or argue about, what to do when resources are scarce. For example, one principle of justice says we ought first to help those who are the least advantaged. We do not often follow that principle.

In the procedure of replacing an aortic valve, it is not the part that is expensive or limited in number: the valve itself is of synthetic, manufactured material. It is the cost of time by medical professionals and hospital facilities that imposes constraints. Typically, a patient has to wait several months for surgery. There is a waiting list. Sometimes a person with connections gets merit points and moves up the list more quickly than others. Therefore, the physician thinks, "I can't operate on this mentally retarded person before Mr. X., who has four children, or Ms. Y., who owns four companies, or Mr. Z., whose sister is a trustee of the hospital." For some physicians, this thought is too distasteful even to acknowledge consciously. The thought becomes progressively masked and translated: the patient is too weak to handle the procedure; the patient will probably not follow instructions and will be worse off after surgery; or the patient's life is so miserable it is a blessing that she will die anyway.

Mr. R. was fortunate to have many determined and resourceful advocates. They continued to push for his operation, but without dominion in the hospital their power for change was limited. One physician at the hospital took an interest in Mr. R.; he wanted to know what Mr. R. was like when he was not sick. He became convinced that Mr. R. did have a quality of life "worth preserving." As an insider in the hospital bureaucracy, this physician was able to arrange for Mr. R. to remain at the hospital for a while. As the hospital staff got to know and like Mr. R., their attitudes changed. Myths were extinguished.

Mr. R. was granted the surgery within a few months. He complied with procedures, with the support of his familiar residential staff. He made a strong and complete recovery and has resumed his life in the community.

Not all people with mental retardation have such support systems. Many have families who are uninvolved. Many live in institutions or residences where the staff are too divided or too unmotivated to be strong advocates. And everywhere, people who are mentally retarded encounter others who are afraid of them, who pity them, or who simply don't know how to be with them.

We need to teach others how to be with them.

56

STAFF TRAINING IN ETHICS

Mary C. Howell and Richard J. Pitch

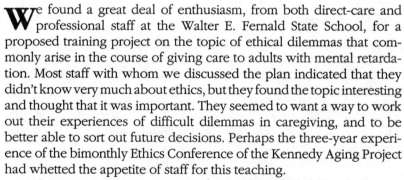

We found a great deal of enthusiasm, from both direct-care and professional staff at the Walter E. Fernald State School, for a proposed training project on the topic of ethical dilemmas that commonly arise in the course of giving care to adults with mental retardation. Most staff with whom we discussed the plan indicated that they didn't know very much about ethics, but they found the topic interesting and thought that it was important. They seemed to want a way to work out their experiences of difficult dilemmas in caregiving, and to be better able to sort out future decisions. Perhaps the three-year experience of the bimonthly Ethics Conference of the Kennedy Aging Project had whetted the appetite of staff for this teaching.

Our contemporary concern about ethics probably reflects two parallel cultural trends. The first is a growing interest in the importance of spirituality in our lives, an interest that makes us want to explore areas of thought and action that reflect our struggle to be spiritually aware and centered.

The second trend is a maturity of intent in human service work, such that there is concern to do the work well—in the sense of "right," beyond the merely technical—with thoughtful reflection and sensitive deliberation. This maturity of intent on the part of caregivers reflects a growing understanding that the work of giving care to other people is of great importance for the "rightness" of our culture as a whole. One consequence of these parallel trends is an appreciation of the complexity of dilemmas where more than one course of action seems to be mostly correct, and no single course of action seems to be entirely correct, in the moral sense.

This interest expressed by staff led us to write a Staff Training Manual on the subject of ethical dilemmas encountered in giving care to people with mental retardation.[1] This manual was then used as a guide for training sessions with staff.

The manual is centered on specific cases, drawn from actual experience and altered only to conceal the identity of the protagonists. The cases are instances in which there were clear-cut dilemmas about the "best" course of action, dilemmas that were related to and centered in opposed ethical principles.

The purposes of the Training Manual and the group staff training sessions were to:

- increase awareness of the frequency and range of ethical dilemmas in everyday caregiving situations;

- give permission to deliberate and discuss the difficulties engendered by ethical dilemmas;

- teach a language of ethical concepts—of principles and rules—and of the issues and contexts surrounding ethical dilemmas commonly experienced in caregiving work with adults who are mentally retarded; and

- create a climate of understanding and tolerance for ambiguity that allows staff to cope with true dilemmas and with the need to take some action, the action that seems most grounded in ethical principles, even when no action is entirely "right."

The content of the Staff Training Manual, and the content of the series of staff training sessions, begin with discussion of the difficulty of selecting a best action in a situation of ethical dilemma. A series of briefly-presented cases stirs interest and gives the trainees a general context for the work to come.

A second session of training is devoted to discussion of the principles of beneficence and respect for autonomy, and also of protection of the vulnerable and equitable distribution of scarce resources. The two pairs of principles are set in opposition to each other, to highlight the tensions that can arise when more than one ethical principle leads to more than one course of action.

This second session continues with a summary of the domains in which these principles are likely to be recognized in opposition, when the human subjects are adults with mental retardation. These domains are (1) whether the subject is competent to make his own decisions or should have the decisions made for him by someone else; (2) who should make decisions (if not the subject) and by what process; (3) what rights the subject is owed, and whether they are being honored; and (4) what retribution or compensation is owed to a subject whose rights have been significantly violated in the past.

The second session concludes with an outline of common contexts in which ethical dilemmas are recognized for this group of clients. These contexts include housing, day-programming, social supports, and medical services. Figure 1 demonstrates visually the intersection of the three elements of principles, domains, and contexts.

Figure 1
Protecting the Vulnerable

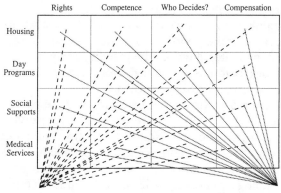

BENEFICENCE
vs
RESPECT FOR AUTONOMY

PROTECTING THE VULNERABLE
vs
EQUITABLE RESOURCE DISTRIBUTION

The rest of the Training Manual, and the remainder of the training sessions, are devoted to discussions of cases. Eight cases are presented, in two parallel groups of four; one or two cases may be taught and discussed at a single session. The second group of four cases could be used for home study, if group teaching time is limited.

Trainees are asked to read cases as if they themselves were direct participants, and to consider what the situation asks of them in terms of decisions and action. A short discussion of "Contradictions" brought forward by each case, and a series of questions based on the case and the surrounding discussion, stimulates engagement by the trainees.

The Training Manual can be used by staff as a personal study-workbook, or as a class text for group teaching. We have no doubt that the stimulation of discussions with other trainees adds to the richness of the training. Because released time for staff training is difficult to arrange, we urge that training take place during times when clinical teams are already scheduled to be assembled, even, if possible, during times that have been set aside for in-service training.

Staff training sessions are probably ideally conducted by someone with special training in ethics—a rabbi, priest, or minister, or a theologian, philosopher, lawyer, or ethicist. But others with less specific training can also lead group sessions. The Training Manual is designed to sensitize staff to the problems and concepts of ethical dilemmas, and can be read even without assistance of a group leader. For instance, a functioning leaderless team could use the Training Manual for group self-instruction, if no ethicist were available to teach.

In pilot training sessions we conducted during the writing of this manual, we found that the people who felt they gained the most were those who read the material before the meeting and who participated actively in the discussion. Such participation made the meetings not only more informative, but also rewarding.

During these pilot trainings we also surveyed the participants. It was commented that staff are not given enough opportunity to learn how to sort out such dilemmas. Nor are they given much credit for attempting to decide on the course of action that seems "most right." The illustrative cases discussed often reminded staff of similar situations in their own buildings. Almost all of these participants felt that this kind of training program was needed at their workplace; if it were made available, they would like to attend.

SERVING THE UNDERSERVED

57

PROTECTING THE RIGHTS OF THE CLIENT WITH ALZHEIMER'S DISEASE

Deirdre G. Gavin

■

In our concern for the safety and physical well-being of a person with Senile Dementia of the Alzheimer's type (SDAT), it is easy to overlook the rights of the patient to self-determination. Protecting the rights of people with Alzheimer's disease requires care and planning so that patients' wishes may be honored when they can no longer make these wishes known.

Three topics relating to patient rights have particular relevance to the person with mental retardation who has Alzheimer's disease: competence, informed consent, and research. Addressing each of these subjects early in the disease and planning for future developments will assist the patient in making many decisions for herself and will also offer protection from exploitation.

■ Competence

The whole issue of competence and what it means has been repeatedly debated, and different experts use very different tests to arrive at a judgment. (See Chapter 23) In the case of Alzheimer's disease, "the notions of limited competence and intermittent competence are useful, because they require a statement of the precise decisions a person can make, while avoiding the false dichotomy of 'either competent or incompetent.' Use of these notions preserves maximum autonomy, justifying intervention only in those instances where a person clearly is of questionable competence."[1]

In evaluating the competence of the person with mental retardation who has Alzheimer's, special consideration must be given to possible limitations in life experience that might falsely suggest incompetence. Past institutionalization, little or no opportunity for education, and the relatively controlled environment in which many people with mental retardation have lived, may limit an individual's knowledge but should not be interpreted as incompetence. Any adult may appear incompetent to respond when unfamiliar language is used to describe situations that have no parallel in prior experience or observation.

In assessing the competence of a person with mental retardation who may have Alzheimer's, effort should be made to communicate in terms that the client himself has used in the past. If new information is introduced, such as alternative living arrangements or proposed medical testing, the use of examples that relate to the client's own experiences would help to clarify explanations. Caregivers are vitally important in the preservation of client rights because they can explain to unfamiliar professionals the client's usual style of communication, her current experiences, and her past history. Thus, competencies may be judged within the context of the individual's life experience.

Probably the most important aspect of protecting the rights of the person developing Alzheimer's is discussion about and selection of an appropriate surrogate decision-maker for a future time when the client may not be considered competent. In the very early stages of dementia the individual could name a person whom she knows well, trusts, and who is capable, willing, and available to make decisions for her, consistent with her wishes. The surrogate could be a relative, a caregiver, an advocate—basically, someone known to the client who would spend time learning what she would want and what she would refuse regarding care and medical treatment. The client may clearly state her desires, and a written record may be established at this time for future reference. For example, an individual may express the wish to continue working as long as possible, or may wish to retire early to pursue enjoyable hobbies. Living arrangements can be discussed, and the client may describe those relationships that are most important in her life. Close friendships and the many years of companionship of a roommate or housemate are important factors in considering environmental changes. While competent, the person should be asked what she wants for herself and should also be offered realistic alternatives.

The client may formalize his choice of a surrogate decision-maker through execution of a Durable Power of Attorney (DPA). (See Chapter 23) The Maryland legislature has extended the use of the DPA (traditionally used for purposes of property management) to allow patients to select a surrogate for consent to procedures in health care.[2] Maryland law puts patient choice of the surrogate before any hierarchy of relatives.[3] To execute a valid DPA, a person must be competent. Thus, it is important to address this issue in the early stages of suspected Alzheimer's disease, before competence is seriously challenged. The concept of "limited" competencies recognizes that a person may be competent to appoint a trusted friend to make medical decisions for him while, at the same time, be incompetent to give his own adequately informed consent to treatment. In today's world of complex medical technology it is difficult for many patients, especially under the stress of illness, to comprehend full explanations of proposed diagnostic and treatment procedures, purposes, and possible consequences. It is, therefore, particularly helpful to the person with mental retardation to appoint a trusted representative to make medical decisions for him when he is incapacitated due to intermittent symptoms of Alzheimer's, or simply when medical information is too complex.

Depending upon the state, the DPA may or may not be used to designate a health care decision-maker. Many statutes simply state that a person may, in writing, designate another to act as her "attorney in fact." In Massachusetts, however, where the statute does not mention health care, an amendment has been filed to extend the Durable Power of Attorney *explicitly* to health care decision-making.[4]

The DPA provides greater autonomy to the client than other forms of proxy decision-making because the person who may later become incompetent may choose the surrogate herself, may authorize specific types of decisions, and may discuss and document her wishes *before* she becomes incapacitated. The DPA also allows her to nominate her own conservator or guardian for the time when she can no longer handle her estate or personal decisions.[5] Other proxy decision-makers are usually appointed when the client has already been found incompetent.

Legally authorized guardians are responsible for making decisions in the "best interest" of the ward[6] rather than by considering what the previously competent person would want on the basis of past history and preferences, expressed or implied, prior to dementia (i.e., substituted judgment). According to a 1986 study of consent by proxy in a nursing home, almost one-third of the proxies who believed that the patient would refuse consent nevertheless gave such consent.[7] Proxies may have no knowledge of the patient's wishes when competent, and thus may not adequately represent the patient as a true "proxy."[8] The solution that most carefully protects the rights of the person with

Alzheimer's provides, through the execution of a DPA, that the still-competent patient appoint an agent who will be empowered with the authority to make future specified decisions.

Presently there are no clear regulations that govern decision-making for people with Alzheimer's disease. Since the illness develops gradually and erratically, it is inappropriate to seek a finding of incompetence and the appointment of a guardian while periods of confusion occur only sporadically. Since there is as yet no real treatment for Alzheimer's disease, one may assume that the term medical "treatment" includes experimental approaches, psychotropic medications to control behavior, and therapy for intercurrent illnesses such as pneumonias. Under such circumstances it becomes particularly important that the Alzheimer's patient have a spokesperson to represent her wishes as faithfully as possible. Ideally the competent patient should make as many important decisions as possible regarding health care while competence is not challenged, and these decisions should be respected.

■ Informed Consent

Non-emergency medical treatment requires the informed consent of the patient; this is a matter of particular concern in protecting the rights of people with mental retardation who have Alzheimer's disease. To be valid, informed consent requires three conditions: first, the patient must be competent; second, consent must be voluntary; third, the patient must be informed of all the risks, benefits, discomforts, and all other likely consequences of the treatment.

The first requirement of informed, competent consent has already been discussed, and every effort should be made to allow the patient to make his own decisions as long as periods of competence continue.

The second requirement, voluntariness, presents a problem for people who are old and live in nursing homes, other institutional settings, or as a household dependent. Authority figures, even family members, may convey a sense of coercion to an elderly person who may also fear punitive consequences for refusal of treatment.[9] An advocate must remain alert to those treatments that do not benefit the patient but are administered for management purposes. One nursing home director described the routine administration of Haldol to all residents as a matter of policy,[10] despite the fact that falls and increased cognitive impairment are listed among the possible side effects of the medication. Caregivers must be watchful that the Alzheimer's patient's right to make treatment decisions is respected or that a legally authorized decision-maker is appointed. In Massachusetts, a *Rogers* hearing is required to authorize the administration of antipsychotic medication to a person who has been found incompetent. (See Chapter 23)

The third component of informed consent requires that the patient be told all the risks, benefits, discomforts, and other likely consequences of the treatment. However, in many states a "therapeutic privilege" allows the physician to withhold information regarding risks and adverse effects which, in his judgment, would be upsetting to the patient, would not benefit the patient, or would provide burdensome and unnecessary information.

In the case of the Alzheimer's victim, information would need to be provided early in the illness, and repeated on a number of different occasions, days or weeks apart, due to variation in comprehension and memory. A considerable amount of data documents the fact that, as the complexity of information increases, the comprehension of a person who is old and ill is likely to decrease.[11] The most successful informed consent processes—that is, those well understood by patients who are old—have employed both written and oral explanations, been presented in simple language, allowed time for questions, not been rushed, and not been extended over a single prolonged period. Written information has been more easily understood by using dark, large, double-spaced type or other simple graphic techniques.[12] For many people with mental retardation who have Alzheimer's, informed consent for medical treatment should be limited to procedures that are familiar or those that can be simply explained.

New York state has recognized the special needs of the person who is mentally disabled, without family member or guardian available, who has been recommended for major medical treatment but is presumed incompetent to give informed consent. Since court proceedings are often lengthy, expensive, and do not necessarily provide much substantive review of the decision about treatment, they are sometimes avoided either by treating patients on an "emergency" basis (which does not require informed consent that cannot be readily obtained), or by leaving patients untreated altogether. In response to this problem, the New York legislature created in 1985 two volunteer surrogate decision-making committees on a trial basis.[13]

Composed of at least twelve members, each committee exercises its decision-making powers through a four-member panel including one member from each of the following groups: (1) health care professionals, including certified psychologists and certified social workers; (2) former patients or relatives of people who are mentally disabled; (3) attorneys admitted to the New York Bar; and (4) advocates and others with recognized expertise or interest in the care and treatment of persons with mental disabilities.[14]

Each committee serves a specific catchment area and is available as an alternative to judicial proceedings to receive applications and make decisions about "major medical treatment" for residents of institutions and licensed community-based programs for persons who are mentally disabled. These medical treatments include medical, surgical, or diagnostic procedures in which general anaesthesia is used, or which involve significant bodily invasion, incision, pain, weakened condition, or a significant recovery period. The committees do not review routine medical diagnoses or treatment, routine dental care, or procedures that are governed by separate statutory or regulatory procedures (e.g., administration of electroconvulsive therapy or antipsychotic medication). Also excluded from consideration are matters that only the court may decide (sterilization and abortion), and those for which new laws are being developed (discontinuation of life-support systems).

The task of each surrogate decision-making committee, in responding to an application for consent to medical treatment, is to consider three questions. First, it must determine whether the patient is competent to give informed consent to the proposed treatment. If the committee finds the patient competent, it makes a formal ruling and provides both the patient and the treatment provider with a legal document to that effect and indicates that the patient's wishes are to be respected. Second, the committee must mail notices to appropriate persons to determine whether a family member or guardian is available and willing to decide about the medical treatment proposed for an incompetent patient. If no other legally authorized surrogate decision-maker is available, the committee will assume that role. The final decision for the committee is whether the proposed medical treatment is in the "best interest" of the patient. The panel does not, however, entirely reject the notion of substituted judgment. It is required to give careful consideration to "evidence of a previously articulated preference by the patient" and to weigh the benefits of treatment against the risks entailed, "taking into account...the personal beliefs and values known to be held by the patient."[15] The panel adapts its approach to the reality that, in the case of some people who are profoundly retarded, there may be no basis on which to determine what the patient would have wanted.[16]

The panel makes its decision by a majority vote of the four members, and the statute protects physicians and hospitals from liability when they rely on the committee's decisions. Committee members are also immune from liability for "conduct within the scope of their duties." It should be emphasized that a determination of incompetence for the purpose of surrogate decision-making is limited to the specific medical treatment that is proposed, unless ongoing or related treatment is necessary. The surrogate decision-making committee does not make general determinations of incompetence, nor do their decisions affect the patient's other rights.

The pilot program's first year results indicate that advocates and health care providers prefer this new and effective approach to the more cumbersome judicial process; in March 1988, the New York legislature voted to continue and expand the program.[17] The surrogate decision-making panels provide "quick yet careful individualized decisions in an informal and accessible forum."[18] Committee decisions in the first year include finding one patient competent, finding legally authorized surrogate decision-makers, denial of consent for various reasons (e.g., patient asymptomatic, risk outweighed benefit, insufficient justification for diagnostic testing), and also consent to treatment, with care to obtain second medical opinions when appropriate. The review process succeeded in some cases in influencing medical care: "as a result of questions from panel members, the proposed medical treatment was modified by the treating physician to reduce risks to the patient."[19]

New York's surrogate decision-making program offers a workable and individualized model for protecting the rights of people with mental retardation who have Alzheimer's disease and no available family member or guardian to assist in major health care decisions.

■ Research

The third and most serious area of concern in the protection of the rights of persons with Alzheimer's disease is that of human experimentation and biomedical research.

The availability of substantial funding, keen interest in and media coverage of research developments, and greater public awareness of Alzheimer's disease as an illness that can strike any aging person, have provided the impetus to seek research subjects wherever consent can be obtained. As yet there are *no* federal regulations specifically for the protection of human subjects of research in Alzheimer's disease,[20] although President Reagan endorsed research into the causes and treatment of the illness.[21] In September 1984 the Department of Health and Human Services issued the Report of the Secretary's Task Force on Alzheimer's disease, which outlined nine main areas of research that it sought to promote. These include: epidemiology, etiology and pathogenesis, diagnosis, clinical course, treatment, the family, systems of care, training of research and clinical personnel, educational materials, and information dissemination for professionals and the public. The report provided information on research findings to date and indicated needed research for the future.[22] It *did not*, however, offer guidelines for the protection of the human subjects of research.

At this point, discussion of research subjects will focus on vulnerable populations including persons with Down syndrome, mental retardation, and those with any past or present history of mental illness. I recommend the exclusion of these individuals from biomedical research and human experimentation relevant to Alzheimer's disease. The reasons for such a recommendation are based on past history, the potential for exploitation, and the long-range social consequences of a utilitarian approach to vulnerable populations.

Institutionalized mentally disabled persons have traditionally been subjects of experimentation. Convenience and stability of subject population over time; relatively uniform diet, daily routine, and sleeping schedule, and, frequently, the legal status of "ward of the state," have provided an inexpensive source of subjects for researchers. Their medical and psychiatric histories are well documented, and their controlled environment offers the appeal of a laboratory to the scientist.[23] It is precisely this "ideal" research environment and its historical significance that dictate the exclusion of mentally handicapped individuals from biomedical experimentation.

The current trend away from institutional living to smaller, more homelike settings or even family home care does not eliminate the coercive implications of dependency. Mental retardation departments provide means for tracking clients who receive department services, thus maintaining ease in locating this population. Institutionalization exerts such a profound effect on a person's decision-making power that ability to give informed consent may be seriously impaired.[24] Even in a more intimate, homelike setting, the person who is dependent and mentally disabled frequently responds to the caregiver's implied wishes. Those who have worked with individuals who are mentally retarded often describe clients' readiness to say or do what the client believes will please the caregiver.

Historically, exploitation of people who are mentally handicapped has persisted for centuries. Reference is often made to Nazi atrocities and inhumane experiments conducted on subjects who were institutionalized and mentally impaired, before their mass murders.[25] However, we need not look to Nazi Germany for models of such exploitation. In the same era, the United States utilized inmates of mental institutions as research subjects in accordance with popular ideas about sacrifices appropriate to the war effort.[26]

The ethics of American research during World War II were frankly utilitarian. Peace did not slacken the pace of biomedical research, but rather brought increased vitality. The Committee on Medical Research received federal support for research after the war, due to its record of accomplishments and in anticipation of even greater achievements. Biomedical human experimentation in the 1950s and 1960s continued with a sense of mission and urgency.[27]

Despite the fundamental research principle of the Nuremberg Code (1948) that "voluntary consent of the human subject is absolutely essential," the use of human subjects for research followed the utilitarian ethic well into the late 1970s, when federal regulations began to emerge.[28]

Today, deeply entrenched attitudes toward medical problem-solving may promote the use of human subjects with Down syndrome for experimental research relating to Alzheimer's. Many practical considerations support such a proposal. First, persons with Down syndrome develop Alzheimer's disease much more frequently than the general population. As discussed in Chapter 36, according to *post-mortem* findings, the rate is nearly 100 percent, although only one in three develop symptomatic behavioral changes before death.[29]

Secondly, adults with Down syndrome age at a faster rate than the rest of the population, and symptoms of Alzheimer's, if they are to develop, will appear 10 to 20 years earlier than they would in non-Down syndrome victims.[30] This might be considered advantageous to researchers.

A third consideration has already been described and relates to many people who are mentally handicapped. State departments of mental health or retardation monitor clients who receive their services, and thus facilitate locating individuals with Down syndrome. This offers an additional convenience for researchers.

Most dangerous of all is the concept of expendability, in past and possibly future application to research subjects. As evidence of expendability, many fetuses diagnosed with Down syndrome are aborted every year. The prospect of utilizing people with Down syndrome as the ideal subjects of biomedical research and human experimentation in Alzheimer's disease raises the specter of the crimes that proved the need for the Nuremberg Code.

Our proposal for the exclusion of individuals with Down syndrome from biomedical experimentation is based on what ethicist Hans Jonas calls the "rule of the ascending order," as described in the following quote:

> Let us note that this is the opposite of a social utility standard, the reverse of the order by "availability and expendability": The most valuable and scarcest, the least expendable elements of the social organism, are to be the first candidates for risk and sacrifice... We feel a rightness about it and perhaps even a higher "utility," for the soul of the community lives by this spirit. It is also the opposite of what the day to day interests of research clamor for, and for the scientific community to honor it will mean that it will have to fight a strong temptation to go by routine to the readiest sources of supply—*the suggestible, the ignorant, the dependent, the "captive"* in various senses. I do not believe that the heightened resistance here must cripple research...; but it may indeed slow it down by the smaller numbers fed into experimentation in consequence. This price—a possible slower rate of progress—may have to be paid for the preservation of the most precious capital of higher communal life.[31]

Philosopher John Rawls's theory of justice supports the exclusion of people who are mentally handicapped from biomedical research on the basis that, since "inequalities of birth, historical circumstance, and natural endowment are undeserved, society should correct them by improving the unequal situation of naturally disadvantaged members."[32] According to Rawls's theory, justice would require protection for people who are mentally disadvantaged.

Protection from biomedical experimentation for people who are mentally impaired is vital today because of the rapid proliferation of medical and surgical innovations to address previously incurable diseases. Fetal brain tissue transplants are currently performed experimentally to treat Parkinson's disease.[33] It may be that similar surgery will soon be performed on the victims of Alzheimer's. Among people who are affluent and professionally and socially successful, less tolerance for this form of dementia is frequently reported than among populations more familiar with adversity. Embarrassment and a sense of degradation among those whose expectations throughout life have remained high may place particular urgency upon the demand for a cure at any cost. Public policy must set the limits for Alzheimer's biomedical research before society adopts, as it has in the past, a purely utilitarian approach to the selection of experimental subjects.

■ Conclusion

The study of history provides a warning that care and vigilance must be maintained if we are to respect the rights of all individuals—particularly people who are old, sick, or disabled.

Today we eagerly pursue dreams we once believed were impossible, looking to research as our vehicle to success. Perhaps this is also a time to pause, reflect, and carefully consider the decisions we urge upon citizens who are elderly and infirm.

Tomorrow, any one of us may develop Alzheimer's disease. We are *now* not simply planning for others; we are determining our own future and the character of our society as a whole.

In the words of Hans Jonas:

> Let us...remember that a slower progress in the conquest of disease would not threaten society...but...Society would indeed be threatened by the erosion of those moral values whose loss, possibly caused by too ruthless a pursuit of scientific progress, would make its most dazzling triumph not worth having.[34]

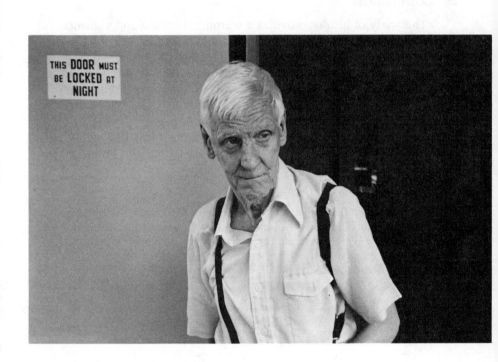

■

DEATH AND DYING

■

58

GRIEF COUNSELING

Mary C. Howell

■

Death is the endpoint of growing old. As children, we can hardly imagine death. In youth, we defy death. By mid-life, we begin to understand death as more than a concept—it becomes an inner reality, an expectation. As old age moves through us, we come more and more to accept the coming fact of our own death, an acceptance that is reinforced by our participation in rituals that commemorate the deaths of others who are close to us.

Cross-culturally, awe is always a central aspect of the human regard for death. But in our culture, we have learned to look at death with different emotions—fear, even loathing. In medical science, death is regarded as the enemy to be vanquished. This cultural perspective makes it difficult for us to do the work that we need to do to prepare for death. Only when we can look on death as the last great transition, the proper end to life, perhaps even the beginning of other unknowns, can we look toward our timely death with a welcome anticipation.

People with mental retardation are no different in this respect than the rest of us. We can realize how strongly our culture disparages old age when we hear a person with mental retardation say, "I don't like [that person]; she's old. I don't ever want to be old." We have very little permission to talk about death in an open and exploring fashion; with people who are mentally retarded, the same pained avoidance usually appears when we open a conversation about dying. Allowing and encouraging talk about death, teaching some words and concepts, demonstrating attitudes of respect and strength, are gifts for someone with mental retardation who is growing old and thus approaching death.

Learning to look at death is part of learning to look at loss and mourning. Mourning is a process, not an illness. Commonly, mourning the loss of someone who is important to us takes a period of about two years. If mourning does not proceed well—if it gets "stuck"—then it can become dysfunctional. Every episode of mourning we enter revives all of our past losses. Mourning can get stuck in feelings of anger, sadness, or denial of the importance of the loss; depression is one common expression of incomplete mourning. It is healthy to review our past losses at the time of a new loss and period of mourning; often those prior experiences of loss can be brought closer to completion and can therefore be less disturbing in everyday events of life.

Experiencing loss and mourning is part of what it means to be a human being, irrespective of one's level of cognitive development and capability. Losses come thick and fast as old age proceeds; understanding about loss and mourning is an important preparation for the last stage of life.

Our most important losses are valued people and activities—our sources of esteem, what we value, and what makes us feel valued. Retirement from work is a loss. Changing our place of residence is a loss. Dropping out of favorite activities—riding a bicycle, playing softball, or manipulating yarn and needles in knitting—are losses. When important people move away, take new jobs, disappear into new intimate relationships, or die, we experience loss. And of course the certainty of death, the loss of this body, the end of this lifetime, is a loss that comes more and more into one's awareness as old age progresses.

In these matters, the person with mental retardation is more like everyone else than she is unlike. Depending on her level of cognitive development, she may or may not understand that death is permanent and universal (See Chapter 59), but she will always have *some* level of understanding about loss and mourning. That awareness will be expressed differently depending on her verbal facility and on whether she has a capacity for symbolic representation or deals primarily in literal, concrete conceptualization. One of our clients, dying and in pain, got comfort from holding a doll and "giving" her pain to the doll. Another, also dying, was able to ask that her favorite song, "You Are My Sunshine," be sung at her funeral.

When we work with a client with mental retardation, we must never assume that he "doesn't know" about the loss and the experience of grieving. Mourning that is not acknowledged may become the kind of mourning that is "stuck," that cannot be run through to any sort of conclusion, that stays in one's life and interferes with straightforward participation in a wide variety of opportunities. We must, in fact, proceed on the assumption that he knows about the loss, that he feels it emotionally, and that it affects his physical body and his spiritual center. We need to learn that there is no "easiest" time to start talking about the pain of a loss, but that the longer we put it off, the more difficult it is likely to be.

Grief counseling is a process that provides both information and support. The person who is grieving is encouraged to recognize emotions and to name them. She is given permission to experience them fully, and is not cut off or distracted from her expressions of feeling. She is taught ways to release anger—to run, scream, pound. Her fears are explored; most likely, she is afraid that she will not be taken care of or will be abandoned, and in this she is like all of us, although perhaps with better cause. Her sadness is validated and given opportunity for expression. For a person who is dying, who is mourning her own death in anticipation, a grief counselor is especially helpful.

Another kind of grief counseling can be done in groups. (See Chapter 67) It is helpful to make a contract with group members, to come to an agreement that these meetings will be useful, that certain topics will be discussed, and that members will attend every meeting. A series of eight or ten meetings is usually enough, but not too much; the goal is not to resolve all conflicts or even to transmit "enough" information, but to give to group members names for feelings and concepts, a realization that *everyone* experiences certain losses and mourns for them, and permission to talk about these matters. After the group has ended, members carry with them some tools for starting again on the next occasion that their lives are touched by loss. If group members remain in contact with each other (if, for instance, they live together or work at the same workshop), then their group process can also continue in a natural way.

In our experience the best topics for introducing discussions about loss and mourning are old age and "ageism," our societal prejudice against getting old. With encouragement, clients will begin to tell how their bodies feel different to them with age than they felt in youth, and will recall the aging of family members such as parents or siblings. The topic of loss is best begun by asking about pets, job changes, and staff turnover. Soon enough death will be brought into the conversation.

It is important to all of us that we have opportunities to take part in the rituals that honor people who have died. Too often, people with mental retardation have been excluded from funerals and memorial services for people who have been important to them. Sometimes the rationale is that the person who is mentally retarded "wouldn't understand" or "wouldn't be able to handle" the sad emotions. But, in fact, we have seen over and over again that *not* being invited to funerals and memorial services is a great injury, and interferes with proper mourning.

A central element in working successfully with people with mental retardation who need to explore their feelings and experiences about loss and mourning is our own progress in coping with past experiences of grief. In this, as in so many aspects of serving our clients, it is essential to recognize how much they are like us, for all their apparent differences of cognitive ability, living circumstances, and worldly sophistication.

We all have known significant losses. Most of us have experienced the death of someone who meant a great deal to us. Grieving is a universal human experience. Every new experience of mourning opens old wounds and asks us to look again at what we have lost and what we have become. Grief also calls us to count what we have now that we *could* lose. All this emotion gets called up as we begin to work with a client who is dying, mourning the death of someone close, or reacting to any of the losses that recur and repeat in a long life. As the end of life approaches, these losses accelerate, as does our awareness of frailty, isolation, and dying. By helping ourselves we learn better to serve our clients.

59

A DEVELOPMENTAL APPROACH
TO COGNITIVE UNDERSTANDING
OF DEATH AND DYING

Gary B. Seltzer

∎

In our society, discussion of death and dying has not been fashionable, comfortable, or safe. Death is the last of a series of points along the life cycle. Our avoidance of the topic of death greatly influences our own lives, and also our ability to work with and care for other people. The ability to come to terms with our own mortality can influence our interpersonal sensitivity to people who are experiencing loss, grief, separation, or imminent death.

Freud[1] held a different view, He suggested that we need to hold onto the belief that we are immortal and reject ideas to the contrary. This formulation of Freud and other similar formulations (e.g., Becker[2]) stresses our inability to recognize the inevitability of death. However, this denial of death exists more at the affective level than at the intellectual level.

It appears that there is developmental progression to our understanding of the construct, death. As a rule, this progression is chronologically-based and dictates when (at what age) we begin to understand the cognitive meaning of the word death. Children at different stages of cognitive development attribute different meanings to the concepts of death and dying.[3]

As adult thinkers we are capable of understanding our mortality, even if we deny it emotionally. Children at various ages of development, however, understand only the meanings for which they are cognitively competent. That is, before adolescence, children do not fully understand that death is a universal phenomenon that happens to everybody and inevitably will happen to them. Similarly, people with cognitive limitations may only be able to understand in an intellectual way that which is consistent with their cognitive developmental level.

For example, a person with mental retardation may not understand the hypothetical construct of "universal." That is, while he may understand that death is something that will happen to all the people he knows, including himself, he may not understand that death is something that happens to everyone, even to people that he does not know.

Being limited cognitively, though, does not mean that people with cognitive impairments do not feel the loss, grief, and bereavement that accompany death and dying. They do. It is important, therefore, to know what the person with cognitive limitations is likely to be thinking, in order to appreciate the meaning of that experience for her.

Interestingly, many of the cognitive errors made by people with mental retardation are similar to those errors that we all make when we are initially struck by the reality that someone we love and care for is dying or is dead. Often we become egocentric and employ magical thinking, a process by which we assume that we have the power to control the welfare of others by our actions. A typical example of magical thinking occurs when we believe that, if only we hadn't done this or that, the deceased would still be alive. The impact of this type of thinking can be dramatic. A spiral of self-blame can follow and other negative thoughts may result. Usually though, people without cognitive limitations or emotional difficulties are able to recover from these distortions. They can employ a more complex logical operation that allows them to understand that they do not have the magical power to control or prevent the death of another person. (See Mike's story in Chapter 67)

This emotionally charged misunderstanding of death is only one example of the many types of thinking errors that can be made by people with mental retardation. Obviously, it is not possible to predict the specific distortions that can occur at every functional level of mental retardation because specific life experiences affect the content of the cognitions. However, there are some general and predictable parameters of the thinking of a person with mental retardation that correspond to his level of cognitive development.

The experience of death and dying for people with mental retardation has been little studied. In order to explain the absence of literature on this topic, we need to take into account both the great ambivalence professionals and parents alike have toward acknowledging that death is a part of our lives, and the tendency we have to protect people with mental retardation from emotionally charged "adult" topics. The long-held paternalistic view that people with mental retardation are "eternal children" lingers on. Many social systems, including some families, religious organizations, and schools, "protect" people with mental retardation against the rituals and realities of death.

■ Cognitive Development and the Construct of Death

There is a relationship between the Piagetian cognitive stage at which a person functions, and her understanding of the meaning of death. I borrow liberally from the child development literature because there are few empirical studies that examine how people with mental retardation think, feel, or act in relation to the topic of death and dying. I use the Piagetian cognitive stages as a device to explore and, I hope, to enrich the varied meanings given to death and dying by people with mental retardation at specific stages of cognition.

The existence of a relationship between cognition and the resultant meaning of the construct of death is not a new idea. Other authors[4] have noted that how much one understands about death is related to cognitive development. That is, cognitive impairments may limit the extent to which a person comprehends the construct of death. As a person develops cognitively, he understands the construct of death in a qualitatively different manner than previously. It is not just that he understands more about death and aging, but rather that he attributes different meanings to death. During the earlier stages of cognitive development, it is quite feasible that a person might mistakenly think that death is reversible, temporary, and impersonal. The application of these erroneous attributes of death to the actual experience of someone dying is likely to foster a very different interpretation of the event. For example, if death is assumed to be reversible and temporary, then it may be thought that one could act instrumentally on behalf of the dead person and he would resume living. Such a bizarre notion may seem like a logical progression to the cognitively limited person.

Odd and bizarre behavior are rather normal occurrences during the grief and bereavement stages immediately following the death of a loved one. For most people, these distortions are diminished as the bereaved person adjusts to the loss. However, for a person who believes that death is reversible and temporary the distortion may go on. Such a person might believe that some gesture, some wishing, some egocentric action may be the right key to unlock the physical barrier between themselves and their loved one. After all, television programming is replete with shoot-to-kill-but-never-die adventures. If death comes and goes so easily on television, why not in reality? If the Road Runner cartoon character can get run over by a truck and come back to life, maybe getting hit by a car is the key to bringing a deceased parent back to life.

As a person develops cognitively, she acquires an understanding that death is actually irreversible, inevitable, biologically-based, and universal. Figure 1 shows the chronological ages that are associated with the development of these concepts, the concepts' relationship to the Piagetian cognitive stages, and the meanings associated with each age and cognitive stage, If, for example, a person with mental retardation functions cognitively at the sensory-motor stage of development, a stage at which objects out of sight are out of mind forever, then separation from significant others is a traumatic, anxiety-provoking event.

In fact, the work of Bowlby[5] and Spitz[6] suggests that separation from attachment figures at this stage of development is associated with significant psychological reactions such as depression and pathological grieving. Bowlby traces the sequences of reactions of a child at this stage as *protest, despair,* and finally, *detachment.* Bowlby suggests that the continual longing for the attachment figure is often mingled with generalized anger and hostility. Spitz notes that extended separations grossly affect the development of object relations and the ability to relate intimately and interpersonally with significant others. Thus, people with mental retardation who function cognitively at the sensory-motor stage of development may be continually limited in their psychological growth and ability to attach to other nurturant figures when separations occur in their lives.

A person with mental retardation who functions at the sensory-motor stage is unlikely to be verbally skilled. Instead, she generally experiences separations due to death by exhibiting excessive behaviors, either too many or too few, such as withdrawal and avoidance of task demands. Behaviors such as self-abuse, aggression, persistent crying, anorexia, and withdrawal are generally assumed to be related to the presence of environmental contingencies. By using these cognitive stages as guidelines for understanding how a person with mental retardation understands loss, the error of assuming that this person does *not* understand the meaning of death is less likely to occur. In contrast,

Figure 1
Development of a Concept of Death

Approx. Age	Developmental Stage	Concept of Death	Age
0-2	Sensorimotor Preverbal Reflex activity to purposeful activity Rudimentary thought	Expresses discomfort with separation Behavioral manifestation rather than verbal	infancy
2-6	Preoperational Prelogical Development of a represen-tational or symbolic language Initial reasoning	Uses word "dead," but only to distinguish "not alive." Limited notion; may express no personal emotion, but may associate death with sorrow of others Avoids dead things; imagines death as a personified being; believes he will always live, only others (especially those older than he) die. Associates death with "old age"; may be violent and emotional about death, including representations (e.g., magazine pictures) or may display intense curiosity about dead things.	3 years 4 years 5 years 6 years
6-12	Concrete Operational Logical Problem solving restricted to physically present, real objects that can be manipulated Development of logical functions (e.g., classification of objects)	Morbid interest in details (e.g., graveyards, coffins, possible causes); seeks answers through observation of decomposition, etc.; suspects he himself may die. Less morbid, more expansive; interested in what happens after death; accepts without emotion that he too will die. Understands logical and biological (e.g., absence of pulse) essentials of death; can accept full and rational explanation of death process	7 years 8 years 9-10 years
12+	Formal operational Abstract Comprehension of purely abstract or symbolic content Development of advanced logical functions (e.g., complex analogy, deductions)	Meaning of death appreciated, but reality of personal death not accepted.	Adol.

Adapted from Sahler and Friedman, 1981.

one is challenged to search for the meaning of the experience, given the mentally retarded person's capacity to think in a limited but still instrumental sense.

At the preoperational stage of cognitive development, a person thinks in categorical terms and egocentrism abounds. A person has the cognitive and affective capacity to appreciate that a loved one exists even though she may not be immediately present. There is a capacity to appreciate that there are gray areas, not only black and white or good and bad ones. Figure 1 describes some of the particular meanings that occur from the ages of three to six. During this stage, a person employs a great deal of magical thinking. Magical thinking influences a person's reaction to death, particularly when it is unexpected. When shocked by the news that someone we love has died, we commonly regress back to our magical thoughts. The "if only's" flows into our consciousness, expressing a power that we erroneously attribute to ourselves. And since we did not use this power, we feel guilty, as if we had done something wrong. Most people who have the capacity to return to a more logical form of thinking do so. However, a person with mental retardation who functions at this cognitive level is likely to maintain these thinking errors. For example, a person living in a community residence may think that, if only he had given his roommate the opportunity to use his stereo, a request that was often made and just as often denied, then he might have prevented that fatal heart attack.

At this stage of cognitive development, a person's capacity to understand that death is final and not reversible is limited. As noted in Figure 1, at this cognitive stage, death is personified so that a person may think that life after death, although not observable, requires the same basic essentials of food, clothing, air, and water. When seeing the corpse in the coffin, a person with mental retardation might worry about the absence of food, water, or other essentials. He may worry about his role in not providing for the deceased. Is the deceased going to be angry or hurt that no food is being provided? Shouldn't he have more clothes than the suit he is being buried in? He must need clothes if he is being buried in that nice suit...and so on. These thinking errors are further complicated by magical thinking, which reinforces a person's beliefs that he can affect the fate of others, even, perhaps, that of a corpse.

Since people who function at this cognitive stage do not appreciate the finality of death, they might be exceptionally frightened if they experience the visual illusion of seeing a deceased relative or friend. People in mourning experience this type of visual illusion as a normal part of the grieving process. These illusions occur when the bereaved person mistakes a shadow or some other object as the figure or face of the deceased. These illusions usually subside after a few days or weeks. However, if the person's reality-testing capabilities are limited by her cognitive abilities, the illusion may persist. Although the person is not psychotic, she may be acting or feeling that way. The behaviors, thoughts, and feelings associated with these perceptual and cognitive errors look bizarre. Sleep patterns may also be disrupted because of confusion surrounding sleeping, dreaming, and illusions. Obviously, lack of sleep will exacerbate the problem.

There is a difference between assuming that the observed behavioral excesses are occurring because the person is not able to understand death, and assuming that the excessive behavior is a function of some misunderstanding of conceptual aspects of death. In the latter case, it is appropriate to help the person with mental retardation to understand death more realistically. In contrast, the former formulation would dismiss the person's ability to understand her feelings. Such a dismissal is characteristic of a paternalistic approach to people with mental retardation.

At the concrete operational stage of cognitive development, a person begins to understand that death is inevitable and, toward the end of this stage, he begins to realize that death is irreversible. As noted in Figure 1, at this stage there is often a morbid interest with what happens to the body.

This interest in the tangible body and its decomposition after death may conflict with the stress that many people place on the spiritual element of death. In many religions, an emphasis on the physical body is shunned in favor of a spiritual emphasis. The soul is thought to exist irrespective of the condition of the physical being.

Abstract constructs such as "soul" are cognitively complex and, as such, they tend to be difficult for people with mental retardation to understand. Religion is often an important part of their community and familial experience, but there may be very little questioning of the issue of body versus soul. People with mental retardation who can reason at the concrete operational stage may have some idea about their own mortality, and may want to discuss this inevitability. Discussions will cover a broad range of thoughts and concerns such as where they will be buried, whether they should leave a will, and who will take care of their things after they are gone.

People whose level of mental retardation is mild may reach the formal operational stage, the stage at which abstract reasoning occurs and people have the ability to think about thinking, to think about the existential self. They would appreciate the universal nature of death and that the same rules applying to all players, even people whom they don't know.

There are few empirical studies that examine the relationships among the constructs of death, cognitive ability, age, and other socio-demographic variables. One intriguing question is whether age affects a person's understanding of death when cognitive ability is held constant. Are people with mental retardation who are old more likely to understand the meaning of death than their younger counterparts? In a well-designed study of 65 mentally retarded adults, Lipe-Goodson and Goebel[7] found that age and, to a lesser extent, IQ were related to understanding the concept of death. It appears that people with mental retardation who are old have a "better" concept of death than their younger counterparts. This is important because it suggests that life experience, as well as cognitive ability, helps us to understand what persons with mental retardation may be thinking and feeling about their mortality or that of someone they care about. Thus, it would seem that opportunities for people with mental retardation to participate in rituals and ceremonies of dying and death may compensate for some of their cognitive limitations.

60

HOSPICE

Mary C. Howell

Hospice is a concept of care. The word comes to us from a medieval institution or way-stations for travelers. In the last several decades it has been used to connote a change in the way we take care of people who are dying.

The single most emphatic focus of hospice care is concern for living. Hospice caregiving seeks to enable the person who is being helped to live the most full, rich, and connected existence that is possible, up to the point of the transition that we call "death."

The paradox is that we are all dying from the moment of birth. Most organ systems steadily lose efficiency. Cells die, one by one; some are replaced by other cells, some are never replaced. Reserves diminish. Our remarkable human resilience, our ability to bounce back after challenge or stress, is reduced year by year. These changes, which we tend to think of as changes of old age, actually begin at birth and proceed through childhood and youth and continue until the end of life.

The process of normal aging is no different for people with mental retardation, except that those with Down syndrome usually experience rapid, telescoped aging beginning in their late thirties or early forties. Ordinarily, death comes when there is a challenge to the system that is too great, and the system reserve is insufficient to meet the challenge. That system of the human organism is, of course, not just physiological but cognitive, social, emotional, and spiritual as well.

From this perspective, death is not a disease, nor is it always the consequence of disease. At the end of the process of normal aging, when organ-system reserves are stretched thin, a small stress can be "too much" and can be followed by death. Death does occur also from illness and injury; we recognize this situation when we see someone who only recently was vigorous and appeared to have great reserve, and who is quickly depleted by an extraordinary challenge.

Sometimes we want to consider the advantages in various scripts for dying. There may seem to be comfort in the idea of sudden, unexpected death; with our cultural tradition of avoiding thinking about death, people often say they hope that they are hit by a truck or suffer a sudden and massive heart attack. We know so little about death (many of us never having watched while someone died) that we think of it as horrible, to be gotten over with as quickly as possible, with as little awareness as possible.

Of course, the problem with sudden, unexpected death is that we have no opportunity to make our "good-byes" nor to put our affairs in order. Sometimes when we understand that any of us *could* die suddenly and unexpectedly, at any moment, we are able to learn that we need to try to keep our affairs in order, as best we can, and leave no relationship untended or in need of repair, lest we die before repairs can be made. We need to say our goodbyes every day.

At the other extreme, people sometimes die so slowly (as with the dementia of Alzheimer's disease) that they lose the capacity to keep their affairs in any order at all, to tend to relationships, and to say good-bye in a meaningful way, long before their physiological reserve is challenged. Between these two extremes, we can die with forewarning and make an orderly transition. This is what hospice care is about—helping someone in the midst of the process of dying to live the end of her life in such a way that she, and those who love her, are as ready for her transition as it is possible to be. The final stage in the process of dying in a way that is aware and ready is sometimes called "acceptance," which does not mean that the emotions of anger and sadness are not also acutely felt, but only that the inevitability and even the "rightness" of the time are understood.

The basic assumptions of hospice care are these:

1) When death can be anticipated, when the person who is in the process of dying is aware of that process, preparations need to be made. Giveaways, forgiveness, farewells—these are all part of the work of making ready. There may be activities or experiences that the person has "always wanted" but never done because the time was just not right. As death approaches the time may become right.

2) The person who is looking forward to death may experience physical changes—weakness, perhaps, or pain—that alter the capacity for self-care as well as for extended reaching-out activities. Social, emotional, cognitive, and spiritual changes may also diminish the person's reserve, will, courage, or energy level.

3) In our present cultural climate other people often turn away from the person who is looking forward to death. We have a special vocabulary about "fighting," "not giving in," and "using all of the weapons at our disposal." Sometimes people who are in the midst of dying get so caught up with fighting and resisting that they cannot either accept the idea of death, nor can they go on living their lives. The only thing they have time or energy or attention to take care of is the fight to outwit death; this sometimes happens to people who become part of cancer treatment protocols at hospitals or clinics.

4) For all of these reasons, hospice care is an invaluable resource to the person who anticipates death and who wants to live, as fully as he can, up to the moment of death. The principles of hospice care are

designed to help make possible the most gracious, aware, and fully engaged connections with life.

There are formal agencies called Hospice Centers. Some of these meet the administrative requirements established for reimbursement by Medicaid or medical insurance plans; others do not, and their (equally good) work cannot be reimbursed by third-party agencies. But hospice is essentially a philosophy, and hospice care can be given by anyone who espouses that philosophy. To this end, training in specific procedures of hospice care is helpful.

Hospice care for people who are mentally retarded is not really different than for anyone else. We must, however, take note of the fact that in the past, and to some extent still in the present, people with mental retardation may be discriminated against in their access to the best of curative medical services. Hospice care is no substitute for cure, when cure is possible. Neglect, and being barred from opportunities for the most sophisticated—and costly—procedures of modern medical care, are contrary to the meaning of hospice care. If, however, we can agree that the hospice model of care is appropriate in some circumstances, then it seems obvious that people who are mentally retarded should have this option, as does anyone else. With this group of patients, also, special training for the philosophy and procedures of hospice care is helpful.

The essentials of training are threefold. Staff who are unfamiliar with this work will want to learn about dying itself; about awareness and elaboration of the details of everyday life that are comforting and sustaining for the patient; and about techniques of care.

■ Dying

In our culture and in the last several decades, most people have died in hospitals; this was different in our past, and is now different in other parts of the world. There is a long tradition, and good rationale, for dying at home. But our convention of dying in the hospital means that most of us have never sat vigil with a person who is near death and have never observed the typical changes that happen as death approaches. Awe is the most common (and appropriate) emotion in the presence of death. When we are unfamiliar with death we may also feel fear, even terror. Knowing something about the actual events of death helps.

We used to define death simply as the cessation of breathing and heartbeat. When there are sophisticated measuring machines available, we now recognize another kind of death, called "brain death." In an instance of brain death there is no evidence (according to electronic measurement) of activity in the part of the brain that can think and feel, but the lower brain centers still function in a reflex way to keep the heart and breathing mechanisms active. When someone dies at home, however, the absence of breathing and heartbeat are still the signs that we use to recognize death.

The heart and lungs work together to pump nutrients to all the cells and organs of the body; without essential nutrients, the cells and organs cannot continue to be alive. The heart and lungs will stop working when the brain centers that control them fail, or when they themselves falter. They can falter as a result of a sudden event (like a heart attack, or trauma to the chest in an automobile accident) or as a result of slow decline (as in emphysema, or chronic congestive heart failure). Some of these causative events cause pain; others do not. The actual failure of brain centers, heart, or lungs (the events of death itself) practically never causes pain. (Pain with cancer, on the other hand, is usually associated with tumors growing bigger and pressing on nerves, or stretching other tissues.) Death most often comes not suddenly but slowly, in sleep or coma or a half-drowsy state, and is a painless letting-go.

There are some common events that will be seen as a person comes very close to death; they are ordinary and expected, and should not alarm the person who is sitting vigil. These include very irregular breathing, with long pauses; a rattle in the throat and upper airways, caused by mucous; an irregular heartbeat; a change in skin color, so it looks pale or bluish, and a change in skin temperature, so that it feels cooler; a slight amount of restlessness, or else an extreme quiet; moaning or calling out quietly. Throughout all of these events the person is likely to appear to be relatively comfortable. If, on the other hand, the person looks or acts in a way that makes one think that there might be pain, fear, or other distress, then help should be offered. The actual dying may go on for only a few minutes, or may last for several hours.

■ Sustaining a Comforting Environment

As death approaches—especially if it is foreseen, can be planned for, and takes some time to happen—most of us are comforted by being surrounded by our most familiar and most loved people and things. Usually, this means staying at home. For the person with mental retardation, just as for all of us, "home" is where we declare it to be. For someone who has lived in a residential institution or community home for a long time, that place is probably home.

Being with familiar and loved people means a comfort of touch and movement, of voice and vision. It means relationships that are known, well-worn, and reassuring. It means a human presence that is companionable and accountable. Similarly, one's own things—pictures, books, records, treasures, the very bed itself and the bedclothes—can be looked at, listened to, touched, and held.

When we take care of someone who is dying we need to think about all of these factors. We need to ask what is wanted, to watch and listen and keep an open mind so intuition can do its work. Often simple objects—one flower in a vase, one seashell—are more comforting, and seem more real, than elaborate arrangements. Remember also that certain objects will have symbolic value, as rewards or treats or promises of comfort. Simple encounters like holding hands, or listening to music together, or sitting in silence, can be the greatest comfort we can offer.

■ Techniques of Care

First and foremost we want to reassure. By predicting death, we have agreed that it will neither be rushed nor held back. For the person who is dying we want to provide the most easy, gentle, and pleasurable passage we can imagine.

Again, the essential ingredient is to keep one's mind open and to search always for ways to give more comfort. Ask always, "Is there any pain?" If there is, pain medicine can be given in a sufficient dose, and on a sufficiently frequent schedule, to take the pain away. Is there thirst, hunger? Skin that wants lotion and a rub? A mouth that wants ice chips, or something nice to taste? Is the room too dark, too bright, too warm, too breezy, or just right? Is it quiet that is wanted, or conversation, or music? What would be nice for the person to look at just now?

For symptoms of discomfort—vomiting, labored breathing, constipation—there are medical remedies. Other remedies will come to you if you let your fancy and your intuition work. Remember that the person who is in the process of dying draws her attention inward, and her energy in also. Less stimulation, more quiet attention, will be appreciated as the process moves along. But remember also that human companionship is very much appreciated at this threshold, and that touch and voice are, at the end, your best means of reassurance that you are there, loving and keeping vigil.

Giving care in a hospice setting almost always arouses old griefs of our own. We need to be ready for these, and to give ourselves time to attend to them, both for ourselves and for the sake of the person we are giving care to.

The experience of working in a hospice setting is rich, profound, and extraordinary, like no other kind of work. Hospice care is part of the panoply that we recommend be available to our clients who are both mentally retarded and old.

61

FULFILLING THE SPIRITUAL AND FAITH NEEDS OF MENTALLY RETARDED PERSONS IN A HOSPICE UNIT

Henry A. Marquardt

■

For people who have moved to a hospice unit, there should be a regular schedule of ongoing religious services, either weekly or bi-weekly. The clergyperson should not appear only when a death has taken place or for a memorial service. It would not take the clients long to say "Here he comes, who died this time?"

Religious services can contribute a very positive force to the clients. Services bring joy, celebration, and strength into their lives. The clergyperson can present a loving image of God and dispel the image of the God of judgment with which most clients were reared. During the service, he can recognize and support the various stages of grieving that the clients are experiencing. Also, he can help the clients to express their feelings and to give affirmation to them.

It would be good to invite friends and volunteers to attend the services. This eliminates some of the feelings of isolation for the clients and continues to challenge the clients in the unit to reach out and contribute to the larger community through prayer and giving of themselves.

As in any service, the homily is of great importance. For the population to which we minister, we should try to incorporate findings of studies into liturgical form. As an example, James T. Mathieu did a study of three communities of old people, asking them to rate the following comfort sources when thinking about death: 1) my religion, 34 percent, 2) love from those around me, 26 percent, 3) memories of a full life, 40 percent.[1] From these results, one should really start with number three and give it more emphasis. It certainly could be linked with St. Paul who said "I have fought the good fight. I have finished the course. Henceforth is laid up for me a crown of righteousness."

The clergyperson should be sensitive to the feelings of the clients and respond to them in the homily—feelings such as segregation, desolation, loss of self, and "transfer" trauma. Also, she should build into the service some outreach, support, and recognition of staff needs. One of the major staff concerns is the worry that a client will die on their shift. Simonton, in his study *Getting Well Again*,[2] says *every* person has some control over his own health history and eventual lethality. This information could ease some staff concerns.

Finally, the religious service can enable clients to retain a sense of continuity in their lives. They can continue to be nurtured in their faith until the very end. Steeped and strengthened in their faith, the clients can maintain greater control over their life and death.

62

FUNERAL AND MEMORIAL SERVICES

Henry A. Marquardt

■

This chapter offers some ideas on developing funeral rites, memorial services, and anniversary services for people who are mentally retarded. Churches and temples can be of great assistance to people suffering the pain of loss and separation through bereavement. One way is by providing the funeral rite. This service is not just for the person who has died but is primarily for the living, for those who are experiencing the deep and pervasive pain of separation. The liturgy or service is not only a ritual to be performed, it is also an instrument to assist those who are suffering to cope, endure, and use this period of pain as a time of growth and personal development.

The liturgy or service should touch the various dimensions of the person—physical, social, psychological, emotional, and spiritual. The development of the service must be a joint effort. It is not the sole responsibility of the clergyperson; family, friends, relatives, and caregivers of the deceased should be involved. It must be a true tribute to the person who has died, and at the same time, a means to assist the mourners on their journey through the bereavement process. It should be both personal and individual. It cannot be a "canned" or pre-packaged liturgy. Everyone has something to contribute.

The following are points to consider when preparing for a service:

1) The service has a twofold purpose: it is both a celebration of the life of the person who has died, and a means of helping the living to work through the grieving process.

2) Clients and staff who knew the person who has died should be informed of the death and should have an opportunity to express their feelings to one another. Be sure that notification of the death reaches all the necessary people with whom the person has lived, worked, or had other significant contacts (such as those in the infirmary and in the transportation unit).

3) Everyone should be aware that he can participate and contribute to the service. Liturgy means "work of the people."

Many funeral rites consist of three parts: the wake period, the funeral or service, and the committal or graveside service. The wake period can be held the afternoon or evening before the burial, or even an hour before the funeral service. It is a time to pay respect to the person who has died and to express personal sympathy to the family and friends of that person. The casket can be opened or closed. If the casket is closed, it would be well to have a picture or photograph of the person who has died nearby. The wake period is a means of helping the mourners bring closure to their loss. Also, it provides opportunities for the clients to share unexpressed feelings and an understanding of death. At a recent wake in the Fernald State School Chapel, a severely handicapped man, who is non-verbal, knelt before the opened casket of his friend. He bowed his head as though in prayer, then reached in the casket to touch the corpse. After rubbing the arm of the deceased, he stood and headed toward the pew. After taking four or five steps, he turned and waved goodby. The staff and I had no idea that this man had an understanding of death. As a result, we took a closer look at his service plan and established more challenging programs for him.

The funeral liturgy provides many opportunities for staff and clients to become involved as altar servers, pall bearers, and lectors, making music and offering tributes to the person who has died. While prayers, readings, and music can support and comfort the grieving, perhaps the most important help the service can afford to those who attend is to give them time to express their feelings, both positive and negative. Doing this in the presence of a clergyperson gives validation to those feelings.

The funeral service will confront many people with their own mortality. Some will be able to discuss their fears and worries about death. It would be helpful to take pictures of the wake, funeral, and burial. They could be used to facilitate a discussion at a later date. Also, the pictures could be shown to those who were unable to attend or they could be shown at the anniversary service. When family members of the person who has died are present, invite them to stand at the Chapel door after the service so that clients and staff who will not be going to the cemetery will be able to share their sympathy as they leave.

The committal service takes place at the cemetery. Attendance should always be optional. Take the time to explain the service beforehand. Going to the cemetery enables the clients to bring closure. It would be beneficial if, before leaving the cemetery, the clients were asked if they had any questions at that point. A meaningful custom is to give each person a flower before returning to the car. They can take it with them as a remembrance of the person who has died.

On return to the building or community residence, have a light meal. This will provide another time for support, sharing, strengthening, and answering questions. Sharing food brings people together at a time like this.

Memorial services are used either when the funeral rite takes place at some place distant from the client's residence, or when it is otherwise impossible for clients and staff to attend the funeral. The service should be interdenominational. It can consist of scripture, prayer, praise, and music. Having it as soon as possible after the funeral is most helpful to the clients. Also, it is important to have a picture of the person who has died at the service. This enables the clients to focus on the person they are honoring. Participation should be open to all. The memorial service, like the funeral rite, allows clients and staff to express their feelings, have them validated by the clergyperson, and bring closure. The clergyperson can do much to bring out the thoughts and feelings of the clients by simply asking "Would you please tell me what this person was like?" or "Would you please tell this person's family what he meant to you?" Having a collation (light meal) at the end of the service will allow clients, family, and staff to share other thoughts and concerns.

The anniversary service usually takes place a year after the death. It will enable some people finally to bring closure to the loss. For others, there may still be some unanswered questions. There also may be a few clients who need to have their feelings reaffirmed and validated, especially if they were negative feelings.

63

TRAINING STAFF TO CARE
FOR DYING CLIENTS

Tom Barbera

∎

How does a developmentally disabled person who is approaching old age perceive death and deal with it? What support can be offered? In discussing the needs of people with mental retardation who are old with regard to death, one must understand the current methods of dealing with their dying. Our discussion will focus on alternatives or choices for the person with mental retardation who is old, emphasizing a hospice model of care. Training and support for caregivers is essential for improving the way we take care of clients who are dying.

There are four areas on which to focus the training: physical plant, medical care, psychosocial care, and administrative issues.

The design of the *physical plant* of a residential center can present many problems for a client who is dying. A staff person should understand what environmental needs the client has. Possibilities for sunlight, a view of the outdoors, relief from mechanical noises (housekeeping machinery, traffic, grounds-keeping machinery), and frequent social contacts should be considered. Decoration with photos, letters and cards, and artwork—the client's own, or those given by friends—is comforting. Flowers and beautiful objects—stones, crystals, patterned scarves—should be easily seen and changed often. In one case, caregivers did all they could for a person who is dying, but because they had no knowledge of what the physical environment could potentially consist of, they were unable to make the changes that were needed. The client's room remained drab, with little privacy.

Medical care has presented a range of problems. Choices about the best medical care for clients who are dying are to some degree optional. Our goal is to choose treatments that are in the best interest of the individual client, if the client is unable to make his own decisions.

If the client is competent, the goal is to provide the treatment of his choice.

> *Donna was a client in her fifties who had terminal and metastatic cancer. She was incompetent to make medical decisions and had limited verbal ability. Her guardian, who was her sister, was out of the country and could not be reached. The team of caregivers knew that her guardian had expressed an opinion that Donna "would want to remain in her own building and die there." She could then remain with her peers and be given supportive, comforting, and familiar care by staff.*
>
> *As the disease progressed, however, a few staff members urged that she be transferred to the infirmary because of their own concerns, which were not clearly specified to the team but had to do with their lack of familiarity with the way a person who is dying might look and act. She was transferred before the caregiver team could meet. Two days later she died, alone, in an unfamiliar room, without her peers or familiar staff.*

Psychosocial care includes support for the client who is dying and for his peers, as well as communication with the individual, his peers, and staff about death and dying. As staff people working with clients who are dying, we should center our attention on offering support, honesty, and consolation.

> *Hattie was a 93 year-old woman. She was institutionally retarded and verbal, but she was also both hearing-impaired and vision-impaired. Her verbalizations were sometimes unintelligible; at other times she could communicate clearly. She was occasionally aggressive and verbally abusive. She was diagnosed as having bone cancer. From my discussion with Hattie, it was clear that she understood the seriousness and consequences of this disease. She asked "Am I going to die?" I wondered, should I lie? Should I tell the truth? I realized that I must respect Hattie, be honest with her, and offer comfort and support. "Hattie, you could likely die from this disease." Hattie said, "Oh God." She bent her head down. I said, "I love you" and she responded, "I love you with all my heart."*
>
> *This discussion was only one of many discussions we had. The situation was difficult for many of the individuals working with*

*Hattie because they did not communicate directly with her. Per-
haps it was too hard, or possibly they didn't believe she could
communicate. Physically, she received the best care imaginable,
but I wonder about the amount of emotional support given to her.
A person should be offered support, a hug or a caressing hand,
whether or not we believe they will understand. In a large institutional setting, all too often physical needs overshadow psychosocial care.*

Caregivers also need to recognize their own sensitivities concerning dying and death. The caregiver usually has had an ongoing relationship or friendship with the person who is. He may be ignored by the
client's biological family members. Thus, caregivers themselves often
do not get the attention and the acknowledgement of emotional connection that they deserve and feel.

There are a number of *administrative issues*. The individual who
is dying presents many specialized needs, including staff resources,
physical plant, training needs, money, legal and medical concerns, that
can only be met through administrative decision-making. My final
example once again involves Donna. One reason for Donna's transfer
out of her residential unit was the need for extra help for third shift
caregivers, who had asked for assistance. Administratively the problem
was to increase building minimums so that there could be one-to-one
staffing with Donna during the third shift. We should anticipate such
situations and plan for them.

Training needs to happen in all settings. When staff members are
first beginning their work experience, death and dying training should
be part of their orientation. Ongoing training should respond to specific
client or staff situations concerning death and dying. Family members
should be offered information and support when a client dies at home
or in a hospital. Death and dying training is an ongoing process and
should be continued after the client has died. Finally, professionals and
non-professionals should request and receive training at conferences
and workshops. Only through education can we learn how best to serve
our clients.

In 1986, a staff training manual about death and dying was written
as a joint project of the Death and Dying Committee of the Fernald
School and the Kennedy Aging Project. This manual has become
valuable as a study guide, source of information, and training tool. The
manual contains information about counseling, legal issues, physical

plant, hospice, and many other topics. The manual can be used for personal reading; it has been used for individual study and training development. The manual has been used in community residences for house or team meetings; families have also used it. Some clients have read the manual to obtain a greater understanding of death and dying.

There are a number of problems for the increasing population of people with mental retardation who are old and dying. The first step is to train caregivers to create comfortable and supportive environments; to offer the best medical care to meet the client's needs; and to deal honestly and compassionately with the client who is dying. Concurrently, the administration must provide a system of support and supervision for grieving caregivers. Then we can begin to offer a place to die in comfort and compassion. (See also Chapter 67)

64

LEGAL CONSIDERATIONS IN THE DECISION-MAKING PROCESS OF THE HOSPICE CARE PROVIDER

S. Charles Archuleta

■

Decision-making in the provision of hospice care inevitably presents issues that are not solely medical, but that present rather a hybrid of medical, ethical, and legal questions. [1] A determination of the purely legal standards and concepts within life-and-death decision-making is, at best, difficult, and must be recognized as a continually evolving process very much alive in the minds of academics, judges and juries, and hospice providers.

In order to provide hospice care, the provider must understand the legal parameters within which she is bound. While these boundaries are far from being settled, the courts have begun to provide definite guidelines; there is also a trend to approve of reasonable freedom in the provision of hospice care. As with any distillation of legal standards of behavior, the relevant questions are of both process (who will decide what, where, and how) and substance (the legal and ethical principles involved).[2]

It must be remembered that a set of general guidelines is vulnerable to the rapid change that is often seen in such a relatively recent field as hospice care. While trends in the court have been toward liberalization, questions of hospice care, like other questions of ethics in the courtroom, remain open to social, political and economic pressures. One must keep up with subsequent decisions and their effect on a growing body of pertinent law.

■ The Substantive Principles

Two principles of greatest concern to the hospice provider, as defined by the court, center on the notions of autonomy and beneficence.[3] (See also Chapter 52) The principle of autonomy concerns the right of each and every person to remain in control of herself. Such individual control is seen as superior to that of any other person or societal institution. This principle forms the basis of the legal notion of a "right to die."

The principle of beneficence holds that society must do what is ultimately best for each individual. This principle incorporates the right to remain free from inflicted harm, while it is also obligates society affirmatively to care for the individuals within it. For example, this principle declares that medical treatment should be provided in the way most beneficial to a patient, without reference to whether that patient desires the particular care.

In the hospice situation it is obvious that the principles of autonomy and beneficence can, and do, come into conflict. In general, there is a trend in U.S. courts toward greater recognition of the principle of autonomy over that of beneficence. Beneficence may, however, become an equivalent or a primary principle when autonomy becomes meaningless, as in cases where a patient is relatively limited in her ability to articulate wishes or desires with respect to her own care.

■ The Constitutional Right to Privacy

Legal decision-making in the area of life-sustaining medical care and treatment termination has borrowed from traditions set forth in the common law, the traditions of ethics in medicine, and particularly the constitutional notion of a "right of privacy." In transplanting the notion of privacy from reproductive freedom cases, the courts have noted three important distinctions that should be of concern in the hospice situation.[4]

In *Matter of Eichner,* a case which will be discussed in detail later, a New York court of appeals disapproved of any legal distinction between withholding and withdrawing treatment from a terminally ill patient.[5] In *Eichner,* the court stated: "It is important that the law not create a disincentive to the fullest treatment of patients...by making it impossible for them...to choose to end treatment which is proven unsuccessful."

A second ethical distinction, also examined by the courts, is that between "allowing to die" and any affirmative act which may be considered proximately to cause death, i.e. those acts that we generally consider "killing." Much of the litigation in the areas of life and death decision-making has addressed this distinction. It appears that the general case removes "withdrawing or withholding" treatment, in appropriate situations, from the general category of actionable affirmative acts.

A third distinction of importance is that between ordinary versus extraordinary treatment, an idea discussed in the Karen Quinlan case.[6] In *Quinlan* and progeny cases this distinction has been minimized with respect to the question of continuation or cessation with respect to the typical hospice patient.

It was in the *Quinlan* case that the application of the right of privacy, recognized by the U.S. Supreme Court in *Roe v. Wade,* was found applicable to decisions about life-sustaining treatment.[7] The New Jersey Supreme Court, in *Quinlan,* borrowed the balancing test, also used in *Roe,* and sought to balance the state's interest in keeping its citizens alive against the individual's application of the right to privacy in decisions concerning termination of life-sustaining treatment. The *Quinlan* court proclaimed that the "states' interest *contra* weakens and the individual's right to privacy grows as the degree of bodily invasion increases and the prognosis dims..."

This question of balance presents one of the more difficult questions to answer, in the legal sense, in the typical hospice situation. Both the courts and the legal scholars have debated the meaning of this balancing test and noted the difficulty in determining exactly when the individual's right to privacy becomes superior to the opposing state interest.

Decision-making under the *Quinlan* balancing test is best done with input from the various parties involved with the patient's care. The parties involved in such a decision should include the patient and the patient's family, if any; those health care providers most familiar with the patient's physical and psychological condition, and an Ethics Committee associated with the health care institution overseeing the particular patient's hospice treatment. (See Chapters 53 and 54)

This group decision-making can contribute to the protection of the individual hospice caregivers from legal liability. The idea of group decision-making makes sense both as a general proposition and because of its inherent compatibility with the legal theory behind the *Quinlan* balancing test. As noted, the right of privacy may conflict with an antagonistic state interest. State interests, however, reflect, or are supposed to reflect, societal interests. By basing hospice decision-making in a group context, the notion of societal input into such decisions is promoted, and the conflict between the individual right at issue and the state interests in opposition to that right is minimized.

Although group decision-making must view each patient as an individual, there are some generalities that may be drawn with respect to the care of patients with particular characteristics.

■ The Competent Patient

The choice to refuse medical treatment by a competent adult patient was addressed in 1984 in *Bartling v. Superior Court*.[8] In *Bartling* a California court of appeals was

> called upon to decide whether a competent adult patient, with serious illnesses which are probably incurable but [which] have not been diagnosed as terminable, has the right, over the objection of his physicians and the hospital, to have life-support equipment disconnected despite the fact that withdrawal of such devices will surely hasten his death.

The court concluded:

> [I]f the right of the patient to self-determination as to his own medical treatment is to have any meaning at all, it must be paramount to the

interests of the patient's hospitals and doctors. The right of a competent adult patient to refuse medical treatment is a constitutionally guaranteed right which must not be abridged.

Of particular note to the hospice caregiver is the reference by the *Bartling* court to the "strong and unequivocal statements" that demonstrated Mr. Bartling's own decision to terminate his life-sustaining treatment. These included:

- A "Living Will" signed by Mr. Bartling, properly witnessed, which stated in general that it was Mr. Bartling's direct wish that he be allowed to die and "not be kept alive by medications, artificial means or heroic measures," upon a determination that there was no reasonable expectation of recovery.

- A written declaration from Mr. Bartling stating in part his full understanding that his request to have medical treatment discontinued would very likely lead to his death and his willingness to accept the risk involved in discontinuation of treatment.

- A "durable power of attorney" for health care executed by Mr. Bartling, directing Mr. Bartling's spouse to "honor my desires...and to refuse ventilator support, at such time that I am unable to do so for myself." Such a durable power of attorney may be executed by any competent adult in states where it is authorized by statute, and provides for the wishes of the patient to be carried out if he should become incompetent. (See Chapter 23 and 57)

- Documents executed by Mr. and Mrs. Bartling and Mr. Bartling's daughter releasing the hospital and its doctors from any potential claims of liability, providing they honored Mr. Bartling's wishes.

Again the decision of the court reflects the idea of group decision-making in the hospice situation. The prepared statements noted in Bartling should be incorporated, when possible, into the record of the decision-making process, both to protect the hospice care provider as well as to document the wishes of the patient.

In a second California case, a court of appeals affirmed the *Bartling* decision and allowed Elizabeth Bouvia to elect "the right to live out the remainder of her natural life in dignity and peace."[9] The *Bouvia* case is important to the hospice case provider because it required the hospital to provide adequate support to Ms. Bouvia during the process of her dying.[10] The court defined the responsibility of the caregiver, in this case the hospital, as that defined by patients themselves and not as defined by physicians or other health care providers. Thus it would appear that a hospice care provider may not only refrain from providing life-sustaining treatment, under appropriate conditions, she may also be required to provide adequate medical assistance to allow the hospice patient to live as comfortably as possible in the absence of any particular life-sustaining treatment.

The *Bouvia* opinion appears to have acknowledged a legal duty applicable to hospice care providers, that is "to alleviate...pain and suffering" to the best of their abilities. To this point the court noted:

> The right to die is an integral part of our right to control our own destinies so long as the rights of others are not affected. That right should, in my opinion, include the ability to enlist assistance from others, including the medical profession, in making death as painless...as possible.

■ Determining Competence (See also Chapter 23)

Although courts have held that the social principle of autonomy is facilitated by allowing a competent adult patient to choose to forgo medical care, even if that choice may result in death, these same courts have been hesitant to define a standard to determine competence. It has been agreed that the autonomy principle is not served by allowing the patient to make a decision he is not competent to make.[11] In general the courts tend to defer to the expertise of physicians, especially psychiatrists, in determining the mental state and thus the competency of the patient.[12]

The demonstration of competency is an unsettled area of law that nonetheless is critical to the hospice care provider. The traditional view, which is to seek a surrogate decision-maker likely to agree with the physician, has passed somewhat out of favor. The so-called "reactionary view" that any patient who could indicate an affirmative response ought to be considered competent, has also been frequently challenged.

In one article prepared by a psychiatrist, a lawyer, and a psychologist, several tests for competency proposed in the literature were outlined.[13] The authors noted that "the search for a single test of competency is a search for a Holy Grail," and that they did not hold much hope for the near development of a clear test for competence that could be easily applied.[14]

The determination of competency to make a life and death decision by a patient must be treated as a legal question by the hospice health care provider, even though the courts tend to refer back to the medical profession in their determination of competency. It is suggested that in questionable cases the legal counsel of the institution sponsoring the hospice care aid in the determination of whether a competency hearing is necessary to the best interests of both the hospice care providers and the patients involved. There is favorable case law allowing a patient who fluctuates between competence and incompetence to make decisions concerning his medical care, even in life and death situations, during a period of competence.[15]

■ Substitution for Patient's Choice (See also Chapter 23 and 57)

As noted, the principle of beneficence becomes primary in the case of a patient not competent to make a reasonable personal choice. Courts have applied two standards, reflecting modern concerns with the premise of autonomy, in the case of an incompetent person. These additional principles are the application of the doctrine of "substituted judgment," or, alternatively, the doctrine of the "best interests" of the patient.[16]

The principle of substituted judgment is most applicable to patients who were formerly competent. Under this doctrine the court may review evidence of the values of a formerly competent patient to determine what the probable choice of that patient would be with respect to the proposed medical treatment.

For the hospice caregiver, the principle of substituted judgment provides a tool to minimize the problems inherent in the issue of competency. The hospice worker should encourage the use of living wills, durable powers of attorney, and other such documentation at an early stage in the hospice care of a patient, when the patient is most competent. Many states have adopted statutes approving of such documentation, and, of course, the hospice care provider should be familiar with any such statute in the state in which care is given.

■ The Incompetent Patient

A hospice caregiver may face a situation where an incompetent patient, in need of life-sustaining treatment, has never executed any documentation during a period of competence, or perhaps has never been considered competent to do so. In such cases the autonomy principle should not be ignored. There is a trend in the courts to apply the principle of substituted judgment in an effort to determine what the patient might have done if that patient were competent.[17]

The courts have looked to the President's Commission concerned with the decision-making process with respect to life-sustaining treatment.[18] The Commission has approved the use of personal knowledge of close relatives and friends of the incompetent patient. The reference to family members and close friends is inherently sensible, and such consultation minimizes potential malpractice complaints, thus making the practice a popular one with health care providers.[19] The hospice care provider must, however, note that a family's conclusions about the probable decisions of a terminally ill patient should not be taken as dispositive, even though they are certainly highly persuasive to a court of law.

For example, in *Matter of Eichner,* a New York State court of appeals allowed Father Philip Eichner a grant of authority to direct the removal of a respirator from Brother Joseph Fox. Brother Fox had been placed on a respirator and was being maintained in a purely vegetative state.[20]

The court noted that "the application was supported by the patient's ten nieces and nephews, his only surviving relatives" and that Brother Fox himself had said that he would want the respirator removed under similar circumstances. The court continued, "more often patients have not addressed the questions that others must decide on their behalf, and there is no dispositive evidence of the subjective desires of the patient. In such cases, courts look wherever they can to determine the patient's wishes." In the case of *Brophy v. New England Sinai Hospital, Inc.,* "the Massachusetts Supreme Court based its conclusions that food and hydration could be withheld from a comatose adult on the substituted judgment analysis done by the lower court."[21]

In *Matter of Conroy,* the New Jersey Supreme Court considered whether a life support system may be removed from a patient who has not expressed, in the past, any desire for or disapproval of such treatment.[22] The Court distinguished two potential scenarios based upon the absence or presence of "trustworthy evidence" that might demonstrate that the patient would forgo the life-sustaining treatment.

The first test was entitled the "limited-objective test," applicable "when there is some trustworthy evidence that the patient would have refused the treatment and...[when] it is clear that the burden of the patient's continued life with the treatment outweighs the benefits of that life for him." The court continued, "this limited-objective standard permits the termination of treatment for a patient who had not unequivocally expressed his desires before becoming incompetent when it is clear that the treatment in question would merely prolong the patient's suffering."

The court defined a second test applicable "in the absence of trustworthy evidence, or indeed any evidence at all, that the patient would have declined the treatment." The standards for the "pure-objective test" included: (1) that "the net burden of the patient's life with the treatment should clearly...outweigh the benefits that the patient derives from life"; and (2) "that the effect of administering life-sustaining treatment would be inhumane."

Along with clarifying the standard to be used in the determination of the use or continuation of life-sustaining treatment with a non-competent patient, the *Conroy* court also rejected any legal significance in distinguishing: (1) active and passive euthanasia; (2) ordinary and extraordinary forms of medical intervention; and (3) the removal of feeding tubes versus the removal of ventilators from patients. In explanation, the court noted: "we emphasize that in making decisions whether to administer life-sustaining treatment to patients...the primary focus should be the patient's desires and experience of pain and enjoyment—not the type of treatment involved."

Despite this clarification of standards involved in the treatment of incompetent patients, the hospice worker must realize that support for the doctrine of substituted judgment as applicable to incompetent patients is certainly not universal.[23] This lack of consensus remains a concern for the hospice care provider. Thus, while the general consensus appears to be consistent with the *Eichner, Conroy,* and *Brophy* cases in the application of the substituted judgment rule as the procedure that ought to be applied in deciding whether to terminate life-support procedures, the burdens of proof to be required by the forum court, and whether the court requires its involvement in the decision-making process at all, may all depend on local interpretation.[24]

Of particular interest to the hospice worker in the State of Massachusetts is the case entitled *Matter of Spring*.[25] In *Spring,* the Massachusetts Supreme Judicial Court appeared to retreat from a previous position that a judicial order was necessary before life-saving treatment could be discontinued.[26]

In general, then, the hospice caregiver must be aware that the debate over the standards required when considering termination of treatment of an incompetent patient continues, and that advice of the legal counsel of the institution providing the hospice care must be sought when faced with this situation.

■ Patients Who Have Never Been Competent

In a situation where the patient has never been competent, the reference case is *Superintendent of Belchertown State School v. Saikewicz*.[27] In *Saikewicz*, the Supreme Judicial Court of Massachusetts noted that "the state must recognize the dignity and worth" of a person who is incompetent "and afford to that person the same panoply of rights and choices it recognizes in competent persons. If a competent person faced with death may choose to decline treatment...then it cannot be said that it is always in the 'best interests' of the ward (i.e., the mentally deficient party) to require submission to such treatment."

The court promulgated a subjective test of "an inquiry into what a majority of people would do in circumstances that truly [are] similar...The goal is to determine with as much accuracy as possible the wants and needs of the individual involved." The court concluded that the general substituted judgment standard is applicable to a mentally deficient and incompetent patient with the single additional factor of the present and future incompetency of the individual taken into account.

There are two important concerns facing the hospice caregiver involved with a patient with a mental impairment. First, it should not be assumed that the patient is incompetent simply because of his mental deficiency. Again, incompetency may only be determined by a court of law. Therefore, the legal (and moral) preference in such a situation is to presume competence, and to attempt to limit the distinction (false or otherwise) between the patient who is mentally deficient, in the hospice situation, and a member of the general public in the same situation.

A second point concerns the fact that not all courts of law have agreed with the rationale behind *Saikewicz*. It is again recommended that the involvement of family, the health care personnel closest to the patient, and the legal counsel representing the institution in charge of the hospice care, as well as the institution's Ethics Committee, all be involved in the decision-making process.

■ The Duty To Resuscitate (See Chapter 54 and 65)

The institution supporting the hospice care provider should implement a formal policy to govern a decision of when not to attempt to resuscitate a dying patient. Such formal policies have been viewed very favorably in recent years and most hospitals maintain such a policy.[28]

■ The Threat of Criminal Indictment

The threat of criminal prosecution for homicide appears to be, at best, highly improbable if the particular precautions outlined in this discussion are followed. Although cases have occurred, including the highly publicized *Barber* case in California,[29] it would appear that such suits are unlikely.[30]

■ Tort Liability for the Refusal To Terminate Life-Support Maintenance Systems

In *Estate of Leach v. Shapiro,* an Ohio court of appeals recognized a civil cause of action with regard to a patient wrongfully placed and maintained on a life-support system.[31] Although the *Leach* case appears to be unique at this time, it has implications for the hospice care provider.

Mrs. Leach was placed on a life-support system after a respiratory and cardiac arrest resulting in a chronic vegetative state. Mr. Leach successfully petitioned the local probate court for an order to terminate the life-support measures and shortly after filed an action seeking damages for the time Mrs. Leach was on the life-support system. The court noted that the refusal to recognize the express wishes of Mrs. Leach and her family in opposition to the life-sustaining measures was an affirmative act, presenting a cause of action based on the treatment of a patient without consent.

The court also noted the long history of the requirement of informed consent and the proposition that when "circumstances may render the patient's consent impossible or impracticable to obtain...an authorized person may consent on the patient's behalf."

Furthermore, the court stated that the doctrine of implied consent in a medical emergency would not satisfy the consent requirement under the circumstances in this case.

Finally, the court stated that the application of the "doctrine of implied consent could effectively nullify...private rights...since a physician could circumvent the express wishes of a terminal patient by waiting to act until the patient was comatose and critical."

The principles announced in the *Leach* case present a potential dilemma to the hospice care provider. A double-edged sword is implied if there is a potential for liability both for terminating life-sustaining treatment and, alternatively, for refusing not to sustain the same treatment. Taken in perspective, however, the *Leach* case apparently reflects the modern trend toward a presumption of patient independence as reflected in the principle of autonomy. With respect to her job, the hospice care provider is best protected from the potential liability expressed by *Leach* by acting quickly and effectively to implement the guidelines suggested herein, either before the hospice care has begun, or certainly shortly thereafter.

■ Conclusion

As the cases and authorities cited and the discussion in general have demonstrated, the proper approach to hospice care with respect to insulation from legal liability appears dependent on openness regarding the treatment of individuals who are terminally ill, and respect for the autonomy of the patient as a human being.

Hospice care should, indeed must, be concerned with the quality of life of hospice patients. The direction of the courts in encouraging the input of the patient herself, and/or her close relatives and friends, is entirely consistent with providing the optimum conditions for a meaningful existence and not simply a prolongation of life.

The legal principles announced by the courts seem to allow the hospice care provider to perform his job without fear of a potential lawsuit lurking around each corner. At the same time, the hospice caregiver must maintain a healthy respect for the continuing evolution of legal premises and principles surrounding hospice situations. An effort should be made to maintain a regularly updated interpretation of case law and local statutory law concerning these questions. Generally the court's present position reflects a reasonably positive attitude when applied to hospice care.

65

MEDICAL ORDERS FOR THE DYING PATIENT: DO NOT ATTEMPT RESUSCITATION, LIMITS OF TREATMENT, AND RECOMMENDATION TO REMAIN IN RESIDENCE

Mary C. Howell

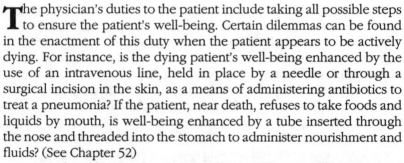

The physician's duties to the patient include taking all possible steps to ensure the patient's well-being. Certain dilemmas can be found in the enactment of this duty when the patient appears to be actively dying. For instance, is the dying patient's well-being enhanced by the use of an intravenous line, held in place by a needle or through a surgical incision in the skin, as a means of administering antibiotics to treat a pneumonia? If the patient, near death, refuses to take foods and liquids by mouth, is well-being enhanced by a tube inserted through the nose and threaded into the stomach to administer nourishment and fluids? (See Chapter 52)

People with mental retardation have, in the past, been deprived of needed and available medical care. This happened for a wide variety of reasons. Sometimes it was felt that the patient's "quality of life," as a person with mental retardation, was not worth living, and therefore no measures should be taken to prolong life. People with mental retardation were often incarcerated in institutions where they were kept out of sight and where adequate medical services were unavailable to them. And individual medical professionals often made judgments, such as "this retarded person is less than human," or "she can't really experience the pain," or "he would never be able to cooperate with the proposed treatment," that have summarily denied medical care to people considered to be intellectually incompetent. Any discussion of limiting medical treatments must be set in the context of this history of denial of care. (See the case of Mr. R, described in Chapter 55)

But the resolution of dilemmas about *how much* and *what kind* of care to administer must center on a consideration of "well-being," which has many dimensions. For instance, a person with mental retardation may have a very strong attachment to her own personal space—her own bed, room, and belongings. The people in her immediate environment—caregiving staff or family members, and peers—may be of great importance to her, and being with other people she does not know so well may make her feel fearful or abandoned. Often these connections are especially strong for people with mental retardation simply because their sphere of awareness is more or less restricted to what they know in their immediate experience; they are not likely to feel involved in national electoral politics, contemporary debates on public policy, or international negotiations. (And lest we think ill of this, we should remind ourselves that this is how human beings lived for most of the time of existence of our species.)

Given, then, a patient with mental retardation with one or more conditions that indicate that an active process of dying has begun (conditions like impaired respiration from cancer metastatic to lung, or progressive congestive heart failure escaping control by drug treatment, or severely compromised kidney function), how can we think about what medical treatments to offer, for what costs and benefits in terms of the patient's comfort and well-being? What medical treatments should be forgone in favor of other, non-medical kinds of care that appear to offer more comfort and promote more well-being? There are three major arenas of decision-making: whether to attempt to perform cardiopulmonary resuscitation, whether to limit some forms of treatment as too burdensome or painful for the patient, and whether to allow the patient to "remain in residence" and die at home.

Leslie Blackhall[1] has argued forcefully that cardiopulmonary resuscitation (CPR) is a medical procedure that was designed for certain types of situations with certain types of patients, specifically the unexpected and acute failure of heartbeat and breathing in a relatively vigorous and healthy person who, if resuscitated, is likely to return to full function. Blackhall argues that CPR was never intended to be attempted with patients who are debilitated, frail, cachectic, or severely compromised in multiple organ systems, as is usually the case when a patient is dying. Research shows that these patients rarely do well after CPR. One must then consider that the procedure is aggressively, even violently, intrusive, and that this may be especially disturbing when the patient is moving toward death. The question always to ask is whether the likelihood of benefits outweighs the likelihood of harms.

In the Commonwealth of Massachusetts at the present time, there is no uniform policy regarding the writing of DNAR (do not attempt resuscitation) orders for a dying person with mental retardation who is in the care of employees of a state-supported institution. It is the opinion of legal counsel in the Massachusetts Department of Mental Retardation that each institution should develop its own policy. (See Chapter 54) At the Fernald School such a policy has been developed and is currently in use. The policy states that if consensus can be reached in a meeting of medical and other caregivers, family, and guardian (if any) on the advisability of forgoing attempts at cardiopulmonary resuscitation, then a Do Not Attempt Resuscitation order can be placed in the patient's medical record. Any possible expression of opinion on the matter by the patient, given verbally or in writing, would be considered at such a meeting. It is always understood that this decision can be overridden if the patient's circumstances change. It is not necessary to bring this consensus decision to court for judicial review.

Orders specifying limitations of treatment must likewise be discussed by all who are involved and invested in the patient's well-being. Treatments to be considered for limitation are those that might be more likely to cause harm (pain, distress, or discomfort) than to do significant good; they include but are not limited to placement of an indwelling intravenous line, by needle or by surgical cutdown, for antibiotic treatment of infections or for administration of fluids; use of a mechanical ventilator; peritoneal or machine dialysis; chemotherapy; frequent taking of blood samples by needle or lancet; and transfer to an on-grounds infirmary or outside acute-care hospital. Again, prior opinions of the patient should be taken into consideration; while the patient may not understand the process of ventilation or dialysis, previous opinions of needles, lancets, and moving to the infirmary or hospital may well have been expressed. Even non-verbal patients may have conveyed anxiety, anger, fear, or depression in response to past medical treatments. These opinions should be taken into consideration when deliberating the question of limitations of treatment. (See also Chapter 23)

It is important to emphasize that restriction of some treatments does not mean neglecting the patient or failing to provide care that is comforting, attentive, loving, and supportive. Good care for a dying patient is labor-intensive and requires staff who are invested in the task and are willing to be inventive and flexible. Nor does a decision to limit treatment mean that *no* "high-tech" medical treatments would be given; for instance, if there is a suspicion that the patient has broken his femur and it appears that splinting or casting would make the patient more comfortable, then X-rays and an appropriate treatment should be undertaken. Similarly, a festering wound might need surgical debriding to increase the patient's comfort.

Once consensus has been reached about treatments that seem likely to reduce well-being more than they increase well-being, it is currently the practice at the Fernald School to bring this decision to a probate court for judicial review; a guardian for medical purposes needs always to have been appointed. Usually such a matter will be heard quickly in the court, but in our recent experience judges are sometimes unfamiliar with this sort of case and wish not to give an opinion until further investigation has been pursued, usually with the appointment of a *guardian ad litem* for the patient and the institution of a process that may take weeks and can cost the family a good deal of money.

The last on our list of special medical orders for patients who are dying is called "Remain in Residence." It has the same effect as deciding to limit medical treatment by not admitting the patient to an infirmary or acute-care hospital, but is expressed not as a negative but as a positive value; that is, it is affirmed that the patient's home means a great deal to her. "Remaining in one's own residential building, while not precisely a treatment in and of itself, is for many clients an important condition of treatment. It means lying in a familiar bed, with familiar walls and furniture surrounding. It means having all one's belongings close at hand. It means always being in the presence of peers who live in the same building. It means being cared for by familiar hands, hearing familiar footsteps and voices, and seeing familiar faces. It means being 'at home'."[2]

At the Fernald School, the Remain in Residence policy, which outlines a process by which the possibility can be considered and debated by all parties involved, is an official school policy. As promulgated, it is not about limitation of medical treatment, but it is usually the case that if someone does remain at home to die, then certain possibilities of medical treatment will be forgone. For instance, at the Fernald School we have the capability of providing clients with oxygen (by using portable machines that concentrate room oxygen) and with nursing services around the clock to give intramuscular or subcutaneous medications in the residential buildings that are their homes. Other kinds of medical treatments, however, including respirators and intra-venous lines, cannot be used in the homes. Therefore, adhering to a Remain in Residence decision may at some point require acknowledge-ment of some limitation of treatment, and then the decision *becomes* one of limiting treatment. In our experience at this time, it is best simply to consider the decision as one about domicile until *and unless* a question of limitation of treatment occurs. In that case, petition to probate court will be necessary. (Of course if the matter is before the court and undecided, many medical professionals will feel legally obliged for the time being to provide all possible forms of medical treatment in the interim.)

Successful enactment of the Remain in Residence decision re-quires careful staff training and support. Many people are afraid of death, have never been close to someone who has died, and will feel very uncomfortable as the client becomes pale and weak, begins to refuse food and drink, breathes with difficulty, has seizures or is intermittently unresponsive, and so on. (See the cases of Donna, in Chapter 63, and of Mr. C, described in Chapter 54) We have used a staff training manual[3] designed for this purpose. In addition we recommend that one staff member become the dying client's special grief counselor. The Committee on Death and Dying, in existence at the Fernald School since 1974, has also been an invaluable resource for staff education; the training manual can be used both for group teaching and as a personal workbook.

As with other orders for limited medical treatments at the end of life, the order for Remain in Residence (which is never absolute, but only a preference "if at all possible") can be overturned when or if caregivers or family members decide to follow another course. If the family feels supported and in good communication with other car-egivers, and if there have been a series of meetings at which family members have had an opportunity to express their feelings and con-cerns, and to ask questions and receive straightforward answers, then about-face decision changes will be few.[4]

These policies and procedures are, of course, made in reference to legislative and case law, which varies from state to state. In Massa-chusetts, as elsewhere, any competent patient can refuse recommended procedures of medical care. As discussed in Chapter 23, being mentally retarded is not synonymous with incompetence, and the notion of decision-specific competencies requires that we ask, "Is this client competent to make this decision, or should we recommend to the court that a guardian be appointed for this purpose?" Medical professionals will usually prefer that a guardian (who may be no more than a *temporary guardian* for medical purposes) be appointed when there is any question of competence. A guardian would usually be a concerned family member, if there is such a person, or a volunteer or court-designated individual, if there is a mechanism for this. In any case, in our experience, except for any delays attendant on court action, the presence of the guardian does not substantially change the process of making decisions nor, in most cases, the decisions finally arrived at.

The case-law standard in Massachusetts for limitation of medical treatment for a dying person who has always been incompetent remains the Saikewicz case, in which the court strongly implied that the authority of the probate court must always be sought. Experts in the legal aspects of biomedical ethics now advise that, with good communication with family and agreement among family members, seeking court approval would probably no longer be seen as required in most cases. (See Chapter 64) Such a case has yet to be tested at the state supreme court level in Massachusetts. In other states, the advice of a knowledgeable attorney should be sought.

We who care for people with mental retardation must be alert to the twin pillars of discrimination in treating the client who is moving toward the end of life. On the one hand, truly life-saving, curative procedures should never be denied because the client has mental retardation. On the other hand, treatments given only because medical professionals are fearful of malpractice litigation, or because treating is easier than limiting treatment, are equally to be avoided. Comfort, freedom from pain, and ample and loving social support are the keystones of care for one who is dying.

66

THE WILL-WRITING PROJECT

Mary Ann DiGiovanni

■

The rationale for exploring the idea of will-writing for people who are old and mentally retarded centers on the concept of normalization. Under this concept, people who are mentally retarded are provided with experiences "which are as culturally normative as possible, in order to establish and/or maintain personal behaviors and characteristics which are as culturally normative as possible."[1] The staff of the Kennedy Aging Project believed that participation in will-writing can contribute to clients' personal dignity and self-esteem. The process provides opportunities for the client to discuss death, loss, significant relationships in her life, and the notion of survivorship. The will-writing process gives permission and legitimacy for the client to discuss these subjects.

This chapter will first briefly describe how the will-writing project evolved. The second part of the chapter will outline the "will-writing process" as developed by participating Aging Project staff.

An attorney, a law student, and a clinical psychologist participated in this project. The plan was to involve these staff members in all phases of will-writing, including all meetings with the client, from the original interview through the actual writing of the will.

The initial stages of research and discussion focused on legal requirements under Massachusetts law (Mass. Gen. Law Ch. 191, Sec. 1.). The primary legal considerations were testamentary capacity, matters of attorney-client privilege, and the manner by which the will-writing service was procured and would unfold. The staff determined that clients without guardians (presumed competent) would become the first candidates for the service.

As to testamentary capacity, the standard that a proponent of a will must meet was set forth in *Tamicone v. Cummings,* (166 N.E.2d 737, 740 (Mass. 1980)). In that case, the court stated,

[t]estamentary capacity requires the ability on the part of the testator to understand and carry in mind, in a general way, the nature and situation of his property and relations to those persons who would naturally have some claim to his remembrance. It requires freedom from delusion which is the effect of disease or weakness and which might influence the disposition of property. And it requires ability at the time of execution of the alleged will to comprehend the nature of the act of making a will.

After discussing this standard, the staff members decided that evidence that the client satisfied these requirements should be provided through affidavits from a psychologist and an attorney, attached to the will.

The question of the attorney-client privilege was also raised. The question centered on the inclusion of a non-legal person, namely the clinical psychologist, in the actual will process--that is, whether non-legal persons could attend meetings in which the client disclosed information, as would occur in the will-writing meetings.

A third problem became apparent as the staff examined the way in which the will-writing service should be offered, and how the will would be written. First, the will-writing service is presented in a face-to-face interview setting. The client is asked whether he has a will and then whether he would want to have a will. The procedure could be viewed as improper solicitation on the part of an attorney and may represent a violation of the Code of Professional Ethics. More trouble-some, from a legal standpoint, was the process the staff envisioned for writing a will. The staff proposed a plan whereby the three staff members and a caregiver would present the idea of a will to the client. The caregiver would take this discussion as a beginning point for further communications about a will. The caregiver would *help* the client generate a list of significant people that would become beneficiaries of the client's possessions. The fact that a caregiver would become actively involved in helping a client generate lists of appropriate people and possessions raises questions of professional conduct for the lawyer.

The staff determined that active participation in will-writing pre-sented potential violations of legal professional ethics. They concluded that the project's goal remained important and could be realized without the necessity of drafting a legal document—a will.

The staff then focused on how the normal process of will-writing could be incorporated in a process that would not result in a legal will. It was decided that the purposes of having a will could be satisfied by having the client write a letter to a significant person. This letter would explain the client's wishes as to the distribution of her possessions after death.

The process by which this letter develops involves a series of meetings over a period of time. It is suggested that three people comprise the team that presents the idea of writing this letter to a client. One person should have daily contact with the client and enjoy a trusting, established relationship—a caregiver. A second person should be someone with a routine professional relationship with the client, such as a doctor, a psychologist, a clergy member, or someone with whom the client has bonded and has established a confident and comfortable relationship. The third person should be an "outsider," in the sense that this person is not known by the client. This person can act as the "legal" person, and in fact could be (but does not have to be) an attorney. This person takes notes, gathers information, maintains communication with the client and caregiver, and writes the letter.

The staff concluded that the meetings should span a period of two to three months, comprising three to five separate meetings. This provides the client with opportunities to discuss the issues surrounding death and to formulate the lists of significant others and possessions. The first meetings involve conversations about death and loss, and explanations about leaving special possessions to significant people. After this meeting, the caregiver reinforces and continues the talks with the client and begins to make the lists of significant others and possessions. The "legal" member of the team communicates with the caregiver about the client's responses to the talks. The team assesses the appropriate number of meetings required for the client to develop his letter. After the letter is drafted it is read to the client and, if it is approved, it is signed by the client.

The team had an opportunity to write such a letter with a client. The client was a 62-year-old man who moved from a state school to a group home seven years ago. He works at a sheltered workshop and also does odd jobs in the neighborhood. The client's father died this past year, at the age of ninety. The psychologist on the team counseled him and, in the course of this grief counseling, he decided that he wanted to write a will for himself. After three meetings with the team and many discussions with his caregiver, he completed his letter. Following is the will addressed to the client's brother. (All names and addresses have been changed.)

■ Sample Will

86 Western Avenue
Dorchester, MA
May 21, 1987
William Burden
Rural Rt. 2
Hamilton, New Hampshire

Dear William,

I've been talking with some people and they have suggested that I may want to think about what I want to happen to my things after I die. I have decided to write this letter to you to let you know about my wishes for some of my things after I die. I am asking you to carry out my wishes to the extent that you are able. Thank you.

1. I would like you, William, to have my watch.
2. I would like our sister, Janet, to have my rosary beads and my Bible.
3. I would like my friend, Tom Wilson, to have my electric toothbrush and razor because he bought me a pair of pajamas.
4. I would like Sam DiVito's girlfriend, Connie Murphy, to have my Irish Record Collection because I know she would like them.
5. I would like the program coordinator to have my television set so he can give it to a client who needs a television after I die.
6. I would like my cab driver, Paul Albertson, to have my radio.
7. I would like my friend, Jim Lee, to have my clothes.

As you can see, I have not talked about all things. William, please take care of the rest of my things as you think best.
Sincerely,

John H. Burden

67

A SUPPORT GROUP ON THE ISSUES OF DEATH AND DYING WITH MENTALLY RETARDED ADULTS

Barbara McDaniel

■

Most people who are mentally retarded and old have experienced many losses in their lives, including the deaths of family members and friends, frequent staff turnovers, and changes in their living circumstances, such as being moved from their homes to institutions and moving again to community group homes. In an effort to address the ways in which a group of people who are mentally retarded and old were coping with loss, and the impact of their losses, a support group was organized to talk about death and dying. The members of the group offered support and counsel to each other and to the group leader, sharing their own pain and their ways of coping with loss.

■ Why a Support Group on Death and Dying?

Establishing a support group for adults who are mentally retarded on the issues of death and dying was a collaborative effort between the Kennedy Aging Project's social work intern and the director of a community-based group home that serves eight people who are mentally retarded and old. The particular group home serves mildly retarded[1] men between the ages of 46 and 65. Just in the past year, these eight men had experienced the death of a fellow resident, one client's mother had died, and another client's brother had died. The director of this group home wanted to offer these clients an opportunity to express their grief. Faculty members of the Kennedy Aging Project provided supervision and consultation to their social work intern.

The purpose of the group was to establish an arena where these clients could express their feelings, receive support, and share their coping skills in dealing with the loss of family members and friends. Eunice Thurman states well the need for such a support group for people who are mentally retarded and old,

> [who] react to interpersonal difficulties, transitions from one living setting to another, or the death of close family members or friends in the same ways as does any adult. They become anxious, fearful, resentful, and grief-stricken…They share identical needs for emotional support with their non-disabled older peers.[2]

■ Developing the Group

The group home's staff input was important to the formation of this support group. In fact,

> enlisting the cooperation of the residential staff was essential to this group process as each staff member was part of the client's network of support and daily activity. Staff attitudes toward grief and dying could facilitate or deter the client's progress to accept death and perceive grief as normal.[3]

Therefore initial work was done with the group home staff by the social work intern to clarify the role of the staff to the support group and to develop the intern's function and role as the group leader.

The mechanics of the group, such as how clients would be recruited, the location of the group's meetings, and how information between the group and the residential staff would be exchanged, were discussed and decided upon with the group home staff. Questions of confidentiality for the group's members were worked out, and the staff cooperated in choosing a time and coordinating house activities to promote optimum participation by the clients in the group. It was agreed that the group leader and the group home director would meet weekly to exchange information necessary to the group's future.

While the group home director and staff had identified grief as an issue for the men in their care, it could not be assumed that these eight adults also identified grief as an issue for themselves. Group participation was not mandatory. An interview was held with each client prior to the group's beginning. During this interview the purpose of the group was stated, the staff's input was shared, and each individual was invited to discuss his own thoughts on how he was coping with grief and was asked if he wanted to be part of a group that would talk about grief and loss.

After these formal interviews were conducted and the client agreed to join the group, the client was asked to sign a form stating his interest in the group and his commitment to attend all ten sessions of the group. Only one client declined to enter the support group.

Prior to the first meeting, clients received cards specifying the time and place of the meeting. Before subsequent meetings the group leader met the seven group participants and walked with them to their meeting place at a nearby office building. The group's sessions lasted for 45 minutes.

■ The Group

Each session began with a review of the last meeting. Juice was served at each meeting. After the first session, one member, Joe, asked if he could serve the beverage. Joe continued to serve the juice to all group members at each meeting he attended.

Four of the men have good expressive and receptive language skills. Three of the seven, Mike, Joe, and Carl, have poor expressive skills. Mike, who had been recently hospitalized, had difficulty speaking but could be understood and led many discussions in the group. Joe has trouble hearing, especially in group settings. While it is difficult for Joe to stay on topic, due in part to his hearing loss, he did respond to other group members in appropriate and caring ways. For example, when Mike was crying during the first and fifth sessions, Joe was visibly involved with the group, offering Mike support. Carl, who takes anti-psychotic medication, was very quiet during the meetings and only spoke when he was asked questions directly. While Mike attended all the meetings, Carl attended only one and Joe was absent for the last three meetings as he was hospitalized for surgery that had been scheduled prior to the beginning of the group. Four clients attended all ten sessions.

Early in the group the men introduced house issues. We agreed as a group to take 15 minutes of our 45 minute sessions for the discussion of house issues. However, after the third session the men no longer brought house issues to the group. The group had begun to focus on loss and grief. This adherence to the topic of loss was influenced by three events: one, the tragedy of the explosion of the Challenger space craft; two, the resignation of a staff member; and three, the death of a former group home worker.

An example of how the group demonstrated ownership in the topic of death and dying is illustrated in an exchange between two group members. While discussing the death of the staff person, Mark began talking about news clippings on local events. John turned to Mark saying, "stick to the topic." This phrase was used throughout the remaining group sessions when a group member would stray from the topic of loss, reminding all present that we were gathered to talk about issues of death and dying.

■ The Group's Discussions

The first three sessions were spent remembering the deaths of family members and friends. Tears were shed. Two themes emerged. First, the men expressed a feeling of being left out of funerals and memorial services: "You're going to find out anyway. Why hide it?," said John. (See Chapter 58 and 62) Second, the men raised the question of who would take care of them when their relatives, especially parents, died.

Mike shared a story that poignantly demonstrated the effect of being left out of the shared experience of someone's death. After he had an argument with a close relative, the relative died. Mike thought their argument had killed his cousin. Three days later at the funeral services, Mike learned that his cousin died of cancer. It was not until Mike learned the facts of his cousin's death that his feelings of guilt began to abate. (See Chapter 59)

From these first sessions, the adult roles these retarded men played in their network of family and friends began to surface. All but one group member had attended the funeral services of relatives and friends. Bob, the one exception, stated he is always "sick with a cold" during the funeral and burial services of family and friends; but Bob does participate in the social gatherings prior to and after the funeral services.

Adult roles included visiting surviving family members and friends, visiting grave sites in memory of the deceased persons, and actively participating in funeral and burial services. For example, Ed led the prayers at his father's funeral. A direct outcome of the group's discussion on adult roles and feelings of exclusion was that two group members, Ed and John, contacted their families and asked that they be told when someone is ill or may be in the process of dying, so that they

(Ed and John) would know and be prepared for the person's possible death.

Coping skills were shared and discussed. Each group member offered concrete examples on how he deals with grief and loss. Bob said he liked to remember the positive, the "good" aspects of the person now dead. Ed said it was important to continue working and "keeping up" with your daily routine. John said it helps to go out, to meet other people. Bob offered that just thinking about the dead person was not good. Rather, you "have to laugh" and enjoy those who were around you.

The tears expressed in the first sessions by Ed and Mike were received differently by each of the group's members. When someone cried, most of the clients sat silent with their heads down. However, John voiced annoyance when Mike cried when sharing the news of the dead astronauts, saying, "there's no use to crying. There's nothing you can do about it. You shouldn't be upset." At a later session when Mike shed tears over the loss of a friendship, John protested, "he's always crying." The group leader suggested that John may be expressing the thoughts of many, that it is hard to be with someone when they are crying. Mike engaged John in conversation:

> Mike: I'm lonely. I cry.
> John: We're all lonely. I go out. I meet people.
> Mike: I haven't seen my brother in two weeks [still crying.]
> John: I've met your brother. Sure, he's nice but you can't just go out with him. Were you lonely with Joan [a staff person at camp]?
> Mike: No.
> John: You can't just go to your family. I go out. I meet people.

The group leader introduced two topics of concern that were discussed during the final group sessions. The first was a conversation on what these men thought happens when someone dies. Three group members offered their perspectives. John said, "It [death] stinks. It's life in the slow lane." A second client, Mike, said, "God calls you. It's a tough life. You're judged. You go to heaven or purgatory." Bob's beliefs drew the most response; Bob said he had been part of a seance and wondered if we could talk to "spirits" (those who are dead). John, Mike, and Ed were quick to say they did not believe in spirits but many shared that they had dreamt of dead loved ones and wondered, after the dream, if the person were still alive.

The second topic introduced by the group leader was a discussion of wills. Each of the men knew what a will was. One of the men had a will drawn up some years ago. Several of the clients said they intended to speak with their families about having a will prepared for them. (See Chapter 66)

These open exchanges among the members of the group demonstrate that as a support group these men were attempting to help each other cope with loss and search together for ways of dealing with grief.

■ Conclusion

The organization, planning, and implementation of this support group entailed cooperation from the group home staff and the Kennedy Aging Project staff, and the willingness of the group members to share their experiences with death, dying, grief, and loss. With a clear purpose and a supportive atmosphere of acceptance the group afforded these people who are mentally retarded and old an opportunity to share their life experiences with death and dying, and to explore and challenge their coping skills while being supportive to each other. As Deutsch has pointed out:

> unfortunately, mentally retarded individuals are frequently unprepared for dealing with their grief, and usually receive little or no assistance through the mourning process. These are individuals whose poor adaptive skills make it difficult to cope with everyday stress, yet they are expected to cope with the loss of a significant interpersonal relationship.[4]

The support group presented here provided a structured setting in which feelings of grief could be expressed, questions could be asked, and coping skills shared. Through the exchanges between and among the group members grief can be seen as one part of our life experiences, common to us all. In fact, the commonality of experiences, like feeling excluded by their families during times of death, and exploring the question of who would take care of them when their parents died, pointed to the need for these clients to find ways of expressing their grief and develop coping skills to deal with loss. In a support group on death and dying, people who are old and mentally retarded can begin to share their feelings of grief, express their anger and sorrow, and begin to accept their own roles as adults in coping with grief.

PART 5
REFLECTIONS AND
RECOMMENDATIONS

68

RESEARCH IN THE CONTEXT OF AN EDUCATIONAL AND SERVICE PROJECT

Edith Finaly and Mary C. Howell

■

Data collection is a requisite of contemporary work. In an undertaking like the Kennedy Aging Project, where the stated goals of the work were to teach health professionals and to provide exemplary service, there is also an expectation that data will be accumulated and analyzed. This is both for the purpose of evaluating the work done and also for sharing the experience of the work with others.

Early deliberations of the Interdisciplinary Team (see Chapter 7) determined the shape, scope, and content of the interview schedule that was the foundation of the data-collection process. Very simply, the information that was collected in the course of client intake became data to be analyzed and reported. As we worked with this data we experienced a variety of dilemmas with regard to the use of data for service (and, by demonstration, for education) and the use of data for research.

In pure research, acquiring data is an end in itself, although the long-range effect of the study may also be beneficial to respondents. Our data collection, on the other hand, focused on establishing a helping relationship and eliciting data in order to provide services to clients.

There are differences between the interviewer-respondent relationship and the worker-client relationship. Research interviews are limited in time and the parameters for the data to be obtained are predetermined. Worker-client interviews can, and should, explore all topics relevant to the client's needs, in as long a period of time as is required. The goal of research interviews is to obtain data about and for a particular population. The research interviewer cannot make promises or commitments about help. The goal of service interviews is to help a particular client system; the service worker represents help offered to the client.

These additional dilemmas came to our attention:

1. The interview schedule was prepared for the "most general client," with questions laid out to cover the broadest range of life contingencies. But in actual practice only some of the questions from the interview schedule were answerable for any given client, and the interview therefore had to be "tailored" to the life circumstances of the individual client in order to be of maximal use in giving service.

2. Data collected for research must be gathered in a consistent format so they are comparable from one subject to the next. In our project, by contrast, the practice of face-to-face responsivity, a requirement for good clinical care, obviated the kind of exceptionless regularity that defines a consistent data-gathering format. Further, it was our intention to promote and encourage each team member (both faculty and students) to develop a manner of interviewing that was stylistically in harmony with that person's own personality, experience, and knowledge. For these reasons, even though each set of data was collected using the predetermined schedule, we acknowledge that there are inevitable irregularities in the manner in which questions were asked, in the question-enlargements that were pursued, and in the way the open-ended responses were interpreted by the interviewers.

3. As a service project, we were not able to control the identity of the informant who came with the client to the intake interview: sometimes this was a family member, sometimes a member of the caregiving staff who knew the client well and over a long period of time, but sometimes it was a staff member, such as a Service Coordinator, who did not have day-to-day contact with the client or who had not known the client for more than a few months. The quality and quantity of information obtained likewise varied.

4. In a project in which our energies were directed to providing service, there was no opportunity to confirm the reliability and validity of data in a way that would have been necessary for confident reporting of research results. Some kinds of data were obviously more valid, in our collection process, than others: dates of the client's birth and of first admission to a state residential facility were likely to be more valid than answers to questions like "is the client able to wear his eyeglasses?" (or his dentures or hearing aid). Especially when clients were failing in their functional abilities, different caregivers might disagree strikingly in their reports of what a client was or was not currently able to do. Our data

summaries (see below) reflect differential confidence in the information obtained.

5. More significant in the workings of the Project was the fact that uncertainties or inconsistencies in data obtained may still have been useful in a *clinical* sense. If important caregivers saw the client's behavior as disruptive to the entire residence, this information was important to our understanding of where help was needed, even if an objective observer would not agree with the caregiver's strongly-expressed negative condemnation of the client's actions. On occasion we were aware that the acute need of the caregiving staff for advice and concrete help led them to describe the situation as more extreme, more disruptive, and more painful than they might have described it if they had not hoped to get help from their encounter with us.

6. Other problems of research in this service setting have to do with technical requirements of survey research. In a project that works with a client group about whom little data are available, the survey has no baseline to work from. No randomization of subjects was possible, nor can a control group be identified, at this stage.

7. Finally, the collaborative nature of the work of the Interdisciplinary Team presents dilemmas with regard to publication of research results in the usual academic fashion of individual work and individual "ownership" of data and published results. In this volume, for instance, it should be clear that although this piece on research results is written by Finaly and Howell, the data collection and interpretation are products of the work of every member of the Aging Project team.

Despite these dilemmas of service *vs.* pure scientific research goals, the team collected important and useful information that helped us to assess clients' needs in a relatively systematic, objective, and scientific manner. If our assessments could have been repeated, we might have taken some measure of the success of our interventions. We are fully aware that we cannot intervene in other people's lives simply on the assumption that good intentions will lead to good client outcomes. Ideally, research and evaluation would be integrated into clinical practice so that we could measure the effects of our helping efforts on clients' outcomes, e.g., well-being.

On the following pages are data about our clients. The purpose of our assessment was to identify the short term and long term needs of people with mental retardation who are old, and to match those needs with the most appropriate services.

■ Methodology

The study population included all the clients who were referred to the Kennedy Aging Project for Interdisciplinary Team evaluation.

■ Data Collection

Interviews were conducted by members of the Interdisciplinary Team, one faculty member and one student for each client. Interviews were conducted between October 1985 and May 1988. Each interview lasted about 45 minutes.

The entire instrument was a 24 page, 522-item questionnaire consisting of both open-ended and close-ended questions. (See Appendix) It was developed in September-October 1985 by the Interdisciplinary Team of the Kennedy Aging Project. The final version was pre-tested. The questionnaire was divided into three parts, telephone interview, mail questionnaire, and in-person interview, with both objective and subjective data recorded. The in-person segment included simultaneously an interview with the caregiver and an interview with the client.

The questionnaire covered the following domains: 1) Health. 2) Activities of daily living: the ability of the individual to perform activities like walking, bathing, dressing, etc. 3) Family and friends: support, intimacy. 4) Housing: living conditions, safety, co-residents, staff. 5) Financial well-being. 6) Mental functioning. 7) Emotional functioning. 8) Legal status. 9) Work and leisure. 10) Spiritual functioning. Each questionnaire was coded by a minimum of two people in order to minimize error and improve reliability, particularly with the open-ended items. All questionnaires were identified by subject number rather than by an individual name, and data were aggregated in the analysis to preserve the confidentiality of the respondents.

Table 1
Major Demographic Characteristics of the KAP Clients:
(in percentages*)
Total (n=104)

Gender:

Male	40.4
Female	59.6

Age:

32-42	10.0
43-53	11.1
54-64	13.3
65-75	40.0
76+	12.3

Religion:

Protestant	21.2
Catholic	52.2
Jewish	6.7

Living Situation:

At home with family	5.8
Sheltered village	1.9
Semi-independent apartment	5.8
Group home	20.2
Special homecare	1.9
Nursing home	55.8
State residential school	1.0
Foster home	1.9

*Note: Percentages may not equal 100% due to missing data

Table 1 shows the demographic characteristics of our clients. We saw for Interdisciplinary Team evaluation 104 clients, approximately 40% male and 60% female. The distribution of ages ranges from 32 to 88, 34.4% in the youngest groups (ages 32-64) and 52.3% in the oldest age groups (ages 65 and older). The majority of clients were Catholic (52.2%); Protestants were 21.2% and Jews were 6.7% of the overall sample. The clients' living arrangements were distributed in the following way: more than half of our clients came from institutions—nursing homes and state schools (56.8%)—and the remaining clients came from community living arrangements (38.5%).

Table 2
KAP Clients' Profile (in percentages*)
Total (n=104)

Diagnosis:

Down syndrome	Yes: 21.2
	No: 76.6
Epilepsy	Yes: 22.6
	No: 77.4
Active seizures	Yes: 19.2
	No: 77.9
Cerebral palsy	Yes: 9.6
	No: 87.5
Depression	Yes: 27.0
	No: 71.2
Anxiety	Yes: 35.6
	No: 61.5

Communication:

Non-verbal	4.8
Single words or signs	9.6
Phrases	12.5
Sentences	13.5
Fully verbal	54.8

Level of Retardation:

Average intelligence or above	8.2
Mild mental retardation	45.9
Moderate mental retardation	29.4
Severe mental retardation	9.4
Profound mental retardation	7.1

*Note: Percentages may not equal 100% due to missing data.

Table 2 presents the KAP client profile. Most clients are classified as mildly or moderately retarded (75.3%), and most of them can perform at a full level of verbal communication (54.1%). Other profile characteristics of our clients were: anxiety (35.6%), depression (27.0%), and Down syndrome (21.2%). A smaller percentage were diagnosed with epilepsy (22.6%) (although only 19.2% of them have seizures), and 9.6 were diagnosed with cerebral palsy.

Table 3
KAP Clients' Reasons for Referral (in percentages*)

Things harder to do past year	Yes: 48.1
	No: 45.2
Behavioral problems	Yes: 51.7
	No: 48.3
Is day program appropriate?	Yes: 48.1
	No: 15.4
Is current residence appropriate?	Yes: 31.4
	No: 68.6
Number of Physical Illnesses:	
No illness at all	15.3
1-4 illnesses	67.1
5 or more	16.4

* Note: Percentages may not equal 100% due to missing data and the fact that most clients had more than one reason for referral.

As seen in Table 3, there are some common reasons for referral to our project. Most of the clients were referred because of questions about whether the living arrangements were appropriate (68.6%), because of behavioral problems (51.7%), or because of decrements in the client's functioning in the past year (48.1%). Fewer Clients were referred because of questions about whether their day programs were appropriate (15.3%). Most clients had more than one reason for referral.

Table 4
The Type of Services KAP Clients Receive (in percentages*)

Receiving recreational services	Yes: 86.5
	No: 5.8
Day program	Yes: 63.5
	No: 26.0
Occupational therapy	Yes: 16.3
	No: 74.0
Legal assistance	Yes: 27.9
	No: 61.5
Transportation assistance	Yes: 88.5
	No: 4.8
Social work assistance	Yes: 72.1
	No: 16.3
Housecleaning assistance	Yes: 71.2
	No: 19.2
Education in community living skills	Yes: 42.3
	No: 46.2
Vocational program	Yes: 63.4
	No: 33.7
Day Program Type:	
Competitive employment	1.9
Sheltered workshop	29.8
Day activity program	18.3
Other	23.1

* Note: Percentages may not equal 100% due to missing data and the fact that most clients receive more than one type of service.

Table 4 displays the services our clients were receiving. Most of our clients were receiving transportation (88.5%) and housecleaning assistance (71.2%). Also, most of our clients attended some kind of day program (63.5%). There were fewer clients who received education in community living skills (42.3%) and legal assistance (27.9%).

Table 5
Mean and Standard Deviation of Level of
Mental Retardation, by Sex and Age, of KAP Clients

Sex:	Mean	SD
Male	2.76	1.06
Female	2.56	0.97
Age:		
0-64	2.92	1.11**
65 and older	2.39	0.69**

** p 0.01

Finally, we may conclude that there is no significant difference between males and females on their level of retardation (Table 5). We have assigned numerical rank to level of retardation, as recorded in clients' records, as follows: 1 = mild, 2 = moderate, 3 = severe, 4 = profound retardation. The mean level of retardation for males was 2.76 and for females the mean was 2.56, with standard deviations of 1.06 and 0.99 respectively. Our younger age group was significantly more retarded than our older age group, mean level of retardation 2.92 and 2.39 respectively with standard deviations of 1.11 and 0.69 respectively.

69

RECOMMENDATIONS FROM EXPERIENCE

Mary C. Howell

■

Most people with mental retardation can be expected to make use of professional services at some time during their old age. Even those who have always lived at home are likely to need residential placement as family caregivers age. If capabilities for productive work decline, alternative daytime occupations are needed. A range of health-related services may be indicated, intermittently or on a regular basis.

In past years, there have been few services well suited to the needs of people with mental retardation who are old.[1] Service providers who are familiar with young people with mental retardation plead unfamiliarity with the characteristics of people who are old and, conversely, service providers experienced with the needs of old people may resist requests for service for clients who have been labeled as mentally retarded.

It is true that state departments of mental retardation (or their equivalents) are obliged to provide services for their clients of every age. Similarly, the Older Americans Act designates its funds for services for needy people aged sixty or older.[2] Policy planners sometimes propose that acceptance of these old and developmentally disabled clients into "generic service systems" (for those who are mentally retarded or for those who are old) is all that is needed to resolve the present problems of service inadequacy.[3] Our experience in the Aging Project, however, suggests that several caveats are in order.

■ Pitfalls To Be Avoided

Age segregation is no more a good arrangement for people with mental retardation than it is for people who are not labeled mentally retarded.[4] While most of us prefer to have some predictable, everyday contact with others of our own age, there are also some compelling advantages to mixed-age groupings. Among these advantages are a maintenance of tolerance and understanding by people of all age groups for each other; exposure to a broad range of interests and activities; and person-to-person bonding that has the character of intergenerational relations.

For caregivers, also, there are advantages in mixed-age groupings of clients. Clients who have different abilities and different kinds of wisdom can help each other. Increasing frailty and increasing need for assistance with activities of daily living (including transferring, lifting, and turning) make care for the very old a difficult physical burden; awareness of approaching death contributes to the emotional and social burden of giving care. But these characteristics also give people who are old and frail a particular value that can be heightened when they are a minority among younger, more physically able clients.

Inappropriate "generic" geriatric services should not be perpetuated on a new group of clients, those with mental retardation. There is much in the current service delivery system for old people that we should fret about; it seems an extreme of short-sightedness to ask that these inappropriate aspects of service be visited on yet another client group. From the deprivations engendered by forced uniform retirement demands, to the demeaning character of medical clinics in acute-care hospitals, to the boring sterility of many "day-health" and "day-activity" programs, there are myriad reasons not to add a new client group—the group labeled as mentally retarded—to those old people who are already at risk of being ill served. This is not because people identified as retarded will not fit in smoothly; after decades of forced participation in group programs, they are usually "good sports" and are inclined to accept whatever is offered. Their inability to envision better circumstances for themselves is all the more reason for those of us who want to understand their needs to continue to struggle for appropriate and individualized services.

Lockstep programs, identical for all members of any group, are unlikely to provide an adequately high level of care. As the numbers of people living into old age increases (in the year 2000, the group of people in the general population older than seventy-five is expected to be as large as the group aged sixty-five to seventy-five[5]), there will be an inclination to respond to service needs by "warehousing": offering services that are not individualized and that are only minimally varied.

This tendency will be reinforced if there are cutbacks of public funds for social programs to families that cannot afford the kind of care they would choose for family members who are old. Those of us who work in the provision of direct care are most acutely confronted by painful gaps when service is given *en masse,* and are most propelled to argue for truly individualized care plans.

Finally, it is unlikely that people with mental retardation will receive optimal care from "generic geriatric service" providers *in the absence of special training.* In keeping with the current fashion in quantifiable training, there needs to be communication of demographics, data, and other numbers. More acute, however, is the need for adjustments of attitudes and beliefs, and for opportunities to reduce long-held negative biases and to overcome narrow stereotypes. These latter challenges will not yield to the conveyance of numbers; they serve as threshold barriers and are probably best overcome by apprentice education, clinically-based and mentor-modeled.

With these caveats as background, the following recommendations represent the experience of the Kennedy Aging Project in specific areas of service needs.

■ Residential Placement

Housing needs are and will probably continue to be major problems for people who are old. Mental retardation only adds to the difficulties.

"Housing" actually means a complex of domestic needs, going beyond the provision of four walls and adequate heat. Grocery and clothes shopping, meal preparation, kitchen clean-ups and laundry, and assistance with activities of daily living all occur within the home. Anyone who is old and frail, arthritic of hand and slow of foot, handicapped by diminished vision and hearing and an unreliable memory, is likely to need the kind of help that can be provided by on-site extra hands. These are not services that will be carried out by professionals whose skills are so pricey they are reimbursed by the quarter-hour.

Our observations about avoidance of age segregation apply very strongly to residential placement. A generational mix brings benefits to both residents and to staff. One kind of co-placement must be avoided, however. People who are old and frail should not have to live with others who are physically strong and impulsively driven to assault and other forms of aggressive abuse. The vulnerability of people who are old and frail is great.

Homes for people who are progressing through old age require certain amenities of convenience. Doors and level changes must be wheelchair accessible. Stairways will inevitably become barriers. Kitchen and bathroom equipment must be reachable and easily operated. Handrails and cleared walking paths are required to minimize the possibility of falls.

The forgetfulness of old age shades into the confusion of dementia. Alzheimer's disease occurs among those with mental retardation at the same rate as among those who are not mentally retarded, with the exception of the group with Down syndrome, who experience Senile Dementia of the Alzheimer type at a rate of about 35 percent after age thirty (see Chapter 36). Experience with dementia teaches that the best chance of slowing the inevitable progression of the disease comes when sameness, familiarity, structure, and simplification of the physical and social environment are deliberately planned.[6,7] For most people, this means continuing to live at home. For most homes, extra hands and extra staff will be needed.

Both, then, for those who are becoming forgetful and confused and for those who are becoming physically frail, a need for a higher staff-to-client ratio should be anticipated. These staffing needs cross disciplinary lines. Nursing visits may be required to administer medications; physical and occupational therapists may be needed to plan programs designed to maintain function or to modify environments to match declining capabilities. Primarily, however, additional staff will be needed because the aging person is slow or weak or has little endurance or is clumsy.

These are not "medical" problems, yet our system provides few routes for extra staff support except in circumstances of medically-defined illness or injury. Nursing home placements, incidentally, are rarely propitious for people with mental retardation, who tend either to become infantilized "pets" of the staff and clientele, or sink into quiet near-neglect, or are given medications to subdue objectionable behavior. Some nursing homes are exceptionally good, but this is not the rule.

■ Day Programming

Everyone needs a daytime occupation, an answer to the question, "What do you do?" For people with mental retardation—except for the fortunate few who are engaged in competitive employment—their occupations are subsumed under the rubric of "day programming." Work is highly valued in our culture, and most of us (those who are retarded are no exception) would prefer that our daytime occupation were a form of work. Although some people with mental retardation look forward to a time of retirement, many more resist that idea. In their work they find a measure of self-esteem, social companionship, a way to earn money, and a sense of productivity.

Workshop positions are often difficult to find and to hold; other clients are pressing to fill them, even though most workshop work is repetitive and boring. The majority of retirement programs, however, are even more dreary and dull. It is our strong recommendation that no one be "retired" from a workshop position until a plan for some better sort of daytime occupation is firmly in place. The best of these plans involve pairing with a community volunteer (such as a "friendly visitor" from a local church) with real opportunities for participation in community activities that are not age-segregated.[8] Warehousing of old people in day programs is a real threat and should be guarded against by carefully designed and individualized retirement plans, to be instituted only when the old person wants to begin to leave work and to move on to other occupations.

A special recommendation has to be made for flexibility in the workshop itself. We know of instances when profit-making companies have extended themselves to accommodate the failing productivity of valued but aging employees. One can easily argue that in sheltered workshops, where workers have invested long hours and years for low wages and no benefits, flexible accommodations for those whose productivity is diminishing ought to be the rule.

■ The Interdisciplinary Team Approach to Assessment and Service Planning

Our work in the Kennedy Aging Project has been rooted in the assumption that there are advantages, when clients' needs are unexplored territory, to working as a team of professionals from a broad swath of disciplines.[9,10] In clinical work on an interdisciplinary team model it is also essential that one person (or, on a teaching model, one student and one supervising faculty member) serve as case coordinator and direct communicator with the client and her caregivers.

The problems and care of people who are both mentally retarded and old are very like those of other old people. But these clients have lived lives of extraordinary experience. Many of them have been institutionalized for no "fault" and without their permission. Some have been neglected or even abused. Enduring into old age has required courage, resilience, and plain stubbornness.

Services for people with mental retardation have improved a great deal in the past several decades. For those who are old, services are still inadequate. They deserve our considered good will and most creative planning. Settling for "generic geriatric services" is not good enough.

70

TRAJECTORY OF A THREE-YEAR PROJECT

Mary C. Howell

■

The beginning of the Kennedy Aging Project suited me exactly. I have long assumed that undertakings that began easily were meant to be, whereas those that had to struggle to get conceived and born were not meant (for me) to do. The Aging Project began from a spark that was so sudden, unexpected, and seemingly inevitable, that I was immediately impressed that it was "a go."

The Aging Project was initiated by Mrs. Eunice Kennedy Shriver and the staff of the Joseph P. Kennedy, Jr., Foundation. The project was envisioned as a mechanism for teaching health professionals about the population of people with mental retardation who were growing old and who were being relatively neglected, both in services provided and in academic interest and prestige. From the beginning, Mrs. Shriver and the Kennedy Foundation recognized that giving Foundation money to a project that *focused* on this population was a way of giving value to these people, both as individuals and as a group.

In the context of this vision, Mrs. Shriver designated the director of the Project (Howell), two faculty members (Beyer and Seltzer), some of the emphases of the Project (for instance, the liaison with Special Olympics, the focus on ethics, and the inclusion of a spiritual component in our concept of health), and the location of the Project in the Eunice Kennedy Shriver Center for Mental Retardation, Inc., in Waltham, Massachusetts. The Kennedy Foundation was also very helpful in recommending the Project to the Massachusetts Department of Mental Retardation for supplementary funding.

In the spring and summer of 1985 the planning took form. My participation in the Project was fixed at 18 hours a week—although certainly the weekly work consumed more than 40 hours of my time from the beginning to the very end. The administrative staff of the Shriver Center was generous from the start, giving me clerical assistance, making office space available, and providing steady encouragement during the planning period.

Most of the faculty and students spent a small part of their week (between four and sixteen hours) with the Project. The two other "regular" staff members (whose hours were full-time, or nearly so) joined the project in September of 1985: Liz DeBrine as the faculty member for Sports and Recreation and also as the Liaison with Massachusetts Special Olympics, and Jerry Cabrera as Chief Administrative Assistant, Intake Worker, Editor, and Jack of All Trades. The ambience of the office was very much determined by the presence of these two remarkable, compassionate, and competent people.

In the first year (1985-1986) we were able to bring together faculty members in eight disciplines and six students. We had assembled the Project in a short time, and were fortunate to have located such a strong staff, devoted both to the educational and the service goals of the work, enthusiastic about the focus of the Project, and willing to invent process and subject matter emphasis as we went along.

The emphasis in that first year was on designing what the Project was about. For instance, on Wednesday afternoons we met as a "Legal Clinic." On a few occasions we did see clients with legal problems—and on those occasions provided needed expert help to unravel their problems. But more essentially we debated and resolved our own views on confidentiality, release-of-records permission, and competencies. Probably it was no accident that in that first year there was a preponderance of attorneys and psychologists on the staff. We laid a groundwork in the first year for a perspective that was central to all of our later work.

We also began in that first year to hold Ethics Conferences. In fact, these were our first "clinical" efforts; Ethics Conferences were held bimonthly from late summer 1985 through to the end of the Project in 1988. Case Conferences, Interdisciplinary Team Evaluation Clinics, and Geriatric Clinics also began in the fall of 1985, after our staff of faculty and students was assembled. The evolution of the Team process is described elsewhere in this book (see Chapter 7).

Also in September of 1985 we began a productive association with the Department of Mental Retardation of the Commonwealth of Massachusetts. Under the leadership of Mary McCarthy, this department later took the opportunity to redefine its focus and responsibilities as it became a separate department, no longer a subdivision of the Department of Mental Health. In the process of "the split" of the two Departments, the commitment of the professional staff in Mental Retardation to respond to the needs of clients who are old gained new impetus. The Department offered our Project not only funding but also cooperation, courtesy, and responsive collaboration.

By the end of the first year our purpose, way of working, and special efforts were established. These special efforts included promotion of confidentiality and respect for client competencies, struggle against "ageism" and a thoughtless acceptance of demeaning and segregated old-only services for our clients, emphasis on maintenance of function, and an effort to find an authentic integration of the cognitive, social, emotional, and spiritual aspects of a "holistic" vision of health and well-being.

As we began our second year we became aware of and impressed with the grace of our funding arrangements with the Kennedy Foundation. Our responsibility to the Foundation was to keep them informed of the direction of our work. In return the Foundation gave us a large measure of trust and confidence. I am grateful to Mrs. Shriver for reading and responding to *all* of the reporting material we sent to her.

By the fall of 1986 we had established rituals of eating together (at Team meetings, lunchtimes, and at our quarterly pot-luck parties) and of bringing each other clippings from our various personal information sources. The second year was the full flower of the Project—far enough into the work so that our procedures ran smoothly and with a minimum of worry, and with the end of the Project not yet in our awareness.

During the second year we had a broader distribution of disciplines represented by both faculty and students. Our list of publications, media projects, and speaking engagements grew. Also during this second year we began a special project for the Department of Mental Retardation, assessing clients who had been placed in nursing homes but whose placement was questioned as possibly inappropriate.

We began our third and final year knowing that there was no certain funding for continuation of the Project. The original proposal of the Kennedy Foundation had been for a three-year demonstration project. On the one hand it seemed that our period of peak productivity would probably correspond to that three-year interval. On the other hand, we were a smooth-functioning team of experts, and there is always regret when an ongoing working group cannot continue. As the year progressed our concern was confirmed by the termination date for the Kennedy Aging Project, August 31, 1988: no funding source had been found to take over its support.

Our awareness of the ending of the Project was crystallized early in the year into an intention to create this Handbook. Max Schleifer and Stanley Klein of *Exceptional Parent* magazine, who had from the start given strong support to our Project efforts, offered to become our publishers. Working with them and their staff has been easy and efficient.

The events of the final year were ritually marked: the last of our scheduled conferences, the last Winter-Holiday celebration in the office, the last nursing-home client, the last client seen for Interdisciplinary Team Evaluation Clinic, the last pot-luck party. In the spring of 1988 we decided to give one more conference, this a "giveaway" (a no-charge event) in the Native American tradition of marking transition by giving our treasures to our friends.

The Kennedy Aging Project is also bracketed by the arrival of Liz's babies: she was pregnant with Andrew when she began this work and delivered William in the penultimate month of the Project. Our devotion to her children is a reflection of our personal attachment to each other, to the importance of families, and to work that allows us to put these values into action.

Good programs thrive with good funding. Good neighbors provide another impetus to well-being, and the neighbors who shared our corridor of the Shriver building were warm, encouraging, and good-natured. Finally, good programs need good energy; it may be that a three-year Project nicely captures a periodicity of human energy that promotes an ability to recognize and respond to challenge, a creative impetus, and a high degree of productivity.

■ Postscript

One of our goals in creating the Kennedy Aging Project (and in writing this book) was to disseminate a model project that could be replicated. Already we know of two spin-off projects, similar but not identical to the Kennedy Aging Project: one at the Shriver Center in Waltham, Massachusetts and a second at the Waisman Center, in Madison, Wisconsin. Most of our faculty and many of our students continue to work with people who are old and mentally retarded.

PART 6
AFTERWORDS

71

WORKING AT THE KENNEDY AGING PROJECT

Gerard Maria Cabrera

■

Working at the Kennedy Aging Project taught me more than organizational and administrative skills. This has also been a period of personal growth. What I learned extends beyond the office and the clinic; it has come home with me, to my relationships, to my outside volunteer work, and to my thoughts and dreams of the future.

Working at the Project prepared me for new intellectual and spiritual challenges. The supportive atmosphere of my colleagues freed me to express myself, knowing that my opinions would be respected. In a mutually sharing environment I learned a little about each of the different disciplines that come together here, and I have been able to put that new knowledge to use.

One of the most valuable and practical things I learned is about the right to refuse medical care, and the complicated legal and ethical issues surrounding life-sustaining treatments. I hope I can apply this to myself and to the people I care for, when and if such decisions have to be made. An appreciation for the process of dying has also formed in my mind. I know better now that how one dies is equally as important as when one dies, and that a spirit at peace with itself and the universe will pass calmly into whatever comes next, if anything.

Also, as the brother of a person with mental retardation, I came to understand more about the developmental issues in my sister's life and the ways that I can be more supportive and responsive to her needs. I have gotten rid of most of the sense of ignorant embarrassment I had growing up with her, and can separate myself from her enough to know that she has her own feelings and beliefs that I must respect.

I saw the Aging Project, through its three years, change and develop in many ways. At the beginning there was a sense of undertaking something unknown and a chance for innovation; at the end, there is a feeling of accomplishment as we compile our bibliography, our statistics, and our papers. It is remarkable that so much has been achieved in so short a time. I am gratified and honored to have been part of such a special Project. I take from this place good memories, good knowledge, and good friends.

72

WHO DO WE BLAME?

Elizabeth J. Debrine

■

Clients and their caregivers, families, and friends came to the Kennedy Aging Project with a list of problems experienced by the client. These problems may have to do with appropriate housing, day programming, disruptive behaviors, or medical matters. The Interdisciplinary Team tried to discover why the client was no longer cooperating at home or at work, why the client was experiencing loss of skills, or why the client and the services appeared to be mismatched.

After a thorough review of the records, intake data, and staff and client interviews, I found myself searching for the one piece of information that indicated who or what was "responsible" for the client's problems. Who or what was not fulfilling the client's needs?

It's easy to find fault with bureaucratic policies that do not allow for flexibility in housing and day programs, agencies that do not provide adequate staff education and supervision, the general lack of funding, families who reject their aging sibling who is mentally retarded, and a society that has little respect for human service workers. In addition to current events, there are events that occurred decades ago, such as institutions that instilled self-destructive behaviors, parents who rejected an abnormal child and placed her in an institution, and a community that ignored people who were different.

SERVING THE UNDERSERVED

It was only this past year that I began to examine why I so desperately needed to blame someone for the present situation: the caregivers, the system, the family, the agency, or even the client. ("If only the client would do X, then we could provide Z services!") At first I thought that I wanted to blame someone because I had spent many years practicing therapeutic recreation in programs that used a medical model; in this model, a disease is identified and a prescribed cure is given. In our work, we offer no cures. But even with this realization, I still had to contend with an overwhelming sense of failure. There was no way that I could ever make up for all of my clients' losses with regard to family, work, education, and community life. I could not compensate for the many abandonments and the inadequate provision of care. How could I say I was sorry for the past fifty or sixty years of their lives?

Then I experienced what I consider to be a crisis of understanding. I began to realize that all of the people involved in the client's life were performing to the best of their abilities, despite what I considered to be the client's needs. Once I was able to forgive *my own* inability to provide total restitution for a client, I was able to have compassion for the staff's and family's limitations as well. Many of the caregivers were looking for a place where they could unburden their feelings of guilt and inadequacy. They were confronted every day with the frustrating reality that situations take a long time to change, if they change at all. As a result I was able to develop a working relationship with the caregivers in a more meaningful fashion. I have learned to try to reaffirm the caregivers' work and dedication as having a positive impact on the client's life.

I feel that it's important to understand that the client has some responsibility in all of this. The client is accountable for his actions. I do not mean that we should blame the victim, because there is no empowerment in that. I think we should view our clients as *survivors* of institutionalization in state schools and nursing homes. When they are given the chance, I hope that clients will choose to re-engage with people and life in general, even though it may mean taking risks. It would be a shame if they chose to continue a safe but isolated life.

It is never too late to try to initiate change, regardless of how old or resistant the client is. Staff attitudes have great potential to initiate transformation. If staff perceive hope and dignity in caring for a client, then they will have compassion for the client and her present position. This empathy will empower the client to realize some measure of her inherent capabilities.

I have learned a lesson at the Kennedy Aging Project. It is not my role to find someone to blame for a client's unpleasant past and less-than-adequate present circumstance. What I must do is move beyond fault-finding to compassion and empowerment with both staff and clients. In such a supportive environment, caregivers and clients have a greater opportunity to realize their potential.

73

PERSONAL REFLECTIONS ON KENNEDY AGING PROJECT FAMILIES

Susan L. Sternfeld

■

Ordinarily one envisions a family as composed of parents and children who live and grow together throughout their individual biological life-cycles. Parents are caregivers when their children are young; then, hopefully, adult relationships develop when the children are grown. Finally the children become caregivers, or oversee the care, of their aging parents.

However, for every family represented by a client in the Kennedy Aging Project, this traditional notion of "normal" family living has been knocked askew by the birth of a son or daughter who is mentally handicapped. The personal histories of some clients are filled with accounts of abandonment at a young age to an institution, lack of any formal education, and little, if any, contact with family of origin during the adult years. For other clients, it was family crisis, such as the premature death of their parents, that cast them adrift from biological family living and shifted caregiving to the state system. Each client's story is a testament to the resiliency of the human spirit, for each client in his unique way has coped with many adversities and survived to old age. It is easy to wonder how people so vulnerable survive in a society that has labeled them as inferior human beings. The following vignettes describe the families of four remarkable people whose lives briefly connected with mine via the Project.

John A. is one of the few people we saw who never "spent time" in an institution, and whose family of origin is still intact and actively involved in his life. Both parents are still living, and both have been assisting with his adjustment to supervised apartment living. John, who has Down syndrome, is 41 years old and lived at home until 5 years ago, when he moved into an apartment which he shares with one other man. John's stable and loving family life is reflected in his easy-going, affable personality and his gentle sense of humor. He is indeed very fortunate that his life has provided him with so much stability, continuity, and loving concern, for even as he attempts a more independent style of living, his parents and three sisters are there offering him encouragement and support. For John's 70 year old parents, the role of caring for their son and planning for his future has changed very little over the past 41 years. When John was small they had to become his teachers as well as his parents, since the public schools offered little or no education; even now they are involved in decision-making on John's behalf. Mr. and Mrs. A. worry about who will carry on their commitment to John when they are gone, but at the same time they are enjoying their new freedom from daily caregiving by taking trips and holidays together.

The family circumstances of Roger B. reveal a more complicated life story. Roger had two brothers and two sisters and he lived at home until his early teens. Caring for Roger, who is diagnosed as having mild-to-moderate mental retardation, must have been a strain for the family because at 13 he was going to be placed in an institution until an uncle in Chicago offered to care for him. Roger lived in the city and worked in the uncle's restaurant until he was 33, at which point he was sent to an agricultural community for able-bodied, retarded men. At age 63, five years ago, Roger moved into a group home and started working in a sheltered workshop. In many ways, Roger has led an active and productive life. He has been able to keep in touch with one of his sisters. He coped with witnessing a tragic accident when his brother was run over by a bus, and he mourns the loss of other family members who have died—his parents and one sister. He visits his surviving sister and her family several times each year for a day and enjoys these visits, but he longs to see his brother whom he hasn't seen for 25 years. At the moment, Roger's housemates and caregivers form his support "family." In addition he has developed a close and special friendship with a woman at the workshop with whom he would like to spend more time, perhaps even marry.

Linda C. has very little recorded family history, and since her father died in 1981, she has had no contact with her family of origin. Linda is 60 years old and has Down syndrome with moderate to severe mental retardation. She lived at home until age 15, when she entered a state school. She has resided there ever since, except for a brief 5-month period in 1987 when she attempted living in an Intermediate Care Facility. Linda has developed a strong attachment to the cottage she has lived in for many years and views it as her home. Other clients and caregivers are her "family" in every sense of the word except the biological. That is, they care about each other, help each other, and share good and bad times together. Thus, when Linda began to experience slight cognitive deterioration over a year ago, an element of denial entered into people's thinking, just as it might when a biologically-related family begins to notice changes in a loved one. Through the best of intentions, Linda was encouraged and supported in a careful attempt to give her a more "normal" life-style in the ICF. Unfortunately for everyone, the attempted move either exacerbated or co-existed with a further cognitive deterioration and dementia and rapid decline in daily living skills, which in the end necessitated Linda's return to the state school. At present, Linda's caregivers and fellow clients are caught in an emotionally-charged moral dilemma wherein administrative needs about staffing are pulling in one direction, while personal feelings and a desire to maximize Linda's present abilities in her familiar setting, a recommended practice for Alzheimer's patients, is pulling in another direction.

Mary D., age 61, spent virtually all of her life in an institution. As a young child she was placed in a state school where she resided for many years before moving to a rest home. Finally, in 1986, when the rest home closed, Mary moved in with a foster family;

here for the first time in her life she is experiencing normal family living and interaction with people of all ages, including young children and babies. Although Mary has three siblings who live within commuting distance, there is very little contact, and Mary shows little emotional attachment to, or interest in, her family of origin, even when the one brother who acts as Mary's legal guardian pays an annual visit. Mary's level of retardation is described as severe, but her present "family" believes she understands far more than she is able to express and that, had she been given appropriate education as a child, she would have been capable of much more than was ever expected of her. This family's loving care and efforts to provide opportunities for Mary's growth are enriching her life. At a time when most people her age are experiencing the loss of loved ones, Mary is experiencing an increase. Mary is the only one of these four people who had virtually no normal family life as a child, and thus it seems particularly right, from a moral standpoint, that she should have found such a happy family experience at the opposite end of her life-span. She has finally found the nurturing and education, the mothering and fathering, one normally has as a child.

This is a microscopic sample of the many family stories told during Kennedy Aging Project team meetings; there has been no attempt to make these four vignettes representative. Rather, these are four people whose stories I came to know, stories that raised within me a particularly poignant reaction. Each shows the emergence of a core value of family living, whether experienced within the biological or formally acquired family system: interpersonal commitment. For John, his parents rejected the personal advice of the day and kept their son at home rather than send him to an institution. Their devoted commitment to his care and education has endured despite the early indifference of both the educational and human service systems. At this stage in their lives together, both parents and son are experiencing more independent life-styles, a development that is due to a more sensitive state system providing new opportunities for people who are disabled. John's parents can now trust the system to assume some of their own personal commitment to John.

Roger's extended family rallied support at a critical point in his life. Through an uncle's willingness to care for Roger as he entered adulthood, Roger learned skills that enabled him to remain in society's mainstream for many of his adult years. When Roger moved into the agricultural community at 33, the state assumed primary responsibility for his care. In spite of this shift in caregiving, from family to state, Roger was able to maintain some family contact which was, and is, very important to him. Now that he has returned to community living, he has been able to develop a strong attachment to a woman in his workshop. Thus, the thread of family care and contact and commitment that has wound through his life will, perhaps, help him form a lasting bond with his new friend. His present caregivers are sensitive to this need in Roger's life and are attempting to support his efforts to increase social and leisure contacts with Jane.

For both Linda and Mary, their primary memories and emotional identities rest solely with paid caregivers and fellow clients, all of whom demonstrate a level of personal commitment that rivals that of biologically related families. These two women have spent virtually all of their lives in institutions; presently their days are filled with the loving concern of individuals who really care about their well-being and are prepared to argue for their right to live with dignity. For Linda this is in her familiar cottage on the grounds of a state school, for Mary in a cheerful, lively foster family.

So the "family" bond that holds folks together and urges them to help each other has taken many forms throughout the lifetimes of John, Roger, Linda, and Mary. Parents, relatives, advocates, employees, and policy-makers have acted out their commitment to four needy individuals in unique and sometimes heroic ways. Their actions transcend legal, biological, and job requirements; there is a spiritual, ethical, and moral quality to their commitment that can only be described as love.

74

FULL CIRCLE AND MORE

Deirdre Gavin

■

As a student at the Kennedy Aging Project, I began with focused goals and specific expectations, unaware that my internship would resurrect the experiences of some twenty years past, enlighten my present knowledge, and expand my vision of future possibilities in health care.

In 1965, as members of the Commonwealth Service Corps, five other volunteers and I lived with the children in Stephen Bowen Hall at the Fernald State School. Our small group of college and graduate students might best be described as "multidisciplinary," for I was a classics major, and others were modern language, history, and English majors. Only our team leader, a doctoral candidate in psychology, had specialized education in mental retardation. We came with the energy and naivete of youth and a creativity charged by ignorance of unwritten institutional "rules."

At that time, we were clearly intruders, watched by security police for several months, and viewed suspiciously by many administrators. Our mission was to provide the children with a varied program of activities, based on the simple assumptions that children need love and encouragement to build trust and to develop self-confidence; need good food, fresh air, exercise, and fun; and need rewards, enjoyable activities to look forward to, and the opportunity to participate in planning for these activities. While choice of activities was part of our original plan, we quickly learned that our children had so little experience that our first task was to introduce many different summer activities. By the end of the summer they would be able to make choices.

When we first arrived at Bowen Hall, the children simply sat on wooden benches and watched television—all day, every day. Medications were prescribed for those who became restless or wished to go outside. Our plans included daily trips off the institutional grounds, arts and crafts in other buildings, and outdoor games. With the daring of novices we insisted that no tranquilizing drugs be given to the children unless required to treat a specific medical condition. We had our meals with the children and learned first hand how very little they had to enjoy. Dinner followed a regular pattern of three menus repeated on specific days and a fourth for Sundays. Ketchup, served twice a week with baked beans, was the most exciting item in their diet, and the children poured it on the square of un-iced yellow cake that faithfully followed the beans. Living in their unit, we learned how little privacy the children (who ranged in age from four to fourteen) had; we requested that some environmental changes be made, as well as changes in daily routines.

The children, who had been treated as a homogeneous group, were remarkably diverse. Some were mentally retarded, others were not; a few had Down syndrome, one child was deaf, another did not speak and apparently did not relate to those around her; several other children had suffered abusive experiences prior to institutionalization.

We forged ahead with our plans, uninhibited by prudence or experience, and brought the children regularly to Beaverbrook Reservation to play in the wading pool, to the swan boats in Boston, to Whalom Park for a day of amusement, taught them group games and songs, and helped them to make marvelous *papier mache* masks and monsters.

The children blossomed. The girl who apparently did not speak came to life and joined enthusiastically in all activities. The deaf child had greater opportunities to communicate. And the children cooperated with one another to make group activities a success.

Our experiences were exciting, but also troubling. While we prepared our reports and recommendations for the Commissioner of Mental Health, we realized that no program was scheduled to succeed ours when we left. As far as we knew, the children would return to the wooden benches to watch television—all day, every day. Had we acted irresponsibly in providing the children with a summer of healthy activities, only to return them to a life devoid of stimulation? Had we raised their expectations without consideration for the consequences they might suffer? Would they be punished for wanting to use their time constructively? I do not know if our children suffered for their exposure to a lively summer of fun, but I learned from the experience to make follow-up plans *before* initiating change in the lives of dependent and vulnerable people.

At the Kennedy Aging Project I learned directly from clients and caregivers that many of the recommendations of more than twenty years ago had been carried out; many who had been institutionalized now lived in group homes or staffed apartments, participated in workshops or competitive employment, and enjoyed healthy recreational activities as well as vacation trips. Although I can take no credit for implementing the positive achievements of deinstitutionalization, I feel a personal joy in each success story. In 1965 we could find no excuse for segregating these children from the community. At the Aging Project I saw clients who were about the age "my children" at Fernald would be today. I was proud to be working on a Team that constantly strove to improve the lives of clients as they grew older.

Participation in the Interdisciplinary Evaluation Team provided me with a series of surprising experiences. First, as a student, I assumed that my role would be that of a silent consumer of expertise. Very quickly, however, students learned that their comments were welcome and that their broad spectrum of experiences could contribute to the problem-solving process. Students were treated with encouragement and respect, which served as an example for evaluation interviews with clients and caregivers and facilitated innovative thought in addressing the issues brought for Team consideration.

Secondly, the Team operated as a real *team*, rather than a hierarchical structure, with medical doctors having greatest authority and other disciplines ranked beneath, according to their proximity to medicine. As a parent, I had learned how intimidating an interdisciplinary team can be to a caregiver, particularly when diagnosis or successful treatment remains elusive. All too often the caregiver is blamed for the doctor's frustration, rather than encouraged to contribute information and observations that may lead to a solution. The Aging Project Team approached each case with questions from every discipline and sought to obtain a total picture of the client in his environment. Attention to each aspect of the client's life often revealed areas for improvement that had not been raised in the initial evaluation request and sometimes disclosed a very different issue from the original presenting problem.

One of my social work advisors had warned me that many interdisciplinary teams do not achieve their goal of serving the client because they are consumed by internal power struggles. At the Kennedy Aging Project not only did the many disciplines of faculty members receive equal time, but students enjoyed the same opportunities to participate as did professionals. Amidst the rich diversity and numerous refinements of proposed solutions, common sense constantly stabilized Team discussions—a rarity among professors gathered to tackle problems of daily life. The practical execution of recommendations was consistently addressed as the various disciplines offered a system of checks and balances to one another, and the real world of the client emerged in focus.

I had originally joined the Team as a client advocate, with the goal of learning lessons from the field of developmental disabilities that could contribute to the success of the protection and advocacy system in the field of mental health. I came with certain biases and tended to support client rights without fully listening to apparently opposing views from Team members experienced in direct care. In time I learned that we were not engaged in "either/or," "right or wrong" arguments. Each Team member had the potential to expand our understanding of the client's situation. It was not necessary to choose *between* opinions, but rather to consider a problem from many different viewpoints and thus develop a more informed and workable set of recommendations. This experience impressed me, because it clearly demonstrated that the Team relied on *teamwork* without sacrificing the individuality of its members.

The third surprising lesson I absorbed from my internship at the Project evolved gradually but relentlessly over time and related to my studies in Public Health. In the beginning I had a limited focus, presuming that my work pertained to the specific needs of people with mental retardation who are old. Soon, however, the Team evaluation process revealed that identification of the *actual* needs of clients and/or caregivers was the primary task, regardless of the reasons given for the requested evaluation. The determination of need started with the client as a total person—his living situation, his work, his leisure activities, his spiritual beliefs and opportunities to practice his religion, meaningful relationships, and special interests or concerns unique to him. Frequently the Team determined that the client lacked an adequately stimulating environment to challenge his potential and recommended a move into the community, as in the instance of many clients inappropriately placed in nursing homes. In other cases the need rested with caregivers who required more staffing, supplemental services for clients, or support and guidance in the care of clients in the early stages of Alzheimer's disease.

Definition of need always started with the client and caregiver interview, with previously obtained information providing the background. For me this offered a model which ought to be applied to health care practices in general. In my studies of health services, definition of need repeatedly had come from experts utilizing charts of area demographics to determine what services a hospital should provide. It would seem that a far more reliable method of defining health care needs in particular locations would begin with the patients themselves, emergency room diagnoses, the reasons for nonelective hospitalization, and whether the patients lived in the area or had come a distance for medical services.

The Interdisciplinary Team approach to the client as a complete person has enormous implications for health care. Much of medicine is so highly specialized today that viewing the body as a functioning unit appears to be a lost art. If the body cannot be seen as a marvelous, synchronized machine, how can the spirit that moves it be recognized as significant to the maintenance of good health? At the Aging Project, the attitudes of clients and caregivers played a vital role in developing recommendations. Self-esteem, a sense of unique personhood, joy in the ability to give love as well as graciously to accept it, a pride in loyalty to friends, a sense of dignity in performing demanding and often unpraised tasks—these are a few of the essential elements the Team sought to nurture to improve the likelihood of a successful evaluation outcome. This holistic approach to the well-being of clients and caregivers alike serves as a model for addressing many aspects of human need, but particularly the delivery of health care in the United States today.

Although it may seem unrealistic to generalize from my internship at the Kennedy Aging Project to recommendations for the delivery of health care and the treatment of the patient as a person, it was also unrealistic in 1965 for a small group of student volunteers at the Fernald State School to write to the Commissioner of Mental Health recommending that the children in Bowen Hall not live in an institution, but rather enjoy a life in the community filled with healthy activity that would challenge their potential. Although I can claim no credit for implementing those recommendations, I arrived at the Kennedy Aging project to learn that they had been accomplished. Even more impressive was the creative energy with which the Interdisciplinary Team attacked the new problems of many clients, formerly institutionalized as children, as they grew old. For all the professional expertise of Team faculty, their resourceful and fresh approach to problem-solving revived my memory of the enthusiastic, though untrained, little band of pathbeaters who lived for one summer, over twenty years ago, on the very same grounds where the Aging Project evolved and flourished.

The lasting message I derive from my internship on the Team is simply that *what ought to be done can be done.* In the delivery of health care *every* patient should be treated with respect, as a complete person—not simply a disconnected anatomical part. If the patient is to be respected as a person, then the definition of health care needs should start with patients, rather than with administrators and the allocation of high technology equipment, which may, in fact, have little positive impact on the general health and well-being of our nation. The Kennedy Aging Project presented a model for dealing with people in need of assistance, and I believe that this model can and should be utilized in addressing health care needs throughout the United States.

75

SPIRITUALITY IN THE SECULAR SERVICE ENVIRONMENT

Mark Hatch

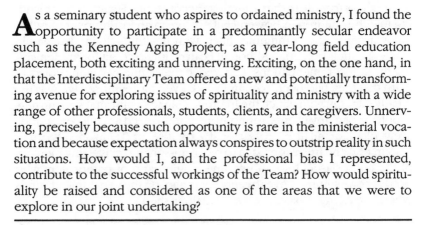

A s a seminary student who aspires to ordained ministry, I found the opportunity to participate in a predominantly secular endeavor such as the Kennedy Aging Project, as a year-long field education placement, both exciting and unnerving. Exciting, on the one hand, in that the Interdisciplinary Team offered a new and potentially transforming avenue for exploring issues of spirituality and ministry with a wide range of other professionals, students, clients, and caregivers. Unnerving, precisely because such opportunity is rare in the ministerial vocation and because expectation always conspires to outstrip reality in such situations. How would I, and the professional bias I represented, contribute to the successful workings of the Team? How would spirituality be raised and considered as one of the areas that we were to explore in our joint undertaking?

As a second year student at Harvard Divinity School, the stated goal of my placement at the Kennedy Aging Project was to try and synthesize academically-oriented, classroom-based learning with ministerial, hands-on experience. This would entail my participation on the Team as a representative, in a sense, of the religious, spiritual, and pastoral dimension within a larger understanding of health care and well-being. My tasks in this regard (shared by a woman religious and a permanent chaplain) would introduce me to a realm of learning and growth which, in the end, was nothing short of transforming. Reflecting on my time as a Team member there are three fundamental discoveries that I made while undertaking this role during the academic year 1987-1988.

The first area of great discovery came through my interaction with clients and caregivers, cases arranged and prepared in advance, interviewed, presented to the larger Team, perhaps visited in the field, and finally reported upon with recommendations and suggestions. Without exception, and much to my amazement and wonder, each client possessed some image of God and some concept of ultimacy which was a part of her world. Such images ranged from the highly doctrinaire and orthodox—God as the person or entity that discerns right from wrong and serves as arbiter and judge of all behavior—to the unusual and the marvelous—gods who are engaging in a colorful, vivid, dynamic fashion. Such figures were often remarkable composites of many facets of a client's life, representing as they do a cumulative and shared experience through the years. In every case, significant and deeply meaningful elements of a client's journey over her particular lifespan were represented in her God. This was "upsetting" to me, in the way that we in religion use that term: it shook me out of my complacency, undermined my dogma, and forced me to reconsider my own theology in a very healthy way. It deeply challenged me to reexamine the various images of God that have become conventional and established. Music and liturgy were also particularly important components of this larger spiritual construct. Many clients exhibited a wondrous capacity to recall tunes and lyrics from many years ago. Throughout their various pasts, the experiences of celebration and worship had remained as special and enhancing. Every client, each in her own special way, was able to share this with me and with others.

The second area of great discovery for me was in the realm of the professional interaction that took place on the Team itself. The very fact that all participants were willing to integrate spirituality and pastoral issues in the overall understanding of well-being and health was unusual. But more fundamental than that, each person with whom I worked revealed and shared his own inner life in the process of fulfilling a special role on the Team. By virtue of the members' individual authenticity in addressing spiritual issues, we as a collective Team were able to examine complex and holistic aspects of our clients' lives and, by extension, our own lives. Given the volatile and often discomforting aspects that can accompany religious discourse, this could only take place in an environment of honest professional trust and genuine respect. I saw my own respect for other professions—law, social work, medicine, psychology—deeply enhanced. And because of this mutual respect we were able to escape the grave danger that so often dooms interdisciplinary endeavors: overspecialization. Spirituality was not relegated to one predetermined corner, competing for attention with psychology. Pastoral issues were not limited to some restrictive definition. Rather, the goal of integration and of genuine equality was realized early on. As a result, all gave of themselves and out of this sincerity, respect, and real listening there emerged growth and health.

Finally, such an undertaking could not be completed without discoveries about myself. While these are certainly subjective—unique to my own path and to my own place in time—I reflect back on the experience with the belief and hope that some universal and transcendent lessons were learned.

There was awesome power and growth in coming to a time and place where I had no answers. It was shattering and then empowering to be able to say to a client or a caregiver "I don't know," "I have no answer for you." Even more empowering, as a result of this impotence, was the emergence of a "ministry of presence." Though it remains novel and frightening to me, learning simply to be human in the face of sadness or tragedy or confusion was uplifting. The learning to be a person, regardless of titles, degrees or aspirations—especially in the face of illness, despair or exhaustion—was transforming.

A corollary to the strange and yet beautiful discovery of personhood was the gift of being ministered to by clients. Their reaching out and caring, their elemental capacity to cut through the pretensions and the defenses with which I always armed myself, was very special. In this way the circle was closed, the brokenness was mended—the minister was being ministered to. The last piece of the puzzle was put in place. Just as it is often said that a doctor cannot be fully trained as a physician until she is a patient, so too the minister cannot be made whole until he (in my case) is on the receiving end of love, grace, and humanness. It is a remarkable experience that ultimately lies outside the realm of words. My life will have been changed irrevocably as a result of such encounters.

All of these discoveries regarding spirituality in the secular service environment reflect what I see as the joy and success of integration between religion, health, and human sharing. Surely each team experience will be unique, each set of persons will possess varying expectations and gifts. From my perspective, the opportunity to apply theoretical knowledge and deeply-felt beliefs in a real world setting proved invaluable to my personal growth and to the evolution of my conception of ministry. The challenge of integrating spirituality with secular care networks remains an important one, especially as research and investigation evolves on the question of the link between health and spirit. My work at the Kennedy Aging Project provided a special prism through which to examine many facets of this question, even as the journey continues.

In this time of growth and challenge a demand for humility emerged, the kind of humility that the prophet Micah shared regarding our place as human beings in the world: "God has showed you, O humankind, what is good; and what does the Lord require of you but to do justice, and to love kindness, and to walk humbly with your God?" (Micah 6:8). It is to this authentic, graceful humanness that we must turn as the joint search for health and spirituality continues.

76

CLOSING THOUGHTS

Bridget Bearss

■

A miracle is something that causes us to wonder, and to stand in awe in the face of a world filled with messages of hopelessness. My involvement with the Kennedy Aging Project has been an experience of the miraculous; coming to value human life in a new way and causing me to feel called to action. It has been an experience of knowing people deeply oppressed, and knowing those who will not allow that oppression to continue.

The Kennedy Aging Project has taught me to believe in miracles, and to hope that collaboration, honesty, and hard work can break the boundaries of a world that has forgotten how to dream. Professionally, I feel privileged to have been a part of crashing the limiting expectations of those who are old, and those who are mentally retarded. Within the context of the Interdisciplinary Team at the Aging Project, I have learned how to believe that we can make impossible things possible, and to see that together—in collaboration with other professionals—we can do more than we ever could have done individually.

Personally, the Kennedy Aging Project has opened new doors for me. In ten years as a professional educator, my world had become consumed with working to provide quality education for children. In the field of special and elementary education, I became focused on developing programs that allowed children to learn. My involvement with the Aging Project stretched that involvement to include adults, and redefined the oppression of those who have been too long without a voice. It has been a life-changing involvement. Pastoral companionship with both clients and Interdisciplinary Team members has allowed me to walk through a door to new understanding, and, having passed through the door, I can never return to the ignorance of believing that there was little work to be done in this field. I have been changed by the sensitivity, the commitment, and the self-giving of caregivers and clients. I have been filled with awe at the depth of intimate relationships developed between clients. And I have become enraged at those within our society who continue to create immobilizing institutions through attitudes. Through all of these experiences, the Interdisciplinary Team has worked with unrelenting hope that the world still has room to believe in the miracle of love.

I find it particularly disturbing that this Project is ending. But, as an educator, I recognize the tremendous learning that has happened because of it. Accepting the responsibility for taking what we have done and learned into new arenas, I will continue to believe that we can make a difference, and that I am called to action, refusing to rest in the despair of realizing the magnitude of the problems, or the insurmountable odds in changing a deeply entrenched system.

I will go forward with deep gratitude to Mary Howell, Liz DeBrine, Jerry Cabrera, the faculty and students, the clients and caregivers with whom I have had the chance to journey. It has been a pathway filled with deep joy and also tears of anguish. Knowing that I cannot remain stationary—in this place and time—I will take these experiences with me, recalling that I do believe in miracles, and that having been a part of a three-year miracle makes me more aware of finding and recreating those moments of wonder.

77

INTERNSHIP AT THE KENNEDY AGING PROJECT (09/87 - 12/87)

Nancy MacRae

■

The Project had an impact on both my professional and personal beliefs. Despite clinical experiences, specifically with clients who are mentally retarded, spanning nearly twenty years, I discovered that I held presumptions about what they could think, feel, and express. Exposure to this Project's philosophy and, more importantly, to the people they serve, has proved my presumptions to be just that.

Validation of the Interdisciplinary Team approach and its ability to utilize collective and individual expertise to assess a client from a holistic perspective; reassertion that each person needs to reconcile, in some manner, his life and what it has meant, in order to live fully until death; and, finally, a widening of my focus, a sensitizing of my expectations, and a humanizing acceptance affecting my ability to practice with this population, have all occurred. Additionally, a new appreciation of community issues for this clientele was developed, in contrast to my institutionally-based experience and knowledge. This has led to a more balanced outlook between the challenges, problems and benefits of institutional *versus* community living.

When the basic approach to a clientele that is both mentally retarded and aging is one of acceptance, positive outcomes are likely. Then clients are able to express themselves fully, with or without language, as human beings of worth. This belief is repeatedly validated by the gifts of insight that reflective practitioners can gain from their interactions with these remarkable clients. When an individual who is severely mentally retarded is given the opportunity to honor his dead peer by spending time with the corpse, appropriately kneeling down, looking at and touching him before walking away to turn back and wave at him, one can only be deeply affected by his intensely felt and simply expressed emotion. Such experiences lay waste to the multiple presumptions we have held regarding certain individuals' ability to feel, to express, to live fully. The Aging Project has numerous examples of such simple but beautiful displays throughout its three years.

The choice of topics for the three conferences sponsored by the project this last year also reflects the holistic nature of the Project. Retirement, Hospice, and Spirituality were the themes of focus, each emphasizing applicability to the population of people who are mentally retarded and old. The Retirement Conference stressed the institutionalization of all of our aged, ageism, the lack of opportunities for the person with mental retardation to assume adult roles, the importance of meaningful work in our lives, and the possibility of integrating this population and providing personalized planning to enhance opportunities for meaningful and self-affirming work. The Hospice Conference discussed the concepts underlying hospice care, developmental concepts of death, grieving stages, and how to help this population to deal with losses, aging, and death. The Spirituality Conference dealt with the need each of us has to make meaning of our existence, and how we can provide opportunities to enhance each person's sense of value, contribution, and dignity. Specific examples of intimacy shared with and by these clients were presented.

The Project has had the luxury of being able to include home visits as part of the assessment process. I had opportunities to visit programs for people who are mentally retarded and old, ranging from institutionally-based programs (one for Alzheimer's clients and one for clients who are old) to a community-based adult habilitation day program. All staff acknowledged the special needs and strengths of these clients and tried to meet or utilize these needs and strengths with varying degrees of success. A particularly meaningful visit to the home of one of the clients who had been referred to the Project occurred during the last week of my internship. This experience highlighted the multiple needs of clients, the tenuousness of many of their living situations—particularly when they reside at home with parents who are old—and the remarkable lengths that caregivers will go to keep them in familiar surroundings.

The Project has not been problem-free. Its short term of existence, the bureaucratic parameters within which it existed, the monumental task of coordinating the multiple schedules of its faculty and students with those of the clients and their caregivers, the small space that was available to them—which limited privacy—and finally, not always knowing whether they have made a difference in their clients' lives, have been difficulties with which the staff of the Project has had to cope.

The leadership at the Kennedy Aging Project is another example of exceptional qualities, personified by Mary Howell. Her strength of character and belief in each person's ability to make changes have inspired a small group of professionals to make a significant and reverberating effect on the lives of many students, students who will go on to enlarge the influence of this Project's conceptions about the dignity and worth of people who are mentally retarded and old. Her acceptance of each student, her encouragement by word and creative example of striving to do one's best, her tact and wisdom in knowing how and when to broach the bureaucracy, and her warmth and sense of humor make the experience at the Kennedy Aging Project one of lasting impression and a true demonstration of ethics and idealism put into practice.

The Project may end this summer, but it will leave behind a rich and vibrant legacy, one of students who can become change agents and advocates for this population within the various bureaucracies in which they work, and one of clients whose level of independence was facilitated or maintained and whose lives were enriched by their exposure to the Kennedy Aging Project. Ultimately, the Project has been able to demonstrate that small and caring, focused, knowledgeable, and ethical efforts can make a difference.

LAST PIECE

Mary C. Howell

■

The most important lessons of the Kennedy Aging Project for me had to do with trust and letting go. First, the grace of being able to work with the Kennedy Foundation, with funds given because we, as individuals, were known and trusted to do our best work, brought forward our very best efforts. This was especially true of the three "regular" members of the staff (Cabrera, DeBrine, Howell), we who spent the most hours, year-round, answering telephones, dealing with correspondence, responding to requests for help, and identifying ourselves with the goals of the Project.

Second, within the Project, a spirit of positive expectation drew a high quality of effort from everyone who participated. Almost every student remarked that being considered a full member of the team encouraged a kind of effort that was involved, creative, and energetic. Faculty, as well, were responsible, engaged, and gave fully, beyond the limited schedules of time that had been agreed to.

Third, it was exciting to see an idea ("teach health professionals...", *et cetera*) be lived out—trying this possibility, then that, to see what worked best—by a group who felt in harmony with each other. I believe that the Project was a nice example of group process at its best, without authoritarian leadership or predetermined, cut-and-dried procedures to curtail exploration and invention.

In a time when we are inclined to be skeptical about the possibility of successful work in any format other than individualistic, competitive effort, it was heartening—and fun—to be a part of a collective effort that was productively successful.

■ References for Chapter 4, Working With People Who Are Old and Mentally Retarded

Edgerton, Robert B., *The Cloak of Competence: Stigma in the Lives of the Mentally Retarded,* Berkeley: University of California Press, 1967.

Erikson, Erik H., *Identity and the Life Cycle,* New York: W.W. Norton & Company, 1980.

Erikson, Erik H., *The Life Cycle Completed,* New York: W.W. Norton & Company, 1982.

Featherstone, Helen, *A Difference in the Family: Living with a Disabled Child,* New York: Penguin Books, 1980.

Maxwell-Scott, Florida, *The Measure of My Days,* New York: Penguin Books, 1968.

Tyor, Peter L. and Bell, Leland V., *Caring for the Retarded in America,* Westport, Connecticut: Greenwood Press, 1984.

■ References for Chapter 5, The Educational Component of the Project

Adams, Margaret, Mental Retardation and its Social Dimensions, New York: Columbia University Press, 1971.

Bruininks, Robert H., C. Edward Meyers, Sigford, Barbara R., and Lakin, K. Charlie, eds., *Deinstitutionalization and Community Adjustment of Mentally Retarded People,* Washington, D.C.: American Association on Mental Deficiency, 1981.

Ernst, Nora S., *The Aged Patient: A Sourcebook for the Health Professional,* Chicago: Glazor-Waldman, Hilda K. Year Book Medical Publishers, Inc., 1983.

Janicki, Matthew P. and Wisniewski, Henry M., eds., *Aging and Developmental Disabilities: Issues and Approaches,* Baltimore: Brookes, 1985.

■ References for Chapter 6, The Context of Exemplary Service

Erikson, Erik H., Joan M. Erikson, and Kivnick, Helen Q., *Vital Involvement in Old Age,* New York: W.W. Norton and Company, 1986.

Justice, Blair, *Who Gets Sick: Thinking and Health,* Houston: Peak Press, 1987.

■ Notes for Chapter 7, The Interdisciplinary Team: Two Perspectives

1. *Model Code of Professional Responsibility,* American Bar Association, Canon 4, Ethical Consideration 4-1.

2. *Ibid.*

3. *Ibid.,* Ethical Consideration 4-2.

4. Although this was true in all cases, it was probably most apparent in tne nineteen cases in which the Mass. Department of Mental Retardation asked the Team's opinion about whether individuals living in nursing homes were appropriately placed and, if not, what would be the constituents of a proper placement.

5. See, generally, Paul R. Tremblay, "On Persuasion and Paternalism: Lawyer Decisionmaking and the Questionably Competent Client," 1987 *Utah Law Review* 515 (1987); Stanley S. Herr and others, *Guide to Representing Individuals in Mental Retardation Admission Proceedings,* prepared for The Section on the Delivery of Legal Services of the Maryland State Bar Association and the University of Maryland Clinical Law Office (1986).

6. See discussion of guardianship in chapter 23.

7. See, for example, Opinion No. 80-4 of the Massachusetts Bar Association's Committee on Professional Ethics (1980): A court-appointed attorney for a patient in an involuntary commitment proceeding "cannot suggest to a third person that a guardian be appointed for the client....[and] cannot initiate guardianship proceedings against the client...."

8. *Model Code,* note 1 above, Canon 7, Ethical Consideration 7-11.

9. *Ibid.,* Ethical Consideration 7-12.

10. 104 Code of Mass. Regulations, Sections 20.11 (1) (c) and 20.05 (8) (a) 2.

■ References for Chapter 7

Bass, R., "A Model for Clinical Team Evaluations in a Clinical Setting," in *Evaluating Mentally Retarded Individuals for Guardianship,* Symposium presented at Region X meeting of the American Association on Mental Deficiency, Montreal, Canada, 1981.

Golin, Anne K. and Ducanis, Alex J., *The Interdisciplinary Team: A Handbook for the Education of Exceptional Children,* Rockville, MD: Aspen Publications Systems, 1981.

Kane, Rosalie A. and Kane, Robert L., *Assessing the Elderly: A Practical Guide to Measurement,* Lexington, MA: Lexington Books, 1981.

Matson, Johnny L. and Breuning, Stephen E., eds., *Assessing the Mentally Retarded,* New York: Grune and Stratton, 1983.

◼ Notes for Chapter 8, The Climate of Our Work

1. The ethical framework used is from Carol Gilligan, *In a Different Voice,* Cambridge, Harvard University Press, 1982.

◼ References for Chapter 9, The Structure of Our Work

Matson, J.L. and Breuning, S.E., *Assessing the Mentally Retarded,* New York: Grune and Stratton, 1983.

◼ References for Chapter 14, Physical Therapy Evaluation

R. Wong, "Geriatrics Emphasis in PT, A Historical Survey," *Journal of the American Physical Therapy Association,* Vol. 68, Number 3, 360-363.

A.M. Jette and J.M. Bottomly, "The Graying of America, Opportunities for Physical Therapy," *Journal of the American Physical Therapy Association,* Vol. 67, Number 10, 1537-1541.

◼ References for Chapter 18, Medical Assessment

Kenney, Richard A., *Physiology of Aging: A Synopsis,* Chicago: Year Book Medical Publishers, Inc., 1982.

Rowe, John W., "Health Care of the Elderly," *New England Journal of Medicine,* Vol. 312, No. 13; pp. 827-34, 1985.

Rowe, John W. and Richard W. Besdine, *Geriatric Medicine,* 2nd ed., Boston: Little Brown, 1988.

◼ Notes for Chapter 19, Assessment of Legal Needs

1. Massachusetts "class members" covered by mental retardation institutional consent decrees are those residing at: Monson State School on or after 9/17/75; Belchertown State School on or after 2/2/72; Dever State School on or after 12/17/75; Wrentham State School on or after 12/4/75; or Fernald State School on or after 7/23/74. The consent decrees, approved by the U.S. District Court for Massachusetts, are: Belchertown: *Ricci v. Greenblatt,* C.A. 72-469-T; Dever: *MARC v. Dukakis,* C.A. 75-5210-T; Fernald: *McEvoy v. Mitchell,* C.A. 74-2768-T; Monson: *Gauthier v. Benson,* C.A. 75- 2910-T; and Wrentham: *MARC v. Dukakis,* C.A. 75-5023-T.

---

2. See, for example, *Wyatt v. Stickney,* 344 F. Supp. 387 (M.D. Ala. 1972); *N.Y. State ARC v. Rockefeller,* 357 F. Supp. 752 (E.D. N.Y. 1973); *Homeward Bound v. Hissom Memorial Center,* No. 85-C-437-E (U.S.D.C., N.D. Okla., 7/24/87).

3. Both verbally and in writing, through the handbook, *Estate Planning for Parents of Persons with Developmental Disabilities,* prepared for the Disability Law Center by the Boston University Center for Law and Health Sciences, Boston, revised Dec. 1986.

4. See *A Handbook on Guardianship, Conservatorship, and Other Options,* Mass. Association for Retarded Citizens and the Mental Health Legal Advisors Committee, Boston, rev. 1984, at 4. This *Handbook* provides an excellent introduction to all aspects of guardianship. Although specific to Massachusetts law, much of its guidance is applicable in all states.

5. See Id., at 23.

6. For a landmark decision addressing similar issues, see *Superintendent of Belchertown State School v. Saikewicz,* 370 N.E. 2d 417 (Mass. 1977).

7. In Massachusetts, the records are kept in the probate court of the county in which the ward lived at the time the guardianship was originally imposed. The records are arranged alphabetically by year, and are open to the public.

8. See *Handbook,* note 4 above, at 26.

9. See S.S. Herr, C. Jacobs, and J. Tyssowski Jr., *Guide to Representing Individuals in Mental Retardation Admission Proceedings,* Maryland Bar Association, Section on the Delivery of Legal Services, and Clinical Law Office, University of Maryland, Baltimore, 1986, at pp.8 and 25.

10. *Halderman v. Pennhurst,* 612 F.2d 84 (3d Cir. 1979), at 115, vacated 451 U.S. 1 (1981), reinstated 673 F.2d 647 (3d Cir. 1982), vacated 465 U.S. 89 (1984); *Homeward Bound v. Hissom Memorial Center,* note 2 above; *Clark v. Cohen,* 794 F.2d 79 (3d Cir. 1986), cert. denied 107 S.Ct. 459 (1986); *N.J. ARC v. N.J. Dept. of Human Services,* 445 A.2d 704 (N.J. Sup. Ct. 1982); *ARC of N.D. v. Olson,* 561 F. Supp. 473 (D.N.D. 1982), affirmed 713 F.2d 1384 (8th Cir. 1983).

11. See, for example, 42 U.S.C. 6010(2); 104 Code of Mass. Regulations 15.02(26).

12. See, for example, *In re Z,* Docket No. MR-87-663 (Mass. Super. Ct., Suffolk Cnty., Div. of Admin. Law Appeals, 12/10/87).

13. Chapt. 796, Mass. Acts of 1985.

14. *Romeo v. Youngberg,* 457 U.S. 307, 319 (1982).

15. *Thomas v. Morrow,* 781 F. 2d 367 (4th Cir. 1986), cert. denied 106 S.Ct. 1992, 107 S.Ct. 235; *Clark v. Cohen,* note 10 above; *Homeward Bound v. Hissom Memorial Center,* note 2 above.

16. See *ARC of N.D. v. Olson,* note 10 above.

17. See, for example, 42 U.S.C. 6011(c); 104 Code of Mass. Regulations 21.42.

18. See H.A. Beyer, "Litigation and the Use of Psychoactive Drugs in Developmental Disabilities," and M.G. Aman and N.N. Singh, "Patterns of Drug Use, Methodological Considerations, Measurement Techniques, and Future Trends," in *Psychopharma-*

cology of the Developmental Disabilities, M.G. Aman and N.N. Singh, eds., Springer-Verlag, N.Y. (1988).

19. See, e.g., *Wyatt v. Stickney,* 344 F. Supp. 387, 400 (M.D. Ala. 1972); *Halderman v. Pennhurst,* 446 F.Supp 1295, 1307-08 (E.D. Pa. 1977); *Gary W. v. Louisiana,* 437 F.Supp. 1209, 1229 (E.D. Ia. 1976); *Morales v. Turman,* 383 F.Supp. 53, 103-05 (E.D. Tex. 1974); *Welsch v. Likins,* 373 F.Supp. 487, 503 (D. Minn. 1974).

20. See, for example, *Wyatt v. Stickney,* id., at 400, sec. 22d. Cf. *Welsch v. Dirskwager,* No. 4-72 Civil 451 (U.S.D.C., D. Minn., consent decree, Dec. 1977), at 17.

21. *Rogers v. Commissioner of Mental Health,* 390 Mass. 489 (1983); Guardianship of Roe, 383 Mass. 415 (1981).

22. See, for example, *Rivers v. Katz,* 67 N.Y. 2d 485 (N.Y. Ct. App 1986); *People v. Medina,* 705 P.2d 961 (Colo. 1985); Matter of Alleged Mental Illness of Kinzer, 375 N.W.2d 526 (Minn. Ct. App. 1985); *Jarvis v. Levine,* 418 N.W. 2d 139 (Minn. Sup. Ct. 1988).

23. See C. Sigelman and others, "When in Doubt, Say Yes: Acquiescence in Interviews with Mentally Retarded Persons," 19 Mental Retardation 53 (1981).

24. For an overview of many of these legal rights that have been judicially recognized, see H.A. Beyer, "Litigation with the Mentally Retarded," in *Handbook of Mental Retardation,* J.L. Matson and J.A. Mulick, eds., Pergamon Press, N.Y. (1983).

25. *In re "AB"* (Mass. DMH, ISP Hearing Decision MR-54, 11/30/87). See also the more recent Memorandum from M.A. McCarthy, Commissioner, to Senior Staff and other administrators of the Mass. Dept. of Mental Retardation, re "Eligibility" (5/23/88): Under the "eligibility criteria contained in our statute and regulations,...IQ should not be the sole consideration in determining eligibility for DMR services."

26. Cf. Compliance Review No. 01-83-7001 (Region I Office for Civil Rights, U.S. Dept. of Health and Human Services, Letter of Findings, 4/16/85), which found that Connecticut "DMR programs would be in non-compliance with Section 504 [of federal Rehabilitation Act of 1973, which bans discrimination on the basis of handicap]... if dually diagnosed persons who could benefit from admission to DMR facilities were denied admission because of mental illness."

27. See, generally, S.S. Herr, *Rights and Advocacy for Retarded People,* Lexington, Mass.: Lexington Books (1983); P.R. Roos, "Advocate Groups," in *Handbook of Mental Retardation,* note 24 above.

28. The fact that family members or other caregivers had taken the initiative of contacting the Aging Project for services indicated that they were probably already engaged in such advocacy.

29. One handbook given to several caregivers was Discrimination on the Basis of Handicap, prepared by the Developmental Disabilities Law Center of Massachusetts and the N. Neal Pike Institute for the Handicapped, Boston University School of Law (revised April 1986).

■ Notes for Chapter 20, Leisure Assessment

1. Dr. Gerald Fain at Boston University and I developed this process while working together at a nursing home in Boston. We found that the categories helped us to find gaps in a person's leisure.

2. See Tom's story, Chapter 51.

■ References for Chapter 21, Assessment by Rehabilitation Medicine

Bates, P. and Wehman, P., "Behavior Management With the Mentally Retarded: An Empirical Analysis of the Research," *American Journal of Mental Retardation*, 1977, 15 (6): 9-12.

Bradley, T.B., "Remediation of Cognitive Deficits: A Critical Appraisal of the Feuerstein Model," *Journal of Mental Deficiency Research*, 1983, 27 (part 2): 79-92.

Capute, A.J. and Biehl, R.F., "Functional Developmental Evaluation: Prerequisite to Habilitation," *Pediatr. Clin. North. Am.*, 1973, 20 (1); pp. 3-26.

Cotten, P.D., Sison, G.F. Jr., and Starr, S., "Comparing Elderly Mentally Retarded and Non-Mentally Retarded Individuals: Who are they? What are their needs?" *Gerontologist*, 1981, 21 (4): 359-65.

Cotten, P.D. and Spirrison, C.L., "The Elderly Mentally Retarded (Developmentally Disabled) Population: A Challenge for the Service Delivery System," in Brody, S.J. and Ruff, G.E., Eds., *Aging and Rehabilitation* New York: Springer, 1986, pp. 159-187.

Davies, R.R. and Rogers, E.S., "Social Skills Training With Persons Who Are Mentally Retarded," *Mental Retardation*, 1985, 23 (4): 186-96.

Gaillard, F., "Recovery as a Mind-Brain Paradigm," *International Journal of Rehabilitation Research*, 1983, 6 (3): 331-8.

Intagliata, J. and Willer, B., "A Review of Training Programs for Providers of Foster Family Care to Mentally Retarded Persons," *Monogr. American Association of Mental Deficiency*, (4): 282-315.

Janicki, M.P. and MacEachron, A.E., "Residential, Health, and Social Services Needs of Elderly Developmentally Disabled Persons," *Gerontologist, 1984, 24 (2): 128-37.*

Killebrew, J.A., Harris, C., and Kruckeberg, K., "A Conceptual Model for Determining the Least Restrictive Treatment Training Modality," *Hospital and Community Psychiatry*, May, 33 (5): 367-70.

Konarski, E.A. and Diorio, M.S., "A Quantitative Review of Self-Help Research With the Severely and Profoundly Mentally Retarded," *Applied Research in Mental Retardation*, 1985, 6 (2): 229-45.

Landesman-Dwyer, S., "Living in the Community," *American Journal of Mental Deficiency*, 1981, 86 (3): 223-34.

Lloyd, L.L. and Karlan, G.R., "Non-Speech Communication Symbols and Systems: Where Have We Been and Where Are We Going?," *Journal of Mental Deficiency Research,* 1984, 28 (Part 1): 3-20.

Luftis, R.L., "Increasing Probability of Sign Language Learning of Severely Mentally Retarded Individuals: A Discussion of Learner, Sign Production, and Linguistic Variables, *Applied Research in Mental Retardation,* 1982, 3 (1): 81-97.

Nardone, M., "Characteristics Predicting Community Care for Mentally Impaired Older Persons," *Gerontologist,* 1980, 20 (6): p. 661-8.

Segal, R., "Trends in Services for the Aged Mentally Retarded," *Mental Retardation,* 1977, 15 (2): 25-7.

Seltzer, M.M., "Informal Supports for Aging Mentally Retarded Persons," *American Journal of Mental Deficiency,* 1985, 90 (3): 259-65.

Seltzer, M.M. and Seltzer, G.B., "Functional Assessment of Persons With Mental Retardation," in Granger, C.V. and Gresham, G.E., Eds., *Functional Assessment in Rehabilitation Medicine,* Baltimore: Williams & Wilkins, 1984, pp. 273-288.

Walz, T., Harper, D., and Wilson, J., "The Aging Developmentally Disabled Person: A Review, *Gerontologist,* 1986, 26 (6): 622-9.

■ Notes for Chapter 22, Serving the Underserved

1. World Health Organization, "Healthy Public Policy—Strategies for Action: The Adelaide Recommendations," Adelaide, Australia, 1988.

2. U.S. Department of Health and Human Services, "Personnel of health needs of the elderly," Washington, USDHHS, 1987.

■ Notes for Chapter 23, Decision-Making by and for Individuals of Questionable Competence

1. See, for example, Mass. General Laws, Chapter 123, Section 24.

2. *Ibid.*

3. See Rogers v. Commissioner, 390 Mass. 489 (1983), at 494-497; *Reise v. St. Mary's Hospital,* 12 Mental & Physical Disability Law Reporter 145 (Cal. Ct. App. 1987).

4. See, for example, 104 Code of Mass. Regulations, Section 20.05(8) (a) (2).

5. The New York State legislature has recently established a pilot program in which volunteer committees are empowered to provide such consent. See C.J. Sundram, "Informed Consent for Major Medical Treatment of Mentally Disabled People," 318 *New England Journal of Medicine,* 1368 (1988). (See Chapter 57 of this book)

6. See, for example, *Kritzer v. Cirton,* 224 P.2d 808 (Cal. Ct. App. 1950); W. Va. Code, Chap. 16, Sec. 4C-11.

7. A good introductory description of representative payees, their responsibilities, and the process for becoming one appears in *A Handbook on Guardianship,*

Conservatorship, and Other Options, by the Mass. Association for Retarded Citizens and the Mental Health Legal Advisors Committee (MHLAC) (rev. Oct. 1984), at p. 6. Available from MHLAC, 11 Beacon St., suite 925, Boston, MA 02108; (617) 723-9130. ("Suggested donation" is $1.50.)

8. A good introductory description of trusts is provided in *Estate Planning for Parents of Persons with Developmental Disabilities*, prepared for the Disability Law Center (DLC) by the Center for Law and Health Sciences, Boston University School of Law (May 1982; rev. Dec. 1986). Available from DLC, 11 Beacon St., Suite 925, Boston, MA 02108; (617) 723-8455 (Voice/TDD).

9. See, for example, Cal. Civil Code, Sections 2430-2444; Mass General Law, Chapter 201B, Sections 1-7; Pa. Consolidated Statutes Annotated, Section 20-5603(h). See also Chapters 57 and 64 of this book.

10. In New York, however, the state attorney general has taken the position that a durable power of attorney cannot be used to delegate generally to an agent the authority to make health care decisions. 1984 Opinions of the N.Y. attorney General F84-16, at 58 (Dec. 28, 1984). Some statutes, however, (e.g., California and Pennsylvania, note 9, above) explicitly authorize the delegation of health care decision making.

11. See *Wittkugel v. State,* 160 N.Y.S.2d 242 (N.Y. Ct. Cl., 1957), affirmed 172 N.Y.S.2d 57; (4th Dept. 1958).

12. See note, "Appointing an Agent to Make Medical Treatment Choices," 84 *Columbia Law Review* 985 (1984); D.L. Moore, "The Durable Power of Attorney as an Alternative to the Improper Use of Conservatorship for Health-Care Decisionmaking," 60 *St. John's Law Review* 631 (1986).

13. See, generally, P.R. Tremblay, "On Persuasion and Paternalism: Lawyer Decisionmaking and the Questionably Competent Client," 1987 *Utah Law Review* 515 (1987). Professor Tremblay, at pp. 564-67, discusses serious ethical problems presented when a lawyer pursues guardianship for his or her client. See also T. Gutheil and others, "Participation in Competency Assessment and Treatment Decisions: The Role of a Psychiatrist-Attorney Team," 11 *Mental & Physical Disability Law Reporter* 446 (1987). See also Chapter 64 of this book.

14. See L. Hipshman, "Defining a Clinically Useful Model for Assessing Competence to Consent to Treatment," 15 *Bulletin of the American Academy of Psychiatry and Law* 235 (1987).

15. *Deciding to Forgo Life-Sustaining Treatment: Ethical, Medical and Legal Issues in Treatment Decisions,* President's Commission for the Study of Ethical Problems in Medicine and Biomedical and Behavioral Research (March 1983), p. 45.

16. C.V. Granger, G.B. Seltzer, C.F. Fishbein, *Primary Care of the Functionally Disabled: Assessment and Management,* Philadelphia, J.B. Lippincott Company, 1987.

17. G.B. Melton, J. Petrila, N.G. Poythress and C. Slobogin, *Psychological Evaluations for the Courts: A Handbook for Mental Health Professionals and Lawyers,* New York, The Guildford Press, 1987.

18. T. Grisso, *Evaluating Competencies: Forensic Assessments and Instruments,* New York, Plenum Press, 1986.

19. A.G. Saunders and M.M. Simon, "Individual Functional Assessment: An Instruction Manual," 11 *Mental and Physical Disability Law Reporter* 60 (1987).

20. Mass. General Laws, Chapter 201, Section 6A. See also N.C. General Statutes, Section 35-1.6(3), (4), & (5). Other Massachusetts statues provide for guardianships for mentally ill persons (Mass. General Laws, Chapter 201, Section 6) and "spendthrifts" (Mass. General Laws, Chapter 201, Section 8).

21. See H. Owens, R. Rosner, and R.B. Harmon, "The Judge's View of Competency Evaluations II," 15 *Bulletin of the American Academy of Psychiatry and Law* 381 (1987).

22. Mass. General Laws, Chapter 201, Section 6A.

23. G. Mesibov, B. Conover, and W. Saur, "Limited Guardianship Laws and Developmentally Disabled Adults: Needs and Obstacles," 18 *Mental Retardation* 221 (1980).

24. A "guardian" is sometimes referred to as a "guardian of the person," whereas a "conservator" may be called a "guardian of the estate." A "plenary guardian" may be referred to as a "guardian of the person and estate." See N.C. General Statutes, Section 35-1.7(9) & (10).

25. See A. Bruggeman, "Guardianship of Adults with Mental Retardation: Towards a Presumption of Competence," 14 *Akron Law Review* 321 (1980).

26. See, generally, *Guardianship & Conservatorship: Statutory Survey: Model Statute,* Commission on the Mentally Disabled, American Bar Association (1979); A. Federman, "Conservatorship: A Viable Alternative to Incompetency," 14 *Fordham Law Journal* 815 (1986).

27. Mass. General Laws, Chapter 201, Section 16B. See also Conn. General Statutes Annotated, Section 45-78c (limited guardianship of the property).

28. See H. Beyer and J. Levine, "Evolving Limits on Guardianship," *National College of Probate Judges Newsletter* (Fall, 1980).

29. See, for example, Alabama Acts of 1982, Act. No. 82-384; Alaska Acts of 1981, Chapter 83; Connecticut General Statutes Annotated, Sections 45-320 through 45-336; Idaho Code, Section 56-239; Maine Revised Statutes Annotated, Chapter 18, Section 3512; Texas Probate Code, Part 5, Section 130A; Vermont Statutes Annotated, Chapter 14, Sections 3060-3080.

30. See, for example, *Guardianship of Bassett,* 7 Mass. App. 56, 385 N.E.2d 1024 (1979); *Guardianship and Conservatorship of Sim,* 403 N.W.2d 721 (Neb. 1987). But see *In re Fabre,* 371 So.2d 1322 (La. 1979).

31. See, for example, Mass. General Laws, Chapter 201, Section 14; N.C. General Statutes, Section 35-1.15 (interim guardian).

32. *Ibid.*

33. See Uniform Probate Code, section 5-312.

34. See generally, E.B. Krasik, "The Role of the Family in Medical Decisionmaking for Incompetent Adult Patients: A Historical Perspective and Case Analysis," 48 *University of Pittsburgh Law Review* 539 (1987).

35. See, J. Seelig and S. Chestnut, "Corporate Legal Guardianship: An Innovative Concept in Advocacy and Protective Services," *Social Work* 221 (May-June 1986); W. Langen, "Public Guardianship: Protecting the Interests of the Ward," 2 *Law and Human Behavior* 267 (1978); Cal. Civil Code, Division 8, Sections 8000-8015; Ill. Public Act 80-1416, Section 30 (1978); Del. Laws, Chapter 12, Sections 3991-3997; Maine Revised Statutes Annotated, Chapter 18, Section 3638; *Exercising Judgment for the Disabled: Report of an Inquiry into Limited Guardianship, Public Guardianship, and Adult Protective Services in Six States,* Commission on the Mentally Disabled, American Bar Association (Sept. 1979). "Support Services and Alternatives to Guardianship," prepared by the American Bar Association's Life Services Planning Project, 12 *Mental and Physical Disability Law Reporter* 202 (1988), profiles more than 100 organizations throughout the country that provide specialized services to elderly persons, persons with disabilities, and families with an elderly or disabled dependent.

36. See, for example, *Corporate Guardianship for Retarded Citizens: A New Concept for Substituted Judgment,* a pamphlet by Greater Boston Association for Retarded Citizens, 1249 Boylston St., Boston, MA 02215 (1985); 1984 Annual Report, Association for the Help of Retarded Children, New York City Chapter.

37. See, for example, Conn. General Statutes Annotated, Section 45-78q; *Matter of Mary Moe,* 385 Mass. 555 (1982); *In re Grady,* 85 N.J. 235 (1981); *In re Hayes,* 93 Wash. 2d 228 (1979).

38. *Price v. Sheppard,* 239 N.W. 2d 905 (Minn. supp. Ct. 1976); *Guardianship of Roe,* 383 Mass. 415, 437 (Mass. 1981).

39. See, for example, *Rivers v. Katz,* 67 N.Y. 2d 485 (N.Y. Ct. App. 1986); *People v. Medina,* 702 P. 2d 961 (Colo. 1985); *Rogers v. Commissioner,* 390 Mass. 489 (1983); *Jarvis v. Levine,* 12 *Mental & Physical Disability Law Reporter* 144 (Minn. Sup. Ct. 1988); *Reise v. St. Mary's Hospital,* 12 *Mental & Physical Disability Law Reporter* 145 (Cal. Ct. App. 1987).

40. See, for example, *Superintendent of Belchertown v. Saikewicz,* 373 Mass. 728 (1977).

41. See Mass. General Laws, Chapter 201, Section 6A(b).

42. *Guardianship of Roe,* 383 Mass. 415 (1981), at 435.

43. See, for example, the Connecticut sterilization standard. Conn. General Statutes Annotated, Section 45-78w.

44. See, for example, *Superintendent of Belchertown v. Saikewicz,* 373 Mass. 728 (1977); *Mildred G. v. Valerie N.,* 707 P. 2d 760 (Cal. 1985) ("court-supervised substituted judgment" for sterilization). See also J. Parry, "A Unified Theory of Substitute Consent: Incompetent Patients' Right to Individual Health Care Decision-Making," 11 *Mental & Physical Disability Law Reporter* 378 (1987). See also Chapter 64 of this book.

45. *Rogers v. Commissioner,* note 3 above, at 500 (1983), citing *Superintendent of Belchertown v. Saikewicz,* 373 Mass. 728 (1977), at 750. See also *In re Jane Doe,* 12 *Mental and Physical Disability Law Reporter* 39 (R.I. Sup. Ct., decided 1987, reported 1988).

46. See, for example, *Guardianship of Linda,* 401 Mass.783 (1988).

47. *Rogers v. Commissioner,* note 3 above, at 505-6.

48. *Ibid.,* at 501, n. 15.

49. See *The Belmont Report: Ethical Principles for the Protection of Human Subjects of Research,* by the National Commission for the Protection of Human Subjects of Biomedical and Behavioral Research (April 18, 1979); Editorial: G. Annas and L. Glantz, "Rules for Research in Nursing Homes," 315 *New England Journal of Medicine* 1157 (1986).

50. *Commonwealth v. DelVerde,* 398 Mass. 288 (1986).

51. At least one court has found that some individuals under guardianship may still possess a right to vote, despite a statutory provision to the contrary. See *In re Guardianship of Bent,* Nos. 88-J-752 and 88-J-753 (Mass. App. Ct., Nov. 8, 1988).

■ Notes for Chapter 24, Confidentiality

1. Mass. General Laws, Chapter 214, Sec.18.

2. *Tarasoff v. Regents of Univ. of Cal.,* 551 P.2d 334 (1976).

3. See, for example, Mass. General Laws, Chapter 111, Sec. 70e.

4. See, for example, Mass. General Laws, Chapter 123B, Sec.17.

5. Cass, L.J. and W. J. Curren. "Rights of Privacy in Medical Practice," *The Lancet,* 2:783-785, 10/16/65.

■ Notes for Chapter 25, What Is Function? How Can It Be Maintained?

1. *International Classification of Impairments, Disabilities, and Handicaps: A Manual Relating to the Consequences of Disease,* World Health Organization, Geneva, 1980.

■ References for Chapter 25

Granger, Carl V., Seltzer, Gary B., and Fishbein, Carol Farb, *Primary Care of the Functionally Disabled,* Philadelphia: J.B. Lippincott Co., 1987.

Marinelli, Robert P. and DellOrto, Arthur E., *The Psychological and Social Impact of Physical Disability,* New York: Springer Publishing Company, 1984.

Williams, T. Franklin, ed., *Rehabilitation in the Aging,* New York: Raven Press, 1984.

■ References for Chapter 26, The Function of Relationships

Dass, Ram and Gorman, Paul *How Can I Help? Stories and Reflections on Service*, New York: Alfred A. Knopf, 1985.

Hussian, Richard A. and Davis, Ronald L., *Responsive Care: Behavioral Interventions with Elderly Persons*, Champaign, Illinois: Research Press, 1985.

Perlman, Helen Harris, *Relationship: The Heart of Helping People*, Chicago: University of Chicago Press, 1979.

■ Notes for Chapter 27, A Conceptual Framework for Policy and Service Design

1. The concept of old age as a devalued status, as used here, describes the outcome of a social process that both stereotypes a person or group as negatively different, and imposes patterns of discrimination on that person or group. For a thorough discussion of this framework see "The Social Construction of Reality" in Estes, Carroll L. *The Aging Enterprise: A Critical Examination of Social Policies and Services for the Aged*, San Francisco: Josey-Bass, 1979.

2. Dowd, James J., "Aging as Exchange" in *he Age of Aging*, A. Monk, ed., New York: Prometheus, 1979.

3. Graebner, William, *A History or Retirement: The Meaning and Function of an American Institution*, New Haven: Yale, 1980.

4. *Estes*, pp. 16-18.

5. Achenbaum, W. Andrew, *Old Age in the New Land*, Baltimore: Johns Hopkins, 1979. pp.39-54.

6. There is a widespread assumption that "the old" prefer age-segregated environments. In the only national survey of such preference undertaken by Menachem Daum as part of the Louis Harris survey, *The Myth and Reality of Aging in America*, Daum found the following: Two out of three persons under 65 (67 percent) and three out of four persons over 65 (76 percent) said they preferred interacting with people of all different ages. Those persons who had attended a senior center in the previous year had a significantly higher preference for interaction with people of all ages (80 percent of this small group) than those who had not gone to a center. Menachem Daum, "Preferences for Age-Mixed Social Interaction" in *Age or Need*, Bernice L. Neugarten, ed., Beverly Hills: Sage, 1982. pp. 247-262.

7. Comfort, Alex, "Age Prejudice in America," *Social Policy*, 7 (3), 1976, 3-8.

8. Krauss, Marty W., and Seltzer, Marsha M., *A National Directory of Programs Serving Elderly Retarded Persons*, Waltham, MA: Florence Heller Graduate School, Brandeis University, 1986.

9. Matthews, Sarah H., *The Social World of Old Women: A Study in the Management of Identity*, Beverly Hills: Sage, 1979.

10. *Estes*, p.228.

11. It is interesting to note the use of language in the description of these practices: Janicki, for example, uses the phrase, "integration into generic services for the elderly." Here, "integration" refers to services that are thoroughly segregated by age, while "generic" describes the categorical services of the aging network, not to the intended meaning—services utilized by all valued members of a community. (Matthew Janicki, Address to Conference on Aging and Developmental Disabilities, University of Maryland, September 26, 1986.)

12. Heumann, Judy, "The Relevance of the Independent Living Model" in C. Mahoney, C. Estes, and J. Heumann, eds., *Toward a Unified Agenda: Proceedings of a National Conference on Aging and Disability*, San Francisco: Institute for Health and Aging, 1986, pp. 9-10.

13. Janicki, Matthew, *Aging and Developmental Disabilities*, Baltimore: Brookes, 1985, pp. 130-37.

14. Haber, Carole, *Beyond Sixty-Five: The Dilemma of Old Age in America's Past*, New York: Cambridge University, 1985. pp.82-107.

15. Grob, Gerald N., *Mental Illness and American Society 1875-1940*, New Jersey: Princeton University, 1983. pp. 180-81.

16. Currently, three State Schools in Massachusetts have substituted "geriatric units" or "cottages" as the only principle of specialization and grouping for "residents" who are above their mid-fifties. This process of "geriatrizing" the state institution is visible throughout the country, especially in the midwest, New England, and the mid-Atlantic states.

17. An analogous situation might be found in our recent social history: norms toward black citizens have been, in themselves, fundamentally inferiorizing. When human services replicated those norms for blacks with mental retardation, they were supporting the normative not the peculiar; they were, however, imposing deeply devaluing life conditions on those individuals.

18. Wolfensberger, W. and Tullman, S.A., "A Brief Outline of the Principle of Normalization," *Rehabilitation Psychology*, 1982, 27, pp. 131-145. Wolfensberger has recently substituted the term *social role valorization* for normalization in order to emphasize the focus upon the valued in contradistinction to the normative. W. Wolfensberger, "Social Role Valorization: A Proposed New Term for the Principle of Normalization," *Mental Retardation*, 1983, 21, pp 234-239.

19. Lippmann, Walter, *Public Opinion*, New York: MacMillan, 1922.

20. Schur, Edwin M., *The Politics of Deviance: Stigma Contests and the Uses of Power*, New Jersey: Prentice-Hall, 1980, p.8.

■ References for Chapter 28, The Perspective of Holistic Health and Well-Being

Dychtwald, Ken, *Wellness and Health Promotion for the Elderly*, Rockville, MD: Aspen Systems Corporation, 1986.

Surgeon General's Workshop: Health Promotion and Aging, Proceedings, Washington, D.C., March 20-23, 1988. U.S. Department of Health and Human Services, Public Health Service (1988).

Wind, James F., *Second Opinion: Health, Faith and Ethics,* Lutheran General Health Care System. Park Ridge Center, Park Ridge, IL: James F. Wind, 1986.

■ Notes for Chapter 29, Primary Health Care Needs of Adults With Mental Retardation

1. See, for example, *Healthy People: The Surgeon's Report on Health Promotion and Disease Prevention,* 1979; DHEW (PHS) Publication No 79-55071.

2. *Ibid.,* p. 10.

■ Notes for Chapter 30, Exercise

1. Conrad, C. Carson, "When You're Young at Heart," *Aging,* Administration on Aging, U.S. Department of Health, Education and Welfare, April 1976, p. 12.

2. Sidney, K.H. and Shepard, R.J., "Perception of Exertion in the Elderly, Effects of Aging, Mode of Exercise and Physical Training," *Perceptual and Motor Skills,* 1977, 44: 1009.

3. Smith, Everett L. and Gilligan, Catherine, "Physical Activity Prescription for the Older Adult," *The Physician and Sports Medicine,* August 1983, 11: 92-93.

4. Cooper, Kenneth H., *The Aerobics Program for Total Well-Being,* Toronto: Bantam Books, 1982, p. 141.

5. Serfass, Robert C., Agre, James C., and Smith, Everett L., "Exercise Testing for the Elderly," *Topics in Geriatric Rehabilitation,* 1985, vol. 1, no. 1, p. 61.

6. Smith, Everett L. and Gilligan, Catherine, *op. cit.,* p. 93.

7. Ostrow, Andrew C., *Physical Activity and the Older Adult: Psychological Perspectives,* 1984, Princeton Book Company, p. 147.

8. Shepard, R.J., "Management of Exercise in the Elderly," *Canadian Journal of Applied Sports Science,* 1984, 9 :3: 117

9. *Ibid.*

10. *Ibid.,* p. 114.

11. Clark, Bruce A., "Principles of Physical Activity Programming for the Older Adult," *Topics in Geriatric Rehabilitation,* 1985, 1 (1) p. 70.

12. Pollack, M.L., Wilmore, J.H., and Fox, M. III, *Exercise in Health and Disease: Education and Prescription for Prevention and Rehabilitation,* 1984, W.B.Saunders, Philadelphia, p. 261.

13. Clark, Bruce A., *op. cit.,* p. 69.

14. Ostrow, Andrew C., *op. cit.,* p. 153.

15. Mobily, Kenneth, "Attitudes of Institutionalized Elderly Iowans Toward Physical Activity," *Therapeutic Recreation Journal*, 1981, Third Quarter, p. 39.

■ References for Chapter 31, Diet and Nutrition

Ballantine, R, *Transition to Vegetarianism: An Evolutionary Step*, The Himalayan International Institute of Yoga Science and Philosophy of the U.S.A., 1988.

Brody, J., *Jane Brody's Nutrition Book*, Bantam Books, New York, 1987.

Chernin, K., *The Obsession: Reflections on the Tyranny of Slenderness*, New York: Perennial Library, Harper & Row Publishers, 1981.

Clark, N.. *The Athlete's Kitchen: A Nutrition Guide and Cookbook*, NY: Bantam Books, 1981.

Danforth, E., *American Journal of Clinical Nutrition*, May 1985, 41: 1132-1145,

Hirsch, J. and Liebel, R.L., "New Light on Obesity," *New England Journal of Medicine*, 318:8, 509-510.

Lappe, F.M., *Diet for a Small Planet*, New York: Ballentine Books, 1982.

Ratto, T., "The New Science of Weight Control," *Medical Self Care*, March-April, 1987; 25-30.

■ Notes for Chapter 32, Safety for Adults With Mental Retardation

1. *Healthy People: The Surgeon General's Report on Health Promotion and Disease Prevention*, 1979; DHEW (PHS) Publication No. 79-55071, p. 15.

■ References for Chapter 36, The Down Syndrome Alzheimer's Disease Connection

Burger, P.C., and Vogel, F.S., "The Development of the Pathologic Changes of Alzheimer's Disease and Senile Dementia in Patients with Down's Syndrome," *American Journal of Pathology*, Vol. 73, pp. 457-76.

The Course, Treatment and Management of Alzheimer's Disease, Geriatric Research, Education and Clinical Center, Veteran's Administration Medical Center, Minneapolis, MN; 20 single-issue pamphlets.

Hurley, A.D. and Sovner, R., "Dementia, Mental Retardation, and Down's Syndrome," *Psychiatric Aspects of Mental Retardation News*, 1985, Vol. 5, No. 8, pp. 39-44.

Katzman, Robert, "Alzheimer's Disease," *New England Journal of Medicine*, 1986, Vol. 314, No. 15, pp. 964-73.

Kolata, Gina, "Down Syndrome-Alzheimer's Linked," *Science,* 1985, Vol. 230, pp. 1152-53.

Losing a Million Minds: Confronting the Tragedy of Alzheimer's Disease and Other Dementias, Congress of the United States Office of Technology Assessment, 1987.

Mace, N.L. and Rabins, P.V., *The 36-Hour Day: A Family Guide to Caring for Persons With Alzheimer's Disease,* Baltimore: Johns Hopkins University Press, 1981.

Miniszek, N.A., "Development of Alzheimer's Disease in Down Syndrome Individuals," *American Journal of Mental Deficiency,* 1983, Vol. 87, No. 4, pp. 377-85.

Reisberg, Barry, ed., *Alzheimer's Disease: The Standard Reference,* New York: The Free Press, 1983.

■ References for Chapter 37, Depression

Beck, Aaron T., et al. *Cognitive Therapy of Depression,* New York: The Guilford Press, 1979.

Busse, Ewald W. and Dan G, Blazer, eds. *Handbook of Geriatric Psychiatry,* New York: Van Nostrand Reinhold Company, 1980.

Knight, Bob. *Psychotherapy with Older Adults,* Beverly Hills, CA: SAGE Publications, 1986.

Rush, A. John. *Short-Term Psychotherapies for Depression: Behavioral, Interpersonal, Cognitive, and Psychodynamic Approaches,* New York: The Guilford Press, 1982.

Salzman, Carl. *Clinical Geriatric Psychopharmacology,* New York: McGraw-Hill, 1984.

The Course, Treatment and Management of Alzheimer's Disease, Geriatric Research, Education and Clinical Center. Veteran's Administration Medical Center, Minneapolis, Minnesota; 20 single-issue pamphlets.

Whanger, Alan D. and Alice C. Meyers. *Mental Health Assessment and Therapeutic Intervention with Older Adults,* Rockville, MD: Aspen Publications, 1984.

■ Notes for Chapter 38, Community Housing

1. See H. Beyer, "Litigation with the Mentally Retarded," *Handbook of Mental Retardation,* J. Mason & J. Mulick, eds., New York, Pergamon Press, 1983, at 88.

2. "Summary and Analysis: Group Homes Overcome Exclusionary Zoning," 6 *Mental Disability Law Reporter* 3 (1982), But see *Garcia v. Siffrin Residential Association,* 407 N,W.2d 1369 (Ohio 1980); *Penobscot Area Housing Development Corp. v. City of Brewer,* 434 A.2d 14 (Me. 1981); *Westwood Homeowners Association v. Tenhoff,* 745 p. 2d 976 (Ariz. Ct. App. 1987).

3. See, for example, *Jackson v. Williams,* 714 P.2d 1017 (Okla. 1985). But see *Zoning Board of City of Hammond v. Tanqipahoa ARC,* 510 So.2d 751 (La. Ct. App. 1987).

4. P. Boyd, "Strategies in Zoning and Community Living Arrangements for Retarded Citizens: Parens Patriae Meets Police Power," 25 Villanova Law Review 273 (1979-80).

5. See, for example, Westwood Homeowners Association, note 2, above.

6. See, for example, Gardner-Athol Mental Health Association v. Board of Zoning Appeals, 401 Mass. 12 (1987).

7. See, for example, Fitchburg Housing Authority v. Board of Zoning Appeals, 380 Mass, 869 (1980).

8. See Mass. General Laws, chap. 40A, sec. 3.

9. City of Cleburne v. Cleburne Living Center, 473 U.S. 432 (1985).

10. Ibid., at 448.

11. Ibid., at 450.

12. Ibid., at 446.

13. See 42 Code of Federal Regulations, Sections 442.400-442.516

14. For further information, contact David or Margot Wizansky, Specialized Housing, Inc., 12 Lincoln Rd., Brookline, MA 02146. Mental Health Law Project, Washington, DC, is reportedly also SSI's "principal residence" exclusion to develop housing for a class of New Yorkers with mental disabilities who have been awarded retroactive disability benefits. See P. Appelbaum, "Housing for the Mentally Ill: An Unexpected Outcome of a Class-Action Suit Against SSA," 39 Hospital and Community Psychiatry 479 (1988), at 480.

15. 20 Code of Federal Regulations, Sections 416.1210(a).

16. See Michael Downey, *A Blessed Weakness*, New York: Harper & Row 1986.

17. One U.S. L'Arche community is L'Arche Syracuse, 1701 James Street, Syracuse, N.Y. 13206.

18. See C.M. Pietzner, *Village Life: The Campbill Communities*, Boston: Neugebauer Press, 1986.

■ References for Chapter 38

Bourey, J.M. *"Cleburne Living Center v. City of Cleburne:* The Irrational Relationship of Mental Retardation to Zoning Objectives," 19 *John Marshall Law Review* 469 (1986).

"City of Cleburne v. Cleburne Living Center, Inc,: Judicial Step or Stumble?" 6 *Northern Illinois University Law Review* 409 (1986).

"Group Homes for the Mentally Retarded in Maine: Legislative Intent and Administrative Process," 37 *Maine Law Review* 63 (1985).

Housing for the Elderly and Handicapped: The Experiences of the Section 202 Program from 1959 to 1977, Washington D.C.: U.S. Department of Housing and Urban Development, Office of Policy Development and Research, 1979 (HUD-PDR-301, Jan. 1979)

Minow, M. "When Difference Has Its Home: Group Homes for the Mentally Retarded, Equal Protection and Legal Treatment of Differences," 22 Harvard Civil Rights-Civil Liberties Law Review 111 (1987).

Mueller, D., Group Homes Do Not Cause Property Values To Decline or Neighborhood Characteristics to Change, Washington, D.C.: Mental Health Law Project, 1986.

Schonfeld, R.L. " 'Five-Hundred-Year Flood Plains' and Other Unconstituted Challenges to the Establishment of Community Residences for the Mentally Retarded," 16 Fordham Urban Law Journal 1 (1988).

Smith, T.P. and M. Jaffe, Sitting Group Homes for Developmentally Disabled Persons, Chicago: American Planning Association, 1986.

Steinman, L.D., The Impact of Zoning on Group Homes for the Mentally Disabled: A National Survey, Chicago: American Bar Association, 1986.

Wolfe, C. , "City of Cleburne v. Cleburne Living Center: In Search of Equal Protection: Are the Mentally Retarded Lost in Wonderland? 54 University of Missouri at Kansas City Law Review 54 (1986).

■ Notes for Chapter 39, Community-Building in Group Homes

1. Stages of community from M. Scott Peck, A Different Drum: Community Building and Peacemaking.

■ References for Chapter 40, Work and Retirement

1. Haber, Carole, Beyond Sixty-Five: The Dilemmas of Old Age in America's Past, Cambridge: Cambridge University Press, 1983, p. 8.

2. Ibid, p. 28.

3. Ibid, p. 41.

4. Graebner, William. A History of Retirement: The Meaning and Function of an American Institution, 1885-1978, New Haven: Yale University Press, 1980, p. 31.

5. Haber, Carole, op. cit., p. 113.

6. Ibid., p. 121.

■ Notes for Chapter 41, Retirement Programs

1. Based on Tibbits, C., "The Evolving Work Life Pattern" in Tibbits C., ed., Handbook of Social Gerontology, Chicago: University of Chicago Press, 1960, pp. 123-125.

■ Notes for Chapter 43, Modifying Religious Services for People Who are Old and Mentally Retarded

1. William Glasser, *Reality Therapy*, New York: Harper and Row, 1965.

■ Notes for Chapter 45, Intimacy Issues of Clients and Caregivers

1. Antoine de Saint Exupery, *The Little Prince*

2. This article utilizes the experience and terminology from Gerald Calhoun, SJ, *Pastoral Companionship*, Paulist Press, 1986.

3. *Ibid.*, from the section entitled "Supporting the Decisionmakers."

4. *Ibid.*, p. 39.

5. *Ibid.* This was adapted from Calhoun's Stages of Prayer.

■ References for Chapter 45

Fisher, Kathleen R., *Winter Grace: Spirituality for the Later Years*, Paulist Press, NJ, 1985.

Lyon, Brynolf and Browning, Donald S., *Toward a Practical Theology of Aging and Pastoral Care*, Fortress Press, 1985.

■ References for Chapter 47, Sexuality

Birren, J.E. and Schaie, K.W., eds. *Handbook of the Psychology of Aging*, second ed. New York: Van Nostrand Reinhold Company, 1985.

Bolnick, J.P.. *Winnie: "My Life in the Institution."* New York: St. Martin's Press, 1985.

Committee on Sexuality and Sexuality Education, *Guidelines for Promoting Responsible Social and Sexual Development: A Reference for all Staff Persons*, Waltham, MA: Walter E. Fernald State School.

Edmonson, B., McCombs, K., and Wish, J., "What Retarded Adults Believe About Sex," *American Journal of Mental Deficiency*, 1979, Vol. 84, No. 1, pp. 11-18.

Erikson, E.H., Erikson, J.M., and Kivnick, H.Q., *Vital Involvement in Old Age*, New York: W.W. Norton and Company, 1986.

Gochros, H.L., "Risks of Abstinence: Sexual Decision Making in the AIDS Era," *Social Work*, 1988; May-June: 254-6.

Maddox, G.L., ed., *The Encyclopedia of Aging*, New York: Springer Publishing Company, 1987.

Marinelli, R.P., Dell Orto, A.E., eds., *The Psychological and Social Impact of Physical Disability*, New York: Springer Publishing Company, 1984.

Whyte, J., "Teaching Safe Sex," *New England Journal of Medicine*, 1988; 318:387.

■ Notes for Chapter 49, Estate Planning: Providing for Your Child's Future

1. In his will, after making various bequests and directing the sale of his Washington residence, Justice Oliver Wendell Holmes gave the remainder of his estate (approximately $230,000) to the U.S.government. See "A Report of the Oliver Wendell Holmes Devise Committee Pursuant to Public Resolution No. 124 of the 75th Congress," U.S. Senate, 76th Congress, 3rd Session, Document No. 197 (5/13/40).

■ References for Chapter 49

For Non-Lawyers (Also useful for lawyers not experienced in establishing trusts for families with a member with mental retardation)

"How to Provide for Their Future: Suggestions for Parents Concerned with Providing Lifetime Protection for a Child with Mental Retardation" (Rev. 1984), a booklet prepared by the National Association for Retarded Citizens, P.O. Box 6109, Arlington, Texas 76011.

For Lawyers (Or non-lawyers who wish to delve into technical details)

"Estate Planning for the Handicapped or Disabled," by Raymond L. Miolla, 26:4 N.H. Bar Journal 297 (Summer 1985). "Estate Planning for Parents of Mentally Disabled Children," by L.A. Frolik, 40 University of Pittsburgh Law Review 305 (1979).

"Consolidated Omnibus Budget Reconciliation Act of 1985," P.L. 99-272, Sec. 9506 (4/7/86) (Medicaid eligibility now affected by some trusts).

"Trusts and Wills in Entitlements Planning for Elders, the Personal Injury Victim, and Families with Handicapped Children," by Donald Freedman, in course materials published by Mass. Continuing Legal Education (MLCE) for course No. 87-202, "Beyond the Safety Net," Available from MLCE, 20 West Street, Boston, MA 02111; (617) 482-2205.

"Estate Planning for Medicaid Coverage of Long Term Care," by Emily S. Starr, in course materials published by MLCE for Course NO> 87-202. (Same Availability as preceding item.)

"Estate Planning for Families with Handicapped Children," by Charles R. Robert, The Complete Lawyer 51 (Fall 1986).

Lang v. Commonwealth of Pennsylvania, 528 A.2d 1335 (Pa. Sup. Ct. 1987).

■ Notes for Chapter 50, Burnout Among Family Caregivers

1. Chernis, C., "Job Stress in the Human Services" in *Staff Burnout*, 1980, Sage Studies in Community Mental Health 2, Sage Publications, Third Ed., 1982.

2. Maslach, C. and Jackson, S.E., (1981), "The Measurement of Experienced Burnout," *Journal of Occupational Behavior,* Vol. 2, pp. 99-113.

3. Potassnik, H., and Nelson, G., "Stress and Social Support: The Burden Experienced by the Family of a Mentally Ill Person," *American Journal of Community Psychology,* Vol. 12, No. 5, 1984, pp. 283-305.

4. Stevens, G.B., and O'Neill, P., "Expectation and Burnout in the Developmental Disabilities Field," *American Journal of Community Psychology,* Vol. 11, No. 3, 1985, pp. 245-268.

■ Notes for Chapter 52, Ethical Dilemmas

1. Aaron, Henry J. and Schwartz, William B., *The Painful Prescription: Rationing Hospital Care,* Washington, D.C.: The Brookings Institution, 1984.

2. Goodin, Robert E., *Protecting the Vulnerable: A Reanalysis of our Social Responsibilities,* Chicago: University of Chicago Press, 1985.

3. Kopelman, Loretta and Moskop, John C., eds. *Ethics and Mental Retardation,* Dordrecht, Holland: D. Reidel Publishing Company, 1984.

4. McCullough, J., "Medical Care for Elderly Patients with Diminished Competence," *Journal of American Geriatrics Society,* Vol.32, No.2; pp. 150-153; 1984.

■ Notes for Chapter 53, Institutional Ethics Committees

1. *In the Matter of Karen Ann Quinlan,* 70 N. J.10, 355 A.2nd 647 (1976).

2. President's Commission for the Study of Ethical Problems in Medicine and Biomedical and Behavioral Research, *Deciding to Forgo Life-Sustaining Treatment,* Washington, D.C., U.S. Government Printing Office, 1981.

3. See Kuhse, Helga, and Singer, Peter, *Should the Baby Live? The Problem of Handicapped Infants,* New York: Oxford University Press, 1985.

4. Cranford, R.E., and Doudera, A.E., "The Emergence of Institutional Ethics Committees," *Hastings Center Report,* Vol. 14, No. 1, 1984.

5. Gibson, J.M., and Kushner, T.K., "Will the Conscience of an Institution Become Society's Servant?, *Hastings Center Report,* Vol. 16, No. 3, 1986.

6. Lo, Bernard, "Behind Closed Doors: Promises and Pitfalls of Ethics Committees," *New England Journal of Medicine,* Vol. 317, No. 1, 1987.

7. Lo, *op. cit.,* p. 49.

Notes for Chapter 54, Impact of an Institutional Ethics Committee

1. *Brophy v. New England Sinai Hospital,* 398 Mass. 417, 497 N.E. 2nd 626 (1986).

Notes for Chapter 55, A Case for Equal Access to Health Care

1. Carolyn Nock, RN, BSN, FNPC, JD, researched and presented the original case for an Ethics Conference at the Kennedy Aging Project. I would like to thank Ms. Nock for allowing me to use this case and for a number of ideas developed in this article.

Notes for Chapter 56, Staff Training in Ethics

1. M.C. Howell and R.J. Pitch, *Ethical Dilemmas In Caregiving,* Boston: Exceptional Parent Press, 1989.

Notes for Chapter 57, Protecting the Rights of the Client With Alzheimer's Disease

1. T.L. Beauchamp and J.F. Childress, *Principles of Biomedical Ethics,* Oxford University Press, 1980, 67-68.

2. Chapter 21, Acts of the General Assembly of Maryland, 1982; Chapters 591 and 540 of the Acts of 1984, Section 20-107, Health—General Article, Annotated Code of Maryland, 1984 Cumulative Supplement,

3. J.C. Fletcher, F.W. Dommel, Jr., and D.C. Cowell, "Consent to Research with Impaired Human Subjects," *IRB,* Vol. 7, No. 6, November/December 1985, 2.

4. Mary Jane Gibson, State Representative, 26th Middlesex District, and assistant majority whip. "The Patient's Right to Refuse Medical Treatment: The Status of the Living Will and the Durable Power of Attorney in Massachusetts," a public discussion of legal, ethical, and legislative issues. June 21, 1988, Belmont, MA.

5. Massachusetts General Laws, Chapter 201B, section 1.

6. *Handbook on Guardianship, Conservatorship and Other Options,* Massachusetts Association for Retarded Citizens; Mental Health Legal Advisory Committee, October, 1984, 16.

7. Robert Abrams, M.D., "Dementia Research in the Nursing Home, " *Hospital and Community Psychiatry,* 259, March 1988, vol. 39, no. 3, 259.

8. We usually use the term "proxy" to describe someone who acts as a substitute for, and in accordance with the wishes of, another—as in voting corporate stock or acting as a "proxy" in a marriage ceremony, when one of the contracting parties

cannot be present but has authorized another to represent him. If, however, a proxy is appointed by a *third* party, such as the court, it may be difficult, and sometimes impossible, for the proxy to know the wishes of the person he represents.

9. Robert Abrams, M.D., *op.cit,,* 257.

10. Lecture on geriatric care, in "Mental Health Systems," Boston University School of Public Health, Spring, 1987.

11. "Do Elderly Research Subjects Need Special Protection?" Excerpts from National Institute on Aging Conference, July 18-19, 1977, *IRB,* October 1980, 5-8. M. Powell Lawton, "Psychological Vulnerability," *IRB,* October 1980, 6.

12. Id.

13. New York Mental Hygiene Law, Chapter 354 of the Laws of 1985. "Promoting Individual Rights," 1986-87 Annual Report, New York State Commission on Quality of Care for the Mentally Disabled, 32-34.

14. Clarence J. Sundram, "Informed Consent for Major Medical Treatment of Mentally Disabled People—A New Approach," Special Article, *New England Journal of Medicine,* Vol. 318, No. 21, May 26, 1988, 1368-1373.

15. New York Hygiene Law, Art. 80.

16. 14 New York Code of Rules and Regulations, Paragraph 27.9

17. Chapter 339 of the New York Laws of 1988 (3-28-88).

18. New York Hygiene Law, Art. 80. *Matter of Eichner and Storer,* 52 N.Y.2d 363 (1981). T.G. Guthiel and R.S. Appelbaum, "Substituted judgment: Best interests in disguise?" *Hastings Center Report,* 1983, 13(3), 8-11.

19. Sundram, *supra* note 14, at 1369.

20. In 1978 the National Commission for the Protection of Human Subjects of Biomedical and Behavioral Research included the elderly in its *Report and Recommendations in Research Involving Those Institutionalized as Mentally Infirm* (DHEW Publication No. (OS) 78-0006, Washington, 1978). This report was subsequently modified and issued by the Department of Health, Education and Welfare (now the Department of Health and Human Services) as DHEW, "Protection of Human Subjects: Proposed Regulations on Research Involving Those Institutionalized as Mentally Disabled" (*Federal Register* 43 (No. 223) November 17, 1978, 53950-56). It did *not,* however, deal with the specific problems of elderly research subjects. Research into diseases associated with aging poses problems because the human subjects are not only sick, they are old. Regulations which may protect a 30-year-old patient, may expose someone who is 60 or 70 to unreasonable risk or intrusive procedures. For discussion, particularly of issues relating to dementia research, see R.M. Ratzan, "'Being Old Makes You Different': The Ethics of Research with Elderly Subjects," *Hastings Center Report,* October 1980, 32-42.

21. *Alzheimer's Disease, Report of the Secretary's Task Force on Alzheimer's Disease,* September 1984, DHHS, ix.

22. Id., x-xiv.

23. George J. Annas, J.D., M.P.H., Leonard Glantz, J.D., and Barbara F. Katz, J.D., *Informed Consent to Human Experimentation: The Subject's Dilemma,* Ballinger Publishing Company, Cambridge, MA, 1977, 140, including citations to: Comment,

Behavior Modification and Other Legal Imbroglios of Experimentation, 52 *J. Urban L*, 155, 157 (1974); and Ritts, A Physician's View of Informed Consent in Human Experimentation, 36 *Fordham Law Review* 631 (1968).

24. Erving Goffman, *Asylums, Essays on the Social Situation of Mental Patients and Other Inmates,* Doubleday and Co., New York, 1961.

25. F. Wertham, "The geranium in the window: the 'euthanasia' murders," in *A Sign for Cain: An Exploration of Human Violence,* Macmillan, New York, 1966.

26. David J, Rothman, Ph.D,, "Ethics and Human Experimentation," *New England Journal of Medicine,* Vol. 317, No. 19, (1987) 1198.

27. Id.

28. Id., 1198-1199.

29. "Research in Progress," vol. 8, no. 1, Summer 1987, 2 (Boston University School of Medicine).

30. Conference on Alzheimer's Disease, Fernald State school, Waltham, MA, December 3, 1987.

31. Jonas, Hans, "Philosophical Reflections on Experimenting With Human Subjects," in *Experimenting with Human Subjects,* edited by Paul A. Freund (New York, George Braziller, 1970), 20.

32. John A, Rawls, *A Theory of Justice,* Harvard University Press, Cambridge, MA, 1971.

33. Correspondence, "Transplantation of Fetal Substantia Nigra and Adrenal Medulla to the Caudate Nucleus in two Patients with Parkinson's Disease," *New England Journal of Medicine,* Vol. 318, No. 1, (1988) 51. Discussion on Nightline, ABC network television, 11:30 p.m., January 6, 1988.

34. Hans Jonas, *op. cit.,* 28.

■ References for Chapter 57

Drane, James F., "The Many Faces of Competency," The Hastings Center Report, April 1985, 17-21.

Dyer, Allen R., "Informed Consent and the Nonautonomous Person," *IRB,* August/September 1982, 1-4.

"Ethical Theory and Bioethics," in *Contemporary Issues in Bioethics,* edited by T.L. Beauchamp and LeRoy Walters, 1982.

Grundner, T.M., "How To Make Consent Forms More Readable," *IRB,* August/September 1981, 9-10.

Jonas, Hans, "Philosophical Reflections on Experimenting With Human subjects," in *Experimenting with Human Subjects,* edited by Paul A. Freund (New York, George Braziller, 1970).

Libow, L.S. and Zicklin, R., "The Penultimate Will: Its Potential as an Instrument to Protect the Mentally Deteriorated patient," *Gerontologist* 13 (1973), 440-442.

Miller, Bruce L., "Autonomy and Proxy Consent," *IRB,* December 1982, 1-8.

The Nuremberg Code, From Trials of War Criminals before the Nuremberg Military Tribunals under Council Law No. 10, vol. II, Nuremberg, October 1946-April 1949.

Relman, Arnold S., "Michigan's Sensible 'Living Will," *New England Journal of Medicine* 300 (1979), 1270-1271.

Tibbles, Lance, "Medical and Legal Aspects of Competency as Affected by Old Age," *Aging and the Elderly*, 127-151.

Veatch, Robert M., "Research on 'Nonconsentables,' " *IRB*, January 1981, 6-7.

Veatch, Robert M., "Three Theories of Informed Consent: Philosophical Foundations and Policy Implications," submitted to the National Commission (February 3, 1976).

■ References for Chapter 58, Grief Counseling

Levine, Stephen, *Who Dies? An Investigation of Conscious Living and Conscious Dying*, Garden City, NY: Anchor Press/Doubleday, 1982.

Morgan, Ernest, ed., *A Manual of Death Education and Simple Burial*, Burnsville, NC: The Celo Press, 1977.

Worden, J. William, Ph.D., *Grief Counseling and Grief Therapy: A Handbook for the Mental Health Practitioner*, New York: Springer Publishing Company, 1982.

■ Notes for Chapter 59, A Developmental Approach to Cognitive Understanding of Death and Dying

1. Freud, Sigmund, *Mourning and Melancholia*, (1917) in *Collected Papers, Vol. IV*, London: Hogarth Press, 1950.

2. Becker, Ernest, *The Denial of Death*, New York: The Free Press, 1973.

3. Piaget, J., *The Origins of Intelligence in Children*, New York: International University Press, 1952.

4. White, E., Elsom, B., and Prawat, R., "Children's Conception of Death, *Child Development*, 1978; 49:307-310.

5. Bowlby, J., *Attachment and Loss: Separation: Anxiety and Anger*, (Vol. 11). New York: Basic Books, 1973.

6. Spitz, R., "Analytic Depression, *Psychoanalytic Study of the Child*, 1946; 2:313-341.

7. Llpe-Goodson, P.S. and Goebel, B.L., "Perception of Aging and Death in Mentally Retarded Adults, *Mental Retardation* 1983; 21:68-75.

■ References for Chapter 60, Hospice

Bowers, Margaretta K., Edgar N. Jackson, James A. Knight and Lawrence LeShan., *Counseling the Dying,* New York: Jason Aronson, Inc., 1975.

DuBois, Paul M., *The Hospice Way of Death,* New York: Human Sciences Press, 1980.

Saunders, Cicely M., ed., *The Management of Terminal Disease,* London: Edward Arnold Publishers, 1978.

■ Notes for Chapter 61, Fulfilling the Spiritual Needs of Mentally Retarded Persons in a Hospice Unit

1. Mathieu, J., "Dying and Death Role Expectations," Unpublished Ph.D. dissertation, University of Southern California Libraries, University of Southern California, Los Angeles, CA 1972, p. 162.

2. Simonton, O.C., *Getting Well Again,* New York: St. Martin's Press. 1978.

■ References for Chapter 63, Training Staff to Care for Dying Clients

Barbera, T.V., Pitch, R.J., and Howell, M.C., *Death and Dying: A Guide for Staff Serving Developmentally Disabled Adults,* Boston: Exceptional Parent Press, 1989.

■ Notes for Chapter 64, Legal Considerations in the Decision-Making Process of the Hospice Care Provider

1. Furrow, Johnson, Jost, Schwartz, *Health Law* (St. Paul: West Publishing Co., 1987), p. 826.

2. Furrow et al., *op. cit.,* p. 827.

3. *Ibid.*

4. Capron, *Borrowed Lessons: The Role of Ethical Distinctions in Framing Life-Sustaining Treatment,* 1984 Ariz. St. L.J. 647.

5. *Matter of Eichner,* 52 N.Y. 2d 363, 438 N.Y.S. 2d 266, 420 N.E. 2d 64 (Ct. App. 1981)

6. *In re Quinlan,* 70 N.J. 10, 355 A.2d 647 (1976)

7. Capron, 1984 Ariz. St L.J. 647.

8. *Bartling v. Superior Court,* 163 Cal.App.3d 186, 209 Cal. Rptr. 297 (1986).

9. *Bouvia v. Superior Court,* 179 Cal. App. 3d 1127, 225 Cal. Rptr. 297 (1986).

---

10. Furrow et al., pp. 835-836.

11. See Furrow et al., pp. 853-854.

12. *Ibid.*

13. Roth, Meisel and Lidz, "Tests of Competency To Consent to Treatment," 134 Am. J. Psychiatry 279 (1977).

14. *Ibid.*

15. *Matter of Quackenbush,* 156 N.J. Super. 282, 383 A.2d 785 (1978). See also *Lane v. Candura,* 6 Mass, App.Ct. 377, 376 N.E. 2d 1232 (1978). In addition, some states have statutes that protect the right to choose of the variably competent patient.

16. Furrow et al., p. 861.

17. Furrow et al., pp. 884-885.

18. President's Commission, *Deciding to Forego Life-Sustaining Treatment,* p. 127 (1983).

19. See Furrow et al., p. 885.

20. *Matter of Eichner,* 52 N.Y. 2d 363, 438 N.Y.S. 2d 266, 420 N.E. 2d 64 (Ct. App. 1981).

21. *Brophy v. New England Sinai Hospital,* 398 Mass. 417, 497 N.E. 2d 626 (1986).

22. *Matter of Conroy,* 98 N.J. 321, 486 A. 2d 1209 (1985).

23. Furrow et al., p. 892. See also the *Brophy* case, (Justice Nolan and Justice Lynch, dissenting).

24. Furrow et al., p. 894.

25. *Matter of Spring,* 380 Mass. 629, 405 N.E. 2d 115 (1980); Cf. *Superintendent of Belchertown State School v. Saikewicz,* 373 Mass. 728, 370 N.E. 2d 417 (1977).

26. *Matter of Spring,* 405 N.E. 2d 115, at 120-121.

27. *Superintendent of Belchertown State School v. Saikewicz,* 373 Mass. 728, 370 N.E. 2d 417 (1977).

28. See, e.g., *Committee on Policy for DNR Decisions, Yale New Haven Hospital Report on Do Not Resuscitate Decisions,* 47 Conn. Med. 478 (1983).

29. *Barber v. Superior Court,* 147 Cal. App. 3d 1006, 195 Cal. Rptr. 484 (1983); see also Furrow et al., p. 919.

30. See L.H. Glantz, "Withholding and Withdrawing Treatment: The Role of the Criminal Law," 15 *Law, Medicine and Health Care* 231 (1987/88).

31. *Estate of Leach v. Shapiro,* 13 Ohio St. 3d 393, 469 N.E. 2d 1047 (1984).

■ Notes for Chapter 65, Medical Orders for the Dying Patient: Do Not Attempt Resuscitation, Limits of Treatment, and Recommendation to Remain in Residence

1. Blackhall, L.J., "Must We Always Use CPR?" *New England Journal of Medicine,* 1987, Vol. 317, No. 20, pp. 1281-85.

2. See the "Remain in Residence" policy in Mary Howell and R.J. Pitch, *Ethical Dilemmas In Caregiving,* Boston: Exceptional Parent Press, 1989.

3. *Op. cit.*

4. Fabizewski, K. and Howell, M.C., "A Model for Family Meetings in the Long-Term Care of Alzheimer's Disease," *Journal of Gerontological Social Work,* 1985, Vol. 9, pp. 113-17.

■ Notes for Chapter 66, The Will-Writing Project

1. Frohboese, R. and Sales, B.D., "Parental Opposition to Deinstitutionalization, *Law and Human Behavior,* 4 (1980), p. 43.

■ Notes for Chapter 67, A Support Group on the Issues of Death and Dying With Mentally Retarded Adults

1. The term "mildly retarded" refers to a classification based on and I.0. score of 55 to 70 derived from Stanford-Binet norms. Adaptive behavior has taken priority over I.Q. scores in recent years as a classification criteria, promoting flexibility within classification parameters. Scheerenberger, R.C., Ph.D. (1983), *A History of Mental Retardation,* Baltimore, MD: Paul H, Brooks Publishing Co.

2. Thurman, Eunice (1986), "Maintaining Dignity in Later Years," Jean Ann Summers, B.G.s., editor, *The Right to Grow Up: An Introduction to Adults with Developmental Disabilities,* Baltimore, MD: Paul H. Brookes Publishing Co.

3. McDaniel, Barbara (1989), "A Group Work Experience with Mentally Retarded Adults on the Issues of Death and Dying," *Journal of Gerontological Social Work,* Vo. 13 (3/4), New York: The Haworth Press, Inc.

4. Deutsch, Henri, Ph.D. (1985), "Grief Counseling With The Mentally Retarded Clients," *Psychiatric Aspects of Mental Retardation Reviews,* Volume 4, No. 5, Brookline, MA: Psycha-Media, Inc.

■ Notes for Chapter 69, Recommendations from Experience

1. Herr S.H., "Legal Processes and the Least Restrictive Alternative," in Janicki, M.P. and Wisniewski, H.M., eds., *Aging and Developmental Disabilities: Issues and Approaches,* Baltimore: Brookes Publishing, 1985.

2. Older Americans Act of 1965 (P.L. 89-73) as amended.

3. Brodsky D., "Future Policy Directions," in Browne, W.P. and Olson, L.K., eds., *Aging and Public Policy,* Westport, CT: Greenwood Press, 1983.

4. Daum, M., "Preferences for Age-Mixed Social Interaction," in Neugarten, B., ed., *Age or Need?* Beverly Hills, CA: Sage Publications, 1982.

5. U.S. Senate Special Commission on Aging in conjunction with the AARP, the Federal Council on the Aging, and the Administration on Aging. *Aging America: Trends and Projections,* Washington, DC: U.S. Government Printing Office, 1985-86 edition.

6. Gwyther, L., *The Care of Alzheimer's Patients: A Manual for Nursing Home Staff,* New York: American Health Care Association and the Alzheimer's and Related Disorders Associations, 1985.

7. Mace, N.L., Rabins, P.V., *The 36-Hour Day: A Family Guide to Caring for Persons with Alzheimer's Disease, Related Dementing Illnesses, and Memory Loss in Later Life,* Baltimore: Johns Hopkins University Press, 1981.

8. Stroud, M., Sutton, E., *Expanding Options for Older Adults with Developmental Disabilities: A Practical Guide to Achieving Community Access,* Baltimore: Brookes Publishing, 1987.

9. Howell, M.C., "Clients Who Are Both Mentally Retarded and Also Old: Developmental, Emotional and Medical Needs," in Gilsons, Goldsbury T, Faulkner E. eds., *Three Populations of Primary Focus: Persons with Mental Retardation and Mental Illness, Persons with Mental Retardation Who Are Elderly, and Persons with Mental Retardation and Complex Medical Needs,* Omaha, NE: Administration on Developmental Disabilities, Department of Health and Human Services, 1987. Grant monograph.

10. Janicki. M.P., Knox, L.A., Jacobson, J.W., "Planning for an Older Developmentally Disabled Population," in Janicki, M.P. and Wisniewski, H.M., eds., *Aging and Developmental Disabilities: Issues and Approaches,* Baltimore: Brookes Publishing, 1985.

INTAKE INSTRUMENT

FOR THE TELEPHONE INTERVIEW

Hi,

    My name is _____. I'm calling from the Kennedy Aging Project at the Shriver Center. Your family member/client has an appointment with our team in _____, as part of our aim to collect as much information as possible about R. I'm calling to ask you several questions about how your family member/client performs his/her daily routines, leisure activities and services and assistance. It will take about 15 minutes to talk with me. Thank you in advance for your cooperation.

Date of interview: _____

Name of interviewee _____

Relationship to the client_____

Interviewer's name _____

At the end of the interview:

Thank you very much for your cooperation.

I AM GOING TO READ YOU A LIST OF COMMON ACTIVITIES. FOR EACH ONE
PLEASE TELL ME HOW WELL YOUR RELATIVE/CLIENT IS ABLE TO PERFORM
THESE TASKS. (Please hand Card #1 with categories to informant.
Then ask questions in order they appear.)

ID # __ __ __ .
        1 2 3
CARD # 0 0
        5 6
PROJ # __ __ .
        8 9

HOW WELL IS R ABLE TO PERFORM THESE TASKS?:

		Not at all	With Physical Assistance	With Verbal and/or Environmental Reminders	Independent	
		(0)	(1)	(2)	(3)	
1.	Undressing	0	1	2	3	__11
2.	Buttons	0	1	2	3	__12
3.	Dressing Appropriately	0	1	2	3	__13
4.	Bathing	0	1	2	3	__14
5.	Grooming	0	1	2	3	__15
6.	Toileting	0	1	2	3	__16
7.	Sweeps/washes floor	0	1	2	3	__17
8.	Self-medicates	0	1	2	3	__18
9.	Performs first aid on self	0	1	2	3	__19
10.	Answers telephone	0	1	2	3	__20
11.	Dials telephone	0	1	2	3	__21
12.	Knows how to walk around neighborhood	0	1	2	3	__22
13.	Takes bus to familiar destination	0	1	2	3	__23
14.	Makes change for dollar	0	1	2	3	__24
15.	Goes food shopping	0	1	2	3	__25
16.	Maintains savings account	0	1	2	3	__26
17.	Cashes checks (e.g., paychecks, SSI checks)	0	1	2	3	__27

HOW WELL IS R ABLE TO PERFORM THESE TASKS?: (continued)

	Not at all	With Physical Assistance	With Verbal and/or Environmental Reminders	Independent	
	(0)	(1)	(2)	(3)	
18. Evacuates building in fire drill/emergency in 2 1/2 minutes	0	1	2	3	28
19. Dials police or fire in emergency	0	1	2	3	29
20. Follows simple one or two part directions	0	1	2	3	30

21. ARE THERE ANY SKILLS THAT YOU ASSES R CAN DO BUT IN FACT HE/SHE DOES NOT DO?

_____ (1) YES _____ (2) NO   31

If YES, PLEASE LIST:

_____
_____   32
_____   33
_____   34
_____
_____

22. (If YES) WHY DO YOU THINK HE/SHE IS NOT PERFORMING THESE SKILLS?

_____
_____   35
_____
_____   36
_____

BASIC NEEDS

NOW I WOULD LIKE TO ASK YOU SOME QUESTIONS ABOUT R'S NEEDS AND
HOW WELL THEY ARE MET.

IN YOUR OPINION, ARE R'S NEEDS FOR THE FOLLOWING BASIC NECESSITIES
BEING WELL MET, BARELY MET, OR ARE THEY NOT BEING MET?

	Not Met (0)	Barely Met (1)	Well Met (2)	
23. Food	0	1	2	37
24. Housing	0	1	2	38
25. Clothing	0	1	2	39
26. Medical Care	0	1	2	40
27. Small luxuries	0	1	2	41

PHONE INTAKE QUESTIONS FOR SPORTS AND RECREATION

28. DOES YOUR FAMILY MEMBER/CLIENT PARTICIPATE IN COMMUNITY RECREATION OR
CLUBS?

_____ Yes _____ No _____ Don't Know   42

Which ones? _____   43

29. DOES YOUR FAMILY MEMBER/CLIENT PARTICIPATE IN TRIPS OR EVENTS PLANNED BY
THE PERSON'S HOME?

_____ Yes _____ No _____ Don't Know   44

Which ones? _____   45

30. DOES YOUR FAMILY MEMBER/CLIENT HAVE HOBBIES OR INTERESTS THAT HE/SHE DOES
ON THEIR OWN?

_____ Yes _____ No _____ Don't Know   46

Which ones? _____   47

31. DOES YOUR FAMILY MEMBER/CLIENT SEEM SATISFIED WITH HOW THEY SPEND THEIR
FREE TIME?

_____ Yes _____ No _____ Don't Know   48

32. ARE YOU, THE CAREGIVER OR THE INVOLVED PERSON, SATISFIED WITH HOW YOUR
FAMILY MEMBER/CLIENT SPENDS THEIR FREE TIME?

_____ Yes _____ No _____ Don't Know   49

33. DOES YOUR FAMILY MEMBER/CLIENT HAVE A SIGNIFICANT OTHER WHO IS NOT A STAFF PERSON OR A FAMILY MEMBER?

_____ Yes _____ No _____ Don't Know

<u>   </u>
50

SERVICES AND ASSISTANCE

I AM NOW GOING TO ASK YOU SOME QUESTIONS ABOUT SERVICES R RECEIVES
OR NEEDS AND WHO PROVIDES THEM. (Please snow Card #2 to informant.)

34. WHO TAKES RESPONSIBILITY MOST OF THE TIME TO PROVIDE THIS SERVICE

    (1) Does or can do alone
    (2) Sibling
    (3) Parent
    (4) Other relatives
    (5) Neighbor or friend
    (6) Paid person arranged for informally
    (7) Formal agency service

SERVICE CATEGORIES	Currently Receives	Who takes Responsibility most of the time to provide this service? (PUT IN NUMBERS 1-7 FROM ABOVE LIST)	(If NO) Is this needed?		(If YES) Receiving but more is needed		
	YES (1) NO (0)		YES (1)	NO (0)	YES (1)	NO (0)	
Assistance in Personal Care	__ __	_____	__	__	__	__	11 12 13 14
Transportation	__ __	_____	__	__	__	__	15 16 17 18
Shopping	__ __	_____	__	__	__	__	19 20 21 2
Housecleaning	__ __	_____	__	__	__	__	23 24 25 26
Legal	__ __	_____	__	__	__	__	27 28 29 30
Individual Counseling	__ __	_____	__	__	__	__	31 32 33 34
Family Therapy	__ __	_____	__	__	__	__	35 36 37 38
Leisure/Recreational Services	__ __	_____	__	__	__	__	39 40 41 42
Day Program	__ __	_____	__	__	__	__	43 44 45 46
Medical or Nursing Assistance in Home	__ __	_____	__	__	__	__	47 48 49 50
Occupational Therapy	__ __	_____	__	__	__	__	51 52 53 54
Physical Therapy	__ __	_____	__	__	__	__	55 56 57 58

34. (continued)

(1) Does or can do alone
(2) Sibling
(3) Parent
(4) Other relatives
(5) Neighbor or friend
(6) Paid person srranged for informally
(7) Formal agency service

SERVICE CATEGORIES	Currently Receives		Who takes Responsibility most of the time to provide this service? (PUT IN NUMBERS 1-7 FROM ABOVE LIST)	(If NO) Is this needed?		If YES Receiving but more is needed					
	YES (1)	NO (0)		YES (1)	NO (0)	YES (1)	NO (0)				
SERVICE CATEGORIES											
Speech Therapy	__	__	_____	__	__	__	__	59	60	61	62
Religious and Spiritual Program	__	__	_____	__	__	__	__	63	64	65	66
Social Work Assistance	__	__	_____	__	__	__	__	67	68	69	70
Dental Health Assistance	__	__	_____	__	__	__	__	71	72	73	74
Educational/Training in Community Living Skills	__	__	_____	__	__	__	__	75	76	77	78
Other	__	__	_____	__	__	__	__	79	80		

MAIL

INTRODUCTION

THIS QUESTIONNAIRE IS ONE OF THE FORMS THAT WE ARE USING TO EVALUATE YOUR
FAMILY MEMBER/CLIENT. THIS IS OUR ATTEMPT AS A TEAM TO ASSIST YOU IN
MAXIMIZING THE QUALITY OF CARE YOU ARE PROVIDONG TO YOU FAMILY MEMBER/CLIENT.
WE WOULD LIKE YOU TO ANSWER THE QUESTIONS AHEAD OF TIME IN ORDER TO REDUCE THE
AMOUNT OF TIME YOU NEED TO SPEND AT THE SHRIVER CENTER ON ANY ONE DAY. ALSO,
SINCE YOU FILLED OUT THE QUESTIONNAIRE, WE WOULD LIKE TO ASK YOU TO ACCOMPANY
YOUR FAMILY MEMBER/CLIENT TO THE APPOINTMENT.

THE TOPICS COVERED IN THIS QUESTIONNAIRE ARE:

1) MEDICAL HISTORY
2) NEED FOR MEDICAL ASSISTANCE
3) RESIDENTIAL/HOUSING HISTORY
4) SPIRITUAL NEEDS
5) INVOLVEMENT IN WORK PROGRAM
6) DIETARY NEEDS

PLEASE ANSWER THE QUESTIONS AND BRING THIS FORM WITH YOU AT YOUR SCHEDULED
APPOINTMENT TIME. IF YOU HAVE TROUBLE ANSWERING ANY OF THE QUESTIONS PLEASE
FEEL FREE TO ASK US WHEN YOU COME FOR YOUR APPOINTMENT OR CALL 642-0101.

THANK YOU VERY MUCH FOR YOUR COOPERATION.

RESPONDENT NAME: _____

RESPONDENT SIGNATURE:_____

INTERVIEW INFORMATION

NAME OF RELATIVE OR CARETAKER: _____

ADDRESS OF RELATIVE OR CARETAKER: _____
                                            Street

_____
                 city   state   zip

TELEPHONE #: (   )_____
              Area code   number

NAME OF ELDERLY PERSON: _____

RELATIONSHIP OF ELDERLY PERSON TO RELATIVE: _____

OTHER CARETAKER: _____

PLEASE WRITE DOWN YOUR FAMILY MEMBER/CLIENT'S ORGANIC DIAGNOSIS.

_____

WHEN WAS HE/SHE DIAGNOSED FIRST?   Age_____

                                        Date _____

ID # __ __ __
1 2 3

CARD # 0 0 1
5 6 7

PROJ # __ __ __
8 9 10

WE WOULD LIKE TO ASK YOU SOME QUESTIONS ABOUT R'S PHYSICAL ABILITY
AND MEDICAL HISTORY

PLEASE RATE THE ANSWERS TO THE FOLLOWING QUESTIONS:
(Please check the appropriate column.)

    (1) Very Poor
    (2) Poor
    (3) Average
    (4) Good
    (5) Excellent

	Very Poor (1)	Poor (2)	Average (3)	Good (4)	Excellent (5)	

1. COMPARE TO OTHER PEOPLE WITH RETARDATION OF R'S AGE, WOULD YOU SAY THAT:

R'S ABILITY TO BE AS ACTIVE AS OTHERS IS: 1   2   3   4   5   __ 11

R'S PHYSICAL ABILITY TO DO THINGS HE/SHE NEEDS TO DO IS: 1   2   3   4   5   __ 12

R'S PHYSICAL ABILITY TO DO THINGS HE/SHE WANTS TO DO IS: 1   2   3   4   5   __ 13

2. IN THE LAST YEAR OR SO, HAVE YOU NOTICED THAT THINGS ARE HARDER FOR R TO DO? (i.e., Is R slowed down in any way, does R get tired, does R not do things at the same pace he/she used to, etc.)

    _____ YES (1) _____ NO (0)   __ 14

3. DURING THE PAST YEAR, HOW MANY TIMES HAS R FALLEN, IF ANY? (If none, please skip to Question #5.)

4. DURING THE PAST YEAR, HOW MANY TIMES HAS R HAD AN ACCIDENT, OTHER THAN FALLING, WHICH REQUIRED MEDICAL ATTENTION?

    __ # times   __ 15

5. ARE THE NUMBERS OF FALLS OR ACCIDENTS INCREASING?

    _____ YES (1) _____ NO (0)   __ 16

6. DURING THE PAST MONTH, HOW MANY DAYS ALL TOGETHER WAS R IN BED ALL OR MOST OF THE DAY BECAUSE OF ILLNESS OR HEALTH CONDITION? (Please circle the most appropriate.)

   (1) none
   (2) a few days
   (3) a week
   (4) 2 weeks   17
   (5) a month
   (6) more than a month

MEDICAL ASSISTANCE

7. WHAT TYPE OF MEDICAL PERSONNEL HAS YOUR FAMILY MEMBER/CLIENT SEEN IN THE LAST YEAR? (Please check the appropriate answer and write on the approximate dates. For example, if your family member/client has seen a psychiatrist in the last year, you would check under the YES column. If he/she has not seen a psychiatrist, check under the NO column.)

	YES (1)	NO (0)	APPROXIMATE DATE	
Psychiatrist	____	____	_____	18
Internist	____	____	_____	19
Neurologist	____	____	_____	20
Orthopedist	____	____	_____	21
Dentist	____	____	_____	22
Other	____	____	_____	23
Who?	_____			24

8. WHO IS PRIMARILY RESPONSIBLE FOR GIVING PRESCRIBED MEDICATIONS? (Please check the appropriate answer. For example, if parents are responsible for giving medication check under the YES column. If parents are not responsible, check under the NO column and so on.)

	YES (1)	NO (0)	
Parents	____	____	25
Siblings	____	____	26
Friends	____	____	27
Client him/herself	____	____	28
Residential Staff	____	____	29

9. DOES YOUR FAMILY MEMBER/CLIENT ACCEPT THE MEDICATION?

_____ YES (1) _____ NO (0)

$\overline{30}$

10. PLEASE COPY THE PRESCRIPTION LABELS FROM THE BOTTLES OF ANY DRUGS WHICH YOUR FAMILY MEMBER/CLIENT IS CURRENTLY TAKING.

PLEASE WRITE IN CAPITAL LETTERS:

DRUG NAME	DOSAGE	
_____	_____	$\overline{31}$
_____	_____	$\overline{32}$
_____	_____	$\overline{33}$
_____	_____	$\overline{34}$
_____	_____	$\overline{35}$
_____	_____	$\overline{36}$

11. DOES YOUR FAMILY MEMBER/CLIENT TAKE ANY OTHER MEDICATIONS?

	YES (1)	NO (0)	
Arthritis Medication	____	____	$\overline{37}$
Pain Killers	____	____	$\overline{38}$
Medicine for Nerves or Depression	____	____	$\overline{39}$
Pills for Water/Fluid Retention	____	____	$\overline{40}$

12. DOES YOUR FAMILY MEMER/CLIENT HAVE ANY OF THE FOLLOWING PROBLEMS? (Please check under each column YES or NO. For example, if the family member/client has "pain in chest", check the YES column. In addition, if this problem has become worse lately, check YES under the second column. Also, if the pains in the chest limit his/her ability to do things he/she wants to do, check YES under the last column.

	HAS PROBLEM		BECOME WORSE		LIMITS HIS/HER ABILITY TO DO THINGS HE/SHE WANTS TO				
	YES (1)	NO (0)	YES (1)	NO (0)	YES (1)	NO (0)			
Pain in chest	____	____	____	____	____	____	$\overline{41}$	$\overline{42}$	$\overline{43}$
Trouble getting breath	____	____	____	____	____	____	$\overline{44}$	$\overline{45}$	$\overline{46}$

	HAS PROBLEM		BECOME WORSE		LIMITS HIS/HER ABILITY TO DO THINGS HE/SHE WANTS TO				
	YES (1)	NO (0)	YES (1)	NO (0)	YES (1)	NO (0)			
Dizziness or lightheadedness	___ ___		___ ___		___ ___		47	48	49
Headaches	___ ___		___ ___		___ ___		50	51	52
Passing out	___ ___		___ ___		___ ___		53	54	55
Confusion	___ ___		___ ___		___ ___		56	57	58
Difficulty sleeping	___ ___		___ ___		___ ___		59	60	61
Incontinence	___ ___		___ ___		___ ___		62	63	64
(1) Bowel	___ ___		___ ___		___ ___		65	66	67
(2) Bladder	___ ___		___ ___		___ ___		68	69	70
Other	___ ___		___ ___		___ ___		71	72	73

13. If OTHER, WHAT? _____
                                                              74

14. DOES YOUR FAMILY MEMBER/CLIENT COMPLAIN OF PAIN?

    _____ YES (1) _____ NO (0)
                                                              75

15. IF YES, WHERE? _____
                                                              76

16. PLEASE CHECK ANY PHYSICAL ILLNESSES OR HEALTH PROBLEMS YOUR FAMILY MEMBER/
    CLIENT MIGHT HAVE. IF ANY OF THESE ILLNESSES OR PROBLEMS PARTICULARLY
    INTERFERE WITH HIS/HER ABILITY TO PERFORM THE DAILY ROUTINE, PLEASE ALSO
    CHECK THE COLUMN TO THE RIGHT. (For example, if he/she has allergies,
    check column 1 AND if the allergies limit his/her ability to do what
    he/she wants to do, check column 2.)

	DOES HE/SHE HAVE THIS PROBLEM?	DOES IT LIMIT HIS/HER ABILITY TO DO WHAT HE/SHE WANTS TO DO?	
	Column 1 Check if YES	Column 2 Check if NO	
Allergies	_____	_____	77
Arthritis or rheumatism	_____	_____	78
Glaucoma or cataracts	_____	_____	79

#16. (Continued)

	DOES HE/SHE HAVE THIS PROBLEM?	DOES IT LIMIT HIS/HER ABILITY TO DO WHAT HE/SHE WANTS TO DO?	
	Column 1 Check if YES	Column 2 Check if NO	
Asthma	_____	_____	11
Emphysema or chronic bronchitis	_____	_____	12
Tuberculosis	_____	_____	13
High Blood Pressure	_____	_____	14
Heart Trouble	_____	_____	15
Circulation trouble in arms or legs	_____	_____	16
Diabetes	_____	_____	17
Ulcers (of digestive system)	_____	_____	18
Other stomach or intestinal disorders	_____	_____	19
Liver disease	_____	_____	20
Kidney disease	_____	_____	21
Other urinary tract diseases	_____	_____	22
Cancer or leukemia	_____	_____	23
Anemia	_____	_____	24
Effects of stroke	_____	_____	25
Parkinson's Disease	_____	_____	26
Epilepsy	_____	_____	27
Skin diseases	_____	_____	28
Renal problems	_____	_____	29
Diseases of female genitals	_____	_____	30
Thyroid or other glandular disorders	_____	_____	31
Pressure sores, leg ulcers or burns	_____	_____	32
Effects of fracture or broken bones	_____	_____	33
Depression	_____	_____	34

CARD # 0 0
         5 6

PROJ # ___ ___
        8   9

#16. (Continued)

	DOES HE/SHE HAVE THIS PROBLEM?	DOES IT LIMIT HIS/HER ABILITY TO DO WHAT HE/SHE WANTS TO DO?	
	Column 1 Check if YES	Column 2 Check if NO	
Fears/Anxiety	_____	_____	35
Cerebral Palsy	_____	_____	36
Seizures	_____	_____	37
Microcephalia	_____	_____	38
Hydrocephalia	_____	_____	39
Spinabifida	_____	_____	40
Down's Syndrome	_____	_____	41
Other	_____	_____	42

17. PLEASE LIST ANY OTHER MAJOR MEDICAL OR SURGICAL PROBLEMS WHICH ARE/IS BEING TREATED:

_____ 43

_____ 44

_____ 45

18. HOW WELL DOES YOUR FAMILY MEMBER/CLIENT HEAR? (Please check the appropriate answer. FGor example, if your family member/client hears normally with both ears, place a check next to #1.)

_____ (1) hears normally with both ears

_____ (2) hears with partial impairment or use of an assistive device (such as a hearing aid)   46

_____ (3) hears with some help from another person to speak extra loudly; or can understand sign language or lip reading

_____ (4) unable to hear, needing complete assistance from another person (meaning profoundly deaf and not able to understand sign language or lip reading)

19. HOW GOOD IS YOUR FAMILY MEMBER/CLIENT'S EYESIGHT? (Please check the appropriate answer.)

_____(1) Sees normally with both eyes

_____(2) Sees with partial impairment such as the use of eyeglasses or use of eye medication

_____(3) Does not see well due to either partial blindness or legal blindness and uses a cane, guide dog or some help from another person

47

_____(4) Does not see at all due to blindness with complete dependence upon another person for assistance

20. DOES YOUR FAMILY MEMBER/CLIENT USE ANY ADAPTIVE EQUIPMENT?

_____ YES (1) _____ NO (0)

48

IF NO, SKIP TO QUESTION #23.

21. IF YES, WHAT EQUIPMENT DOES HE/SHE USE? (Please answer all questions in each category that applies. For example, if he/she is using a wheelchair, answer all the questions under the wheelchair category.)

ID # 1 2 3
CARD # 0 0
PROJ # 5 6
         8 9

	CAN R TAKE OFF/PUT ON DEVICE?		IS DEVICE IN GOOD REPAIR?		DOES DEVICE FIT?		IS IT COMFORTABLE?		IS IT SATISFACTORY?						
	YES	NO	YES	NO	YES	NO	YES	NO	YES	NO					
Wheelchair	__	__	__	__	__	__	__	__	__	__	11	12	13	14	1
Walker	__	__	__	__	__	__	__	__	__	__	16	17	18	19	2
Cane	__	__	__	__	__	__	__	__	__	__	21	22	23	24	2
Dentures	__	__	__	__	__	__	__	__	__	__	26	27	28	29	3
Glasses	__	__	__	__	__	__	__	__	__	__	31	32	33	34	3
Hearing Aid	__	__	__	__	__	__	__	__	__	__	36	37	38	39	4
Prosthesis, e.g., leg	__	__	__	__	__	__	__	__	__	__	41	42	43	44	4
Colostomy, ileostemy equipment	__	__	__	__	__	__	__	__	__	__	46	47	48	49	5
Other	__	__	__	__	__	__	__	__	__	__	51	52	53	54	5

22. IF YES (TO QUESTION #20), WHAT OTHER EQUIPMENT DO YOU THINK HE/SHE SHOULD HAVE? _____

56

23. IF NO (TO QUESTION #20), DO YOU THINK YOUR FAMILY MEMBER/CLIENT NEEDS ADAPTIVE EQUIPMENT SUCH AS:

	YES (1)	NO (2)	DON'T KNOW (9)	
Wheelchair	_____	_____	_____	57
Walker	_____	_____	_____	58
Cane	_____	_____	_____	59
Dentures	_____	_____	_____	60
Glasses	_____	_____	_____	61
Hearing Aid	_____	_____	_____	62
Prosthesis, e.g., leg	_____	_____	_____	63
Colostomy, ileostomy equipment	_____	_____	_____	64
Other	_____	_____	_____	65

RESIDENTIAL/HOUSING

24. WHERE IS YOUR FAMILY MEMBER/CLIENT LIVING NOW? (Please circle the appropriate answer.)

       (1) At home with the family
       (2) Sheltered village
       (3) Semi-independent apartment
       (4) Group home   66
       (5) Specialized home care
       (6) Institution

A Handbook for Caregivers

25. PLEASE FILL IN THE DATES THAT YOUR FAMILY MEMBER/CLIENT HAS LIVED IN EACH OF THE FOLLOWING PLACES. (For example, if he/she has lived in a group home from August 1984 to September 1985, write these dates in the columns provided. If one (or more) of the categories do not apply, do not write in any dates for that category.)

	FROM: MONTH	YEAR	TO: MONTH	YEAR	
(1) At home with the family	_____	_____	_____	_____	
(2) Sheltered village	_____	_____	_____	_____	11 12 1
(3) Semi-independent apartment	_____	_____	_____	_____	14 15 1
(4) Group home	_____	_____	_____	_____	17 18 1
(5) Specialized home care	_____	_____	_____	_____	20 21 2
(6) Institution	_____	_____	_____	_____	23 24 2
					26 27 2

26. HAS YOUR FAMILY MEMBER/CLIENT LIVED IN AN INSTITUTION OR NURSING HOME?

_____ YES (1) _____ NO (0) IF NO, SKIP TO QUESTION #31.
                                       29

27. (IF YES), HAS HE/SHE BEEN IN AND OUT MORE THAN ONCE?

_____ YES (1) _____ NO (0)
                                       30

28. (IF YES), HOW MANY YEARS IN TOTAL DID YOUR FAMILY MEMBER/CLIENT LIVE IN AN INSTITUTION? (Please write in the number of years.)

_____ years.
                                   31 32

29. WHEN WAS YOUR FAMILY MEMBER/CLIENT RELEASED MOST RECENTLY TO THE COMMUNITY? (Please write in month and year.)

_____ _____
Month   Year
                                   33 34 35

30. PLEASE LIST ALL THE PLACES IN WHICH YOUR FAMILY MEMBER/CLIENT HAS LIVED DURING THE PAST 5 YEARS.

Type of residence: _____ 37

_____ 38

_____ 39

_____ 40

                                             41

                                             42

31. WHAT IS THE COMPOSITION OF YOUR FAMILY MEMBER/CLIENT'S PRESENT HOUSEHOLD?
(Please check the appropriate answer for each category.)

	YES	NO	
(1) Lives alone	____	____	43
(2) Lives with parents	____	____	44
(3) Lives with other relative(s)	____	____	45
(4) Lives with other non-relat/ e(s)	____	____	46
(5) Lives in community residence	____	____	47
(6) Lives in institution or nursing home	____	____	48
(7) Other	____	____	49

SPIRITUAL NEEDS

32. WHAT IS YOUR FAMILY MEMBER/CLIENT'S RELIGION?

_____ 50

33. DOES YOUR FAMILY MEMBER/CLIENT ATTEND WORSHIP SERVICES?

_____ YES (1) _____ NO (0)   51

IF YES, PLEASE SKIP TO QUESTION #36.

34. (IF NO), DO YOU THINK YOUR FAMILY MEMBER/CLIENT WOULD LIKE TO PARTICIPATE
IN WORSHIP SERVICES?

_____ YES (1) _____ NO (0)   52

35. IF YOUR FAMILY MEMBER/CLIENT WOULD LIKE TO ATTEND WORSHIP SERVICES, WHY IS
HE/SHE NOT PARTICIPATING IN WORSHIP SERVICES CURRENTLY? (Please check the
appropriate answer.)

_____ Needs assistance and none is available

_____ Appropriate services are not available   53

_____ Church/temple does not welcome persons with mental retardation

_____ Other, specify _____

_____

36. (IF YES TO QUESTION #34), DO YOU THINK YOUR FAMILY MEMBER CLIENT IS
SATISFIED WITH HIS/HER LEVEL OF INVOLVEMENT IN SPIRITUAL ACTIVITIES?

_____ YES (1) _____ NO (0)   54

37. IS A PASTOR/RABBI IN REGULAR CONTACT WITH YOUR FAMILY MEMBER/CLIENT?

_____ YES (1) _____ NO (0)

38. IS YOUR FAMILY MEMBER/CLIENT VISITED BY LAY REPRESENTATIVES OF A LOCAL CHURCH/TEMPLE?

_____ YES (1) _____ NO (0)

39. (IF NO), DO YOU THINK YOUR FAMILY MEMBER/CLIENT WOULD LIKE TO SEE THEM?

_____ YES (1) _____ NO (0)

40. IS YOUR FAMILY MEMBER/CLIENT INCLUDED IN PARISH/TEMPLE ACTIVITIES OTHER THAN WORSHIP SERVICES?

_____ YES (1) _____ NO (0)

41. (IF NO), DO YOU THINK YOUR FAMILY MEMBER CLIENT WOULD LIKE TO BE INVOLVED?

_____ YES (1) _____ NO (0)

DIETARY NEEDS

42. IS YOUR FAMILY MEMBER/CLIENT ON A DIET PRESCRIBED BY A PHYSICIAN OR ON ANY OTHER SPECIAL DIET?

_____ YES (1) _____ NO (0)

43. (IF YES), WHAY TYPE OF DIET? (Please check as many answers as appropriate.)

(1) Low fat   _____

(2) Bland   _____

(3) Low-salt or no salt _____

(4) Low caloric   _____

(5) Diabetic   _____

(6) Ground food   _____

(7) Vegetarian   _____

44. DOES YOUR FAMILY MEMBER/CLIENT APPEAR TO BE EATING WELL?

_____ YES (1) _____ NO (0)

45. WHAT IS THE CONDITION OF YOUR FAMILY MEMBER /CLIENT'S TEETH? (Please check the appropriate answer.)

(1) has his/her own teeth _____

(2) has dentures _____

(3) neither _____

44. HOW WOULD YOU RATE YOUR FAMILY MEMBER/CLIENT'S APPETITE? (Please check the appropriate answer.)

(1) Excellent _____

(2) Good _____

(3) Fair _____

Poor _____

WORK/VOCATIONAL PROGRAM

47. IS YOUR FAMILY MEMBER/CLIENT INVOLVED IN A WORK OR A VOCATIONAL PROGRAM?

_____ YES (1) _____ NO (0)

48. (IF YES), WHAT TYPE OF PROGRAM OR INVOLVEMENT? (Please check the appropriate answer.)

(1) Competitively employed - full time _____

(2) Competitively employed - part time _____

(3) School program _____

(4) Sheltered workshops _____

(5) Day activity program _____

(6) No day program _____

(7) Other, specify _____

49. IS THE WORK/VOCATIONAL PROGRAM APPROPRIATE FOR HIM/HER?

_____ YES (1) _____ NO (0)

50. (IF NO), WHY NOT?

_____

_____

_____

INTRODUCTION

THE AIM OF THIS INTERVIEW IS TO ASSESS THE STRENGTHS OF YOUR FAMILY MEMBER/CLIENT. THIS IS ONE OF OUR ATTEMPTS AS A TEAM TO ASSIST YOU IN YOUR EFFORT TO IMPROVE THE QUALITY OF YOUR CAREGIVING.

WE WOULD LIKE TO COVER THE FOLLOWING FOUR TOPICS WITH YOU TODAY:

1. SOME LEGAL AND FINANCIAL QUESTIONS

2. THE ROLE YOU AND OTHER FAMILY MEMBERS OR CAREGIVERS PLAY IN OBTAINING AND COORDINATING SERVICES FOR YOUR FAMILY MEMBER/CLIENT.

3. THE KIND OF SOCIALIZING YOU AND YOUR FAMILY MEMBER/CLIENT TAKE PART IN.

YOUR PARTICIPATION IS TOTALLY VOLUNTARY AND YOU CAN CHOOSE NOT TO ANSWER ANY QUESTIONS THAT I ASK.

THANK YOU FOR YOUR COOPERATION.

CLIENT NAME: _____

CARETAKER'S NAME (1) _____

(2) _____

NAME OF INTERVIEWERS: (1) _____

(2) _____

DATE OF INTERVIEW: _____

THIS SET OF QUESTIONS HAS TO DO WITH THE FINANCIAL ASSISTANCE WHICH YOUR
RELATIVE/CLIENT IS RECEIVING.

1. DOES R RECEIVE ANY ASSISTANCE, ALLOWANCES (FINANCIAL HELP) FROM ANYONE?
    (Do not include public assistance or social security; only money or help
    from family/friends.)

PARENTS	SIBLINGS	OTHERS
YES NO	YES NO	YES NO
(1) (0)	(1) (0)	(1) (0)
____ ____	____ ____	____ ____

30 31 32

DOES R CURRENTLY RECEIVE ANY INCOME FROM THE FOLLOWING SOURCES?

	CURRENTLY RECEIVING (2)	NOT CURRENTLY RECEIVING (1)	DON'T KNOW (9)	
2. Medicaid	2	1	9	__33__
3. Medicare	2	1	9	__34__
4. Food Stamps	2	1	9	__35__
5. Social Security income or alternative, public pension	2	1	9	__36__
6. Supplemental security income (includes old age assistance, disability assistance, and aid to the blind)	2	1	9	__37__
7. Private Insurance	2	1	9	__38__
8. Wages	2	1	9	__39__
9. Dividends, Interest, Trust Funds, etc.	2	1	9	__40__
10. Other Please specify	2	1	9	__41__

_____

FINANCIAL (cont'd)

	YES (2)	NO (1)	DON'T KNOW (9)	
11. DOES R HAVE ANY BANK ACCOUNTS?	2	1	9	42
12. IS THERE ANYONE WHO USES HIS/HER ACCOUNTS?	2	1	9	43
13. IS THE BANK ACCOUNT IN HIS/HER NAME?	2	1	9	44
14. DOES HE/SHE HAVE TO ASK SOMEONE FOR MONEY WHEN HE/SHE NEEDS IT?	2	1	9	45
15. IS HE/SHE GIVEN THE MONEY WHEN HE/SHE ASKS FOR IT?	2	1	9	46
16. DOES R HAVE A REPRESENTATIVE PAYEE?	2	1	9	47
17. WHAT IS R'S MONTHLY INCOME? (Specify) _____	2	1	9	48

THE NEXT SET OF QUESTIONS HAS TO DO WITH LEGAL ISSUES. (Some of the questions may be inappropriate for some clients. If so, check NO. You can do this before or after the interview according to the background information.)

	YES (2)	NO (1)	DON'T KNOW (9)	
18. DOES R HAVE A GURADIAN?	2	1	9	__49__
19. (If YES) HAS TERMINATION OF GUARDIANSHIP EVER BEEN RECOMMENDED?	2	1	9	__50__
20. (If NO) HAS GUARDIANSHIP/ CONSERVATERSHIP EVER BEEN RECOMMENDED?	2	1	9	__51__
21. HAS ANYONE INITIATED LEGAL PROCCEDDINGS SEEKING AUTHOR- IZATION TO TREAT R?	2	1	9	__52__
22. DOES R AGREE TO THE PROPOSED TREATMENT?	2	1	9	__53__
23. HAS R EVER BEEN FOUND TO BE INCAPABLE OF MAKING TREATMENT DECISIONS IN EITHER ISP OR A PERIODIC REVIEW?	2	1	9	__54__
24. HAS A COURT EVER AUTHORIZED TREATMENT WITH ANTIPSYCHOTIC MEDICATION?	2	1	9	__55__
25. DOES R HAVE A WILL?	2	1	9	__56__
26. (If NO), DO YOU THINK R WOULD LIKE TO MAKE A WILL?	2	1	9	__57__
27. HAS ANYONE DONE ESTATE PLANNING OR DRAWN UP A WILL THAT BENEFITS R?	2	1	9	__58__

28. (If YES to #27) WHAT IS THE RELATIONSHIP BETWEEN R AND THAT PERSON?	PARENTS		SIBLINGS		OTHER RELATIVES				
	YES (1)	NO (0)	YES (1)	NO (0)	YES (1)	NO (0)	__59__	__60__	__61__

SOCIAL RESOURCES

I WOULD NOW LIKE TO ASK YOU SOME QUESTIONS ABOUT THE SOCIAL RESOURCES
AVAILABLE TO YOUR FAMILY MEMBER/CLIENT.

29. IS THERE SOMEONE (Outside of this CR or your home) WHO WOULD TAKE
    RESPONSIBILITY FOR YOUR FAMILY MEMBER/CLIENT IF NEEDED?

    (1) YES _____   (0) NO _____

__ 62

30. If YES, WHO IS THIS PERSON?

PARENT	GUARDIAN	SIBLING	OTHER RELATIVES	FRIENDS
YES NO	YES NO	YES NO	YES NO	YES NO
(1) (0)	(1) (0)	(1) (0)	(1) (0)	(1) (0)
__ __	__ __	__ __	__ __	__ __

63 64 65 66 67

SOCIAL CONTACT

I HAVE SOME QUESTIONS ABOUT YOUR FAMILY MEMBER/CLIENT'S FAMILY AND FREINDS.

31. DOES R HAVE THE FOLLOWING RELATIVES: (Please check appropriate column)

MOTHER	(1) YES _____	(0) NO _____		
FATHER	(1) YES _____	(0) NO _____		
SISTERS	(1) YES _____	(0) NO _____	IF YES, HOW MANY? _____	
BROTHERS	(1) YES _____	(0) NO _____	IF YES, HOW MANY? _____	

__ 68
__ 69
70 71
72 73

Instructions: Please use the code for every question and check the appropriate
              column.

32. DOES R HAVE ANY OF THE FOLLOWING
    CONTACTS WITH:

	PARENTS	SIBLINGS	OTHER RELATIVES	FRIENDS
	YES NO	YES NO	YES NO	YES NO
	(1) (0)	(1) (0)	(1) (0)	(1) (0)
	__ __	__ __	__ __	__ __

ID # __ __ __ __
       1 2 3 4
CARD # 0 0 6
       5 6 7
PROJ # __ __ __
       8 9 10

11 12 13 14

33. HOW OFTEN DOES R HAVE CONTACT
    WITH THESE PERSONS? (Please show
    card #3 to informant.)

    (5) very frequently (at least daily)
    (4) frequently(at least weekly)
    (3) some contact (at least monthly)
    (2) little contact (less than monthly)
    (1) no contact

__ 15

34. (If YES to Question #32)
DO YOU THINK R SHOULD HAVE
MORE CONTACT WITH THESE
INDIVIDUALS?

	PARENTS		SIBLINGS		OTHER RELATIVES		FRIENDS	
	YES	NO	YES	NO	YES	NO	YES	NO
	(1)	(0)	(1)	(0)	(1)	(0)	(1)	(0)

—— —— —— —— —— —— —— ——

16 17 18 19

35. (If YES to Question #33)
HOW WOULD R DESCRIBE THE
QUALITY OF THESE RELATIONSHIPS?

    (1) very good
    (2) good
    (3) so-so
    (4) not so good
    (5) bad

20

36. HOW MANY RELATIVES DOES R HAVE LIVING NEARBY? (Nearby includes all who
live within 1 hour's drive.) (Circle the most apprpriate.)

    (1) None
    (2) One
    (3) Two
    (4) Four
    (5) Five or more

21

37. AT PRESENT, HOW MANY CLUBS OR ORGANIZATIONS DOES R BELONG TO?
(Circle the most appropriate.)

    (1) No clubs or organizations
    (2) One club or organization
    (3) Two or more

22

BEHAVIOR

NOW I WOULD LIKE TO ASK YOU SOME QUESTIONS ABOUT YOUR FAMILY MEMBER/
CLIET'S BEHAVIOR IN HIS/HER ENVIRONMENT. I AM GOING TO READ YOU A LIST
OF SOME COMMOM PROBLEMS. SOME MIGHT BE TRUE OF YOUR RELATIVE/CLIENT,
OTHERS MIGHT NOT. IF ANY OF THESE PROBLEMS DO OCCUR, I WILL ASK YOU TO
TELL ME HOW OFTEN, HOW INTENSELY AND HOW CONFIDENT YOU FEEL IN HANDLING
THE PROBLEM.

Instructions to interviewer: For every behavior we would like to know at what
frequency the problem is occuring, what the severity of the problem is and
how confident the caregiver is in handling the problem. Each one of the
measures will be measured on a five-point scale:

Frequency	(1) never occured
	(2) has occured, but not in the past week
	(3) has occured 1-2 times in the past week
	(4) has occured 3-6 times in the past week
	(5) occurs daily, or more often
Severity	(1) not severe at all
	(2) not severe
	(3) somewhat severe
	(4) severe
	(5) very severe
Confidence	(1) none at all
	(2) very little
	(3) moderately confident
	(4) confident
	(5) extremely confident

Please circle the most appropriate answer for each question. (Hand out Card #5)

38. BEHAVIOR	FREQUENCY	SEVERITY	CONFIDENCE	
(1) Asking repetitive questions	1 2 3 4 5	1 2 3 4 5	1 2 3 4 5	23 24 25
(2) Losing or misplacing things	1 2 3 4 5	1 2 3 4 5	1 2 3 4 5	26 27 28
(3) Not completing tasks	1 2 3 4 5	1 2 3 4 5	1 2 3 4 5	29 30 31
(4) Destroying property	1 2 3 4 5	1 2 3 4 5	1 2 3 4 5	32 33 34
(5) Doing things that embarass you	1 2 3 4 5	1 2 3 4 5	1 2 3 4 5	35 36 37
(6) Waking you up at night	1 2 3 4 5	1 2 3 4 5	1 2 3 4 5	38 39 40
(7) Agression	1 2 3 4 5	1 2 3 4 5	1 2 3 4 5	41 42 43
(8) Withdrawn	1 2 3 4 5	1 2 3 4 5	1 2 3 4 5	44 45 46

#38. (continued)

      Frequency   (1) never occured
                              (2) has occured, but not in the past week
                              (3) has occured 1-2 times in the past week
                              (4) has occured 3-6 times in the past week
                              (5) occurs daily, or more often

      Severity   (1) not severe at all
                              (2) not severe
                              (3) somewhat severe
                              (4) severe
                              (5) very severe

      Confidence   (1) none at all
                              (2) very little
                              (3) moderately confident
                              (4) confident
                              (5) extremely confident

BEHAVIOR	FREQUENCY	SEVERITY	CONFIDENCE	
(9) Attention seeking	1 2 3 4 5	1 2 3 4 5	1 2 3 4 5	47 48 49
(10) Bizarre or inappropriate language	1 2 3 4 5	1 2 3 4 5	1 2 3 4 5	50 51 52
(11) Self-abuse	1 2 3 4 5	1 2 3 4 5	1 2 3 4 5	53 54 55

39. HOW DOES R COMMUNICATE?

(1) no verbal or sign ability
(2) single word or sign ability
(3) phrase
(4) sentences
(5) fully verbal
                                                    56

40. IS R'S EMOTIONAL HEALTH BETTER, ABOUT THE SAME, OR WORSE THAN IT WAS
A YEAR AGO?

(3) better
(2) about the same
(1) worse
                                                    57

41. IS R'S ABILITY TO THINK AND REASON ABOUT THE SAME OR WORSE THAN IT WAS
A YEAR AGO? (Circle the most appropriate)

(2) about the same
(1) worse
                                                    58

I WOULD LIKE TO ASK YOU TO DESCRIBE IN MORE DETAIL YOU FAMILY MEMBER/CLIENT"S
PRESENT BEHAVIOR PROBLEMS.

42. DESCRIBE THE BEHAVIORAL PROBLEM(s).

_____

_____

_____   59

_____

43. WHAT IS THE HISTORY OF THE BEHAVIOR PROBLEM(s)?

_____

_____   60

_____

_____

44. WHAT IS THE OCCURENCE OF THE BEHAVIOR PROBLEM(s)?

_____

_____   61

_____

_____

45. HOW DO YOU AND OTHERS IN HIS/HER ENVIRONMENT REACT (TREAT) TO THE BEHAVIOR?

_____

_____   62

_____

_____

46. HOW EFFECTIVE IS IT?

_____

_____   63

47. DOES YOUR FAMILY MEMBER/CLIENT HAVE A HISTORY OF PSYCHIATRIC PROBLEMS?

_____ Yes _____ No   64

48. If yes, WHAT WAS THE PROBLEM? (ASK ABOUT THE MANIFESTATION OF THE PROBLEM.)

_____

_____ 65

49. HOW WAS HE/SHE TREATED?

_____

_____ 66

ID # ___ ___ ___ ___
          1   2   3   4
CARD # 0 . 0 . 8
          ___ ___ ___
          5   6   7
PROJ # ___ ___ ___
          8   9   10

FAMILY BURDEN INTERVIEW

I AM GOING TO READ YOU A LIST OF STATEMENTS WHICH REFLECT "HOW PEOPLE SOMETIMES FEEL WHEN TAKING CARE OF ANOTHER PERSON. AFTER EACH QUESTION, TELL ME HOW OFTEN YOU FEEL THAT WAY: NEVER, RARELY, SOMETIMES, QUITE FREQUENTLY, OR NEARLY ALWAYS." (Please show Card #6 and write the number to each answer in the blank space.)

> Scoring: (1) never
> (2) rarely
> (3) sometimes
> (4) quite frequently
> (5) nearly always

50. DO YOU FEEL THAT R ASKS FOR MORE HELP THAN HE/SHE NEEDS?

___
11

51. DO YOU FEEL THAT BECAUSE OF THE TIME THAT YOU SPEND WITH R YOU DON'T HAVE ENOUGH TIME FOR YOURSELF?

___
12

52. DO YOU FEEL STRESSED CARING FOR R AND TRYING TO MEET OTHER RESPONSIBILITIES? (e.g., family, job)?

___
13

53. DO YOU FEEL ANGRY WHEN YOU ARE AROUND R?

___
14

54. DO YOU FEEL THAT R CURRENTLY AFFECTS YOUR RELATIONSHIPS WITH OTHER FAMILY MEMBERS OR FRIENDS IN A NEGATIVE WAY?

___
15

55. ARE YOU AFRAID OF WHAT THE FUTURE HOLD FOR R?

___
16

56. DO YOU FEEL THAT R IS DEPENDENT ON YOU NOW?

___
17

57. DO YOU FEEL THAT YOUR HEALTH HAS SUFFERED BECAUSE OF YOU INVOLVEMENT WITH R?

___
18

58. DO YOU FEEL THAT YOU DON'T HAVE AS MUCH PRIVACY AS YOU WOULD LIKE?

___
19

59. DO YOU FEEL THAT YOUR SOCIAL LIFE HAS SUFFERED BECAUSE YOU ARE CARING FOR R?

___
20

60. DO YOU FEEL UNCOMFORTABLE ABOUT HAVING FRIENDS OVER? (If subject says, "No one comes over," ask "WOULD YOU BE UNCOMFORTABLE......"?)

___
21

61. DO YOU FEEL THAT R SEEMS TO EXPECT YOU TO TAKE CARE OF HIM/HER AS IF YOU WERE THE ONLY ONE HE/SHE COULD DEPEND ON?

___
22

62. DO YOU FEEL THAT YOU DON'T HAVE ENOUGH MONEY TO CARE FOR R IN ADDITION TO THE REST OF YOUR EXPENSES?

___
23

63. DO YOU FEEL UNCERTAIN AS TO WHAT TO DO ABOUT R?

___
24

64. DO YOU FEEL THAT YOU SHOULD BE DOING MORE FOR R? $\overline{25}$

65. DO YOU FEEL THAT YOU HAVE MADE ADJUSTMENTS IN YOUR
    PROFESSIONAL CAREER PLANS BECAUSE OF R? $\overline{26}$

66. DO YOU FEEL COMPLETELY OVERWHELMED BECAUSE OF WORRY
    ABOUT R; AND CONCERNS ABOUT HOW YOU WILL MANAGE? $\overline{27}$

67. DO YOU FEEL THAT YOUR SLEEP IS DISTURBED (because R is
    in and out of bed or wanders around at night)? $\overline{28}$

68. ARE YOU CONCERNED ABOUT THE PHYSICAL STRAIN INVOLVED IN
    PROVIDING CARE FOR R? $\overline{29}$

69. DO YOU FEEL THAT RELATIONSHIPS WITHIN YOUR FAMILY HAVE
    BEEN STRAINED AS A RESULT OF TRYING TO PROVIDE CARE FOR R? $\overline{30}$
    (No privacy, or a disruption in the family routine)

70. PLEASE TRY TO SUMMARIZE WHY YOU DECIDED TO COME TO OUR PROGRAM AND WHAT
    YOU HOPE WILL HAPPEN AFTER OUR EVALUATION.

_____

_____

_____ $\overline{31}$

_____

_____ $\overline{32}$

_____

_____

_____ $\overline{33}$

_____

_____

_____

_____

_____

_____

CAREGIVERS BURDEN INTERVIEW

I AM GOING TO READ YOU A LIST OF STATEMENTS WHICH REFLECT "HOW PEOPLE
SOMETIMES FEEL WHEN TAKING CARE OF ANOTHER PERSON." AFTER EACH QUESTION,
PLEASE TELL ME WHETHER ANY OF THESE APPLY TO YOU. (Please circle the
appropraite column.)

	YES (1)	NO (0)	
71. DO YOU FEEL THAT R ASKS FOR MORE HELP THAN HE/SHE NEEDS?	1	0	34
72. DO YOU FEEL STRESSED CARING FOR R AND TRYING TO MEET OTHER RESPONSIBILITIES?	1	0	35
73. DO YOU FEEL ANGRY WHEN YOU ARE AROUND R?	1	0	36
74. DO YOU FEEL THAT R IS DEPENDENT ON YOU?	1	0	37
75. DO YOU FEEL THAT YOU CAN'T TAKE CARE OF R MUCH LONGER?	1	0	38
76. DO YOU FEEL UNCERTAIN AS TO WHAT TO DO ABOUT R?	1	0	39
77. DO YOU FEEL THAT YOU SHOULD BE DOING MORE FOR R?	1	0	40
78. DOES R'S BEHAVIOR UPSET YOU?	1	0	41
79. DO YOU FEEL FRUSTRATED WHEN CARING FOR R?	1	0	42
80. DO YOU FEEL OVERWHELMED (e.g., concerns about how you will manage R's behavior)?	1	0	43

THIS PART OF THE QUESTIONNAIRE IS ADMINISTERED TO THE CLIENT ACCORDING TO
HIS/HER ABILITY TO ANSWER THE QUESTIONS.

THE CLIENT INTERVIEW SHOULD BE ADMINISTERED BEFORE THE LAST PART OF THE
CAREGIVER'S BURDEN INTERVIEW.

ID# $\overline{1}$ $\overline{2}$ $\overline{3}$ $\overline{4}$

CARD# $\overline{0}$ $\overline{0}$ $\overline{7}$
$\overline{5}$ $\overline{6}$ $\overline{7}$

PROJ# $\overline{8}$ $\overline{9}$ $\overline{10}$

CLIENT'S INTERVIEW

I WOULD LIKE TO ASK YOU SOME QUESTIONS ABOUT WHERE YOU LIVE AND THE PEOPLE YOU
LIVE WITH. (Positive satisfactions are coded as 1; dissatisfactions are coded
as 0.)

Code 1 or 0

1. DO YOU LIKE WHERE YOU LIVE? OR   —— $\overline{11}$

   DO YOU WANT TO LIVE SOMEWHERE ELSE?   —— $\overline{12}$

2. WOULD YOU RATHER BE LIVING WITH OTHER PEOPLE? OR   —— $\overline{13}$

   DO YOU LIKE THE PEOPLE YOU LIVE WITH?   —— $\overline{14}$

3. DO YOU THINK THEY ARE NOT TRUSTWORTHY? OR   —— $\overline{15}$

   CAN YOU TRUST THE PEOPLE YOU LIVE WITH?   —— $\overline{16}$

4. ARE THE PEOPLE YOU LIVE WITH GOOD FRIENDS? OR   —— $\overline{17}$

   ARE THEY NOT GOOD FRIENDS?   —— $\overline{18}$

5. DO YOU WISH YOU HAD MORE FRIENDS?   ——
                                                     $\overline{19}$
6. DO YOU HAVE ENOUGH FRIENDS?   ——
                                                     $\overline{20}$

AUTONOMY

7. ARE THERE RULES ABOUT SPENDING YOUR MONEY? OR   —— $\overline{21}$

   DO YOU SPEND YOUR MONEY THE WAY YOU WANT TO?   —— $\overline{22}$

8. DO YOU SPEND YOUR MONEY WHENEVER YOU WANT TO?   —— $\overline{23}$

9. DO YOU HAVE TO CHECK WITH SOMEONE BEFORE YOU LEAVE YOUR
   HOUSE? OR   —— $\overline{24}$

   CAN YOU DECIDE TO GO OUT WHENEVER YOU WANT TO?   —— $\overline{25}$

10. WHEN YOU WANT TO HAVE A BEER OR OTHER ALCOHOLIC DRINK,
    CAN YOU? OR   ——

    DO YOU HAVE TO CHECK WITH SOMEONE?   —— $\overline{26}$

A Handbook for Caregivers

11. DO OTHER PEOPLE TELL YOU WHAT TO DO TOO MUCH?   OR

    _____ 27

    CAN YOU DO WHAT YOU WANT?

    _____ 28

12. DO YOU THINK THERE ARE TOO MANY RULES WHERE YOU LIVE?   OR

    _____ 29

    ARE YOU FREE MOST OF THE TIME TO DECIDE FOR YOURSELF WHAT
    YOU WANT TO DO?

    _____ 30

13. CAN YOU MAKE UP YOUR MIND WHETHER OR NOT TO GO TO
    CHURCH (SYNAGOGUE)?   OR

    _____ 31

    ARE THERE RULES ABOUT GOING?

    _____ 32

NOW I HAVE A FEW QUESTIONS ABOUT WHERE YOU WORK.

Code 1 or 0

14. (ROUTINE): DO YOU FIND YOUR WORK TO BE THE SAME DAY
    AFTER DAY?

    _____ 33

15. (SATISFYING): DOES YOUR JOB MAKE YOU FEEL GOOD?

    _____ 34

16. (BORING): DO YOU THINK IT IS BORING (DULL)?

    _____ 35

17. (RESPECTED): DO OTHER PEOLPLE THINK YOUR JOB IS A GOOD ONE?

    _____ 36

18. (CHALLENGING): DOES YOUR WORK EXCITE YOU SO THAT YOU
    WORK HARD?

    _____ 37

19. (ENDLESS): DO THE DAYS SEEM VERY LONG, LIKE THEY WILL
    NEVER END?

    _____ 38

CO-WORKERS

20. (STIMULATING): DO YOU THINK THE PEOPLE YOU WORK WITH ARE
    VERY INTERESTING?

    _____ 39

21. (BORING): DO YOU EVER FIND THEM BORING (DULL)?

    _____ 40

22. (SLOW): ARE THEY SLOW?

    _____ 41

23. (AMBITIOUS): DO THEY TRY HARD TO DO A GOOD JOB?

    _____ 42

24. (RESPONSIBLE): DO THEY MOST OFTEN DO WHAT THEY ARE
    SUPPOSED TO DO?

    _____ 43

25. (INTELLIGENT): ARE THEY SMART?

    _____ 44

26. (EASY TO MAKE ENEMIES): IS IT EASY TO MAKE ENEMIES
    WITH THE PEOPLE AT WORK?

    _____ 45

27. (TALK TOO MUCH): DO THEY TALK TOO MUCH?

    _____ 46

CO-WORKERS (Continued)

28. (LAZY): ARE THEY LAZY? _____
   47

29. (NO PRIVACY): DO THE PEOPLE AT WORK MAKE IT DIFFICULT
   (HARD) TO WORK BY YOURSELF? _____
   48

30. (LOYAL): DO YOU THINK THEY WILL STICK BY YOU WHEN YOU
   NEED THEM (VERY GOOD FRIENDS)? _____
   49

NOW I HAVE SOME QUESTIONS ABOUT YOUR FREE TIME AND HOW YOU SPEND YOUR DAY
AFTER WORK.

Code 1 or 0

31. IN YOUR FREE TIME, DO YOU FEEL THAT YOU HAVE ENOUGH TO DO? _____
   50

32. WOULD YOU LIKE TO BE DOING MORE FUN THINGS THAN YOU ARE
   DOING NOW? _____
   51

33. WOULD YOU LIKE SOMEONE TO TEACH YOU MORE THINGS TO DO
   WITH YOUR FREE TIME? _____
   52

34. WHAT IS YOUR FAVORITE THING TO DO IN YOUR FREE TIME?

_____

GENERAL PSYCHOLOGICAL WELL-BEING

HERE ARE SOME THINGS THAT PEOPLE FEEL ABOUT THEMSELVES. TELL ME WHICH IS MORE
LIKE YOU, NOT JUST RIGHT NOW, BUT USUALLY HOW YOU FEEL. (Positive
satisfactions are coded as 1; dissatisfactions are coded as 0.)

Code 1 or 0

35. DO YOU FEEL THAT YOU HAVE A LOT OF FRIENDS, OR _____
   53

   DO YOU FEEL LONELY? _____
   54

36. DO YOU OFTEN FEEL SICK, OR _____
   55

   DO YOU FEEL STRONG AND HEALTHY? _____
   56

37. DO YOU MAKE UP YOUR OWN MIND, OR _____
   57

   DO YOU DO WHAT YOU'RE TOLD? _____
   58

38. DO YOU OFTEN FEEL NERVOUS AND UPSET, OR _____
   59

   DO YOU USUALLY FEEL CALM? _____
   60

39. DO YOU FEEL YOU CONTROL YOUR TEMPER, OR   _____
    DO YOU THINK YOU LOSE YOUR TEMPER TOO OFTEN?   _____

40. DO YOU WORRY ABOUT THE WAY YOU LOOK, OR   _____
    DO YOU THINK YOU LOOK AS NICE AS OTHER PEOPLE?   _____

41. DO YOU OFTEN FEEL PROUD OF YOURSELF, OR   _____
    DO YOU FEEL ASHAMED OF YOURSELF USUALLY?   _____

42. DO YOU FEEL YOU GET INTO A LOT OF FIGHTS, OR   _____
    DO YOU FEEL YOU ARE EASY TO GET ALONG WITH?   _____

43. DO YOU FEEL YOU GET ALONG WITH YOUR FRIENDS, OR   _____
    DO YOU HAVE A HARD TIME GETTING ALONG WITH FRIENDS?   _____

44. DO YOU HAVE TROUBLE SLEEPING, OR   _____
    DO YOU HAVE NO TROUBLE SLEEPING?   _____

45. DO YOU FEEL THAT YOU DO NOT GET ALONG WITH PEOPLE AT WORK, OR   _____
    DO YOU FEEL YOU GET ALONG WITH THEM FINE?   _____

46. DO YOU FEEL YOU TALK TOO MUCH, OR   _____
    DO YOU TALK THE RIGHT AMOUNT?   _____

47. DO YOU THINK ABOUT PEOPLE WHO HAVE DIED, OR   _____
    DO YOU FIND DEATH TOO SCARY TO THINK ABOUT?   _____

48. DO YOU SEE YOURSELF AS OLD, OR   _____
    DO YOU SEE YOURSELF AS YOUNG?   _____

49. WHOM DO YOU KNOW THAT IS OLD?

_____

50. WHAT DOES IT MEAN TO BE OLD?

_____

_____

_____

_____

Column codes (right margin): 61, 62, 63, 64, 65, 66, 67, 68, 69, 70, 71, 72, 73, 74, 75, 76, 77, 78, 79, 80

S. Charles Archuleta, B.S. I received my B.S. in Biology and Anthropology from the University of New Mexico. I am currently a third-year student at Boston University School of Law.

My introduction to the problems faced by people who are old and mentally retarded has come as a result of my student internship with the Kennedy Aging Project. My interest in the potential legal issues of hospice care providers results from my general interest in questions of medical ethics and their legal consequences. My work on the Hospice Care Committee of the Fernald State School gave me the opportunity to combine my concerns for people who are less fortunate, and my interest in the medical-legal field, via preparation of a review of the current case law and its meaning with respect to hospice caregivers.

Thomas V. Barbera, Jr. I was a student at Boston College School of Management from 1977 to 1980. In 1980 I left school to care for my dying brother. In 1982 I returned to Boston and began working at the Fernald State School, in a residence serving twenty people who were mentally retarded and old. I am presently a Habilitative Coordinator at Fernald. Along with other team members, I developed several senior citizen programs at Wallace Building.

I am currently enrolled in the University of Massachusetts Boston School of Public and Community Service. I have been affiliated with the Kennedy Aging Project for its entire three years. I have served on the Aging Committee and the Death and Dying Committee of the Fernald State School for the past four years. I am also a member of the Department of Mental Retardation Advisory Council on Elder Services.

My interest in aging and death and dying comes from my personal experience and current academic pursuits. I have worked as a grief counselor with several people who were old and mentally retarded who have died. I have developed, implemented, and evaluated several programs for clients who are mentally retarded and also old. I am an author of the Death and Dying Handbook and have conducted training sessions in death and dying and program development in a number of settings.

Bridget M. Bearss, M.Ed., RSCJ. I received my B.A. in Elementary-Special-Early Childhood Education from Maryville College, my

M.Ed. in Educational Administration from Washington University, and am currently studying Pastoral Ministry and Theology at Boston College.

Originally from the midwest, I arrived at the Aging Project with a history of involvement in the field of elementary/special education. I came to Boston to prepare for first vows with the Religious of the Sacred Heart, through participation in the novitiate program. Part of my preparation included a ministry component. I chose the Aging Project because it involved working with a different age group, and included diagnostic, intervention and advocacy. In addition, it allowed for the flexibility of being able to create new programs and develop a new format for evaluation of clients.

As an elementary and special educator, I have long been involved in seeking to make education institutions places where all children have the opportunity to learn, without regard to physical, emotional, or intellectual ability. Upon moving to Boston, while studying theology at Boston College and completing the novitiate program with the Religious of the Sacred Heart, I hoped to expand my understanding of people with developmental disabilities by working with adults, rather than children. Through the Kennedy Aging Project, as well as in my role on the Pastoral Care Team at the Fernald State School, I became involved in understanding the developmental pathway of the adult with mental retardation, and in focusing on the spiritual development of aging. It has called for an integration of theological study, an understanding of the developmental process of aging, and consistent reflection in light of that which is most spiritual and fundamental to all life experience. As I return now to the elementary school, I will continue my involvement in the field of mental retardation, both with a more focused desire to create schools that open themselves to children without regard to labels and limitations, and by continuing to be involved in pastoral care visitation to adults with developmental disabilities.

Henry A. Beyer, J.D. I received my B.S. from Duquesne University in Pittsburgh in 1954. I am the Director of the Pike Institute for the Handicapped at Boston University School of Law. I directed the legal component of the Kennedy Aging Project since its inception. As part of my work at the Pike Institute, I lead an annual seminar on legal issues of importance to people with disabilities, and publish a bi-monthly Disability Advocates Bulletin.

My degree is from Harvard Law School. I have worked with and for people with mental retardation since 1976 in various capacities, including: director of projects providing technical assistance to the President's Committee on Mental Retardation and to advocates for individuals with developmental disabilities in the six New England states; director of a project providing training to human rights committees of the Massachusetts Department of Mental Health; member of the Human Rights Committee and the Board of Trustees of the Walter E. Fernald State School for people with mental retardation; member of the Board of Directors of Delta Projects (community services for people with mental retardation); and chair of the State Schools Committee of the Massachusetts Long-Range Planning Task Force on Mental Retardation.

I have also written extensively in the field, including a chapter on litigation in the *Handbook on Mental Retardation,* J. Matson and J. Mulick, eds. (1983). and a chapter on legal issues involving the use of psychotropic drugs in *Psychopharmacology of the Developmental Disabilities,* M. Aman and N. Singh, eds. (1888). I live with my wife, Janet, in Concord, Massachusetts, where we have raised five sons and assorted garden vegetables.

Bruce C. Blaney, M.A. I have an M.A. from Harvard University with a concentration in the social history of total institutions, especially state hospitals and state schools. In the 1970s I was a social worker in several nursing homes, housing many people who had spent most of their lives in institutions for people labeled "mentally retarded." In the mid 1970s I designed and taught the social gerontology curriculum at Lesley College. From 1979 through 1982, I directed the Gerontology Training Project for the Massachusetts Department of Mental Health. Since 1982 I have developed training materials and presented workshops throughout the country on issues of aging and mental retardation. I am also a principal author of the Massachusetts Department of Mental Retardation's recent policy handbook on aging and mental retardation, *Challenges and Opportunities.* I have learned most of my useful knowledge from people with mental retardation who have lived long lives, especially from Mr. Elmer Lewis.

Stephanie A. Bowen, B.S. I am a 1985 graduate of the Boston Bouve School of Human Development Professions, Northeastern University, where I received my B.S. in Physical Therapy. I am currently a Clinical Supervisor in Physical Therapy at the Fernald State School.

I began working with people who are old and mentally retarded as a new graduate in a program called "The Alzheimer's Group," which was serving 4-5 clients. In my two and a half years with the program, it doubled in size and we further developed the curriculum.

I have worked with the Kennedy Aging Project as a speaker at conferences and with Dr. Mary Howell in the Health Focus Day Program. I am also a member of the Fernald Aging Committee, which is developing recommendations for program and residential placement of Fernald's aging population.

Alison Boyer, R.N.C., A.N.P. I am a certified nurse practitioner; I received my Nurse Practitioner certificate from Upstate Medical Center in Syracuse, New York, and have been employed by the E.K. Shriver Center to provide medical care to the residents at the W.E. Fernald State School since 1978.

Gerard A. Cabrera, B.A. I received my B.A. in English and American Literature from Brandeis University in 1985. I was the recipient of the Jacob and Bella Thurman Award for Social Responsibility. After I graduated I began working in the position of Administrative Assistant at the Kennedy Aging Project. I have performed a variety of tasks in my three years here, from word processing, writing and research, to mediating disputes and making friends. I have developed a remarkable capacity for remembering telephone numbers.

During the time I have worked here, I also was involved in a local theatrical troupe and served on the Board of Directors of a small local newspaper. I am very happy to have worked with such dedicated, compassionate, and truly thoughtful people. The scope of interests has broadened my perspective and nourished me both intellectually and spiritually.

Linda S. Corman, O.T.R./L. I received my B.S. degree in Occupational Therapy from Boston University Sargent College of Allied Health Professions. I have continued my education in the areas of Gerontology, Mental Health, and Clinical Education. Currently, I am a Clinical Supervisor of Occupational Therapy at Fernald State School.

It was as a staff therapist that I began to be interested began in programming for people who are mentally retarded and old. Drawing from the residents on my caseload, I saw a need for creative and alternative programming that enhanced and maintained skills, self-esteem, and dignity. I have advocated for, developed, and implemented a Senior Program for basic skills/prevocational residents. Through my interest in residents who are old and mentally retarded, I became the

Occupational Therapy Consultant for the Kennedy Aging Project. I have also consulted to nursing and group homes and have lectured at local universities on the Occupational Therapist's role with people who are mentally retarded.

I feel that Occupational Therapists have a great deal to offer people who are mentally retarded and old through their knowledge of purposeful activity, adaptive equipment, therapeutic interventions, and environmental modification.

Elizabeth J. DeBrine, M.Ed. , C.T.R.S. I graduated from Boston University School of Education with an M.Ed. in Leisure Studies with a therapeutic recreation concentration in May 1985. I was awarded a Louis Lowry Certificate in Gerontology upon graduation. I have been working at the Kennedy Aging Project for the past three years as the Supervisor of Sports and Recreation and as a liaison to Massachusetts Special Olympics.

I began working with people who are old thirteen years ago as a nurse's aid in a large nursing home. Over the years, I worked with old people in adult day health centers and various nursing homes as Director of Activities.

I describe myself as a strong advocate of recreation for people who are old and mentally retarded. Most of the Kennedy Aging Project clients spent many years in institutions where they had little or no exposure to recreation and leisure. The best results of our recommendations are stories of clients who are trying new activities such as horseback riding, vacations to Disney World, swimming for the first time, and finding an unpaid friend.

I live a leisurely life in Reading, Massachusetts with my two young sons Andrew and William, and my husband Jim, who is building a professional croquet court in the backyard.

Mary Ann DiGiovanni, M.Ed., J.D. I received my B.A. from Emmanuel College in Boston in 1970, my M.Ed. in special Education from Boston College in 1978, and my J.D. from Boston University in 1987. From 1972 to 1984, I was a Special Education teacher in the Framingham Public Schools. During that time I worked on a panel at McGraw-Hill Publishers to advise and consult on adapting learning materials for children with special needs. I was a member of the Kennedy Aging Project as a legal intern during my third year as a law student. I have worked as an associate at a small law firm in Boston. Professionally and personally, I benefitted tremendously from working with the Interdisciplinary Team, both personally and professionally.

Edith Finaly-Neumann, R.N., M.Sc., Ph.D. I received my Ph.D. in Sociology from Boston University and am an Assistant Professor in the School of Social Work at Boston University. My areas of expertise include medical sociology, human behavior, health and human services, and evaluation research. I was on the faculty a and research associate in the Kennedy Aging Project from 1985 to 1988. Among my previous positions, I was a faculty member in the School of Allied Health Professions at Ben-Gurion University-Israel. My publications include articles in the social sciences, health, and life satisfaction.

Arianna Fucini, Ph.D. I received my doctorate in Natural Science from the University of Rome in 1965, my M.A. in Psychology from Northeastern University in 1976, and my Ph.D. in Experimental Psychology from Northeastern University in 1982. I have worked intensively with people who are mentally retarded since 1978 in varying capacities, and I have worked with people who are old in nursing homes and other institutional settings for the past four years. I was the Kennedy Aging Project team psychologist for the past two years and I am currently in private practice, offering cognitive behavior therapy.

Deirdre Gavin, M.P.H., M.S.W., M.A.T. I received my B.A. from Manhattanville College, my M.A.T. from Harvard University and my M.P.H. and M.S.W. from Boston University.

In 1965, shortly before the implementation of deinstitutionalization in Massachusetts, I was a volunteer in the Commonwealth Service Corps, and served as assistant director of a pilot activities program at the Fernald State School. I and other college and graduate students lived with clients at Fernald, planned activities, organized recreational trips off institutional grounds, and submitted team reports and recommendations to the Commissioner of Mental Health. Subsequently, I taught special classes for the City of Boston.

In the 1980s, I advocated for a victim of Alzheimer's disease who lived alone in the community. I arranged medical, psychiatric, and neurological evaluations and initiated legal proceedings for the appointment of a conservator. Educating family members regarding the symptoms and course of Alzheimer's disease, the needs and rights of the patient, and the necessity to plan for future care proved a challenge. This experience, together with advocacy for hospitalized psychiatric patients, persuaded me to enroll in the Boston University School of Social Work. After an internship in the Office for Human Rights of the Massachusetts Department of Mental Health, I also enrolled in the B.U. School of Public Health as a Health Law concentrator and focused my studies on the legal and ethical aspects of human experimentation in health care.

In 1987-1988 I fulfilled my second year field education in social work as a student intern at the Kennedy Aging Project.

In September 1988, I entered law school to further my goal of advocacy for the human rights of underserved and vulnerable populations.

Eric Harris, Ed.D., J.D. I received my J.D. from Harvard University in 1969 and my Ed.D. from Harvard University in 1978. I was admitted to the Massachusetts Bar in 1970 and I was licensed as a psychologist in 1980. I am currently the Director of Professional Affairs for the Massachusetts Psychological Association and a faculty member of the Massachusetts School of Professional Psychology. I served as a psychologist/lawyer in the first year of the Kennedy Aging Project. I have been working in clinical-legal issues involving mental health treatment since 1976.

Mark H. Hatch, M.A. I received my B.A. from Dartmouth College in 1980, my M.A. from the University of Massachusetts in 1987, and I am expecting to receive my M.Div. in 1989 from Harvard Divinity School.

In the past ten years I have worked on the national staff of Greenpeace, the national staff of Physicians for Social Responsibility, and have been involved in local, state, and national politics. Being part of the Kennedy Aging Project was my first experience with people who are old and mentally retarded.

I recently moved to rural North Carolina with my wife, Dr. Patty Dilley, and my 13-month-old daughter, Ruth. I am also preparing for ordination in the Episcopal Church.

Mary Raugust (Howell), M.D., Ph.D. I consider myself fortunate to have had wonderful jobs, from practicing pediatrics in a small New England town, to being the first woman Associate Dean at Harvard Medical School, to helping design a comprehensive infant day-care system, to working in a community health center in a Haitian neighborhood. While I have taken on every job with gusto and relish, being associated with the Kennedy Aging Project has been the very best work so far.

My training in medicine and developmental psychology will soon be enriched by additional training in law, as I move toward work in my long-held interest in biomedical ethics. As the Aging Project ends, I treasure in memory a collaboration that was full of growth, good fellowship, and intense effort.

Deborah Lynch, J.D. I received my B. A. in Government and Sociology from Wheaton College in 1983, my J.D. from Boston University in 1988, and am expecting my M.B.A. in Health Care Management from Boston University in 1989. I was a legal intern with the Kennedy Aging Project in its third year.

Nancy MacRae, M.S., O.T.R./L. I received my B.S. in Occupational Therapy from the University of New Hampshire in 1966. I have been working with people who are developmentally disabled my entire professional career, starting with children, then adults, and now people who are old. I was the Director of the Occupational Therapy Department at Pineland Center, Maine's only state facility for mental retardation. I am now a Program Services Director for people who are old and mentally retarded at Pineland where I direct both programmatic and residential services. I just finished a four year term as President of the Maine Occupational Therapy Association and am one of two representatives from the American Occupational Therapy Association to the Accreditation Council on Services to People with Developmental Disabilities where I serve as acting secretary. Finally, I have just received a Masters of Science in Adult Education from the University of Southern Maine.

Fr. Henry Marquardt, M.Ed. I was ordained a Roman Catholic priest for the Archdiocese of Boston in 1957 and served in parishes throughout the diocese until 1973. During that time, in each parish, I established a religious education program for people with special needs. In 1973 I earned my M.Ed. degree in Rehabilitation Administration from Northeastern University. In the same year, I became full-time Catholic chaplain at the Fernald State School. I have been a faculty member of the Kennedy Aging Project since its beginning, and working with the Aging Project has been one of the highlights of my ministry.

Barbara McDaniel, M.S.W. I received my M.S.W. from Boston University School of Social Work and am currently employed at WORK, Inc. in Quincy, Massachusetts, as a Program Manager for Residential Services. I was the first social work student of the Kennedy Aging Project. My working roots are as a van driver for seven retarded people who taught me to laugh and who taught me the highways and byways of northern California.

My topic interest is grief counseling. My own journey taught me the importance of sharing the grief process, a process many retarded people experience with family and caregivers.

Carolyn L. Nock, R.N.C., F.N.P., B.S.N., J.D. I received my R.N. from the Liliane S. Kaufmann School of Nursing in 1967, completed the Family Nurse Practitioner Program at Worcester Hahnemann Hospital in 1978, received by B.S.N. from Boston College School of Nursing in 1981, and my J.D. from Suffolk University School of Law in 1987. My present employment is as a Nurse Practitioner on the Shriver Medical Contract at the Fernald State School.

I chose to work with people who are both mentally retarded and old because they presented a challenge to my skills as a nurse practitioner. Because they are old they experience all of the problems of aging, and because they are retarded they present special problems in communicating health needs and understanding care and treatment.

I was invited to join the Institutional Ethics Committee of the Fernald State School. I gratefully accepted. While I was working as a nurse practitioner, I was attending law school. Many of the health issues I dealt with had legal and ethical ramifications. A chance to work with others—staff, family and other professionals—in sorting out these issues was a wonderful opportunity to grow, learn, and solve problems. To reflect on the evolution and work of the committee has been helpful in assimilating and (I hope) sharing that growth and learning.

Richard J. Pitch, B.A. I received my B.A. in anthropology from Wesleyan University. I worked for two years at the Fernald State School for Mental Retardation, first as a direct care worker, then as an adult educator. There I became involved with the Kennedy Aging Project, first as an author of the training manual on death and dying, and then of the companion manual on ethical dilemmas. I am now a medical student at SUNY-Brooklyn (Downstate Medical Center).

Keith Michael Robinson, M.D. I am currently an Assistant Professor of Rehabilitation Medicine at Boston University Medical Center and Director of Rehabilitation Services at Jewish Memorial Hospital, Boston, Massachusetts. I received my B.A. in Urban Studies with Specialization in Gerontology from the University of Pennsylvania in 1976. I received my M.Sc. in Sociology of Medicine as a Thouron Fellow at the University of London in 1978. I also received my M.D. from the University of Pennsylvania in 1981. I was Board Certified in Internal Medicine in 1985, and in Physical Medicine and Rehabilitation, 1988.

I began working with people who are mentally retarded and old through the Kennedy Aging Project. I am interested in the integration of knowledge between the areas of rehabilitation and mental retardation. My relationship with the Kennedy Aging Project is as a clinical consultant in Rehabilitation Medicine.

Sharon B. Roth, M.S., R.N.C. I received my M.S. in Gerontological Nursing from Boston University and my B.S. in Nursing from Marquette University. I am now employed as Practitioner-Teacher in the Department of Geriatric/Gerontological Nursing and as an instructor in the College of Nursing at Rush-Presbyterian-St. Luke's Medical Center and the Johnston R. Bowman Health Center for the Elderly, in Chicago, Illinois.

I began working with people who are both old and mentally retarded as part of my student affiliation with the Kennedy Aging Project in 1985-86, to fulfill requirements of the gerontological nurse practitioner program at Boston University. Since my background is in acute care, I was intrigued by the stress people who are old and retarded experienced when hospitalized, as well as the lack of knowledge most health care providers had of people who are both mentally retarded and old.

In my work as a gerontological nurse and educator, I continue to act as a spokesperson and advocate for people who are old and mentally retarded.

Majorie L. Rucker, L.P.N., Roman Catholic Lay Minister. I received my Nursing degree from Winthrop Community Hospital School of Practical Nursing in 1965, and my Lay Ministry Training from the Paulist Leadership Renewal Project in 1982. I have worked at the Fernald School for the past eleven years as a staff nurse.

I came to work at Fernald in 1977 quite by accident, after work in Medicine/Surgery, Nephrology, Ophthalmology, Pediatrics, and Gerontology. Over the years, I have found myself working with clients who are old. It has been a very rewarding experience both professionally and personally, especially to be able to be a part of the clients' spiritual life, since I am a very spiritually oriented individual myself. Participating in daily and weekly Mass has been an enriching experience, enhancing my own spiritual journey through the example of others.

Gary B. Seltzer, M.S.S.W., Ph.D. I received my B.A. from the University of Wisconsin in 1970, my M.S.S.W. also from the University of Wisconsin in 1971, and my Ph.D. in Clinical Psychology and Public Practice from Harvard University in 1978.

From 1971 to 1981 I ran support and behavioral groups for families with members who are mentally retarded. I have been the Director of Clinical Services for people with developmental disabilities and other chronic neurological impairments at the Lincoln Hill Camp in Massachusetts and Brown University in Providence, Rhode Island.

I have written on the day-to-day, quality of life issues consequent to developmental disabilities and other neurological impairments. I am currently writing about the psychological implications of caring for people who are both old and mentally retarded. At present, I am participating in a research and training center consortium on aging and developmental disabilities at the Waisman Center, a University Affiliated Program and Mental Retardation Research Center, located at the University of Wisconsin at Madison. In addition, I am an Associate Professor in the School of Social Work at the University of Wisconsin in Madison.

Susan L. Sternfield, M.Ed., M.S.W. I am currently a doctoral candidate in Special Education at Boston University. I am combining personal family experience in raising a mentally and physically handicapped son with my professional social work training and present research interests in social skills and social cognition. The developmental issues for families with disabled members over an entire lifespan, from birth to old age, are of particular interest to me.

Kathy Wilkie Kossey, B.A. I attended Bennington and Simmons College and received a B.A. in Psychology in 1975. I have been working as a Behavior Specialist providing psychology services at the Fernald School since 1976. Together with Alison Boyer I have been conducting a desensitization program helping clients become familiar and comfortable with physical examinations and medical procedures.

Frank Wills, M.D. I trained at Boston University School of Medicine, Boston State Hospital, Judge Baker Guidance Center (Boston), and Pasadena (California) Child Guidance Clinic. After nearly twenty years of child psychiatry practice with children who are retarded and nonretarded, I came to the Eunice Kennedy Shriver Center in 1978. I have worked in the Center's Community Health Clinic and, in its programs at the Dever and Fernald Schools, with patients from age 8 to 92. I served as psychiatric consultant to the Kennedy Aging Project since its founding. A particular interest has been assisting with making the distinction between depression and dementia in the Project's patients with Down syndrome. Currently, I am working at Children's Hospital, Boston, in their program at the Wrentham State School.

Frances Wiltsie, R.N.C., M.S.N., A.N.P. My concern for people who are mentally retarded began in high school, when I helped care for a neighbor's son with mental retardation and cerebral palsy. I worked as a camp counselor for several summers with young women who are moderately to severely mentally retarded.

My education includes a B.A. in Psychology from Brown University, a B.S. in Nursing from Cornell University-New York Hospital School of Nursing, and an M.S. in Nursing from Boston College. I am presently a student in the American Sign Language and Deaf Studies Certificate Program at Northeastern University.

My nursing experience has been almost entirely in community health and primary health care. For six years I have worked as a Nurse Practitioner at the Fernald State School, presently part-time. I have been a faculty person with the Kennedy Aging Project during its three year history. In addition, I have been a consultant to the Eastern Middlesex Association for Retarded Citizens for the past one-and-a-half years.